Cultivating Development

Anthropology, Culture and Society

Series Editors:
Professor Vered Amit, Concordia University
and
Dr Jon P. Mitchell, University of Sussex

Published titles include:

Home Spaces, Street Styles:
Contesting Power and Identity
in a South African City
LESLIE J. BANK

On the Game:
Women and Sex Work
SOPHIE DAY

Slave of Allah:
Zacarias Moussaoui vs the USA
KATHERINE C. DONAHUE

A World of Insecurity:
Anthropological Perspectives
on Human Security
EDITED BY THOMAS ERIKSEN,
ELLEN BAL AND OSCAR SALEMINK

A History of Anthropology
THOMAS HYLLAND ERIKSEN
AND FINN SIVERT NIELSEN

Ethnicity and Nationalism:
Anthropological Perspectives
Third Edition
THOMAS HYLLAND ERIKSEN

Globalisation:
Studies in Anthropology
EDITED BY THOMAS HYLLAND ERIKSEN

What is Anthropology?
THOMAS HYLLAND ERIKSEN

Anthropology, Development
and the Post-Modern Challenge
KATY GARDNER AND DAVID LEWIS

Corruption:
Anthropological Perspectives
EDITED BY DIETER HALLER AND CRIS SHORE

Anthropology's World
Life in a Twenty-First Century Discipline
ULF HANNERZ

Culture and Well-Being:
Anthropological Approaches to
Freedom and Political Ethics
EDITED BY ALBERTO CORSÍN JIMÉNEZ

Cultures of Fear:
A Critical Reader
EDITED BY ULI LINKE
AND DANIELLE TAANA SMITH

Fair Trade and a Global Commodity:
Coffee in Costa Rica
PETER LUETCHFORD

The Will of the Many:
How the Alterglobalisation Movement
is Changing the Face of Democracy
MARIANNE MAECKELBERGH

The Aid Effect:
Giving and Governing in
International Development
EDITED BY DAVID MOSSE
AND DAVID LEWIS

Cultivating Development:
An Ethnography of
Aid Policy and Practice
DAVID MOSSE

Anthropology, Art and
Cultural Production
MARUŠKA SVAŠEK

Race and Ethnicity in Latin America
Second edition
PETER WADE

Race and Sex in Latin America
Peter Wade

Anthropology at the
Dawn of the Cold War:
The Influence of Foundations,
McCarthyism and the CIA
EDITED BY DUSTIN M. WAX

Learning Politics from Sivaram:
The Life and Death of a Revolutionary
Tamil Journalist in Sri Lanka
MARK P. WHITAKER

Cultivating Development

An Ethnography of Aid Policy and Practice

David Mosse

PlutoPress
www.plutobooks.com

First published 2005 by Pluto Press
345 Archway Road, London N6 5AA and
175 Fifth Avenue, New York, NY 10010

www.plutobooks.com

Distributed in the United States of America exclusively by
Palgrave Macmillan, a division of St. Martin's Press LLC,
175 Fifth Avenue, New York, NY 10010

British Library Cataloguing in Publication Data
A catalogue record for this book is available from the British Library

ISBN   978–0–7453–1798–4 paperback

Library of Congress Cataloging in Publication Data
Mosse, David.
Cultivating development : an ethnography of aid policy and practice /
David Mosse.
       p. cm. – (Anthropology, culture, and society)
    Includes bibliographical references and index.
    ISBN 0–7453–1799–5 (hbk) — ISBN 0–7453–1798–7 (pbk)
1. Rural development–Sociological aspects. 2. Economic
development–Sociological aspects. 3. Economic assistance–Social aspects.
4. Economic assistance–Political aspects. 5. Rural development
projects–India–Case studies. 6. Economic assistance, British–India–Case
studies. I. Title. II. Series.
    HN49.C6M67 2004
    307.1'412–dc22

                                                              2004004512

This book is printed on paper suitable for recycling and made from
fully managed and sustained forest sources. Logging, pulping and
manufacturing processes are expected to conform to the environmental
standards of the country of origin.

10   9   8   7   6   5

Designed and produced for Pluto Press by
Chase Publishing Services, Sidmouth, England
Typeset from disk by Stanford DTP Services, Northampton, England
Simultaneously printed digitally by CPI Antony Rowe in England, UK
and by Edwards Bros in the United States of America

For Siobhan

Contents

Preface

During the 1990s I worked as an anthropologist-consultant on a British aid project in rural India. From the first design of the IBRFP project in 1990 until 1998 I was a regular visitor as the project's expatriate 'expert' in social development, participation or local institutions (I also undertook separate assignments in 2001–3). In the highly fragmented world of development consultancy such continuity is rare. Partly for this reason, but also because of the particular importance of this project as a 'flagship' within the 1990s British aid programme – demonstrating a new commitment to participatory and poverty-focused interventions – DFID (the UK Department for International Development) agreed to support an analysis of the project experience from my particular anthropological perspective. For me, this was a chance to reflect on what had been a rich, challenging and frustrating experience, through which I learned much about bilateral aid, participation, project management and the livelihoods of very poor 'tribal' communities in a politically and administratively marginal region of India.

This book is the result of that reflection, now placed in the wider context of international aid. Its focus is on the period of my direct and regular involvement (1990–97) during the project's Phase I (although I also draw on materials for the years up to 2001). I would visit the project for several weeks three or four times a year (more in the earlier, and less in the later years) along with my consultant colleagues – specialists in forestry, crops, irrigation, soil conservation or gender – spending time with project staff, in office meetings or workshops, at their homes, on long journeys and in the scattered villages of the Bhil ('tribal') region undertaking planning or reviews with farmers. These were intense periods of interaction from which grew personal relationships of understanding, trust and respect. This is the first source for my research. The second is a series of reports and studies that came out of my various engagements in planning, monitoring, social research and impact studies. These are part of a larger body of project documentation (for 1990–98) that I have reviewed for this book, including village-level records, project monitoring data, meeting minutes, workshop reports, consultant and donor documents, the published results of technical research and impact assessment studies, and more. As a third layer of research, in

2001 I returned to India to carry out a series of interviews (including over 30 taped) with a representative selection of project workers and ex-staff at different levels, as well as with India- and UK-based DFID officials and consultants. The aim was to test and verify my understanding of project processes, to decentre my own view and to extend the analysis to the wider context of British aid in India.

This has been an unusual type of social research; complex, long-term, multi-sited and initially unintentional, drawing on insights as a participant-insider. It is both social investigation and lived experience. It is based on the best available evidence, but does not cease to be a personal analytical account – an ethnography in which I am myself the principal informant.

There is a fourth and important methodological level. This concerns the response that the analysis received from those who shared the experience and about whom I write. Such ethnography courts controversy and is likely to produce objections. These are themselves part of research which emerges from, and reflects on, relationships in development. And here I concur with Bruno Latour's (2000) view of 'objectivity', which derives not from standing above the fray or suppressing subjectivity, but from maximising the capacity of actors to object to what is said about them (see Chapter 1).

So I shared my writing with 'informants', collaborators, colleagues and friends who possessed a capacity to object. Most who responded to the drafts in fact gave strong endorsement to my analysis, often amplifying it in their commentary. They said that the book was 'a truthful introspection', 'very insightful', 'a balanced feedback', even 'over-cautious' some thought. 'This is my experience you have written', said one, 'on all points we are at par.' But a number of key actors (those in managerial positions) took strong exception to my account saying that it had 'many incorrect statements', was 'too negative and unbalanced', 'unfair and disrespectful', 'out of date' and even 'damning of all our work'. They disagreed fundamentally with my conclusions and considered that many sections of the book needed to be re-written. Such a reaction should disturb any ethnographer. I held to the truthfulness of my analysis, but offered to record alternative points of view in a postscript. My refusal to suspend publication, to consider revising my analysis in substance and to meet the concerned group with that objective, provoked written complaints to my academic managers, my university's research ethics committee, the Chair of my anthropological association (the ASA) and my publisher, stating that the book provided an 'unbalanced and damaging account of the project and will harm the professional reputations of many of those who worked at the project' and the future work of the agency with poor tribal communities in India. Eventually, a group of four project managers (former managers and field staff among them) flew to London and joined some of my UK-consultant colleagues to present their objections to the manuscript to myself, the university, the ASA and others in a day-long meeting.

Now, I defended the veracity of my account and felt that it was quite mistakenly regarded as professionally damaging. Indeed, I believe that my colleagues and co-workers were unjustifiably offended by a misunderstanding of my project and a misreading of my analysis as damning criticism. Let me offer three clarifications to pave the way for the chapters ahead.

First, as an ethnography, this book does not aim to provide a comprehensive record of the project and its achievements. On the one hand it concerns an historical moment in a continuing institutional process. On the other, it offers a perspective on policy and practice as a contribution to the social anthropology of development. This means that its argument is of relevance to *all* aid project interventions – the complexities and contradictions of this one standing for many that have to advance donor agendas ('designer development') within national agencies having different organisational mandates, with outsourced strategic leadership from overseas experts. It does not preclude other accounts of the same institutional processes and outcomes framed in other ways and from other perspectives.

Second, as an ethnographic account, the book does not follow the logic of the consultancy report, the donor mission memorandum or the evaluation study. It does not make a judgement about success, does not aim to explain outcomes in terms of design, to prescribe solutions to problems or to conclude with recommendations. In short, it departs from a managerial view (which is surprisingly difficult in writing about project communities), because its interest is in relationships and the unfolding of events. Anyone who reads this book as an evaluation or a negative judgement on a particular project or its actors has profoundly misread my argument. In fact the book is about the social construction of success, and the IBRFP project lends itself to the argument because it was a successful project with significant achievements; indeed it was probably one of DFID's best.

Third, I place myself firmly within the network of relationships that constituted the project. I take my responsibility for shaping the project's design, for the naivety, over-ambition, ignorance and wrong-headedness of my own contributions. I can admit these as personal failings, but also see them as prefigured by the structural and discursive conditions of a development project. I appear as a Foucauldian subject within, as well as outside the discourse. Of course, I do not wish my own sincerity and commitment or the belief and hope in my actions to be questioned; and I do not in the least question that of any of the other actors in the story. This is not what critical reflection implies.

My colleagues and critics may or may not be satisfied with these explanations, but I am indebted to them for their objections. Indeed, *objection* is crucial, and to my mind has a threefold significance: first, as research method, second concerning research relationships and, third, as project practice.

On the question of method, the objections of some of my informants helped to disturb the analysis. Another round of research and reflection began, taking me back from the text to my fieldnotes, to the interview tapes, to the records and the shared experiences that underpin it, to verify and clarify. An analysis that exists within a field of objections has to be sure of itself. Re-examining my book in the light of a vehement and detailed critical response in fact affirmed my belief that the account was well-founded. In the end, I have not changed my analysis, although I hope that I have clarified its purpose as well as indicating alternative points of view, correcting factual errors and changing phrasings that offended.

However, the objections revealed something else, namely that ethnographic writing opens a rift between different epistemologies, meanings and views of responsibility, between the domains of managerial optimism and critical reflection; a gap which now separated me from some other members of the project community. Ethnographic writing had ruptured relationships and broken the rules of fair play within a development team. Project managers/consultants wrote, and at our last meeting spoke, of the loss of trust, of being hurt by a valued friend and respected colleague of long association with whom they had worked closely. I did not intend this, I regret it; but perhaps it is inevitable. The dilemmas of the politics of representation are only amplified by ethnographies of our own professional communities. To reflect and to write means striving to break free from, or at least become sensitised to, the discursive hold of even one's own cherished policy discourse, to try to understand perceptions and actions from another perspective (of course having its own context). Unsurprisingly this is resented, by some, as the individual appropriation of a collective experience, a team effort, that substitutes 'stand-alone arguments' for collectively defined and sustained representations, that extracts from the 'participatory process' and renders 'we – his colleagues – as objects of study'.

But there is third issue here. This book argues that interventions in development are importantly about establishing, promoting and defending significant interpretations (of actions and events), and moreover that this is social as much as conceptual work; that is to say it involves sustaining supportive networks that constitute a project's 'interpretive community' (Chapter 7). If the ethnography offers a representation that refuses (even competes with) authorised interpretations, then correspondingly the use of available channels by project management to mobilise objections can itself be regarded as a key development intervention. The implication is that the ethnographic representation is not *external* to a project's development action. Not only the author, but also the book itself is uncomfortably part of the world that it describes. It is not just a text (separate from action) but is performative. Indeed, it may be read less in terms of its ideas – for development managers the theoretical and comparative significance of my analysis was irrelevant – and more in terms of its capacity to disturb social relations linked to ruling representations; its potential to affect reputations and materially to influence fund flows. While few would doubt that social relations are shaped by writing about them, ethnographers of development know that they are neither 'shielded from the complicated negotiations of social life' nor 'absolved from assuming an implicated responsibility for their words, images and actions' (Stoller 1994: 357).

Anthropologists concerned with public policy have conflicting responsibilities and accountabilities, shaped by the insider/outsider roles they play. Here, as ethnographer my responsibility is to represent development processes in the light of the broad experience of project workers including myself, even if this destabilises policy representations. The social sciences, Latour (2000) argues, 're-present the social to itself':

> What [they] can do is to represent those things in all of their consequences and uncertainties to the people themselves ... that is, not to define the unknown structure of our actions (as if the social scientist knew more than the actor) ... but [to] modify the representation the public has of itself fast enough so that we can be sure that the greatest number of objections have been made to this representation.

Indeed, this is a precondition for learning and insight, and for development effectiveness. But then a precondition for critical analysis, and indeed for this book, is the joint effort and collaborative work of the project.

All those who worked as part of the IBRFP project have contributed to this book. I am privileged and grateful to have been part of such a rich and rewarding development intervention for more than 13 years. I have benefited hugely from the assistance and encouragement of collaborators, co-workers, colleagues and friends. Even though some disagree with what I write, or regard my indulgence in analysis as delinquent, they have honoured my work with detailed critical attention. Special thanks to P.S. Sodhi, Steve Jones, John Witcombe, Meera Shahi and Paul Smith. My understanding of the local dynamics of project processes owes a great deal to working with Mona Mehta, Supriya Akerkar and Anil Bhatt and the very many present and former staff, consultant colleagues, DFID advisers and KBCL officials whom I interviewed but will refrain from naming. The work of Sanjeev Gupta, Vidya Shah and Julia Rees on the project's migration and livelihoods studies was invaluable, and excellent recent PhD research by Celayne Heaton, Ian Harper, Disa Sjöblom and Marc Fiedrich has informed my analysis. This book would not have got off the ground as a piece of research but for the backing of Rosalind Eyben, Aryan de Haan and Michael Shultz at DFID, and the Social Development research grant that gave me time for writing. Of course, the views expressed are my own and do not necessarily reflect those of DFID, 'KBCL' or the IBRFP project. A glance at the bibliography will reveal my intellectual debts. For inspiration, through both writing and conversation, I am especially grateful to Raymond Apthorpe, Philip Quarles van Ufford, Norman Long, Arun Agrawal, K. Sivaramkrishnan and Tania Li. I am thankful for moral as well as intellectual support from Johan Pottier, John Campbell, John Peel, Richard Fardon, Subir Sinha and Kit Davis at SOAS, to Alan Rew at CDS Swansea, to David Lewis and Sarah Ladbury. Amita Baviskar whose knowledge of adivasi western India was a touchstone, gave the manuscript a generously careful reading. Anne Beech and the team at Pluto have been wonderfully supportive. The book finally came together over two Canadian summers in the supportive company of Peggy Stamp, the Mackenzies and the haunting call of loons across Stoney Lake. Jake and Oli have been in the thick and thin of it, my father Charles is a rock of support, and I have been sustained and loved throughout by Siobhan to whom I dedicate the book.

Abbreviations and Acronyms

ARM	Annual Review Mission
ATP	Aid for Trade Provision
CD	Community Development
CO	Community Organiser
CPA	Community Problem Analysis
DDO	District Development Officer
DFID	UK Department for International Development
DFO	District Forestry Officer
DPAP	Drought Prone Areas Programme
DWCRA	Development of Women and Children in Rural Areas
FAMPAR	Farmer Participatory Agricultural Research
FS	Field Specialist, or Farming System
GOs	government organisations
GoI	Government of India
IA	Impact Assessment
IBFEP	Indo-British Fertiliser Education Project
IBRFP	'Indo-British Rainfed Farming Project'
ICRISAT	International Crops Research Institute for the Semi-Arid Tropics
IDS	Institute of Development Studies
IGP/IGA	Income Generation Programme/Activity
IIED	International Institute for Environment and Development
IRDP	Integrated Rural Development Programme
JFM	Joint Forest Management
KBCL	a national fertiliser cooperative, DFID partner agency implementing IBRFP project
LFA	Logical Framework Analysis
LIS	Lift Irrigation Scheme
M and E	Monitoring and Evaluation
MFI	Micro-Finance Institution
MPR	Monthly Progress Report
NABARD	National Bank for Agriculture and Rural Development
NGO	non-governmental organisation
ODA	UK Overseas Development Administration
PEC	Project Evaluation Committee (of ODA)

PLA	Participatory Learning and Action
PMU	Project Management Unit
PPA	Participatory Poverty Assessment
PPB	Participatory Plant Breeding
PPP	Participatory Planning Process
PRA	Participatory Rural Appraisal
PRS	Poverty Reduction Strategies
PRSP	Poverty Reduction Strategy Paper
PTD	Participatory Technology Development
PVS	Participatory Varietal Selection
QPR	Quarterly Progress Report
SDA	Social Development Adviser
SHG	Self-Help Group
SRL	Sustainable Rural Livelihoods
SWC	Soil and Water Conservation
TC	Technical Cooperation
TOR	terms of reference
VDS	Village Development Society
VFC	Village Forest (Protection) Committee
WIRFP	Western India Rainfed Farming Project

Glossary

adivasi	aboriginal, tribal
Banswara	a predominantly adivasi (Bhil/Mina) southern district of Rajasthan state in which IBRFP works
bund	ridge for soil and water conservation or field marking
chandla	an indigenous financial institution based on reciprocal lending and high interest repayment (esp. among Gujarat Bhils)
Dahod	a district centre in largely adivasi (Bhil) eastern Gujarat and site of IBRFP Phase I project office
daru	distilled liquor
devi	the goddess
falia	Bhil hamlet/territory of a patrilineage
gram sabha	village council
haat	local market
halmo	a Bhil system of reciprocal labour exchange
jankar	village volunteer ('knowledgeable person')
Jhabua	a predominantly adivasi (Bhil/Bhilala) western district of Madhya Pradesh state in which IBRFP works
kharif	monsoon crop
Logframe	Logical framework
Mahua	a tree whose flowers are used to make liquor (*Madhuca indica*)
mandali or *mandal*	society or association
mataji	the goddess (mother)
mukkadam	gang leader, labour contractor or broker
Myrada	a Karnataka-based NGO
nallah	stream or stream bed, valley bottom land
notra	like *chandla* but in Madhya Pradesh Bhils often restricted to raising funds for brideprice
panch	informal council
panchayat	statutory institution of local government
patel	Bhil village headman
patwari	village-level revenue official

rabi	winter crop
sahukar	moneylender
samiti	society, e.g. NGO-promoted
sarpanch	head of the statutory panchayat
subabul	a fodder tree species (*Leucaena leucocephala*)
talati	local revenue official
taluk	sub-district

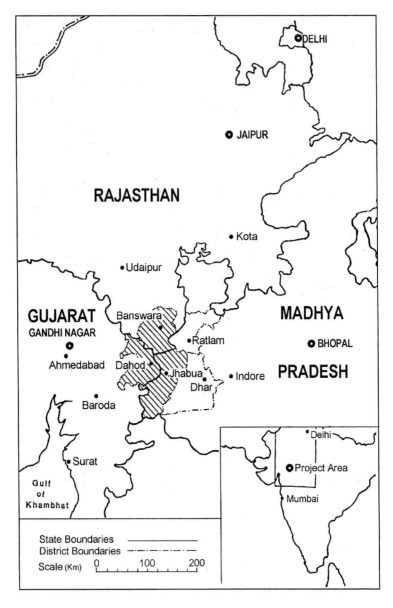

Map 1 Location of the IBRFP project showing Phase I districts (shaded) and adjacent districts for expansion in Phase II

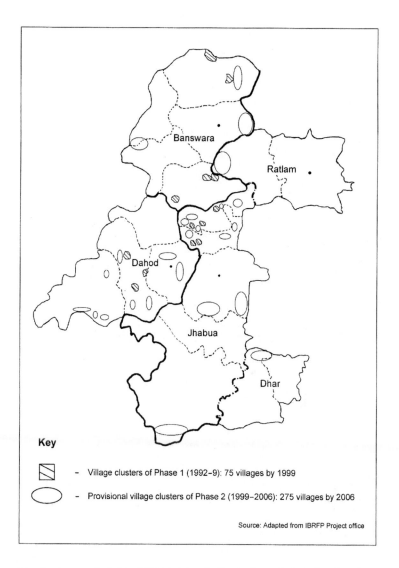

Key

◨ – Village clusters of Phase 1 (1992–9): 75 villages by 1999

⬭ – Provisional village clusters of Phase 2 (1999–2006): 275 villages by 2006

Source: Adapted from IBRFP Project office

Map 2 Area included in IBRFP (with sub-district boundaries) showing the location of village clusters (not to scale)

1
Introduction:
The Ethnography of Policy and Practice

For 50 years 'development' has provided a remarkably stable framework within which the relationship between the affluent West and its 'others' has been understood. But at the start of the 21st century this framework is subject to unprecedented critical scrutiny. While radicals question the relations of global inequality and cultural dominance implied in the idea of development itself, agencies for international development devote their policy processes to constantly revising and re-framing development so as to shore up their legitimacy in a fast-changing political environment. No longer moored to the assumptions of the old colonial and Cold War world order and its 'science of development', notions of growth, progress, modernisation, aid or development demand constant conceptual work to remain politically and morally viable. Western agencies such as the UK's Department for International Development (DFID) and their policy advisers direct huge energy to re-framing development, discarding the signs of a colonial past or present-day commercial self-interest (i.e. tied aid), finding new focus and political legitimacy in the international goal of reducing global poverty, in the language of partnership and participation, citizens' rights and democracy. An abundance of government White Papers, mission statements and strategic plans, 'joined-up' thinking, civil society consultations and policy forums all indicate a striving for coherence in development policy; and there are allied concerns with exerting influence over policy, linking research to policy and of course with implementing policy around the world. For many working in development, getting theory right is the key to addressing the failures and disappointments of development; although the policy process ensures that policies do not command loyalty for long. Better theory, new paradigms and alternative frameworks are constantly needed. In the development policy market place the orientation is always 'future positive' (Edwards 1999).

Despite the enormous energy devoted to generating the right policy models, strangely little attention is given to the relationship between these models and the practices and events that they are expected to generate or legitimise in particular contexts. The intense focus on the future, on new beginnings, is rarely moderated by an analysis of the past in development (Quarles van Ufford et al. 2003: 13). At best, the relationship between policy and practice is understood in terms of an unintended 'gap' between theory and practice, reduced by better policy more effectively implemented. But what if development practice is not driven by policy? What if the things that make for good policy are quite different from those that make it implementable? What if the practices of development are in fact concealed rather than produced by policy? What if, instead of policy producing practice, practices produce policy, in the sense that actors in development devote their energies to maintaining coherent representations regardless of events?

This book asks such questions of international aid, in particular of British aid for rural development in India; and does so by examining the ten-year experience of one project as it falls under different policy regimes. It takes a close look at the relationship between the aspirations of policy and the experience of development within the long chain of organisation that links advisers and decision makers in London with tribal villagers in western India. Its purpose is not to produce a project overview, a commentary on appropriate approaches or 'best practice', nor make an evaluation, or pass judgement; it does not ask whether, but rather *how* development works. The approach is *ethnographic*; and this means examining the making and re-making of policy as well as the practices that policy legitimises as social processes.[1]

INSTRUMENTAL AND CRITICAL PERSPECTIVES ON POLICY AND PRACTICE

Understanding the relationship between policy discourse and field practices has been hampered by the dominance of two opposing views on development policy. These can be caricatured as follows. On the one hand, there is an *instrumental view* of policy as rational problem solving – directly shaping the way in which development is done. On the other hand, there is a *critical view* that sees policy as a rationalising technical discourse concealing hidden purposes of bureaucratic power or dominance, which are the true political intent of development (e.g. Escobar 1995, Ferguson 1994; cf. Shore and Wright 1997). Neither of these views does justice to the complexity of policy making and its relationship to project practice, or to the creativity and skill involved in negotiating development.

First, from an instrumental view, the usual concern is how to define the problem and realise the programme designs in practice. Implicitly, policy makers and project managers are attributed a perfect hegemony over other development actors. In recent years the international development shift away from narrow technology-led micro-managed projects to the wider programme goals of sector and state-level reform has required more sophisticated models capable of dealing with development as a transactional process linking policy goals and outcomes (see Brinkerhoff 1996, Mosse 1998a); but the approach is no less managerial, no less concerned with bringing institutional reality into line with policy prescription. Indeed, the more complex development problems become, and the more uncertain the relationship between policy prescription and development outcome, the more necessary are simplifying models of change and detailed planning and management procedures (cf. Rondinelli 1983: 90).

Arguably, international development is characterised by a new managerialism, driven by two trends: on the one hand, a narrowing of the *ends* of development to quantified international development targets for the reduction of poverty, ill-health and illiteracy (OECD 1996);[2] but, on the other, a widening of its *means*. Whereas until the 1980s technology-led growth or the mechanisms of the market provided the instruments of development, today good government, prudent fiscal policy, political pluralism, a vibrant civil society and democracy are also pre-requisites of poverty reduction.[3] In the extreme, nothing short of the managed reorganisation of state and society is necessary to deliver on the enormously ambitious goal of eliminating world poverty (and ensuring global security, since underdevelopment is now dangerous; Duffield 2001).[4] And as social life is instrumentalised as 'means' in the new international public policy, donor-driven ideas such as social capital, civil society or good governance theorise relationships between society, democracy and poverty reduction so as to extend the scope of rational design and social engineering from the technical and economic realm to the social and cultural, assisted, Fine suggests, by an imperialist economics freed from the constraints of neo-classical models (2002). While taking on the 'the burden of Atlas' (Eyben 2003) donors have a confidence in management through policy that has never been greater. The consequence is persistent optimism about the power of policy design to solve problems, evaluations that confirm self-fulfilling prophecies about viability, and the renewed support of failing programmes (precisely *because* they fail but still affirm goals and values, Long 2001: 35–7). Such confidence in policy is ensured in two ways: first by what Quarles van Ufford et al. (2003) call the 'morality of the black box' which conceals the relationship between development policy and effects; and second, by the logic of the project cycle which ensures the separation of planners and implementers (Biggs and Smith 2003). As the story unfolds in the chapters of this book, these themes will return. But at the centre will be the point that donor policy fails to recognise its own autonomy from events, and therefore misunderstands the significance of its pronouncements. My aim is to encourage reflectivity and to dislodge 'that unscrutinised sense of being in control' (Eyben: 2003: 2) among policy professionals.

The second, critical, view of policy works from opposite assumptions. It takes the failure of development interventions as self-evident. Here there is no surprise that management models which isolate interventions from the history and social and political realities of the 'third world', or bend these realities into the discipline-bound logics of diagnosis and prescription (whether in health, agriculture or education), do not achieve their stated ends (Long 2001: 32–4). However, the critics do not really dispense with the instrumentality of development so much as substitute a set of real, undisclosed or unintended ends or effects for the stated goals of development planning.[5] A now extensive literature argues that, like those of colonial rule, development's rational models achieve cognitive control and social regulation; they enhance state capacity and expand bureaucratic power (particularly over marginal areas and people); they reproduce hierarchies of knowledge (scientific over indigenous) and society (developer over the 'to be developed'), and they fragment, subjugate, silence or erase the local, all the while 'whisk[ing] these political effects out of sight' through technical discourses that naturalise poverty, objectify the poor and depoliticise development (Ferguson 1994; see, for example, Cowen and Shenton 1995, Escobar 1995, Long 2001, Ludden 1992, Scott 1998, Skaria 1999, Tsing 1993).

Recently the critical eye has turned on policy which labels itself participatory, bottom-up or even indigenous (e.g. Chambers 1983, 1997, Chambers et al. 1989), which does not reverse or modify development's hegemony so much as provide more effective instruments with which to extend technocratic control or advance external interests and agendas while further concealing the agency of outsiders, or the manipulations of more local elites, behind the beguiling rhetoric of 'people's control' (Cook and Kothari 2001, Mosse 2001). 'Community', 'indigenous', 'local knowledge', 'people's planning' – these categories which promised keys to counter top-down technocratic approaches and to unlock the power of development for the poor turn out to be dangerous counterfeits, products of modernity, trailing colonial histories of bureaucratically invented custom and tradition and providing, as Li (2002) notes, 'exemplary [foci] for the exercise of governmental strategies'[6] (although in relation to international discourses, national policies or local dynamics, poor people have also revealed a capacity to position themselves so as to acquire rights or resources by becoming 'communities' or adopting 'indigenous' identities; see Li 1996, 1999: 51, Karlsson 2002). Moreover, the techniques of participation themselves (such as PRA) turn out to be disciplinary technologies deployed to produce 'proper' beneficiaries with planning knowledge out of local people and their ways of thinking and doing. (These themes will be explored in some detail in the chapters that follow.)

In short, for the critics, development and its various discourses (that is policies and practices) have both institutional effects – maintaining relations of power – and ideological effects – depoliticisation (Ferguson 1994). Power manifests itself as the cunning of reason *and* populism (cf. Agrawal 1996: 470). Development is not policy to be implemented, but domination to be resisted. And such resistance is celebrated, for example in the activist documentation of social movements against resettlement schemes, or large dams, or the logging of the forest, or a multitude of smaller acts such as uprooting trees, pulling down fences or destroying irrigation ditches in order to protect rights to land, grazing or water.

These contrasted instrumental and critical views have blocked the way for a more insightful ethnography of development capable of opening up the implementation black box so as to address the relationship between policy and practice. Instrumental views are only too obviously naïve in relation to the institutional politics of development. But the critical turn in the anthropology of development is also an ethnographic blind alley, which merely replaces the instrumental rationality of policy with the anonymous automaticity of the machine. Development's effects occur, James Ferguson writes, 'behind the backs or against the wills of even the most powerful actors' (1994: 18). The relentless Foucauldian micro-physics of power occurs beyond the intelligence of the actors; although not, it seems, that of the decoding anthropologist. This is a 'new functionalist' sociology that, as Latour (2000) puts it, *substitutes* false objects with real ones – development with social function (for instance, the extension of bureaucratic power) – and therefore destroys its object.[7] Once the substitution is complete, there is nothing to say. Little wonder that critics such as Ferguson apparently spent so little of their time talking to development workers. My aim in this book is to reinstate the complex agency of actors in development at every level, and to move on from the image of duped perpetrators and victims caught up in a sort of 'space- age juggernaut on auto-pilot' (Sivaramakrishnan and Agrawal 2003 [draft]; see also Grillo 1997: 21), as well as to revise the false notion of all-powerful Western development institutions (Cooper and Packard 1997, Watts 2001: 286). Indeed, in different ways both the critical and the instrumental perspectives divert attention from the complexity of policy as institutional practice, from the social life of projects, organisations and professionals, from the perspectives of actors themselves and from the diversity of interests behind policy models.

CONCERNS OF A NEW ETHNOGRAPHY OF DEVELOPMENT

Recent ethnography of development has begun to blur the bold contours drawn by both rational planning and domination/resistance frameworks. Some has drawn on Foucault's notion of governmentality – 'a type of power which both acts *on* and *through* the agency and subjectivity of individuals as ethically free and rational subjects' (Shore and Wright 1997: 6) – to show how policy regulates social life and makes subjects and citizens, not by repression and overt control, but through a *productive* power which engenders subjectivities and aspirations (Foucault 1979a: 194, Li 1999: 296, 2002). Others, also arguing that the domination/resistance frame is too restrictive to grasp the nature of agency from below, point out that amidst even the most extreme forms of development imposition such as the forced resettlement of 'indigenous' people following dam construction, along with those who confront the contractors out of anger or frustration, there will be some who say 'This will mean a new day for us', 'We will be much better off' (Fletcher 2001). In a variety of ways the new ethnography of development is distinctly uncomfortable with monolithic notions of dominance, resistance, hegemonic relations and the implication of false consciousness among the developed (or the developers).

Michel de Certeau has added subtlety to the understanding of agency by alerting us to the devious, dispersed and subversive 'consumer practices' which are 'not manifest through [their] own products, but rather through [their] *ways of using* the products imposed by a dominant economic order' (1984: xiii, emphasis in original). In other words, while 'beneficiaries' (or project workers) may consent to dominant models – using the authorised scripts given them by projects – they make of them something quite different (1984: xiii). And it is in this sense that we can think with James Scott (1990b) in terms of the existence of 'hidden transcripts' alongside the 'public transcripts' of development policy. What is of interest is less the relationship between policy and implementation, or dominance and resistance, and more that between public and hidden transcripts; between the '"monotheistic privilege" of dominant policy models and the "polytheism" of scattered practices' surviving below (de Certeau 1984: 48).

Another thing the new ethnography of development shows is that governance brought by development schemes cannot be imposed; it requires collaboration and compromise. Reputation and legitimacy (upon which governance depends) are scarce resources for governments, donors, state development agencies or even NGOs operating in competitive environments (Li 1999).[8] Claims to success are always fragile, and counter-claims about development outcomes are 'points of political leverage' (1999: 297). There is always 'the possibility of exposure and disgrace ... [there is an] uneasy sub-text of political jokes and cynical reflections on the pomposity of a speech, the tedium of a spectacle or the stupidity of a plan – reflections that, while they criticise another also implicate the self' (1999: 299). Since success is fragile and failure a political problem, hegemony has to be worked out not imposed; it is 'a terrain of struggle' (1999: 316). The critics of development, Li points out, emphasised the *project* of rule, but missed the political contests, the feigned compliance, the compromises and contingencies involved in the *accomplishment* of rule (1999: 295). Here 'policy' appears in older guise as the pejorative 'stratagems, trickery, cunning, deceit, or hypocrisy' (Shore and Wright 1997: 19). And this (*pace* Ferguson) makes development's promises and practices themselves deeply political (cf. Gupta 1998; Moore 2000). Amita Baviskar (2004) working on decentralised natural resource development in India shows how schemes work so as to secure political consent, while Tania Li studying state resettlement programmes in Indonesia reveals the inherent vulnerability of policy models and 'bureaucratic schemes for ordering and classifying populations [which] may be secure on paper, but are fragile in practice' (1999: 298). Programme success depends upon the active enrolment of supporters including the 'beneficiaries'.

So, to reiterate, the ethnographic question is not whether but *how* development projects work; not whether a project succeeds, but how 'success' is produced. Given that (as later chapters will reveal) the different parts of a project system – donor policy makers, agency managers, consultants, field staff, farmers – operate with considerable autonomy from one another, the operational control which bureaucracies or NGOs have over events and practices in development is always constrained and often quite limited; regardless of whether they are disciplining or empowering in intent (cf. Quarles van Ufford 1988b). What is usually more urgent and more practical is control over the *interpretation* of events. As the critical analysts of policy discourse rightly argue, power lies in the narratives that maintain an organisation's own definition of the problem (also Roe 1994) – that is, success in development depends upon the stabilisation of a particular interpretation, a policy model – but they fail to examine the way in which policy interpretations are produced and sustained socially. As Bruno Latour reminds us, the success of policy ideas or project designs is not inherent (not given at the outset) but arises from their 'ability to continue *recruiting* support and so impose ... [their] growing coherence on those who argue about them or oppose them' (1996: 78). In other words, development projects need interpretive communities; they have to enrol a range of supporting actors with reasons 'to participate in the established order as if its representations were reality' (Sayer 1994: 374, cited in Li 1999: 298–9). Indeed, effective agency (and power) in development requires the strategic generation/manipulation of a network of actors within different discourses 'who become partly, though hardly ever completely, enrolled in the "project" of some other person or persons' (Long 1992: 23). There is always need for translating one set of interests into another. Donor advisers, consultants and project managers are able to exert influence only because the ideas or instructions they purvey can be translated into other people's own intentions, goals and ambitions.

Now, the more interests that are tied up with their particular interpretations the more stable and dominant development's policy models become. A powerful development narrative, such as that of African deforestation and savannah-isation challenged by

Fairhead and Leach (1996, 1997) is buttressed by many interests. It not only secures media-fed constituencies for Western governments, or financial solvency for a Guinean government reliant on green-conditional aid, or routine revenue for officials in a Prefecture from a system of fines, bribes and exclusions, but also underpins professional identities for junior foresters disciplining 'irresponsible villagers', and even the ethnic identity of 'savannah' against 'forest people' (1997).[9] To this set could be added donor advisers, consultants, researchers and many more whose interests come to be tied up with ruling models.

Clearly, common narratives or commanding interpretations are supported for different reasons and serve a diversity of perhaps contradictory interests. The differentiation of practical interests around 'unifying' development policies or project designs is a consequence of successful enrolment, and a condition of stability and success. This is possible because of the productive ambiguity that characterises development policy's 'master metaphors'. But it also requires the constant work of *translation* (of policy goals into practical interests; practical interests back into policy goals), which is the task of skilled brokers (managers, consultants, fieldworkers, community leaders – the subjects of this book) who read the meaning of a project into the different institutional languages of its stakeholder supporters, constantly creating interest and making real (cf. Latour 1996: 86).

The problem is that this diversity and the multiplicity of interests (and needs to be met) itself destabilises and militates against coherence. A postmodern emphasis on fragmentation and the endless multiplicity of actor perspectives, however, provides only half the picture; and is only a partial correction to the reductive analysis that explains away a development project by substitution; that debunks, blames or destroys its object (Latour 2000). The ethnographic task is also to show how, despite such fragmentation and dissent, actors in development are constantly engaged in creating order and unity through political acts of *composition* (Latour 2000). It involves examining the way in which heterogeneous entities – people, ideas, interests, events and objects (seeds, engineered structures, pumps, vehicles, computers, fax machines or databases)[10] – are tied together by translation of one kind or another into the material and conceptual order of a successful project (Latour 2000).[11] So, the coherence attributed to a successful development project is never *a priori*; never a matter of *design* or of policy. As Latour notes, 'If we say that a successful project existed from the beginning because it was well conceived and that a failed project went aground because it was badly conceived, we are saying nothing, we are only repeating the words "success" and "failure", while placing the cause of both at the beginning of the project, at its conception' (1996: 78).

The double effect of ordering and disjuncture, unity and fragmentation, is at the heart of the social processes of development analysed in this book. The book will show how subordinate actors in development – tribal villagers, fieldworkers, office staff, even project managers and their bosses in relation to donors – create everyday spheres of action autonomous from the organising policy models (in the manner of de Certeau's analysis), but at the same time work actively to sustain those same models – the dominant interpretations – because it is in their interest to do so. The social processes which multiply interests and experiences and those which unify and strengthen authoritative representations are the same. It will become clear how, paradoxically, the *practices* of project workers erode the models that they also work to reinstate as representations; and, moreover, that because it rests on disjuncture and contradiction, the coherence and order of a successful project is always vulnerable; interpretations can fail.[12]

My account will draw on a now strong tradition in the sociology of development that is interactionist or 'actor-oriented' focusing on project interfaces, or 'front lines', the lifeworlds of workers and the interlocking intentionalities of the developers and the 'to-be-developed'.[13] However, interactionist approaches often lose sight of the 'problem of policy', in the sense of failing to ask how ideas with power and social practice interact, once simplistic notions that development action is the product of policy intention (a narrow instrumental view) or arranged to resist it (a populist view) are discounted. Addressing the problem of the relationship between ideas and actions in fact returns to well worn issues in social anthropology. For as long as the discipline has existed it has challenged the view that ideas have a life of their own, that they can be mapped apart from institutions, persons and intentions, or be observed influencing institutions ; 'in all cases it is people who have ideas and who influence institutions' (Douglas 1980: 60). The accounts of Wittgenstein on language games, Evans-Pritchard on Azande witchcraft or Latour on scientists, commonly concede that the meanings of words and concepts are located in social activity (Douglas 1980: 36). My intention in this book is to show how, in the arena of development too, ideas have to be understood in terms of the institutions and social relationships through which they are articulated,[14] *and* how relationships have to be understood in terms of ideas. The way that we think, the premises we hold, the theories of cause and effect we invoke, the gaps in our curiosity are patterned by social actions and accountabilities. And, at the same time, policy ideas provide the idiom for alliances and divisions within donor consultant or project teams; farmers negotiate claims on project resources in terms of the classifications and identities offered by policy; and around policy's powerful metaphors wider networks of support are mobilised. As Mary Douglas has demonstrated in remarkably diverse fields, commitment to thought and commitment to social relations are inseparable (see Fardon 1999 for an overview).

POSITIONALITY – ETHNOGRAPHY FROM WITHIN

One final aspect of the new ethnography of development is the fact that increasingly it is multi-*positioned* as well as multi-sited (Marcus 1995). Anthropologists write from inside development (or donor, or project, or professional) 'communities' as well as from outside them. They research not just in, but as *part of*, donor policy-making bodies, consultant design teams, project meetings, village events and the writing or 'emancipatory reading' of texts (Apthorpe 1997). Outmoded conceptions of 'field' separate from 'home' are necessarily abandoned (Gupta and Ferguson 1997) as anthropologists try to explore rather than conceal the personal connections and affinities that tie them to their field of study (Marcus 1998: 16). And this means exploring a new kind of anthropology, one which situates the production of knowledge about other people, and places it explicitly within the framework of international relations, analysing the political and historical relations of power, and the systems of values which shape representations. Moreover, it does so in a way that places the anthropologist within this frame, and turns a self-critical lens onto the anthropologist-actor as member of a transnational community, speaking from within and in the first person.

There is no position from which I can analyse the circuitry of project and policy processes that follows which does not place me within it as a member of the 'communities' I describe. For over ten years, I was a visiting anthropologist consultant, variously labelled as a specialist in participation, institutions or 'social development'. Arguably the social processes of organisations are better understood from within. Certainly for outsiders access to the workings of development agencies is difficult. For one thing, such agencies operate within a nexus of evaluation and external funding which means that effective mechanisms for filtering and regulating the flow of information and stabilising representations are necessary for survival. Here, information is a private good rather than a public asset. Junior staff withhold or reveal information strategically in order to secure reputations, conceal poor performance or to negotiate position in the organisation or with outsiders (donors, villagers); while professionals and bureaucrats hide behind official models and policy jargon – the 'discursive glue' holding policy communities together, while anonymising remarks and distancing outsiders (Kaufmann 1997: 112).[15] 'Studying up' anyway involves studying those with the 'power to exclude themselves from the realm of the discussable' (Cooper and Packard 1997: 5). Nonetheless, the impression that development agencies (donors, field agencies or others) always feel they have something to hide, or that confidentiality and proprietary claims over knowledge inevitably characterise the relationship between agencies and their contracted consultants or researchers (Panayiotopoulis 2002) is wrong.[16] Development organisations are in the habit of dealing with criticism and the questioning of their claims and actions (e.g. through reviews and evaluations). However, they are less tolerant of research that falls outside design frameworks, that does not appear to be of practical relevance, is wasteful of time or adds complexity and makes the task of management harder (see discussion in Mosse 1998a). It is this that makes it virtually impossible to sustain long-term participant observation in the absence of making a practical contribution (whether as an engineer, a medic or anthropologist), being a member of the community and having a certain status (cf. Grammig 2002, Harper 2002). In any case, I for one would not have wanted the role of passive observer. My primary commitment was to promoting desirable development ends, as I understood them, rather than research.[17]

Methodologically one might speak of the category of 'participant comprehension' (Wood 1998: 55, citing Mikkelsen 1995) in relation to my various action-research roles. Through a constructive role in framing policy and project design and through engaging in impassioned contests over strategies and which model to apply, I acquired a performative knowledge of the discourses and relationships of development. But this also constrained the interpretive possibilities. As an actor along with others, I had to operate within what Quarles van Ufford (1993) calls a 'system model' of the project, where there is a necessary assumption of means–ends rationality, integration and manageability. I was an optimist, a positivist, a modernist; I deployed sociology of a classical kind in which groups and structures existed, new ones had to be built, and I forgot to observe myself (Eyben 2003: 6). But this was not my only mode of work. As the programme unfolded, I could use my part-insider/part-outsider position to engage in 'participant deconstruction' (Shore and Wright 1997: 16–17), trying to wrest my thinking free from prevailing models and means–ends rationality in order to offer critical insight. Here a 'sceptical model' applied in which competing interests and contradictory strategies came to the fore (Quarles van Ufford 1993). Setting aside the demands of problem solving or strategic negotiation, the struggle for order and coherence, I become more interested in locating pragmatic rules of project behaviour than arguing over normative ones.[18] This placed me at the margins of the project community – perhaps reincorporated as a means for self-critical learning, but also at risk of being excluded as an irrelevant, not to say disruptive, academic outsider.

Writing this book has been an extension of this role. It has in mind a 'relativist sociology' (Latour 1996)[19] in which I am a project actor like others; my policies and points of view stand with theirs; and so too does my analysis. My colleagues and associates are also social analysts offering theory, explanations, trying to stabilise the project world from their different points of view. The interviews that I undertook (largely in 2001) aimed to draw these out, while (for most interviewees) offering a rare opportunity to reflect candidly on work and its frustrations with an insider/colleague having common goals and shared experience. Depending on with whom I spoke, the story was part of the history and trajectory of British aid to India, part of the history of a para-statal cooperative or the Government of India ministry to which it is accountable; it was part of the history of crop research in India; part of the career of an individual plant breeder, a soil scientist, forester, project manager or fieldworker; the story concerned a project that came into being as a particular moment in the history of individual villages and farmers in a 'remote' tribal region of western India. It was part of my career as a development anthropologist, although its telling would depend on how I was positioned as positive practitioner or critical researcher. Potentially there were at least as many stories and as many co-authors as actors to be contained in this book.

But, as Van Maanen puts it, 'the unblinking ethnographic eye celebrated in Latour's (1993) much mentioned call for "symmetrical anthropology" is not so easy to bring off in those highly segmented worlds of self-interested organisational actors' (2001: 237). In reality, while I draw from the stories of other actors, it is my experience, values and interpretations, my self-critical (or therapeutic; see Pels 2000, cited in Eyben 2003: 6) judgements, my historical sense derived from being part of the originary design team, and my continuing involvement that impose coherence; it is my narrative that becomes the meta-narrative. Mine is an interested interpretation not a scientific judgement; it adds interpretations to those of actors whose experience I share (cf. Latour 1996, 2000). Ultimately, the objectivity of my analysis cannot be that derived from standing above the fray or of suppressing subjectivity, but rather that which comes from maximising the capacity of actors to *object* to what is said about them (to raise concerns, insert questions and interpretations) (Latour 2000).[20] For this reason, drafts of this material have been widely circulated amongst my 'informants' at every level. The analysis has been accepted and challenged, endorsed and dismissed, recognised and unrecognised; it has intrigued and depressed, provoked incandescence and been utterly ignored. Some reactions have deepened my analysis, some I have felt unable to draw into it. In the book's Preface I noted how one group of actors raised objections to my manuscript. When published there will be further responses – 'objectivity' in Latour's sense is a process that will have only just begun. It refuses closure to the analysis. Since, ultimately, the interpretive account that is 'anthropological', always 'coexists with other forms of knowledge' (Gupta and Ferguson 1997: 39), 'the political task [is] not "sharing" knowledge with those who lack it, but forging links between different knowledges that are possible from different locations ... '

THE STRUCTURE OF THE ARGUMENT:
FIVE PROPOSITIONS ABOUT POLICY AND PRACTICE

It remains to introduce the structure of this book and to present its argument in the simplest terms. This I will do by way of five propositions about the relationship between policy (by which I mean all kinds of development models, project designs and strategies) and development practices.

Proposition 1: *Policy primarily functions to mobilise and maintain political support, that is to legitimise rather than to orientate practice.* Anybody who has been involved in project formulation knows that this is work which is technically expressed (as project designs) but politically shaped (by the interests and priorities of agencies). Project design is the art, first, of making a convincing argument and developing a causal model (relating inputs, outputs and impacts) oriented upwards to justify the allocation of resources by validating higher policy goals, and, second, of bringing together diverse even incompatible interests, for example those of national governments, implementing agencies, collaborating NGOs, research institutions or donor advisers of different hues. One could summarise by saying (a) that the discourse of policy acts internally and has internal effects (it is donors who are disciplined by their own discourse, Johnston 2002); and (b) that development policy ideas are important less for what they say than for *who* they bring together; what alliances, coalitions and consensuses they allow, both within and between organisations (cf. Latour 1996: 42–3).[21]

Chapter 2 examines the process of design of a British aid project in these terms. It looks at the conceptual and linguistic devices that inspire allegiance, conceal ideological differences and thereby generate political legitimacy, and successfully enrol the different interests, across organisations, nations and cultures, that are necessary to bring a new project into existence (cf. Apthorpe 1997, Dahl 2001, Shore and Wright 1997). The chapter draws on the analysis of key policy texts, but tries to avoid the sort of 'discursive determinism' (Moore 2000: 657) that results from giving pre-eminence to texts as representations of discourse.[22] Texts are important, but precisely because such a large proportion of the time and expertise of development personnel is organised with reference to writing and negotiating texts, they cannot be read at face value without reference to the arguments, interests and divergent points of view that they encode and to which they allude.[23] Instead, I show that project design texts have to be interpreted backwards to reveal the social relations that produced them, the future contests they anticipate and the wider 'discourse coalitions' (Fairhead and Leach 2002: 9) they are intended to call forth. In short, a sociology of the document is needed to 'dispel the discursive hold of the text' (Apthorpe 1996a: 16).

Chapter 3 turns to the places and people that find strategic representation in project design texts – 'tribal' communities in western India. It shows that policy models which function internally to mobilise resources and political support are not best suited to understanding the social and historical context of development action. Ideas like 'participation' or community, which are strategically or politically useful (cf. Li 1996), lack conceptual clarity and are descriptively weak. To provide background for later discussion, the chapter turns instead, first, to recent subaltern history that views 'tribal' identity and livelihoods as the product of relationships with non-tribals over centuries, challenging standard representations of tribal isolation and underdevelopment. Second, the chapter explores the complex of kinship, land and livelihoods of the people with whom the project interacted, indicating the way in which policy concept and social context diverge.

Proposition 2: *Development interventions are not driven by policy but by the exigencies of organisations and the need to maintain relationships.* The point here is that policy models which work well to legitimise and mobilise political support do not provide a good guide to action, nor can they easily be turned into practice. The logic of political mobilisation and the logic of operations are different. The scope for control in development organisations is limited. International donor policy on, say, 'participatory development' only has effects through the interests, operational systems and culture of collaborating agencies, their workers and those recruited as beneficiaries. Chapters 4 and 5 reflect on a decade of project-level work to show that it is not policy models that make practice intelligible, but rather the political logic and culture of specific organisations. Projects are sites of social and institutional reproduction. Policy models (in this case participatory ones) do not and *cannot* shape actual practice in the way that they claim. They are ignored, resisted, 'consumed' or tactically used in ways that make them irrelevant in the face of more urgent relational demands. There is always the possibility that, as Heyman puts it (citing Perrow 1986), 'organisational masters prefer unofficial goals over official ones and may even make sure that official goals are not achieved' (1995: 264). Development organisations, then, have to be understood in terms of what they do as well as what they say, which involves paying attention to the internal aspects of organisational politics, the relations between managers and the 'street level bureaucrats' (Lipsky 1980) who interface with non-bureaucratic society, and the accommodations and resistances of the latter.

Chapter 4 takes a close look at the village-level encounter between fieldworkers and tribal farmers under the framework of a 'participatory planning process'. It shows how, as it became embedded within both village society and the institutional procedures of the project agency, this process was manipulated by local interests and external agendas, which in various ways constituted and validated themselves as 'local knowledge'. Administrative systems and local compliance pushed participatory planning towards closure. Chapter 5 continues the analysis of the social relationships of this development project, but shifts from planning to implementation, and from village to office. It shows how development practices were shaped less and less by the formal goals (of policy) and increasingly by the organisation's 'system goals', which revolved around the preservation of rules, administrative order and relationships of patronage. The chapter shows that a project regime is as much about sustaining relationships as implementation – as much relating as doing – in order to secure identity, status and the flow of resources. In both of these chapters, ethnographic material shows that as 'participation' – with its implication of local control or autonomous action – becomes institutionalised as policy, part of the 'language of entitlement' rather than the 'tactics of consumption', it too is colonised and eroded from within (de Certeau 1984: 49). Authorised models of 'participatory' development are subject to a multitude of hidden tactical readings. This practical logic is not just unacknowledged, it is hidden by the active promotion of official policy models.

Proposition 3: *Development projects work to maintain themselves as coherent policy ideas (as systems of representations) as well as operational systems.*[24] Despite the fact that the logic of practice routinely contradicts policy models, development projects are constrained to promote the view that their activities are the result of the implementation of official policy. Indeed, projects do not 'work' because they turn policy into reality, but because they sustain policy models offering a significant interpretation of events (which is not the same as operational control over events or practices).[25] Such models reveal and conceal, explain, justify, label and give meaning. It is through them that chaotic practices are stabilised, made coherent and validated for a project's various publics (donor managers, politicians, professionals); that progress is measured and success proclaimed; and that the gap between policy and practice is constantly negotiated away. They are woven thickly into professional practice and the identity of workers as habitus, and organisational survival depends upon them.

In Chapter 6 I reflect on the work of international development consultants including myself, concluding that expertise, as the conceptual work of policy, largely did not precede or direct action but followed it, providing an authoritative framework of interpretation for practices ordered by organisational routines and political relationships (cf. Heyman 1995: 265). The chapter illustrates the manner in which expertise unintentionally serves to stabilise frameworks of interpretation that measures performance but crucially misrepresent practice in terms of socially disembedded generalised models. Chapter 7 concerns the social production of 'success'. It shows the importance, first, of stabilising authoritative interpretations in terms of official project models that conceal the contradictions and weak causal connections between project activities and claimed outcomes; and, second, of enrolling supporters and creating a robust 'interpretive community' for the project, through the work of writing, hosting and organising public rituals. The argument is that projects are *made* successful by social processes that disperse project agency (Li 1999: 304), forge and maintain networks of support, and create a public audience for their drama of social transformation.[26] In short, the point will be that policy models do not generate practices, they are sustained by them. Development proceeds not only (or primarily) from policy to practice, but also from practice to policy.[27]

Proposition 4: *Projects do not fail; they are failed by wider networks of support and validation.* It follows from the above that project failure is not the failure to turn designs into reality; but the consequence of a certain disarticulation between practices, their rationalising models and overarching policy frameworks. Failure is not a failure to implement the plan, but a *failure of interpretation.* The final part of Chapter 7 describes a process of interpretive failure arising from a project evaluation but linked more fundamentally with shifts in donor policy. Chapter 8 documents a process of politically generated changes in the British aid framework which 'failed' the project, and examines the social dynamics of failure as rupture of an interpretive community. The response to failure (or the risk of it) is the re-articulation of project practice in terms of new favoured policy models. During its first ten years, the project in question would bear the imprint of successive international development fashions: beginning in 1990 with technical rainfed farming and the participatory 'farmer first' approach, by 1993–4 watershed development had gained primacy; by 1995, trends towards micro-finance and 'self-help' groups were strongly mirrored in the project; from 1998 the project was to exemplify DFID's new Sustainable Rural Livelihoods (SRL) framework; and, finally, an aid framework focused on governance and partnership with the state. Chapter 8 considers the costs of rapid policy change and of a new convergence of aid policy internationally onto singular models, placing the local project processes within a wider framework of the structuring power relations of aid.

Proposition 5: *'Success' and 'failure' are policy-oriented judgements that obscure project effects.* Apthorpe points out that, 'even if projects fail as practice they may nonetheless succeed as code or policy argument in the wider arena' (1997: 44). The reverse is equally true, namely that projects may have positive effects while being declared, or declaring themselves, as failures.[28] Chapter 9 leaves the 'upstream' world of donor aid frameworks to explore the social experience of being a beneficiary, and the relations and meanings obscured or misconceived by policy models. It draws on village-level research to show that, despite a development project's upwardly oriented obscuring policy vision, it may still have a positive socio-economic effect upon the lives of thousands of people. But the effects are often equivocal, unexpected, contradict legitimising policy models (or are unnoticed by them), and have more to do with infusion into regional and historical processes of change. They concern aspirations to modernity and reflect the historical reality that, for marginal tribal communities, economic survival has long depended upon forming alliances with those with better access to resources (see Chapter 2 this volume, Weisgrau 1997: 9). The difficult fact for participatory or community-driven models of development is that people become 'empowered' not in themselves, but through relationships with outsiders; and not through the validation of their existing knowledge and actions, but by seeking out and acknowledging the superiority of knowledge technology and lifestyles construed as 'modern'. Development rarely works counter to existing patterns of power, and project systems obscure the autonomous generation of meaning. At the same time, an intense emphasis on 'current policy' burdens programmes with new models which may have little bearing on the actual relations and practices of development or the socio-cultural effects they may have, which must be understood historically and ethnographically.

These days, projects are not very fashionable as instruments of policy in international development agencies. They have lost ground to the greater ambitions of sector-wide approaches, state-level partnerships, budgetary assistance and poverty-reduction strategies as the means to reduce global poverty (see Chapter 8 this volume). As the UK Secretary of State for International Development recently put it, 'the effective use of aid means moving away from funding a proliferation of projects to backing poverty-reduction strategies drawn up by developing countries themselves'.[29] The contention of this book is that there is still much to be learned from projects about the nature of the policy process and its relation to practice, about the politics of partnership, the coexistence of divergent agendas and interests, about the production of success or failure, or about the consequences of policy change and convergence. These are issues that have a greater not a lesser significance with a move 'upstream' in international development that only increases the size of the black box of unknowing between development policy and its effects – a point to which I will return in Chapter 10.

I hope that this book will show that, as a window onto larger processes, and as an historically specific set of relationships between policy trends and organisational dynamics, projects can be subject to ethnographic exploration. The conclusion of my argument will be that policy is more not less important than we imagine; and important in more ways than we realise. But most agencies are bound to a managerial view of policy which makes them resolutely simplistic about (or ignorant of) the social and political life of their ideas. What ethnography can offer the policy process is an element of critical reflection, a means to understand in individual cases how, as Mary Douglas writes, 'the work that thought does is social ... thought makes cuts and connections between actions' (1980: 54). Perhaps good policy is not implementable, but it is absolutely central to what happens in arenas of development, and it is important to know how it is so.

2

Framing a Participatory
Development Project

In August 1992 an agreement was signed between the Government of India and the Government of the UK which inaugurated a new Indo-British Rainfed Farming Project (IBRFP) under grant aid of £3.4 million. This was an experiment in agricultural development, which had by 1999 evolved into a much larger (£25 million) flagship British aid project in India. The basis of the agreement was a carefully crafted Project Document which established the purpose, methods, outputs and costs of the project. Most development projects begin as texts, perhaps like this one written by a team of project design consultants and aid agency administrators. These statements of policy involve a special kind of writing that, while preserving the appearance of technical planning, accomplish the social tasks of legitimation, persuasion and enrolment, becoming richly encoded with institutional and individual interests and ambitions and optimisms. The purpose of this chapter is to describe the processes of project design and so reveal the social life of a policy text; it is an ethnography of one moment in the public policy process (cf. Wood 1998).

Aid projects do not originate from design, but in the policy processes of donor agencies. The chapter therefore begins by describing the conundrums of British aid in the late 1980s from which the IBRFP project idea emerged, before turning to project design and asking *how* knowledge was constructed in the work of the UK consultancy team involved. The third section looks at *what* analysis of local problems and solutions resulted, and the fourth examines the interplay between ideas and their social effects as the project design is set to work enrolling a variety of goals, perspectives and interests, securing coherence and legitimacy while burying conflicts which become set as hidden fault lines as the narrative hardens into text, project model, legal agreement, organisation, rules and tasks (cf. Latour 1996). The final section identifies an important Indian partner agenda subjugated by the asymmetrical international relations of aid and its 'cultural nexus of conditionality' (Moore 2001).

MADE IN BRITAIN: POLICY MAKING AND UK AID IN INDIA IN THE 1980s

Long before they meet the livelihood needs of poor people, aid projects satisfy the political needs of Western development agencies. A new project conveys a donor's organisational identity, its favoured policy ideas, and is a site on which internal battles are fought. The question is, what shifting agendas, conflicts or crises facing British aid were written into the IBRFP project design narrative in the late 1980s?

Well, for one thing, there was a growing view at the time that British aid should be about addressing poverty, but was not. Over 30 per cent of the world's poor lived in India; but although India received more British bilateral aid than any other country (around £100 million annually), in 1990–91 only 14 per cent of actual annual disbursements went to projects with 'poverty potential', and only 6 per cent towards reducing poverty in rural areas, where 80 per cent of India's poor still lived, through natural resources development. Instead, the aid programme was dominated by capital aid to large infrastructure projects, especially in the power or (coal) mining sectors which accounted for around 40 per cent of the aid commitments.[1]

The problem was that poverty reduction was only one of several aid objectives, including economic growth and reform, environmental protection, good government and human development. Moreover, aid itself was part of a wider set of diplomatic and especially commercial relations between UK and India.[2] India was not only a powerful non-aligned giant in the Asian region to which Britain had historical ties, but also a major destination for commercial investment and a growing market for British goods and services. Indeed, the value of British exports – £1.3 billion in 1994 – was thirteen times the annual aid budget. In the early 1990s, UK aid helped trade indirectly by supporting India's economic liberalisation with balance of payments assistance, but throughout the 1970s and 1980s most aid was more directly tied to British exports, sterling being used to purchase imports to upgrade capital items in infrastructure projects (Lipton 1996: 510). Indeed, aid for anti-poverty programmes was limited by the fact that the 'local costs' involved could not be tied to packages of British exports (Lipton 1996). Local cost anti-poverty projects (including IBRFP) only became possible (after 1979) under a Retrospective Terms Agreement, a form of debt relief whereby local costs were raised in lieu of official interest payments (specifically for projects with a poverty focus).

In the late 1980s, a British public more concerned about international aid was scandalised by this state of affairs. The stagnation of aid allocations at less than half the UN target of 0.9 per cent of GDP had become an electoral issue, and blatant abuse of aid to India to protect British industry, for example in the notorious Westland helicopters project, put new pressure on the government's Overseas Development Administration (ODA)[3] to change its way of doing business and increase the poverty-focus of its aid.[4]

A second concern, however, was that 'poverty-focused' aid itself should actually benefit the poorest rather than provide commercial opportunities for rural elites. Indeed, the ODA's anti-poverty projects in the forestry and agriculture sectors were heavily criticised in the 1980s for failing on these grounds. The critical attention of Indian and British media and NGOs (including Oxfam for whom I worked in Bangalore at the time) focused, for example, on a large ODA/World Bank 'social forestry' project in Karnataka which, instead of meeting the fuel and fodder needs of the poor and of women, appeared to subsidise commercial planting of water-thirsty eucalyptus by large farmers and absentee landowners, displacing food crops, tenant farmers and farm labourers in a drought-prone region. The project was further tainted by an activist campaign and public interest litigation against eucalyptus plantations supplying the Indian state-subsidised pulpwood and polyfibre industry on common lands, which deprived the poor of access to basic fuel, fodder, fruits and raw material (SPS 1988).

At around the same time, in eastern India, the ODA was promoting 'green revolution' agriculture to raise rice and wheat production through large-scale block demonstrations and subsidised fertiliser inputs (Sharrock et al., 1985). The Indo-British Fertilizer Education Project (IBFEP), the ODA's leading agricultural project, which had its origins in a late 1970s scheme to supply £30 million worth of British fertiliser, was strongly criticised for providing input-subsidies to better-off farmers with irrigated land, for excluding women and the poor, and for a non-participative top-down technology transfer approach. By the late 1980s, senior ODA advisers themselves found little justification for using aid to subsidise commercial production (of crops or trees).[5]

In both forestry and agriculture projects, the critics put many failings down to the problems of working with government systems that were inflexible, top-down, had a narrow focus on increasing commodity output (trees or crops) and technologies for high-potential areas (or commercial forestry) which were ill-suited to work with the poor in marginal rainfed environments. ODA advisers began to conclude that government was part of the problem not the solution; its departments were inefficient, over-staffed, infected with corruption, and 'any benefits available through [them] would be subverted by the way the system worked'.[6] Encouraged by NGO critics and a new 'Washington consensus' on reducing the role of the state in favour of the market, there was a strong view, as one senior adviser put it, 'that governments should not be involved in rural sector activities; this was left to the private sector ...'. NGOs used the space opened up by this language of privatisation, institutional pluralism and 'rolling back the state' to lobby for alternative participative, community-based models of development, attentive to indigenous knowledge and involvement of communities in project design.[7]

At the time (the late 1980s), the ODA was remarkably responsive to such external lobbying. For one thing, the agency lacked an overall strategic policy, and, as one adviser put it, 'policy statements were made in response to international concerns about issues – holes in the ozone layer, carbon, environmental concerns, human rights concerns, famine, drought', or ministerial pronouncements (for example, Margaret Thatcher's 1989 Conservative Conference speech which committed a hundred million to forests). For another, shifting power and influence *within* ODA, and especially the rising importance of the Social Development Advisers (SDAs) under new leadership from 1987, meant that external pressure on matters of poverty, participation or gender, could for the first time be registered as strategically important. The influence of this advisory group within ODA's project cycle management increased steadily from 1987.[8] SDAs began to set the agenda and lead project design teams (rather that merely reacting to 'social issues' or side-effects in technical advisers' programmes).[9] They contributed significantly to changing the status of the issue of poverty from being a social development specialism (in the mid-1980s) to a British aid programme goal.

So, a new project for the India programme in 1990 would carry a weighty policy agenda. It would have to (1) demonstrate a new commitment to poverty reduction in the largely unattended rural and agricultural sector; (2) involve private sector agencies outside the state system; (3) signal the move away from old 'blueprint' projects, delivered in specific form and to a fixed timeframe, and towards 'process projects' in which technical interventions were not defined in advance, and objectives and strategies could be revised as the project proceeded through negotiation with project participants;[10] and (4) adopt a participatory approach and involve a design process which was itself consultative and attentive to the experience of British and regional NGOs (e.g. making the critics into stakeholders by recruiting NGO workers, such as myself, onto design teams). Projects were key, the emerging ODA view in India being that 'to maximise the effect and influence of our (relatively) small programme we will design projects to demonstrate innovative, sustainable and replicable approaches' (ODA India: Country Review Paper 1993). While clearly human-resource intensive, projects provided models with 'bulking-up' potential.

These mandates were not of course uncontested within the ODA in 1990. So, project designs were strategic in that they provided the means by which key players or subgroups within the agency, such as the Social Development Advisers, could consolidate and demonstrate their influence. Exploiting the opportunity for untied poverty-focused aid afforded by the debt relief agreement (RTA), SDAs were able to use a project such as IBRFP 'as a mobiliser for policy change back in London' (DFID SDA). Such project designs were of course also subject to contest from disciplinary or ideological opponents, although differences were quickly concealed behind the logically and sequentially organised plans that established the scientific rationality and legitimacy of donor policy (Wood 1998: 56). The success of the IBRFP project design and the aid policy agenda it articulated were mutually constituted.

But the new British aid policy could not be realised without an Indian partner. So, when in 1987 the state/private sector hybrid KBCL – a large national agro-input manufacturing and marketing cooperative, promising to combine flexible independence from government with a scale of operation and a national network which no NGO could match – approached the ODA with an agricultural extension project focusing on rainfed farming in western India, the ODA's advisers were predisposed to show interest.[11] The point was *not* that KBCL had the necessary experience in participatory development – the fertiliser company had none – but rather that here was an organisation onto which ODA advisers could strategically inscribe their emerging agenda; one with 'a cheerful preparedness to be a clean slate' (senior ODA adviser). Asked why KBCL was chosen as a project agency, another key adviser involved at the time said:

I think probably because it was there, to be quite honest ... You know there were the positives of being able to find an Indian institution that was able to do what you wanted it to do rather than what it wanted to do, like KBCL. With that sort of set-up you can really set the agenda for the whole project in a way that you couldn't with an NGO ... who have their own agenda and certainly with government ... We could impose our own ideas from the beginning on KBCL, set up a separate organisation and get a [consultant] in and he'll tell you how to go about it.[12]

KBCL was an agency willing to enter into a relationship with the donor ODA as 'partner'– an ambivalent concept that, as Dahl notes in the context of aid relations, conveys the ideal of equality, while allowing the asymmetries of tutelage or clientship, 'the best client [being] the client incapacitated ... [by] structural constraints' (2001: 20). The intensive use of expatriate consultants to design, instruct and guide in this kind of project was itself part of a new assertion of donor control that came with the 1990s emphasis on participation, poverty and equity.[13] Turning to *how* the internal policy processes of the ODA became a project design imposed upon an Indian organisation and region takes us to the work a team of such consultants.

THE PROJECT PREPARATION MISSION – A DIARY

In June 1990, unexpectedly I found myself on an expatriate consultancy team (of the University of Wales) that had won the ODA contract to design and prepare the new project in western India. We were a fairly typical aid consultancy team: British 'experts' from different disciplines (economics, soil science, plant genetics and social anthropology) brought together into a 'transitory knowledge building community' given an authority symbolised by access to the time of top people, short time-frames, 'frenetic working displays', privileged transport and communications, receptions and numerous expressions of deference (Wood 1998). Beyond personal commitment to particular development goals and to the new project as their vehicle, our broad ambition (in my view) was to demonstrate professional competence and so secure an enduring relationship with the donor and project agency/area. This offered sites and access for natural resources and social development research/learning, as well as consultancy income (working under a university contract the former was of far greater value than the latter; cf. Goldman 2001, Wood 1998). We each brought our own preoccupations to the project design process. I was working for Oxfam at the time and viewed the consultancy as an opportunity to connect the ODA's new approach to that of Indian grassroots NGOs and to validate a certain approach to participatory development, collective action and sustainability. Another colleague, until recently a research scientist millet breeder at ICRISAT,[14] saw the project as 'a heaven-sent opportunity' to apply new methods of participatory evaluation of crop varieties emerging out of his frustration with official systems of running and analysing crop trials. A third of our company brought professional concerns relating to work on low-cost soil and water conservation in East Africa.

Our 'terms of reference' from the ODA were characteristically ambitious *and* prescriptive – not in the methods, sources (or ownership) of data, but in the time-frame and style of presentation. We had six weeks 'to review all available information which may be relevant to the formulation of the approach and technical content [of the project] ... and to produce a detailed proposal for ... a fully participatory and poverty-focused rainfed farming project'.[15] Let me recall something of the process.

We begin, as most development designs do, in the capital city. Meetings with top government officials, aid agencies, NGOs and academics establish the prevailing rural development discourse, its key players and those who need to be enrolled as supporters of the ODA's agenda. Senior officials are invited to an inaugural workshop on 'participatory approaches'. Robert Chambers, premier ideologue and key speaker, stands in front of an inverted map of India. The message: participatory and poverty-focused development involves a reversal of dominant technocratic 'green revolution' ideas and practices. In the heady atmosphere of irreverence and reversal, senior bureaucrats (from the Ministry of Agriculture among others) speak of 'farmer priorities', 'government participation in people's programmes', 'simple technology at eye level', 'gender consciousness'; consultants chip in with 'historic opportunity' for neglected dry uplands. For a moment the ODA's consultants have set the terms of the design debate ...

Three days later a jeep rattles through the richly green monsoon landscape of rural Bihar carrying our group of consultants on a field trail of development experience in search of storylines from other ODA ventures or from famous NGO projects. A cavalcade of jeeps roars into a small village on the edge of the forest. The trajectories of international consultancy and farming routines intersect briefly, confusingly. A ploughman waylaid in the monsoon rain. The mutual bewilderment of a rice-field encounter between farmer and foreigner: questions and answers, frantic notebook scribbling. Fragments of an agrarian survey – land, crops, inputs, yield, prices, livestock, grazing – interspersed with development stories of hardship and impacts, new crop varieties, training attended, wells deepened, hopes for more. In the characteristically vertical encounter intimate household details of unknown 'project people' are made public, or become elements in establishing position and negotiating analysis within the interdisciplinary consultancy team.

In the shelter of her village home/office a community worker, in the habit of being monitored, explains the work routines and lays out as evidence the documentary products and supervisory instruments of social work – registers, diary, pass-books, ledgers. I wonder whether such order will ever reveal what is going on; then on a walk between hamlets fieldworkers confide unhappiness, excessive workloads, the burdensome demands of outsiders, harassment from senior, technical or male staff, uncooperative villagers, failed experiments, low pay, isolation, insecurity and lack of appreciation. These impressions, too, are stored for later use. We move on from the village to more senior staff who provide us with explicit strategies that explain and give meaning to it all. A multiplicity of schemes unfolds, quantified inputs and illustrative successes. Uncertainty is stabilised as a rational process and bureaucratic structure – at least long enough for the passing attention of transitory consultants. These, and countless meetings like them, leave a spidery trail across the pages of my notebooks capturing fragments of conversations shouted against the roar of engines and the blaring of horns. And then there are the impressions of people, staff, personalities, organisations, hierarchy and deference, managerial cultures – the visible, the normative, the confided, the assumed, condensed ingredients for negotiation and project-making …

The trail leads on. It takes us from rural Bihar through Rajasthan to western Gujarat, to state agricultural universities, tribal research institutes, and activists of various kinds. Meetings in the chambers of senior officials, rural bank managers, breakfast with the District Magistrate, receptions with local dignitaries signal the authority of our knowledge production. Ubiquitous strong tea and sweet biscuits provide a prophylactic against sleep during long hot meetings with district officials under rattling fans after late nights shuffling through the endless piles of official reports, project documents, research papers, statistics, or ethnographies in search of information, inspiration or legitimisation for project making …

In the identified 'project area', with our various professional collaborators, we criss-cross a rolling agricultural landscape of the inter-state borderlands, home to fleetingly encountered Bhil cultivators – our intended beneficiaries – as yet only a shadowy presence in the collective mind of the consultancy team; repeatedly invoked as the underdeveloped tribal 'other' through official meetings with the agents of the state, yet concealed by the order and etiquette of formal development encounters. In a village pre-selected by KBCL staff we sit as honoured guests on a raised dais along with district agriculture officials and cooperative mangers in front of another type of beneficiary – members of the hosting cooperative society, without exception progressive commercial male farmers in a largely subsistence region. We are invited to put our questions to the disciplined crowd. Otherwise we divert from the pre-planned schedule and become uninvited interlopers in villages en route, sitting by the houses of the majority poor, barred by bad debts from cooperative membership, bewildering them with questions framed by our own preoccupations with the agro-ecology and socio-economics of the region. During the day we profile selected villages and landscapes, and in the evenings meet to exchange information/impressions and ideas.

From these diverse encounters we separately drew storylines, plots, characters and scenes for the project we were making. Our methods were frankly crude, *ad hoc*, and qualitative; our 'findings' structured by our different experiences, disciplinary viewpoints, values and interests, and by the separate professional networks to which they connected us. Bound to tight time-frames we depended substantially upon working assumptions, borrowed ideas or past experience.[16] The analyses we produced were equally influenced by the social dynamics of this small but intensely interacting interdisciplinary group (cf. Wood 1998). Patterns of leadership, acknowledged expertise, coalitions of opinion, the division of labour, difference and deference – all established through mutual appraisal over days and weeks – established who would attempt to define the overall discourse, who would retreat into technical speciality, who would contest or concede which points. The policy process was never independent of the contingencies of social relationship (cf. Wood 1998). Small alliances, compromises or adjustments of opinion were mediated by a multitude of small hospitalities and obligations as we tried to reconcile different perspectives in meetings, over meals, during long journeys (cf. Wood 1998). In practice it was not difficult to reach consensus in the written output. ODA policy concerns had virtually pre-defined which perspective could lay claim to the overall project approach (the NGO participatory development one); and the terms of reference were sufficiently broad to allow considerable autonomy to the different expert spheres of soil science, plant genetics or farm economics. Serious conflicts over design options within the team were rare, conflicts with the project agency were suppressed (see below) and with the donor's agenda ruled out.

As Bruno Latour suggests, little separates the work of the engineer, economist (or anthropologist) writers of technical designs, and that of the novelist or scriptwriter, except that the former 'novel' circulating from meeting to meeting, office to office as report or plan might also become a world in which people circulate (1996: 240). The different character-plots provided by members of the team – crop trials, participatory planning, runoff plots, village volunteers – were assembled and reassembled into a shared abstraction, the project narrative, that gradually came to impose its own order on the bewildering variety of encounters and ideas. But this story would only become real if it effectively legitimised policy; if it became an exciting story, a persuasive argument justifying the investment of public money; if it successfully recruited influential supporters, connected to institutional trajectories and personal ambitions (cf. Latour 1996, Wood 1998). I will shortly examine how these demands shaped the expression of this project design. But first I need to explain the analysis through which policy assumptions, interests and priorities (of donor, consultants and others) were naturalised as the problems and prospects of a particular underdeveloped place and people – the Bhils of western India.

'DESIGNER PROBLEMS': TECHNOLOGY AND PARTICIPATION

Several anthropologists have argued that project designs involve representations of places and people as embodiments of those development problems which are amenable to a donor's currently favoured technical solutions (Ferguson 1994). Accepting this simplification for the moment, and applying it to the ODA IBRFP project design, two 'solutions' stand out: the first was 'the introduction of improved agricultural *technology*' and the second 'the enhancement of farmer capacities through *participation*'.

First then, the IBRFP project arose from the ODA's historical concern with agricultural productivity now extended to upland rainfed ecologies in western India. Here, poverty was 'ecologised' as the effects of erratic rainfall, undulating topography, or shallow soils,[17] amplified by the effects of demographic pressure (land fragmentation, reduced fallows and deforestation) and by deficient farmer management practices, knowledge and technology: cropping maize on slopes which encouraged erosion, inadequate use of areas of soil deposition, the lack of improved varieties, low levels of fertiliser use, poor grain storage, or weak draught animals kept in excessive numbers.[18]

Now, these and countless other failings of the existing local farming system made it an arena with almost unlimited 'tappable potential for improvement' through *technical* innovations drawn from an international agricultural science repertoire, by means of which 'the incomes of farm households could at least double in real terms over 5 to 10 years'.[19] They included improved cultivars, seed treatment, methods of fertiliser application, crop protection, improved farm implements, irrigation efficiency, livestock improvement and soil and water conservation techniques – an inventory extended by a series of (always hopeful) consultant experts throughout the life of the project.[20] Note that what counts as innovation and 'technology' (as opposed to timeless 'existing practice' or 'unimproved tradition') comes by definition from outside expertise.[21]

But while the project area was readily understood as the environmentally degraded home to a catalogue of correctable deficiencies, in this case development problems were not, and *could* not legitimately be traced to farmer ignorance and traditional agriculture – as they had been by earlier generations of developers and colonial administrators. This was a project in the new 'Farmer First' mould. Drawing on the work of Paul Richards (1985) and Robert Chambers et al. (1989), among others, indigenous farming practices were now understood as complex, sophisticated and adapted to resource systems which were complex, diverse and risk-prone. Farmers were not seen as ignorant and conservative. They flexibly combined multi-crop regimes, livestock and trees in order to reduce risk, and were themselves experts, active experimenters and critical judges of modern technology.

The real problem, we judged, was that tribal cultivators were victims of a defective state system of agricultural research and extension. Centrally defined research priorities focused on narrowly defined problems (such as 'breeding groundnut for iron clorosis resistance') resulting in recommended technology packages suited to simple, uniform, high-input, risk-free irrigated monoculture agricultural environments – those which resembled the research station – but irrelevant and ill-adapted to the needs of poor upland tribal farmers. Here the husbanding of *more* not fewer species and varieties of plants and animals, increasing complexity and widening choices was required (Jones et al. 1994). Conventional systems of seed development, testing and release applied over-stringent and uniform standards (for example, prioritising yield over duration, fodder, pest resistance or other farmer-relevant criteria) restricting the range of new genetic material reaching poor farmers.[22] Regulations discouraged adaptation to local circumstances, and restricted extension support to officially state-released varieties, excluding seeds developed by NGOs, the private sector or even other states. Matters were worsened by the weak link between research and extension staff, and the assumption among officials that non-adoption meant farmer backwardness, which precluded exploration of the valid reasons for which upland farmers rejected new 'improved' technology.

At its boldest our critique reversed standard flows of expertise, redefined professional profiles and implied that technology developed by formally qualified scientists would no longer, by that fact, be counted as 'improved'; quite possibly the reverse (cf. Appadurai 2004, Crewe and Harrison 1998: 104).[23] Bhil farmers were not unskilled but had been denied access to appropriate modern technology and kept in an agricultural backwater by inefficient science and researchers ignorant of farmers' own innovations, and their capacity to experiment with new technology in their fields.

So while it challenged green revolution approaches to technology transfer, the IBRFP design consensus firmly rejected the antipathy between new technology and indigenous knowledge found in environmentalist and political ecology writing (e.g. Shiva 1989, Yapa 1996).[24] The problem was not modern technology *per se*, but the systems of technology development that excluded farmers. Similarly, Bhils were not destroyers of soil or forest resources, but victims of centrally planned state soil and water conservation programmes implemented on their land without their involvement and without regard to local practices, land-holding patterns or field boundaries; or they were victims of state forestry which enclosed forest areas irrespective of their needs or rights, and an official culture of exclusion and rent-seeking which only encouraged pilfering from 'open access' forests; or victims of the promotion of farm forestry narrowly focusing on commercial exotics (eucalyptus) that exhausted scarce water from the land. To the landscapes of tribal underdevelopment embodying correctable problems, our project design narrative added vivid landscapes of bureaucratic corruption and inefficiency. Indeed, prevailing national development regimes were de-legitimised, and human agency was relocated from the state to the project, its people and donor. So it was not technological invention at all, but institutional change that would improve Bhil agriculture.

This leads, then, to the second project 'solution' namely *participation*. Improved technology would overcome a cycle of inefficient resource use and low production, but it would be farmer *participation* – in setting the research agenda, experimentation and evaluating technology – that would renew farmers' interest in their land, develop and deliver a basket of relevant technologies to choose from, and promise a positive spiral of improved productivity and reduced out-migration, returning Bhil tribals to their vocation as settled agriculturalists (while avoiding the conventional incentivising through subsidies on technology which created unsustainable dependency, prevented learning, perpetuated error and benefited the well-off). So, the policy model framed the problem of increasing agricultural production so that farmer participation itself would be accepted as an autonomous causal link.

But the concept of 'participation' extended further. The project districts were 'an area without participation', in the sense that they were remote not just from agricultural technology and inputs, but also from institutional credit, markets, government administration and services; and their inhabitants dependent upon intermediaries. In fact, within our design team, the language of participation provided a bridge between two development perspectives: on the one hand a 'productivity view' focusing on technology, and on the other an 'entitlement view' that stressed unequal access to resources and services, and the marginality of a *people* rather than a place and ecology.

In the latter view, tribal poverty and vulnerability were understood as historically rooted relations of exploitation involving moneylenders, traders, urban labour contractors, brokers and local agents of the state that for decades conspired to exclude Bhils from the benefits of the state's anti-poverty schemes and circumvent laws for their protection. Marginality was signalled by the everyday absence of teachers from schools, doctors from clinics, extension workers from villages, and the brutality and corruption of police, forest guards and usurers, as much as by official statistics on poor infrastructure and health services, or low literacy rates (close to zero in the case of rural women). The analysis fell short of describing tribal underdevelopment as the direct *result* of colonial and postcolonial state policy towards adivasi areas, and the exclusion of tribals from real political power (e.g. Jones 1978).[25] Nonetheless, participation did mean more local access and power, and a project which did not emphasise new technology so much as enhanced individual and group capacities, increased awareness, skills, social capital and self-reliance generated through the work of Community Organisers and village volunteers, and sustained by farmer institutions for savings and credit, input supply or marketing. Not only was this 'a way of addressing powerlessness and isolation as aspects of rural disadvantage',[26] but also without it few sustainable gains were to be had from new technology itself, which might in fact only increase risks among food-insecure poor tribals; so cautioned the 'social development' counterparts to the project's technical reports.[27]

THE SOCIAL WORK OF POLICY IDEAS: ENROLMENT, PERSUASION, AGREEMENT AND ARGUMENT

As consultants we appeared to have done our job well, to have produced a singular knowledge system providing a coherent project analysis. In fact, there was no such system. We had no single view; for example, no common representation of the identities and problems of the project's future beneficiaries, who were sometimes isolated, culturally other and historically exploited tribals; sometimes modernising farmers and partners in technology development. Sometimes they were imagined living in cohesive subsistence communities characterised by limited desires or market involvement, and charged with conserving resources and lifestyles (cf. Li 1997); sometimes in dynamic and divided villages pursuing the fruits of commercial agriculture and expanding markets and links to the state.[28] I need to turn, then, to the social work of enrolment, persuasion, agreement and argument that lies behind the consensus and coherence demanded of project designs by the politics of aid.

Enrolment: There is a subtle relationship between the framing of problems and the social process of enrolment in the design of a development project. The way in which we conceived the IBRFP project served to accommodate not just our own personal and disciplinary differences, keeping us interested and engaged, but also the larger constituencies who gave us ideas and storylines and who we worked hard to enrol so as to legitimise our effort, and in whose name we claimed to speak: including ODA technical or social advisers, district collectors, NGO managers, social researchers, activists, crop science, rural markets, the environment ... We were like Latour's 'assemblies of spokespersons who bring together, during a single meeting, around a single table different worlds' (1996: 42–3). And our draft paragraphs called forth these wider communities of interest. Indeed, project designs *need* many supporters in order to come into existence, they need to become part of overlapping regional networks and transnational knowledge communities (of agricultural research, participatory development) contending for influence within national or international policy arenas (cf. Biggs 1995). And those who supplied the characters and storylines for our project narrative would soon be needed in support roles (in research, recruitment, training, lobbying). They would be more or less critical to turning the project as a world of signs into a world of objects (Latour 1996) and would be needed to sustain it in future.

So, a project design is itself a bid for political support, a site for coalition building at different levels (that continues beyond design). But as the design wins more supporters, it also takes on more agendas; it is 'a sentence that becomes more and more complex and more and more reasonable ... it becomes so complete, so comprehensive, so enveloping, so detailed, that volumes of reports and specifications are needed to contain it' (Latour 1996: 103). The corollary of enrolment is, of course, the exclusion of other frames, perspectives and approaches – technical, commercial and political. And there were strategic silences on questions such as land reform or conflicts over tenure, or local corruption or state violence against tribals (especially of the police or Forest Department).

In order to attract interest and support, a project design becomes complex and contains irreconcilable perspectives; but in order to persuade it requires unity, coherence and simplicity. A clue as to how this tension can be reconciled is found in the mediating function of the key polysemic and ambiguous concept of 'participation' within our consultancy team and the IBRFP project design. The notion of participation (in this case referencing both better technology and social power) allowed opposed views to be brought together. It was a *necessary* concept in framing IBRFP that rapidly became the 'master metaphor' in terms of which we were able to (re-)frame and inter-translate a variety of technical, economic and political goals and strategies so that we could talk to each other and to donor advisers, government officials, NGOs or scientists.[29] As a goal/strategy, participation had the necessary high degree of *ambiguity*, which in project discourse (as in cultural systems) facilitates and helps maintain consensus, and conceals ideological differences, setting limits to the struggles over meaning (Dahl 2001: 20, Osella and Osella 1996). As Latour notes, 'different groups with different interests will conspire with a certain amount of vagueness ... on a [common] project, that then constitutes a good "agency of translation," a good swap shop for goals' (1996: 48, citing M. Callon). In project plans, ambiguity provides room for manoeuvre, allows compromise, permits the multiplication of the criteria of success and the accommodation of shifting policy agendas; and it distributes agency by allowing various actors to isolate and claim credit for desirable change (Li 1999).[30]

Persuasion: In order to persuade, to sell a problem-solution, to widen the appeal, development designs have to meet other criteria which the IBRFP proposal illustrates. First, a project has to be *consequential*, it has to have big effects. The IBRFP project 'aimed to improve the long-term livelihoods of poor farmers in a drought prone region' and 'promote a replicable participatory poverty-focused and environmentally beneficial approach to farming systems development elsewhere'.[31] Its design told stories that linked specific technical interventions to larger schemes of social change and visions of the future. It involved an arresting narrative of disaster averted – the reversal of agricultural collapse or the transformation of marginal migratory tribal people into a citizenry of locally self-reliant settled agriculturalists. An aid project is a 'globalising technology' (in its way like the media or migration) whose art of persuasion works through projecting the lives of its remote tribal beneficiaries onto metropolitan imaginations (Appadurai 1997, Luthra 2003). Over-ambition holds together internal diversity, and helps conceal the self-evident fact that 'no country in the world has ever developed itself through projects' (Edwards 1989: 119 in Grammig 2002).

Second, a project has to be *innovative*. It needs the quality of novelty, and has to mark a new beginning. This theme reverberates through IBRFP's initial documentation. Third, innovative projects also have to be *replicable* and involve approaches which can, for instance, be taken up by government. Indeed the economic and financial justification of IBRFP relied upon the replication of project initiatives.

Fourth, the designed interventions have to be seen to be *technical*. Policy aims to marshal political support, but always behind empirical facts, science and profession; never openly (Apthorpe 1996a: 20). The flaunting of the technical expertise of foreign consultants and references to participation or 'farmer first' as globally valid technical approaches helped to conceal the political nature of project choices, goals or critiques of existing state programmes. It also served to de-author potentially threatening change that still had to be negotiated within the large bureaucratic project agency (cf. Porter 1995: 79). More broadly, the language of international development consensus (and ultimately legal and intergovernmental agreement) is always technical and never political. To retain its legitimacy and support the project had to be represented at one level as if it had no political or institutional context.

Finally, projects have to be conceived of as predictive *models* in which the elements are systematically and causally related, and where outcomes of actions are certain (Stirrat 2000: 36). So, the IBRFP narrative was expressed as a 'model of change', a simplified set of problem–solution linkages that connected activities to key results (or 'outputs', see Box), and outputs to impacts as cause and effect. These established, for example, the autonomous relationship between farmer-managed trials (activity), widening cultivar choice (outputs) and crop yield increases (impact); or between soil and water conservation measures and yield stability/increase; or between farmer organisations, access to institutional credit and empowerment. Above all, the project model was defined by a 'theory of participation'. This was a depoliticised causal theory asserting that persisting poverty and isolation, and inappropriate and unsustainable development were

---

Key IBRFP Project Outputs

- a *participatory planning system* in which poor women and men are involved in the identification and design of project interventions to meet their needs and the development of village workplans;
- *participatory technology development* and the testing and adoption of low-cost technologies identified as appropriate for broad farming systems development (crops, agro-forestry, horticulture, livestock, soil and water conservation, minor irrigation); collaborative pro-poor research with state agricultural universities on rice and maize breeding.
- the *development of local institutions* for credit, income generation or the management of common property (forest protection, irrigation); the training of a cadre of village volunteers;
- an *autonomous project management unit* with its headquarters in the centre of the project area, headed by a project manager having a core of technical and social science specialists supporting male and female Community Organisers (COs) based in individual village clusters.[32]

Source: paraphrased from project documents and logframes.[33]

the consequence of top-down planning and the non-involvement of farmers in need identification, design and technology development; and, correspondingly, that maximising farmer participation in these (including the specific involvement of women), and enhancing skills and capacities, would result in better designed, more effective programmes and sustainable improvements to livelihoods.[34] Or, as the project document put it, *'the basic premise is that sustainable development can only be achieved by enhancing local self-reliance through institutional and community development'*.[35]

The project design was synthesised into the project management tool – the Logical Framework (or logframe) – which summarily conveyed to outside decision makers the rationality (and manageability) of a scheme with logically related and technically specified activities, measurable outputs, an ordered sequence and the functional integration of different components and institutional actors (donors, implementing agencies, field staff and villagers). The IBRFP logframe went through successive re-workings but remained the point of reference to explicate the approach, to report achievements and negotiate changes in strategy as the project went along. The logframe was itself part of a carefully negotiated and drafted project document which stood for and justified the project in prescribed textual form, with key sections and appendices dealing with economic cost–benefits, technical and institutional viability. Using linguistic and stylistic conventions that 'invoke codes operating beyond the reading' (Apthorpe 1996a: 18), this text established the scientific validity and policy acceptability (its poverty or gender focus) of the project, effectively bringing it into existence. Once its elements – an approach, roles and activities – were present in the text, the project existed in our minds and in our conversations, independent of the actuality of events.

Agreement: The IBRFP project document gave stability to the cacophony of ideas and voices. It was also the basis of a formal agreement between the governments of UK and India. It was a contract that conveyed the fiction of the 'determining present', as opposed to an unfolding performance (Alexander 2001: 478). This was expressed materially when the bound project document (with logframe) reappeared in the hands of visiting consultants and ODA review teams as a constant point of reference. It was a reminder of the obligations of the project agency and a means for the foreign donor to assert authority in the spirit of partnering (2001: 476); or, as Latour says of a legal contract, it offered a 'recall effect' of the interlocking interests maintained in the project (1996: 45).

Argument: But the corpus of IBRFP design documents was only partly and imperfectly written for internal coherence and the enrolment of supporters. It was also a container for wider policy debate and a negotiating tool for future arguments. Recall, for example, that the project narrative contained an argument for the scientific status of farmer knowledge and a critique of centralised Indian agricultural research (Witcombe et al. 1998) which would be used in relations with collaborating bureaucrats and scientists. Moreover, contradictory points of view or arguments between consultants and their collaborators, or within the consultant or donor adviser teams were not resolved (by the mediating notion of participation) but written into the design of the project. After the initial design, when the project was appraised and its texts revised, further disagreements and debates were added. Indeed, as with any policy text, key sentences can be read as bargaining positions in ongoing disputes over strategy within the agency or project teams. When, for example, the ODA Appraisal Mission (1991) report states that 'the team stress the need for the project to help farmers develop solutions to their problems which depend primarily on their own abilities and sources of funding', this is to be read as a response to one of the senior advisers who earlier wrote of 'the need for large and sustained capital and recurrent injections to stabilise soil [and] establish a rural and farm infrastructure' (ODA Technical Adviser's report 1991). Such policy texts are scoreboards of relations of influence in an organisation. In this case the appraisal report clearly reflects the power of an influential coalition in ODA (SDAs and administrators) to distance itself from old big investment projects and to be seen to be getting the participatory process right; even though in doing so it comes close to undermining the justification for the project: why exactly was a multi-million pound British aid project required for poor farmers to help themselves with their own or government resources?

PARTNERS IN DESIGN?

Development policy texts, then, are both the outcome of social processes of enrolment, persuasion and dispute, and contain contradictions which are points of reference anticipating future policy arguments. But the negotiations around policy representations are never between equals. In planning IBRFP, the coalitions within the ODA and its consultants holding favoured policy positions dominated others, including the Indian partner agency. For sure, donor power and imposed designs had to be veiled behind the rhetoric of 'partnership' and through rituals of collaboration, including carefully orchestrated joint planning workshops.[36] Moreover, the independent rationality of donor designs was symbolised by technical studies, reports and accumulated data of various kinds, and references to national policy, and made more palatable by manipulating the rhetoric of the implementing agencies themselves.[37] Despite this, the voice of the ODA's Indian partner agency (KBCL) is virtually absent from project design documents. Its interests in package-based extension, strengthening cooperatives and a role for KBCL itself as input supplier and marketer were excluded. KBCL's own written proposals were ignored, and their people in the field felt more like translators and water carriers than colleagues. 'I felt like a marginalised person at that time', recalls one, 'whenever there was a discussion, I was always at the outskirts, you know [like] the poor [person] or the woman in the village meeting'.

We are reminded that the authoritative knowledge of donor advisers and ourselves as design consultants was produced within development as 'a regime of unequal international relations' (Cooper and Packard 1997: 5). The authority and importance of our ideas had as much to do with *who* we were (Euro-Americans) as what we knew. Our privileged status came from the reduced transaction costs that ODA advisers perceived they derived from engaging individuals broadly familiar with their priorities, language, etiquette, systems and procedures, writing genre and reporting norms, able to articulate current policy in operational form – the same conditions which allow expatriate consultant expertise to reproduce itself as a closed shop (cf. Crewe and Harrison 1998).

The elevation of consultant expertise and the muting of Indian partner points of view derive from the same 'cultural nexus of conditionality'. But while the acceptance of external policy initiatives is demanded, compliance cannot be ensured. Donor designs such as IBRFP's only *appear* to be hegemonic. Indeed, for a project to work at all, its official model has to be porous to the interests of the full range of actors and institutions involved. There *has* to be a *single* project model – given privilege in the text – but there are always several readings of it, several shadow or subordinate models and rationalities validating action from different points of view or operational positions (of fieldworkers, managers, consultants, etc.). I can illustrate this by asking what precisely the project meant to KBCL, the implementing agency. Why would its managers sign up to the external donor-driven development agenda anyway? What interests did KBCL have in a participatory poverty-focused project, and how was it to make this project a successful part of its own organisational goals? On such matters there was silence. KBCL had neither the means to express its opinion on project design, nor even to make itself the object of others' opinions (cf. Latour 1996: 79). The few critical questions raised about KBCL as an organisation were removed from the final draft of the report.

KBCL was a leading national commercial organisation involved in the production and marketing of fertiliser with a firm commitment to agricultural development through 'scientific management' and the 'transfer of modern technology'. Its nationwide marketing operations were concentrated in the same broad region as the project, although its clients were not the poor farming communities ODA intended as the project's focus. As a cooperative, KBCL had only one legitimate channel of distribution, namely local cooperative societies, 2,000 of which from different parts of the country were its members. KBCL marketed its government-allocated quota of fertiliser[38] through apex cooperative societies or directly to lower-level societies at government-fixed prices. Its strategy focused on increasing its share of cooperative sales by retaining farmer loyalty. But the only difference between KBCL urea, and that of its competitors was the KBCL name and logo printed on the bags. There was therefore a fundamental organisational imperative to promote itself and enhance the emotive content of its brand name, through serving the wider interests of farmers both as its shareholders and its market.[39] For this reason various farmer services (ranging from warehousing to soil testing), technology promotion, assistance with accessing government expertise or bank loans and educational and welfare activities were central to KBCL's work. These were offered through a network of client-service centres, an expanding 'village adoption' programme, and KBCL's extensive cadre of field representatives who maintained strong relationships with the leaders of their cooperative clients. As a measure of the success of these strategies, in 1990, KBCL's share of cooperative fertiliser sales was 35 per cent and increasing, despite a fall in the overall cooperative sector share of fertiliser sales due to price competition from other manufacturers and private traders.

In 1990, when the ODA project was being considered, KBCL had an interest in long-term expansion of its sales in Gujarat where its production unit was based (as against Punjab, Haryana and W. Uttar Pradesh, its traditional market), but where strong competition had kept their share of the cooperative market relatively low (24–30 per cent).[40] Clearly a new British aid project might (in the view of some) offer KBCL opportunities to prime this market by enhancing its image as a concerned farmers' organisation and generating new demand through rainfed farming development. It might extend KBCL's expertise in delivering agricultural inputs and services, or increase its capacity to build long-term relationships and trust (a scarce resource upon which client loyalty depended). KBCL's notes and draft proposals of the time reveal such interest, as well as a firm commitment to development through the transfer of technology for scientific agriculture: through demonstrations, soil testing or subsidised input packages.[41] KBCL management were also hopeful of new commercial openings in forestry/wasteland development or from the processing and marketing of project seed or new crop outputs (e.g. safflower oil extraction) with farmers as shareholding business partners. Certainly their principal representative to ODA at the time, Mr P explained to me that, for him, sustainable development meant a commercial relationship with farmer clients as consumers of inputs and suppliers of raw material, and a permanent presence for KBCL in the project area as provider of inputs, services and market.

Along with promoting its relationship with farmer clients, KBCL needed to build its image more generally; and preserve and enhance its profile in relation to the government, which at the state level controlled the allocation of fertiliser quotas and (at the centre) other commercial projects in which KBCL might be interested.[42] Senior managers considered that by handling a donor-aided project with a social responsibility theme and promoting productivity in rainfed areas, they could affirm KBCL's commitment to the national interest.[43] Indeed, in practice, they were far more interested in the value of the IBRFP project as a high-profile, high-prestige, internationally funded venture able to promote KBCL's image and relationship with government than with any potential it had in establishing a (very low value) local market for fertiliser. KBCL may have been part of the ODA's conception of private sector efficiency and accountability in the delivery of rural development, but the ODA project itself was part of KBCL's idea of building political capital for business.

Now, KBCL's project vision – increased inputs for commercial agriculture and spin-offs into agro-based industries linking KBCL to farmer clients – differed fundamentally from the ODA's new participatory poverty-focused agenda. Indeed it was hard to reconcile KBCL's strong marketing agenda and its understanding that input supply was the principal constraint to agriculture (and low input demand a constraint to market development) with a project model which stressed low/no-cost low-input technology and response to the demands of very poor farming communities (with negligible demand for fertiliser); hard too, to reconcile the promotion of a corporate image and relationship with villagers as clients with the idea of farmer self-reliance. Moreover, some of us pondered, how could a fertiliser company with staffing and procedures evolved to meet the considerable logistical demands of transporting and supplying 1.5 million tonnes of fertiliser (yearly) to a precise schedule, with tight systems of control and accountability, manage to respond flexibly to the range and complexity of needs within tribal farming communities while devolving responsibility for programme planning and execution to farmers themselves? And why, senior KBCL finance and personnel staff asked, should the organisation be burdened with an undertaking that would involve new obligations, in particular to retain new project staff in the future, and de-stabilise the rank and order of existing operating systems?[44]

Few observers of bilateral aid would have been surprised if this conflict of organisational objectives was the preface to a tale of project failure, bureaucratic inflexibility and top-down planning; another failure of development to reach the poor. But, on the contrary, what was surprising was not the failure, but the overwhelming *success* of the KBCL host agency in promoting the ODA's participatory development project. The reasons for this will unfold in subsequent chapters. For the moment it is enough to note that IBRFP's design was ambiguous enough to allow very different organisational interests to translate into the same project model, and that these interests in the project were sufficiently strong to override potential conflicts.

The only strategic matter that generated disagreement was the question of the location of the new project. KBCL managers hoped for some commercial farming clients while ODA (through us, its consultants) insisted on selecting the most remote and very poorest adivasi villages in the poorest districts. For KBCL there were political as well as commercial issues at stake. KBCL was a product of India's post-1970s agrarian populism. Its cooperative members were better-off non-tribal farmers, beneficiaries of the green revolution who under the political influence of Charan Singh had re-framed questions of poverty and underdevelopment in the country in a way that suppressed attention to rural caste-class inequality (created by the technologies of capitalist agriculture) (Gupta 1997, 1998). By deploying a polarity between 'India' (urban-biased, elite) and 'Bharat' (the underprivileged, rural sons of the soil) this political leadership re-worked and appropriated Indira Gandhi's populist 'remove poverty' (*garibi hatao*) campaign so as to support claims for the extension of fertiliser and electricity subsidies, irrigation, debt waivers and a good support price for outputs for all farmers (Gupta 1997, 1998).[45] It is unlikely that the political interests and pressures that bore on KBCL were predisposed either to focus on socio-economic inequality, or to share a view of remote and marginal 'tribals' as preferred development beneficiaries on the grounds of their poverty perpetuated through inappropriate state agricultural policy and science, or exploitation by state agents and usurious moneylenders and traders. However, KBCL itself is *not* a political organisation. Indeed senior managers expressed the view that an aid-funded project in an inaccessible tribal area would enable the organisation to pursue its promotional/commercial objectives with greater independence from political pressures that were normal in its core marketing regions such as Uttar Pradesh.

Still, as KBCL staff clambered out of jeeps where the tracks ended and accompanied us across the rolling barren landscape to meet people well beyond the reach of the local cooperative society, and listened to narratives of displacement from flooded valleys, failed milk cooperatives, empty schools and usurious moneylenders, they not only wondered 'where was our technical and commercial advantage' and 'how long it would take to make commercial partners of such people' (senior manager) but also how the project could reach people where there was no access; how staff (especially women) could work in such an area, where government extension staff are not even to be seen? Questions were asked in KBCL's Board.

Through such forays into the Bhil country, the ODA made it clear that 'their' project would depart sharply from KBCL mainline business, and that separate project structures and systems would be needed. Indeed, any divergence of opinion on administrative matters between donor and host agency were rarely discussed but 'resolved' (or distanced) in the principle of the project's 'functional autonomy' from mainline KBCL. Negotiation focused, then, on the systems and rules (financial, personnel, etc.) of a new project management unit (PMU – the project's operational core), located in the middle of the project area and headed by a middle-ranking KBCL area manager, immediately accountable to the marketing division hierarchy and, formally, to a steering committee with representatives from the ODA, Government of India and independent experts. Its team of office-based administrators and field specialists, and village-based Community Organisers, was composed of a mixture of KBCL employees (for administrative, and agronomy/crops technical roles), NGO professionals (institutions, monitoring, gender specialists) and male and female postgraduates.[46] This carefully selected collection of young, broadly middle-class, men and women (mostly 25–35 years old) from eleven different states and a variety of educational, economic and caste backgrounds (all-India without being metropolitan) were rapidly inducted in project principles and participatory techniques.[47] Working in remote Bhil villages, or out of the project's rented office above a private hospital on the edge of the bustling border town of Dahod, they were given the immediate task of facilitating village-level planning, fostering location-specific natural resource development plans, such that their role was redundant after 3–4 years. Initial recruitment and training for the ODA's state-of-the-art participatory project was carefully controlled by its University of Wales consultants who, while outside the team, assumed the role of professional leadership and 'technical' accountability to the ODA. Like the project texts, the project organisation was a hybrid compromise between diverse interests and secured on ambiguity. It contained many of the disjunctures and contradictions that shaped the design process, and that would re-emerge later.

CONCLUSIONS

This chapter has explored how a multitude of contradictory interests and cross-purposes get translated into a single technical-rational, politically acceptable, ambitious and ambiguous project model. The process is planned by the donor and negotiated by its field consultants. Consultants are not involved in any straightforward exercise in rational planning (Chapter 6 will explore the role of consultant knowledge further), but neither can their contribution to development to be judged merely in terms of cultural performance or the aesthetics of the final reports (Stirrat 2000). Consultants are 'significant framers of knowledge, discourses and the legitimisation for allocating sets of resources in particular ways' (Wood 1998: 55). Moreover, to claim that project design involves the subjugation (or cooption) of local or specialist knowledge to policy goals, terms of reference (TORs) and donor reporting formats (Escobar 1991, Goldman 2001) is an oversimplification. Analysis of the interplay between policy ideas and their social effects (enrolment, persuasion) demonstrates that 'the framing of a "development" intervention is a delicate cultural operation' (Li 1999: 298) – more political and less instrumental than is commonly thought.

Project design produces technical cause–effect models; but like an international regime (on say trade),[48] these have the primary social function of bringing diverse people, interests and viewpoints together to facilitate cooperation and create constituencies of support. It is precisely the ability to achieve a high degree of convergence of disparate interests, contained in the official language of a single validating model, that characterises successful policy and project ideas. To achieve this the policy process requires ambiguous concepts like 'participation' which mediate or translate between divergent interests. Recall Latour's conclusion that the success of policy ideas arises from their 'ability to continue recruiting support and so impose ... [their] growing coherence on those who argue about them or oppose them' (1996: 78). Consultants make policy successful by building ambiguity and interpretive flexibility into project designs, thereby opening them up to diverse interests. The relationship between the success of policy ideas and project designs (in these terms) and their practicability is the subject of later chapters of this book.

This chapter has looked at the institutional world that produced a project design text; the next turns to the world that it framed and was intended to transform.

3

Tribal Livelihoods and
the Development Frontier

The development policy models through which resources and political
support are so successfully mobilised are rarely those best suited
to understanding the social and historical context of development
action. Indeed standard intervention models and project cycles are
designed to take out history, to exclude wider economic and political
analysis, and to isolate project action from 'the continuous flow
of social life' (Long 2001: 32). They erect (conceptual) boundaries
around projects and communities and demand the continuous
production of dichotomies, for example, between insiders (the locals)
and outsiders (the project) (2001: 34), and discontinuity between
the past and the present and future. It is necessary to go behind the
simple model of community and change produced by the powerful
metaphors of intervention and impact, first to explore the society,
locality and history within which a development project is situated
(the task of this chapter) and, second, to reflect on the agency and
political relationships of development projects themselves which
are routinely concealed by policy models (the task of the following
two chapters).

I will begin here by showing how the stereotypes and simplifications
through which the IBRFP project apprehended its underdeveloped
beneficiaries drew on historically embedded representations of one
of the nation's frontier places, the society of 'Bhil tribals' (cf. Watts
1992: 116–17 in Li 2000). I will then set the stereotype of Bhil society
– isolation or essential wildness 'civilised' through the projects of
outsiders – against a subaltern history that looks at the way in which
Bhil identity was and is the product of relationships with outsiders:
the colonial state and its systems of taxation and forest demarcation,
usurious moneylenders, reformers or nationalists. State, market and
political party are not external to Bhil identity and community but
constitute them internally and historically, and so do development
projects such as IBRFP (which are as much about forging relationships
as the introduction of schemes). In other words, as Pigg puts it,

'locality is constituted in and through relations to wider systems, not simply impinged upon by them' (1996: 165).

The remaining sections of this chapter offer an interpretation of Bhil society informed by ethnography and our own interactions as project workers. One sketches the structural relations of kin and gender that have a bearing on the way in which project resources were appropriated locally and their political effects. The next turns to land and cultivation to show that agricultural practice is contextualised in a way that contradicts the general prescription (cf. Pigg 1996) and thwarts the ambitions of the project model to hugely increase production (see Chapter 9). The final section discusses debt, usury and labour migration. The argument is not only that Bhil identity is a product of historical connections, and that livelihoods are woven from threads trailing along railway lines to urban construction sites, but also that this determined the way in which the project was understood and the effects it had (discussed in Chapter 9).

WILDNESS AND THE COLONIAL MAKING OF BHIL MARGINALITY

Even before the members of the new IBRFP project team arrived in the inter-state border districts of Banswara (Rajasthan), Jhabua (Madhya Pradesh) and Dahod (Gujarat) they knew they were going to as remote, poor and ecologically degraded an area as they cared to imagine. What signalled this as an underdeveloped place above all was that it was a 'tribal area'.[1] As they first settled in the larger non-tribal villages and towns of the region, our project workers readily adopted the stereotypes used by their urban upper-caste neighbours. The surrounding Bhils were an uncultured 'hand-to-mouth' people, driven by immediate appetites and the compulsions of subsistence survival, without thrift or thought for the future, ignorant and fearful of new technology. These were innocent people, cheated and exploited by usurious moneylenders and traders, by junior state officials, especially forest guards and the police. They were culturally other, unclean, 'not at all civilised in my eyes', one Community Organiser confided of her first impressions of the people she was sent to work with. But equally these were a dangerous, liquor-drinking and wild people of the forest, armed with bows and arrows, highwaymen, thieves and dacoits, a source of insecurity to newly recruited field staff. These images not only coloured the early impressions of middle-class project workers, they also added a cultural significance to their development efforts. Here were places where the social worker or Community Organiser could make history by animating and releasing those imprisoned in material and cultural poverty (cf. Hardiman 1987a: 8, Scheper-Hughes 1992: 53ff). Their inputs, whether soil conservation, seeds or savings, could be symbols of cultural reform, betterment, perhaps 'civilisation'. Even without the explicit missionary concept of 'conversion', project workers could tacitly understand their role in terms of saving, rescuing or lifting a backward people 'up to our level' (Padel 2000: 297).

Implicitly, IBRFP staff drew on the mutually enforcing tribal stereotypes of an earlier century's administrators, missionaries and anthropologists.[2] As writers, these colonials regularly succumbed to fantasy in their descriptions of Bhil tribal exotica, the innocent lack of restraint in their fairs and feasts, their colourful female adornment, their sexual liberty and spontaneous elopement, and their passion for liquor; although the authors invariably return to sober judgement on the 'rude habits' and 'wild vagabond life' of the criminal Bhils, on whom civilisation's core moral and social institutions (of property, cultivation, marriage or the sanctity of life) had a dangerously weak hold; and whose 'sole occupation was pillage and robbery, whose delight alone consisted of murderous forages' (Sherring 1974/1872: 291).

These images of 'wild hill tribes' were firmly rooted in a colonial discourse which contrasted the ordered society of the plains under Rajput royal authority with the unruly hill tribes and forest dwellers (*jungli log*). They drew on a history that viewed Bhils as a people forced by the rising power and tyranny of pre-British Rajput or Maratha rulers into the cultural periphery of the remote forest tracts, from where they became a source of raiding and dacoitry (Chauhan 1978, Doshi 1997, Mathur 1988, all cited in Sjöblom 1999: 37). The idea that loyal Bhils were 'rendered savage and driven to lawlessness' by the oppression of their Rajput overlords (who exacted forced labour – *begar* or *veth*, excessive rents, and tricked them of their land) lent ideological justification to the rule of the British who would rescue and tame them under their just rule of law (Sherring 1974/1872).[3]

Recently, subaltern historians such as Ajay Skaria, have challenged this legitimising colonial narrative of Bhil oppression and rescue (and the development narratives of marginality they anticipated), by invoking the idea of autonomous 'forest polities' and a 'Bhil raj'. Skaria (1999) describes the power wielded by sovereign Bhil chieftains (*naiks*) from medieval times, both within mobile forest communities (living from swidden and gathered forest produce) and in relation to the settled plains people with whom they had military and marital alliances.[4] Bhils – here a loose category of hill and forest dwellers rather than a racially, linguistically or ethnically distinct tribe[5] – had political dominance of many western Indian hilly and forested regions well into the 19th century. Economic redistribution rather than systems of taxation characterised Bhil raj, and power was decentralised or dispersed throughout the *jati* (caste/tribe) by the ties and alliances of chiefly kin-groups, who struggled for prominence and drew together bands of bowmen for defence or for raiding the neighbouring plains (Hardiman 1987b: 29, Skaria 1999). Plains rulers jostled for the support of powerful Bhil chiefs who held rights to collect dues (*giras*) from villages; rights that were periodically 'renegotiated' through raids (*dhad*) which expressed Bhil claims to sovereignty. Perhaps most significantly, Bhil chiefly power operated through a discourse of 'wildness' that was a mode of kingship and dominance as distinctive as those of Kshatrya (warrior kingship) or Brahman (priesthood) (Skaria 1999).

Now, the consolidation of British dominion transformed 'wildness' from a discourse of power into a discourse of marginality; and the relationship between plains and hills from one of structured interdependence (in which raiding was a political act) to one of antagonism (in which raiding was a criminal practice contained by 'punitive expeditions'). British rule required the control and disciplining of the lawless Bhils. In the western Indian princely states British Agents themselves meted out brutal and capital punishment to Bhils suspected of theft, lending support to the Rajput ruling structure and its local *thakurs* (nobles) through whom they governed (Baviskar 1995: 49–64, Weisgrau 1997: 35). The 'Bhil problem' was also addressed through opening schools, the encouragement of settled agriculture with allotments of wasteland, equipment and animals, and (from 1825) the formation of a Bhil Corps which turned hill-men criminals into a disciplined constabulary serving the princely rulers. The Corps supported the settled agrarian lives of its members by advancing loans, discouraged alcohol and promoted education, all with 'the object of weaning a semi-savage race from its predatory habits' (Erskine cited in Weisgrau 1997: 36).[6] The Corps was also closely associated with missionaries who were attracted by the hope of mass conversions among the Bhils, which never materialised (Weisgrau 1997: 36–7). These are familiar attempts by a government to incorporate its 'non-state fringes' (see Scott 1998).[7] The result was that by the 20th century Bhil forest polities had lost influence and become marginal – the social and ecological antithesis to the revenue-paying agricultural plains.

The changing identity of Bhil communities was particularly closely related to their loss of control over forest resources (Skaria 1999). The former abundance of the forest is prominent in present-day Bhil narratives of their past: a wealth of fruits, leaves or flowers to barter, houses with teak pillars, bamboo poles and sleeping areas raised above the cattle sheds away from wild monkeys, boars or tigers which could damage crops or kill cattle. First merchants, and then the British, took leases on the forest from Bhil chiefs. Skaria argues that these new leases, backed by surveys and written contracts, were impervious to the old Bhil chiefly view of such transactions as the means to create alliances with plains powers. Instead, the colonial power set about 'civilising' the tribes and the forests by keeping both apart. Unruly mosaic forests were disciplined into ordered high-value timber-producing reserve forests of teak, protected from Bhils and their hunting, gathering and shifting cultivation (1999: 205–7). Bhils lost the forest by stealth, as colonial knowledge ('scientific forestry') created Bhil ignorance.

Drawing on oral traditions (*goth*) in the Bhil Dangs region of Gujarat, Skaria reveals an enduring social memory of the loss of forest livelihoods, the expansion of colonial forest regimes of demarcation and exclusion, and the extraordinary brutality of their enforcement. Villagers in the IBRFP project area to the east also narrated histories of state discipline and forest loss. They recalled a 'time of fear of patrolling guards on horseback, constant surveillance [when] all households had to cut fodder and give it to officials as a form of tax, [when] British officers would search [their] bags, and punish them if they were caught drinking, [when] guests that came to the village had to be registered'.[8]

While Bhil access to the forest was restricted, outsiders took lucrative timber contracts from the government and felled the forest. Commercial felling escalated between the 1930s and 1950s as rulers and landowners of the minor princely states sought to profit from the trade in timber or charcoal on the eve of post-independence land reforms (Sjöblom 1999). The disappearing forests were cut with Bhil labour, often forced.[9] Indeed, in the 1940s, Bhils in eastern Gujarat depended upon *kabadu*, the felling and transporting of logs for contractors, for 30–40 per cent of their income (Naik 1956). The erosion of livelihoods that followed forest demarcation had, by the 20th century, generated its own long history of Bhil uprisings, involving attacks on government offices, and protests against the Forest Department by setting fire to the forest (Hardiman 1987a: 181, Skaria 1999: 270ff).

Along with state monopoly over timber, colonial forest policy involved an administrative turn against Bhil shifting cultivation and gathering. Lopping or the use of fire was banned, mobility was restricted by permits, and the earlier practice of allotting usufruct rights for unoccupied land by mutual agreement was replaced by the registration of land as private property. 'Under the steady influence of a British officer, it was envisioned that tribes would abandon their wild and wandering ways, take to settled agriculture, and become steady, yeoman cultivators' (Skaria 1999: 198). As forest forms of subsistence were made unviable, many were indeed forced into settled cultivation, such that by the end of the 19th century Bhils (at least in the IBRFP districts) occupied well-defined villages and cultivated with bullock-drawn ploughs (Hardiman 1987b: 6).

With settled agriculture Bhil communities developed their long historical relationship with traders/moneylenders, or *sahukars*. In fact, already in pre-British times *sahukars* had a critical role in the expansion of settled agriculture in the forested Bhil domains. From as early as the late 15th century, Bhil cultivators established relationships with *sahukars* – Das Nimas Baniyas and Muslim Daudi Bohras – who had settled in the small towns and former military outposts of Dahod and Jhalod (Hardiman 1987b). Bhils in the immediate vicinity of such towns bartered grain for salt, iron and cloth from traders who both offset fluctuations in market prices and supplied credit or seed grain for cultivation or to tide them over lean periods. Indeed, the acreage cultivated would vary with the availability of *sahukar* finance, although overall it expanded during the 18th and 19th centuries (Hardiman 1987b). Variable farm productivity and the need to pay fixed revenue in cash (after the consolidation of systems of state revenue extraction, both Mughal and British) enhanced the role of a range of middlemen, traders and usurers. *Sahukars* traded grain and paid tax assessments for cultivators, or acquired direct tax-collection responsibilities from upper-caste officials unwilling to work in remote tribal areas. 'In effect', Hardiman suggests:

... the [British] government machinery hardly stretched to the [Bhil] village, and it was left to the sahukars to appropriate the peasant's surplus and hand over a share to the state at the headquarters town. In this respect, the sahukars were far more important to the colonial state than its own petty officers. (1987b: 36)

Nineteenth-century state revenue systems increased the power of *sahukars* in relation to Bhil cultivators, making relatively equal relationships of trade more definitely hierarchical and exploitative. But *sahukars* had a business interest in keeping Bhil cultivators (their debtors) on the land. Their interest was in controlling the crop (and to some extent labour through debt bondage[10]) not acquiring the land itself, and they would even intervene in civil court cases to prevent the alienation of Bhil property (Hardiman 1987b: 36). This is not to say that the judicial system was not used to deprive Bhils of large tracts of their land – it was (Hardiman 1987b: 15). The relationship of credit and dependence between Bhils and *sahukars* changed little in the 20th century, and was largely unaffected by post-Independence legislation through which tenancy was abolished, share-croppers gained property rights, and the transfer of land from adivasis to non-adivasis was, in theory, prevented.[11] As Hardiman points out, *sahukars* maintained a hegemony through economic compulsion and paternalism rather than coercion. While clearly exploited, Bhils were not bitter towards *sahukars* as a class; the relationship with their *sahukar* was a valuable asset, it was necessary and 'natural' (1987a: 96–7).[12]

The transformation of 'wildness' from a discourse of rule to one of exclusion, the historical substitution of forest livelihoods for *sahukar*-financed cultivation, and the move from independence to debt and dependence, together had the effect of turning 'Bhil' and *jangli* into negative ascriptions. People themselves began to reject such identities in what Skaria describes as a 'deep malaise among forest communities' (1999: 255). Several 'Bhil' communities came to prefer identities like Mina or Bhilala, which emphasised connections (historical or mythical) with the regionally dominant Rajputs (Baviskar 1995, Deliège 1985). A few converted to Christianity. The 'Bhil malaise', together with intensified exploitative economic relations, also contributed to a series of social reform and religious movements or rebellions from the mid-19th century, most of which focused on self-improvement and living pure and clean lives, eliminating meat-eating, alcohol and animal sacrifices to animist deities and ancestral spirits as aspects of 'inferior' Bhil culture (Jain 1991). The Bhil reformer Surmaldas (d. 1898) encouraged devotion to the Hindu god Ram, and another, Govindgiri, added the goal of creating a Bhil raj in 1910s south Rajasthan.[13] However, most adivasi religious movements, notably the one of 1922 analysed by David Hardiman (1987a), aspired to neither the worship of Hindu gods nor political autonomy, but involved new manifestations of the *devi* or goddess who, possessing her devotees, demanded (i) reform of cultural practices, including regular bathing, giving up alcohol or meat, brideprice or widow remarriage, (ii) retaliation against exploitation by striking for higher wages and boycotting Parsi liquor traders, and even (iii) support for the nationalist non-cooperation movement (1987a). These movements suggest (to Skaria) simultaneously a distancing from 'wildness', now associated with marginality, and hostility to (although cultural emulation of) upper castes in relation to whom Bhils suffered new forms of subordination (1999: 256). The goddess cults flowed into the stream of Gandhian nationalist reforms, which left their mark in the form of adivasi schools, *bhajan mandlis* (devotional groups), changed dress or dietary codes. In some villages today, followers of reformed practices identify themselves as *bhagats* claiming status over 'ordinary Bhils', emphasising education, thrift and prosperity, and in some areas *bhagat* Bhils now constitute a separate *jati* restricting marriage with non-*bhagats* (Rao 1988). Even if they did not 'awaken' Bhils themselves, these pre-Independence movements awakened political organisations to the need to mobilise adivasis in order to capture power (Sharma 1990, in Weisgrau 1997: 41). In the 1990s, Hindu nationalist organisations (the Sangh Parivar and its affiliates) found fertile ground in the 'Bhil malaise' for the political rhetoric of pan-Hindu unity (1997: 70) which took a violently communal form in April 2002, when adivasis were mobilised to attack Muslim (Bohra) moneylenders and traders in eastern Gujarat (see Lobo 2002).[14]

Bhil identity, then, has been forged from a complex history of forest livelihoods, rule and resistance, and a history of relationships with dominant groups in society. It has contended with the categorisations of dominant others, whether British officers, Gandhian nationalists, contemporary politicians or agents of rural development. Bhils have been patronised and disciplined (as barbarous and *jungli*, as the 'naughty school boys' of the empire, Skaria 1999), displaced or protected, integrated or excluded, reformed or rescued, ennobled or accused in colonial or postcolonial policies on the 'tribals'[15] or in contemporary environmental debates on deforestation or dams (see Baviskar 1995, Skaria 1999). They have endured intimidation, exploitation and violence as much as protection from state institutions, especially Forest Departments and the police.[16] For Bhil communities, economic survival itself has long depended upon external patronage and social protection, and on forming alliances with those with better access to resources whether Rajputs or *sahukars*, reformers or developers (Weisgrau 1997: 9). At the same time Bhil cultural practices have signalled power, resistance or stigma. Reform movements have democratised the values of dominant groups and challenged Bhil marginality (Hardiman 1987a: 158ff), but also led to the adoption of non-Bhil identities, internal differentiation and rank at the margins of Bhil society (Deliège 1985). Bhils are *adivasis*, a term now stripped of its literal meaning of 'original inhabitants', which has become an adopted identity of people with a shared historical experience of the loss of forests and the alienation of land, an identity which 'both points to subalterneity and refuses to accept that subalterneity' (Skaria 1999: 281, cf. Hardiman 1987a: 12–17). It would be surprising indeed if we did not find these historically determined factors shaping the relationship between Bhil communities and their new development project patron IBRFP and its discourse of improvement; or that through this relationship representations of self and other were forged both by Bhil villagers and project workers. But in order to make sense of the interactions between a development project and its adivasi participants, we first need to know more about the social lives and livelihoods of Bhil communities in the early 1990s; or at least the interpretation of them derived *in the end* from these same interactions, and through which I will analyse the project's process.

LAND, KINSHIP AND AUTHORITY IN BHIL VILLAGES

Today, Bhil villages[17] in the IBRFP project area comprise scattered homesteads situated among their cultivated fields, often on top of a hillock to afford protection and separated from others by ridges of a hill, although generally within shouting distance. These are settled cultivating communities structured by patrilineal kinship in relation to land (cf. Baviskar 1995: 115). As a rule, all men in a lineage have title to land in a village and transmit this to their sons. Ideally (and often actually) a village is composed of a single patrilineage – the core institution of Bhil social organisation – and the practice of village exogamy expresses the tacit view of the village as a large unilineal group, the descendants of an original settler notionally four to six generations back (Deliège 1985, cf. Mosse and Mehta 1993). In principle this gives the village a strong, ritually expressed, corporate identity.[18] The village is also, independently, a territorial identity involving rights to land, a moral unit with honour to protect (or be compensated in case of conflict); it is shared water, soil and residence, and a mode of reckoning social relations apart from kinship, especially for women (cf. Lambert 1996).

Villages are divided into hamlets (*falia*) comprising sections of the dominant lineage or members of other lineages (often affines, or distant agnates) adopting distinct clan names.[19] The social composition of *falias* reflects a history of settlement, land being allocated to men invited to marry and stay in the village in order to clear forest, expand cultivation and increase security, or offered in lieu of brideprice (Sjöblom 1999: 180–1). Even though the association of lineage with territory is weakened today, dominant founding lineages (*bhai-beta*) often still have larger holdings of the best land and rights over trees, while affinal (*karhan*) lineages, matrilocal households and later settlers are to a degree dependent and inferior (cf. Sjöblom 1999: 182). As resources become scarcer, position in the patrilineage becomes more important in struggles over power and land (e.g. over field boundaries, grazing or forest 'encroachments'). As one of Sjöblom's Bhil informants commented, 'to have the right relations in the *phala* [*falia*] is ... more important than earlier. If a woman lives with her husband in her parents' village, both will have less power' (1999: 183–4). *Falias*, then, provide both the units of everyday social exchange, and the fault-lines in factional divisions in Bhil villages. It will become clear that this had an important bearing on IBRFP's practice.

Typically, it is dominant lineages that promote individuals to positions of village leadership. Official links between the village and the colonial government were provided by the headmen (*patel, tadvi* or *rawat*) who, together with the upper-caste plainsmen officials (*talatis* or *patwaris*), were responsible for revenue collection, records and law and order. Other men of influence were the *bhangjadia* – negotiators in dispute resolution, and the priests (*pujaru* or *bhopa*, often from a *karhan* lineage). While no longer government servants, hereditary village headmen remain key mediators between villagers and outsiders, and 'contact persons' for officials or project staff. Their authority operates through informal village councils (*panch*s) comprising five or six hamlet leaders who resolve disputes over land, marriage payments and such matters. Statutorily, local authority rests with the *sarpanch*, the elected head of the gram panchayat, which groups three to five villages together. Educational opportunities have broadened the range of social backgrounds from which *sarpanchs* come (and recent provisions reserve a proportion of positions for women), but many are still Bhil headmen or their kin (including their wives in reserved panchayats).

For several decades now, the *sarpanch*, the headman and richer farmers have constituted a village elite which has replaced the non-Bhil *sahukars* as the brokers (*dalal*) through whom villagers interact with the wider region and its still socially distant institutions and functionaries (cf. Rajora 1987).[20] The procedural difficulties involved in obtaining any of the increasing flows of state resources directed to tribal districts has ensured the continuity of such 'rent-seeking' brokerage roles, and obstructed the delivery of schemes to meet the needs of the poor.[21] As village-level studies throughout the 1970s and 1980s testify, mediated and uneven access to tribal development benefits was the norm (Doshi 1978, Rajora 1987, Rao 1988), accentuating differences based on resource endowments.[22] A large proportion of agricultural loans and subsidies were channelled into the dominant or roadside villages of panchayats, to larger farmers with influence, or to the kin and political clients of *sarpanchs* and party bosses. These adivasi elites established links which took them into fields of political action at the regional level. They were coopted into alliances with non-adivasis with whom they shared class interests, and were unwilling to act against the lower levels of the state that exploited Bhil villagers.[23] Political decentralisation in the 1990s was intended to reduce these effects by increasing resource allocation decisions at panchayat level, and even (in the case of Madhya Pradesh) introducing direct accountability to general village assemblies (*gram sabhas*);[24] but in the 1980s party political mobilisation based on the manipulating role of middlemen ensured that the process of political penetration preceded or replaced the penetration of 'development' resources (Breman 1985). While Bhil political leaders may have imparted knowledge to kinsmen, they did not mobilise adivasis to obtain the benefits of development; arguably the contrary (Breman 1985). Instead this role was largely taken up by non-adivasis: Gandhians, NGOs, left-wing activists and militant peasant workers' unions (Baviskar 1995, Bhatt 1989, Eldridge nd).[25]

The core structures of kinship-in-relation-to-land which shape resource endowments and access to state benefits or political participation, also give rise to systems of marriage, labour and property that define the position of women in Bhil society. Women experience exclusion from the public and political domain, from membership of the *panch*, or from negotiations surrounding marriage or property. The exceptional women with status, independence and voice in village matters are often those living in their natal villages and who stand as sole inheritors of family property. Such women have identities in their own right and the capacity to act as 'operative subjects' (Moore 1988: 72).[26] Usually, however, women's identity and their property rights are not independent but derive from men's. 'A woman's capacity to "own" things', Whitehead notes more generally:

> … depends upon the extent to which she is legally and actually separable from other people … the extent to which forms of conjugal, familial and kinship relations allow her an independent existence so that she can assert rights as an individual against other individuals. (cited in Moore 1988: 72)

In Bhil society women rarely have the capacity to act in this way. Women *are* rather than *have* property and Bhil brideprice (*dej*) traditions and negotiations clearly express this condition. Through these payments women's labour is bought for work on men's land.[27] A woman is an economic asset of the male lineage. As a bride, her incorporation into the household is 'marked by her bowed submission to all the men of the lineage' (Baviskar 1995: 119). The public transactions and disputes of marriages, separations or elopements set in play negotiations in which women are the absent objects, and end in financial compensations which ultimately serve to reaffirm the collective unity, identity and honour of the male lineage and its relationship to others, and to underline the understanding of women as its property (1995). Should her husband die, a woman remains 'property' of the lineage and would, as a matter of preference (though not strict obligation), marry her husband's younger brother (1995). If she leaves to live with another man, her husband's kin will come to demand compensation. Even where assets such as farm wells and houses are created through women's labour and the sale or mortgage of their jewellery, the ownership is ascribed to men. Women only have rights to land, or indeed to their own children, to the extent that they are incorporated into the male lineage. In short, the structure of male lineages that provides the basic architecture of community in Bhil villages gives women a peripheral position and a subordinate identity.

But such a reading of kinship and gender relations denies Bhil women the agency and power that they manifestly have. According to stereotype (at least partly true) Bhil women have a liberty of movement, a lack of seclusion and observe weaker social restrictions, indicated by the absence of menstrual taboos or a high value set on chastity, compared to women of the surrounding plains. It is fairly common for Bhil women to elope with men, and the individual choice and sentiment allowed in selecting partners is institutionalised in the celebrated *bhagoria hat*, an annual 'elopement fair' in February/March. Women are not, in practice, objects defined by male kinship ideology, but subjects constructing their own, different, social worlds. Despite their subordinate position within patrilineages, Bhil women maintain their own independent social networks through ties with men and women from their natal villages, or seek to extend them by exerting influence over marriages in order to bring female kin to their marital villages. Women find ways to subvert the patrilocal family, remaining connected to their natal families and returning home at times of conflict or separation, or because of illness or spirit possession (Mosse and Mehta 1993).[28] Indeed the marriage tie is relatively loose and separation (initiated by women as well as men) is common. Women are capable of manipulating dominant notions to serve their own interests. They can 'refuse to respect rules of male domination which emphasize marriage as a transaction between men ... By eloping, women make men into weaklings and cuckolds, objects of scorn and mockery' (Baviskar 1995: 131–2); although such room for manoeuvre is not unqualified: sexual choice can be asserted in youth, but 'the freedom to resist fades swiftly as women age and bear children and develop ties through their offspring with the village into which they have married' (1995: 132). Finally, as will become clear, women exert power and assert interests as economic agents. Bhil women's formal control over household property and spending (on jewellery, clothing, livestock) may be weak, but their informal influence is significant. As one put it, 'Our husbands don't ask too much where new things come from, because they know we would leave the house and they can't survive without us.'[29]

LAND, CULTIVATION AND CATTLE

Subsequent chapters will show how the contours of lineage, authority and gender reappeared in encounters with the IBRFP project and its field staff. For now I want to turn to the Bhil farming system through which relations with this agricultural project were mediated. The cultivated area (40–55 per cent) of the project districts is overwhelmingly (90 per cent) devoted to food crops, and only 10 per cent is irrigated, mostly by hand-dug wells. In these predominantly hilly uplands, in recent times farms typically comprised three parts: first, the 'old field' or fertile black soil valley land (*nallah*) growing rice and winter wheat; second, poorer stony red soil slopes on which sorghum and millets were grown, now largely displaced by the staple maize[30] and intercropped cash-crop pulses (e.g. pigeon pea); and, third, uncultivated grass and woodland, much of it officially 'forest' although without tree cover. In every generation, jointly cultivated land of each type in the micro watershed (*pani-dhol*) has to be divided and apportioned.[31] Successive partitions intensify cultivation and bring ever-steeper land under the plough (Sjöblom 1999). The fertility of land is increased by 'bunding', clearing stones, constructing stone soil traps, and manuring, which allows a shift from grassland to sorghum or millet, and then to higher-yielding maize crops (1999). The experience is one of intensification and increasing productivity not, as we outsiders usually assume, degradation from population increase (cf. Tiffin and Mortimore 1994). But, as each domestic cycle pushes cultivation further up the hillside there is less grazing, fewer cattle, reduced manure and less crop diversity. Few can now afford to fallow fields with sunhemp (for rope or green manure) as they used to. More households depend upon new sloping land, which takes longer to make and keep fertile, rather than the 'old field' valley bottom, and are forced to plant it with the more demanding (and soil eroding) subsistence maize crop rather than various millets (Sjöblom 1999). Also, more of this 'new field' (*nevad*) is cleared Forest Department land over which tenure is contested or branded as 'encroachment'.

The clear emphasis on making and keeping land fertile rather than preventing erosion means that Bhil farmers speak of productivity decline in terms of the lack of manure dung, ash or green leaves (and the cost of bought fertiliser), rather than soil loss.[32] Narratives of environmental change collected in Bhil villages therefore give first emphasis to the loss of forests and the dramatic decline of cattle herds arising from restricted access to the forest, and the reduction in grazing land and fallows. Some now even travel by train to weed the fields of distant people in exchange for fodder in order to maintain their cattle.[33] Everywhere, the ownership of cattle (especially buffalos giving the best manure) and trees (especially the possession of now rare private protected woodlots) are sure signs of wealth and power.

Fewer cattle means 'less milk to drink, less ghee to sell', but most importantly less manure for the fields;[34] and this is exacerbated by the shortage of wood which means that dung is burned for fuel. Cattle are central to keeping land fertile and productive, and the need for manure is a major reason for keeping and increasing herds, along with their draught power and the security they offer as assets.[35] The poor, who lack the labour and fodder to support them, have few cattle and more precarious cultivation and livelihoods.

Today land and water too are scarce. With the exception of a few small wells, the odd portable pump-set or larger lift irrigation scheme,[36] cultivation in the summer *kharif* season depends upon monsoon rains, and in the winter *rabi* season crops draw on residual moisture in the soil in the valley bottoms. Farm holdings average about 1 hectare, and families with 1.5 hectares of good land are considered well-off. The history of inheritance has fragmented the land of some lineages less than others. Some also have the influence necessary to sustain 'encroachments' onto forest land and so extend their holdings;[37] but many households have less than half a hectare to farm.

Each season presents a complex scenario in which families have to feed themselves and earn income, meet fodder needs and maintain the fertility of the soil. They have to judge the likelihood of rain, the availability of credit, the capital of social obligations yielding labour and support on which they can draw, and in light of this choose the combination of crops to grow and the how to fertilise the soil. Each field involves a complex ecological and social reckoning, a performance not easily put into words (cf. Bloch 1991, Richards 1985). The result is a pattern of cropping, rotation and crop-patch mosaics designed to maximise output for given soil/slope conditions for minimum cost. Sometimes cropping will have to change mid-season. No two fields will be the same: those close to the homestead may be richly manured to grow maize; more distant sloping fields will be intercropped with pigeon pea; more fertile valley bottom lands will be sown with wheat after the rice harvest; and good maize land will be sown with chickpeas in winter. There will always be trade-offs across fields, crops or years, and always questions: 'Our rice will yield, but only if the rains hold, should we risk expensive fertiliser? Drought-resistant millets are safer; maize is easier to plant and harvest, but hard on the soil.' No two households face the same dilemmas. Where one family chooses to grow maize on poor soils applying fertiliser, another whose cash has run out and who cannot afford high-interest *sahukar* credit goes for black gram, which will grow without inputs. The house with only one bullock will concentrate manure in the most productive field; the one with a small herd will manure all their fields. Others will manure fields in rotation. Some will be able to fallow fields, or restore the land with sun-hemp one year in five; others will draw nutrients from the land year on year with a monocrop staple, and even then fail to feed the family for more than three or four months each year. The poorer the household – in terms of access to cattle, land, water, labour and finance – the less room for manoeuvre, the higher the risks and the greater the skill required to maximise output for minimal cost. Rainfed upland environments such as this have recently been characterised as 'complex, diverse and risk-prone' (as in our project design).[38] While in any given village, ecological diversity and the need for highly specific adaptation produces a complex and risk-averse pattern of cropping (in contrast to the monocultures of the irrigated plains), the poorest farmers, cultivating eroded sloping land, actually have a *narrower choice* of crops, varieties or animals. Poor soils and low rainfall mean *less* rather than more diversity. Poor farmers have fewer cultivation options, and can only grow drought-tolerant short-duration varieties as a single food crop to feed their families from their small plots (Witcombe 1999). As my consultant colleague pointed out, 'the more marginal your agriculture becomes, the *less* diverse it is, because the less options you have'.[39] It is a romantic fiction that upland 'tribal' livelihoods choose diverse intercropping rather than a sole food crop staple (maize and rice) and, as we will see, a dangerous simplification to suggest that there is a wide gap between actual and potential output which can easily be plugged with new technology extending farmer choice.

GENDERED AGRICULTURAL PRACTICE[40]

In Bhil society important aspects of gender relations are articulated through agricultural practices. In most respects the farming unit is now the nuclear family with the husband–wife pair at its centre, and women are fully conversant with all farming operations – with the exception of ploughing, which is surrounded by a male mystique (Sjöblom 1999). But while household decisions are ordinarily made jointly, certain operations including seed management (selection, grading, preparation, storage and sowing), weeding, harvesting and post-harvest operations, the management of livestock (including animal health),[41] fodder[42] and manuring, and vegetable production (aubergines, tomatoes, beans, gourds and spices) fall primarily within women's domain. Along with the supply of water and fuel, and feeding the family, these are gendered *responsibilities* rather than simply tasks, in that they involve mobilising labour or other inputs to achieve particular ends. Gendered responsibilities in agriculture imply gendered interests that come to bear on decision making on cropping priorities, inputs, marketing, storage or consumption (along with interests derived from factors such as wealth, landholding or household size). Simply illustrated, because they have responsibility for feeding the family, women might try to ensure that coarse millets (*kudri* or *banti*) are grown in addition to maize and rice because they grow on poor lands, alleviate hunger in smaller quantities, and can be consumed in the slack season saving maize for the labour-intensive cultivation period. Men, because they have responsibility for getting and maintaining assets (ploughs, draught cattle or wells), earning income, and acquiring prestige and status in the community (necessary to mobilise credit or reciprocal labour), might opt instead for income-maximising crop or tree options.[43] Now, because they are differently interested and affected, for example in terms of food security, labour demand or income potential, men and women would evaluate the new technology of the project differently (Chapter 9).

Two further points need to be made. The first is that typically, the structure of gender responsibilities produces an unequal distribution of tasks and workloads.[44] Rising at 4 a.m. and eating last and late at night, most Bhil women undeniably have fearfully heavy workloads, short nights and little sleep or leisure, irrespective of the season. And successive droughts, long-term deforestation, pressure on water sources, increased trade of goods and migrant labour have measurably increased their workloads, while reducing the sources of cash they control (for example, from fuel wood). Licensed to speak out by project workers, women proclaimed:

> We have to do everything. We collect the cow dung for fuel, search for firewood [for three hours a day] fetch water from [far] four or five times a day. We give fodder to the cattle, milk the cows, and hand-grind the food grains. Our hands get cut weeding, and we get thorns in them when we are harvesting; afterwards, we prepare food. When we are sowing seeds, the children cry, when we harvest the fodder we work for a long time bending and our backs and necks hurt. We collect all the grass together and carry it on our heads and our necks again hurt. The men are stupid

and lazy, they don't work much, just waste time. We work continuously, looking after the children, the cattle and other work.

Of course the burden of labour varies with age, marriage, motherhood, residence and wealth. It falls most heavily on young married women living away from their natal home. Relative wealth (more cultivation or cattle) can bring more work to women, although it also offers the ability to forgo migration or hire labour.

The second point is that, despite the fact that women share agricultural tasks, exert decisive influence over farm management based on distinct interests, deploy specialist knowledge, expertise and skill in key areas, and use their own networks to obtain resources (credit, wood, grain, labour), their roles are socially constructed (by themselves as well as by men) as unskilled, manual, ancillary and low status, as menial 'housework' which does not imply technical skill. The gender division of labour is an ideological structure that naturalises gender-based inequality rather than a functional allocation of tasks. It is Bhil men and not women who occupy the social roles of holders of knowledge, decision makers, as farmers or herdsmen; by definition, women do not know or decide about farming matters. Moreover, this male privilege in agriculture is conveyed to outsiders. Men dominate interactions with the market, moneylender, input supplier, cooperative, bank, government extension or IBRFP worker. It is men who are contacted regarding new technologies. And their appearance in public as sole decision makers simply underlines cultural ascriptions of women as dependent labour.[45] Just as the domestic roles of women are emphasised over their productive roles, so the pervasive view of women as labour diverts attention from women as sources of farming knowledge and expertise. When Bhil women exert influence and meet their gender needs, they have to do so by manipulating dominant notions that deny their agency.

WEALTH IN PEOPLE: LABOUR AND SOCIAL CAPITAL

Since Bhil cultivation is self-evidently labour intensive, wealth in people is a critical determinant of economic success (as indicated in IBRFP 'wealth ranking' exercises). It can come from good marriages and bridewealth strategies that secure rights over a woman's labour and access to that of her female kin;[46] but it is also influenced by domestic-cycle shifts. The joint household with married sons or second wives contrasts sharply with that of the widower or the couple

with young children.[47] Wealth in people also means the capacity
to host a *lah* or *halmo* – reciprocal labour arrangements in which
eight to ten households contribute work teams for the weeding or
harvesting of kinsmen's land, or house building, and are provided
with food and liquor; or, for larger capital outlays such as brideprice
payments (or starting a business), the ability to call a *chandla* or *notra*,
in which feasted friends and kin contribute cash sums which must be
reciprocated with at least a doubling of the previous increase at the
next invitation.[48] *Chandla* networks (obligations) are strengthened
through increase in the scale of transactions, while reduced *chandla*
offerings signal weakening ties, and the failure to reciprocate amounts
to social boycott. Networks are built over time: a well-established
one could easily raise Rs 20,000–25,000, that of a newly independent
household with fewer transactions only a few hundred rupees. Strong
social networks of mutual obligation through which loans, seeds,
bullocks or grazing as well as labour can be mobilised are essential
to the success of seasonally concentrated cultivation; they are also
the means by which women whose husbands have migrated manage
agriculture.[49] Support networks have to be maintained through help,
gifts, favours or visits to the sick. They can be deliberately extended (to
affines, or by extending loans to poorer clients) or disrupted through
dispute. A household's ability to generate support (labour, cattle or
finance) at times of need – 'to attach labour without incurring the
costs of maintaining that labour throughout the long production
period' – depends upon its accumulated 'symbolic capital' of prestige,
status and goodwill (Baviskar 1995: 124, after Bourdieu 1977). And
this itself depends upon having the necessary resources to invest in
building up networks and obligations among agnates and affines, to
keep up payments in *chandlas*, or to control others' labour.[50] Such
strategies conceal competition, accumulation and socio-economic
inequalities between Bhil households behind ideologies of kinship,
norms of reciprocity and disinterested generosity between kinsmen
and within the unified Bhil community (1995: 124). Poor families
with few kin, which are unable to maintain their connection to
networks of support and exchange, become excluded, socially
marginal and dependent upon external moneylenders, income from
forest collection or migrant labour.

The 'social capital' theme can, however, easily be overstated.
Farmers who are able avoid dependence on others: they grow maize
and rice from saved seed, only buying for crops which they can
sell for cash (pulses or wheat), and work their fields with their own

bullocks and labour, or through immediate reciprocity. But complex webs of dependency grow around the poor, who are forced to eat last year's seed, or to sell after harvest at low prices to pay off debts, or to wait to borrow someone else's bullocks, or to repay borrowed labour, or to negotiate loans for new seed or fertiliser. For the poor, each season brings new layers of dependence, uncertainty and anxiety. Some will fail. Lacking labour, seed, fertiliser, draught power or the symbolic capital to draw on others' support, their fields will remain uncultivated, and the family will be found working for wages on construction sites in distant cities.

INEQUALITY AND DEBT

Clearly, Bhil villages are not the socially homogeneous places often imagined. Unequal control of labour is one factor. A generation ago it was probably the most important one. A 1960s study in Jhabua noted that since 'most families have more land than they can look after properly' the number of adults in a household rather than landholding correlated positively with income (Aurora 1972). Today, the quantity and quality of land available is far more important and, together with access to cattle, fodder and credit, influences the capacity of a family to meet its food needs in any one season (cf. Doshi 1971, Rao 1988). People in IBRFP villages judge those few households that generate a comfortable surplus as 'better off', but data from project research suggest that 76 per cent of families fall well below this standard, being able to meet their basic food requirements for only six months in a year, and the poorest for as little as three months.[51] Even the better off can descend into poverty in a single season. Literacy and waged employment, or investments in livestock and silver, may secure more enduring social respect, but capricious factors like the loss of bullocks, ill-health, disability, drink, marital failure or the death of a spouse feature prominently in villager self-assessments of ill-being.

Cultivation is highly seasonal and, as noted earlier, has always depended upon external finance for seeds and other inputs at the start of the monsoon season. This is a time when reserves are low, and further drained by the demands of the previous month's festivals and marriages and the dispute resolution payments that they invariably entail. A few farmers are able to raise cash from the sale of small livestock, grams, chickpea or other cash crops. For the majority borrowing is essential, not only for cultivation inputs, but also for food grains once the last of the stored grain has been eaten. Better-off households borrow extensively for agro-inputs and cattle, for life-cycle rituals or to contribute to *chandlas* and service outstanding debts. Their borrowing peaks in the pre-monsoon season. They turn to neighbours and kin. A few who are sufficiently connected to negotiate the hazardous approval procedures and the grasping lower-level bureaucracy, borrow at subsidised rates from banks and cooperatives for wells or bullocks.[52] Most turn to local Soni goldsmiths and Baniya or Bohra merchants and shopkeepers (the *sahukars*), and because they are well-known, these families can borrow against mortgaged silver at relatively low monthly interest rates of 2 to 5 per cent.

Poorer households, by contrast, borrow to meet food requirements and medical emergencies as well as for cultivation inputs. Borrowing peaks in the monsoon season when prices are highest. They cannot afford the risks and costs of institutional credit from banks or co-ops, which lacks the flexibility to meet their urgent need for cash and consumption (cf. Gupta and Schroff 1990), and from which most are anyway barred as defaulters on old loans.[53] Many also lack the necessary financial or social capital to participate effectively in the *notra* or *chandla* systems or reliably to raise loans from kin. They therefore depend upon *sahukars*; but, without a credit standing or collateral in the form of jewellery, they pay a far higher interest rate (12.5 per cent per month). Moreover, they can access loans only through the services of intermediaries (e.g. better-off relatives) willing to negotiate the loan or lend silver, and who also have to be compensated with cash, liquor or chickens. The whole transaction may take several days to complete, adding hugely to the risks of farming where the timing of seed or fertiliser inputs is critical. This is one reason why many Bhil cultivators forgo purchased inputs. Poor women face even greater obstacles to credit from banks or *sahukars* and have to rely on male kin.

Bhils do not default on *sahukar* loans. *Sahukars* recover marketable crops after harvest when prices have halved, or renegotiate repayment at higher interest. In many cases repayment is made from migrant labour wages. Poorer Bhil families, then, find themselves tied into a cycle involving the advance sale of crops, and seasonal or long-term borrowing for consumption and production that ensures the continuing importance of relationships with *sahukars* who take on the multiple roles of credit and input supply, the marketing of produce (reducing the prices farmers get) and (as will be explained) labour contracting.[54] Many who borrow from one source to keep up interest payments on another find themselves tied into an expanding network of credit-dependency while closing off avenues of credit in the future. Access to credit is a huge problem for the poorest, and it is for this reason that families increasingly meet urgent needs through cash advances on their own migrant labour.

With deficit agriculture and acute seasonal food shortages, inflating brideprice demands (anywhere between Rs 2,500 and Rs 40,000 including the feast), rising medical costs (the second most important cause of borrowing and debt), and the periodic need to replace bullocks, deepen wells, pay bribes and service old debts, almost all Bhil households borrow (on average Rs 3,740 per annum in one village) and have outstanding debts (averaging Rs 5,000 in another).[55] For those without agricultural surpluses, small livestock or cash crops to sell, credit payments and emergencies demand the mortgaging of ornaments, bullocks and land (in that order), often to better-off members of the same village. Earning from migration is necessary not only to service existing debts but also to repossess mortgaged assets. In more extreme circumstances debt requires the advanced sale of labour through one or other form of attached labour or 'bondage', the marriage of daughters (in return for brideprice) or the sale of land.[56]

NON-AGRICULTURAL LIVELIHOODS AND SEASONAL LABOUR MIGRATION

Given the precariousness of cultivation, it is not hard to see why Bhil farmers have long sought supplementary sources of income to meet family subsistence as well as to 'feed the Baniya' (Hardiman 1996). Surveys show that only between 12 and 20 per cent of households can rely solely on cultivation for their livelihoods.[57] And even successful cultivators year on year fail to meet basic food needs or to save sufficient maize seed for next year's staple crop. In many villages, the collection and sale of forest produce remains a seasonally important source of gathered food for consumption (tubers, leaves, fruits, honey, medicinal plants, *mahua* flowers for liquor), produce for sale (fuel-wood, fodder grasses, *timru* leaves, *khakhra* leaf plates, bark, gum, medicinal plants) and raw material for handicrafts.[58] Women and children have key responsibilities for forest collection and a measure of control over income from sales. Despite state regulation of commercial forest produce, and the monopoly of State Forest Development Corporations (SFDC) on their purchase at fixed prices at collection centres, local *haats* have a brisk trade in forest produce. This often passes through the hands of traders/*sahukars* who, doubling up as SFDC agents, extract produce from Bhil collectors at less than fair prices against outstanding debts. From the mid-1980s, in some Bhil districts, forest produce and forest workers' unions enrolled men and women to press for fair prices and fair wages, and in 1990 succeeded in increasing the official rate for collected *timru* leaves by nearly 55 per cent.[59]

More important for income than forest gathering is waged labour, in forests and elsewhere.[60] After the post-Independence ban on commercial logging, labour for forest contractors (*kabadu*) was replaced by local work on canals, railways or other public works, or drought relief. By the late 1970s and 1980s Bhil farmers had to go further and further afield to secure employment. At first this migration was to the adjacent regions of commercial agriculture for harvesting, but with the expansion of the urban-industrial corridor extending from Ahmedabad to Mumbai, Bhil migrants were more likely to be found labouring on distant urban construction sites than in either timber yards or irrigated paddy fields. As the result of a gradual upward trend in seasonal labour migration from the 1970s, today, at a conservative estimate, around 65 per cent of Bhil households (up to 95 per cent in some villages) and 48 per cent of the adult population are involved in seasonal migration, which has become the primary source of cash for Bhil families (contributing 86 per cent of cash income).[61]

Seasonal labour migration from these Bhil villages, overwhelmingly for casual urban construction work, is complex and the subject of a separate study undertaken in 1996–7 (see Mosse et al. 2002). By then, with an average of half of the adult population of Bhil villages migrating for half of the year, leaving only the old, the ill or the injured, migration had become a massive event in rural life. A highly segmented casual labour market in the major destination cities of Ahmedabad, Baroda or Surat excludes Bhil migrants from skilled work as masons, carpenters or textile workers, and ensures that they are absorbed almost entirely as the lowest-paid, unskilled casual labour. In particular, it is recruitment through a multi-tier system of labour gang leaders, jobbing recruiter-supervisors and labour contractors that reproduces this segmentation (as well as freeing the owners of capital from the obligations of employer, Breman 1996: 157–61) and ensures that Bhil migrants follow well-defined and repeated routes from particular villages to particular urban work sites.

As with other aspects of Bhil livelihoods, the experience and outcome of labour migration is differentiated. Crudely speaking, migration is shaped by three kinds of strategy. In the first, young men from relatively better-off households take turns to migrate opportunistically for interrupted periods to maximise cash earning, in order to manage the inter-year fluctuations in farming, to meet the need for investment (in wells, house-building, marriages, etc.) or to repay loans. They travel to relatively nearby towns and cities, where they are recruited as daily wage labourers through informal urban labour markets (*nakas*). Second, people with direct contacts with well-known builders/contractors travel in groups. These are usually kin groups with women too, often comprised of affinal relations,[62] a practice which serves to protect the core patrilineage from the divisiveness of unequal and individualised migration earning (and gives women more liberty than among their nuclear kin).

Third, people are mobilised in their own villages by gang leaders/ brokers (*mukkadams*, often former Bhil labourers)[63] who negotiate with contractors/employers, arrange cash advances and long-term work. These migrants are those for whom migration is a defensive survival strategy; people who in the lean season trade their labour in distant urban sites for cash to meet the urgent need for food, and who are most completely tied into relations of dependence and exploitation. They migrate furthest, for longest and with least reward. This is a price paid for the relatively greater security of work, for protection (including shelter at work sites) and patronage offered by ties to *mukkadams*. Larger established builders and contractors (for instance working under contract for state housing or telecommunication schemes, Mosse 2002) most often opt for the dependably compliant, vulnerable and hard-working labour force recruited in this way, in preference to the more independent labour available through urban daily labour markets. Because whole families migrate via *mukkadams*, women migrants, who in our study were 42 per cent, tend to be poorer, older and married with children. While the extent of the first kind of positive or opportunistic migration varies with the availability of household labour in any year/village (influenced by domestic cycles), the extent of the last, survival migration, is a factor of poverty.[64]

By whatever route they get there, at work sites migrants experience long hours, hard work, harsh conditions, injuries (with inadequate medical help or compensation), and social isolation and humiliation. Water, fuel, sanitation and security are major problems, both at work sites and encampments (amplified for women by their gender roles), and the sexual exploitation of women by masons, contractors, the police and others is routine but silenced by fear and economic or marital insecurity. Even when paid in full, migrant wages fall well below the legal minimum (especially piece-rate jobs), but more importantly work is irregular, and payment often late or withheld, especially towards 'the end of the season when the balance of power has firmly shifted from employee (coaxed with advances) to the employer, and when migrants are under pressure to return home for the cultivation season' (Mosse et al. 2002: 75). Unpaid workers have no power of redress. It is because of this uncertainty that poor Bhil migrants place great store on the reputation of reliable if exploitative *mukkadams* and contractors. But for the latter, advances are a mechanism to cement control over a fluid labour force, and debt is 'an instrument of coercion' involving a kind of 'neo-bondage' which only differs from the older agrarian type of clientship in the absence of compensating security (Breman 1996). In other words, the dependence relationship that historically Bhils had with their moneylending *sahukars* has developed and diversified in ways that weaken or eliminate elements of patronage and protection.

The economic and social outcomes of labour migration are as differentiated as the systems of recruitment and employment. For a few, migration provides cash income to supplement agriculture and allow savings and investments (in wells, pumps or good marriages), and sometimes upward mobility as gang leaders and 'recruiters'. It allows investment in social networks, increases social prestige and creditworthiness. For a majority, however, labour migration is linked to long-term indebtedness and fails to generate net cash returns. The poor find it impossible to work themselves out of debt. To give just one example, after three months 'slab work' in Surat a young Bhil couple from a Madhya Pradesh village were able to contribute only Rs 4,000 towards the Rs 7,500 interest due on a Rs 15,000 family loan taken to cover marriage expenses. In the meantime fresh debts were incurred to meet subsistence and medical needs. Long absence and dependence on distant patrons reduces status, erodes social capital, makes the poor marginal to the networks through which credit (or marriages), or benefits from projects such as IBRFP are obtained. Migration, then, is both determined by and amplifies existing social inequalities. People associate repeated seasonal migration with changes that are potentially disruptive of cooperative agricultural life: increased monetisation and the need for cash in Bhil villages; the increase in wage labour at the expense of systems of reciprocal exchange; decline in joint cultivation or well management; and significant strains on intra-household relations (gender, marital and inter-generational).[65]

DE-PEASANTISATION?

For some commentators, growing environmental pressure, deforestation and soil erosion, agricultural deficits, defensive integration into markets (i.e. selling subsistence grain to cover debts), land fragmentation and mortgage, together with labour migration combine to produce a gradual 'de-peasantisation' of adivasis (Breman 1974, Rao 1988: 178), who become 'ecological refugees' (Gadgil and Guha 1995), or a new itinerant proletarian underclass bivouacking under plastic sheets on the urban fringe (Breman 1996). For others, talk of the erosion of agricultural livelihoods in such adivasi uplands is unfounded and reliant upon a mistaken linear view of livelihood change (Sjöblom 1999: 93). After all, cultivation remains economically primary for Bhil communities, many have managed to maintain food security, and population pressure leads to the intensification of land management and not simply degradation, they argue (1999: 93).

Certainly in the villages where IBFRP would work, there was little to suggest that migrating Bhil men and women had ceased to identify themselves primarily as cultivators, and their ideas of well-being remained grounded in the satisfaction of the subsistence lifestyle of past generations (Sjöblom 1999: 132). It is true that, in various ways, migration made villages more cosmopolitan by introducing new kinds of consumption. And for a few, it provided positive opportunities to experience life in the city, in the sense that, as Farley puts it 'migration is mostly about survival, but also a bit about adventure' (cited in Gidwani and Sivaramakrishnan nd: 13); although several years of hard conditions, high cost, and lack of mobility usually challenged such youthful enthusiasm. When given the opportunity to increase agricultural earning, those who could afford to would divert their energy from migration to their land. This is still a society where an interest in land and involvement in agriculture is necessary to retain social position (or symbolic capital); just as social relations are necessary to cultivate. As a Bhil man from a village in nearby Dungarpur district told Disa Sjöblom,

... if you neglect coming to the village for important events in the village or [in] other households, people will speak badly of you. If you do not show your presence [to] *mataji* [the goddess] during Navaratra, people will think you are not interested in village life ... life here is such that you cannot manage on your own. (1999: 178)

Ultimately, for most Bhils migration is not an external factor engendering non-agrarian identities. Migration and cultivation are interdependent. Effective labour migration is hardly possible without *village*-based networks and contacts through which to 'cultivate' urban employment; and cultivation is scarcely feasible without migration earnings to manage uncertainty and make agricultural and social investments including *chandlas*.[66] Migration is a means to support and reproduce agricultural livelihoods and build status in the community. This said, there is a minority of households whose landholdings are so small as to have forced some members (especially younger sons) to move into full-time waged work; and with continuing land partition, in the next generation the number for whom the village is 'a receding point of reference' and the urban connection a source of income and status, will surely rise (Baviskar pers. comm.). Still, from another point of view, survival that is dependent upon migration, individualised earning or the loss of reciprocity is transgressive and brings moral risk. Rather like impoverished Brazilian women who attributed chronic food shortage caused by macro transformations in the rural economy to punishment from God for illegal abortions and tubal ligations (Scheper-Hughes 1992), Bhil women interviewed by Maxine Weisgrau expressed poverty and shortage of water in terms of the increase in sin and the loss of religion (1997: 162) associated with the individualised economic lifestyles of migrants.

In fact, the Bhil agricultural villages studied here have long involved simultaneous connections to the land and to external patrons, and with the advent of the IBRFP project they would continue to do so. Past livelihoods have been forged between the oppressive demands of forest officers and beat guards on the one hand, and usurious *sahukars* on the other; and cultivation has depended upon both the forest and credit. As local sources of fodder, cash or credit have dwindled in relation to demand, people have ventured further and further, and entered into an ever-widening network of alliances and relations (including with development projects) in order to sustain agrarian livelihoods. Some have succeeded; others are pressed to the limits of survival.

Few outside agencies have bothered to penetrate the complexity of Bhil society and the intractability of poverty, preferring their own simplifications. And Bhil communities themselves are no strangers to the manipulating interests of outsiders; they have forged livelihoods and identities in the context of them and the negative stereotypes they purveyed. How would a British-funded participatory development project engage with this complexity; and how would Bhil communities use the project to forge alliances, livelihoods and identities? Of course we project makers were predisposed to view interactions with Bhil society in terms of *our* reading of donor priorities, tribal needs and project narratives of change. At the outset we emphasised yield- and income-increasing crop technologies, soil and water conservation and farmer self-help institutions, and above all 'people's participation'. Bhil villagers, on the other hand, viewed interaction with the project in terms of *their* own priorities and experience of state schemes – as a source of waged labour, credit and external patronage. But this was a *participatory* project whose first obligation was to learn from the people, to deploy techniques of participatory planning so that villagers themselves would give shape to the programme. These were our lofty ambitions as the project settled into remote corners of the Bhil country. The next chapter will examine the dilemmas and contradictions contained in this goal.

4
The Goddess and the PRA:
Local Knowledge and Planning

23 August 1992: With the jeep packed with cooking materials, stationery, bedding, and enthusiasm for the first PRA, seven of us leave the small-town noise and crowds of Dahod and travel across the undulating monsoon green of the Jhabua landscape with its scattered Bhil settlements. We head for Bharola,[1] a Bhil village that meets our criteria as a good place to begin project work. We have been invited to conduct our PRA (Participatory Rural Appraisal) by Mansulbhai one of the leaders of this 'single-clan, faction-free' village, from which we believe agricultural innovations will spread. Our heads are full of plans. We will stay in the village for 3–4 days and carry out a sequence of PRA techniques (interviews, social mapping, matrix ranking, transects, etc.)[2] through which villagers themselves will speak, draw and document their knowledge and practice in relation to the local farming system, and identify priorities for project intervention. As we share informal time and food, listen and learn, through the PRA we will build rapport and communicate the participatory and 'bottom-up' approach of our project to the villagers.

We reach Bharola in the late afternoon and unpack into the school building where we stay. We have already announced a village meeting to explain the event and we expect to move swiftly to organise villagers to prepare social maps of their settlement, to chart 'time-lines' of village history that evening. In the morning villagers will explain their agro-ecology, record local problems of soil erosion, deforestation, indebtedness, education and the like. These will help determine a village plan for project work, and maybe even the location and costs of various soil and water conservation structures will be agreed.

We wait for villagers to arrive for the meeting. For a long time nobody comes. Eventually Mansulbhai arrives with Tersingh a Panchayat Ward Member and seven or eight young men. They are quiet, reserved and unwilling to enter into discussion with the outsiders. Our team members are not sure how to speak about the project. It is all more difficult, more awkward. It is dark, a few villagers have come, sat down and watched, said little and then wandered off. Mansulbhai announces that there will be a meeting in the morning. A young man who has been tending livestock sits and plays a long wooden flute. We exchange melodies. It is now late. We sleep, hoping that the morning will bring more 'participation'.

We are up early. There is nobody else. By 8.15 we can see figures in the distance moving towards us; groups of women. But they are carrying pots with coconuts on their heads. They stop short of where we are waiting, by a shrine in a grove of trees. More and more women come. Now they have two new terracotta figures. They have brought *mataji*, 'the goddess' from a neighbouring village. The goddess manifests herself by possessing a young woman who shakes and, beyond our earshot, begins an argument with another *mataji*-medium. In turn, women pour libations and mark the offered pots with vermilion before laying them at the tree-shrine. (The arrival of the *mataji* is a local instance of the latest goddess movement – begun a few months previously with the miraculous birth of a child from a buffalo; like other goddesses to visit the Bhils in this way she calls for moral betterment and cultural reform, telling people to give up alcohol and animal sacrifice, wash regularly and wear non-tribal dress: dhotis and saris.)

At 9.00 Mansulbhai and Tersing arrive. They say the meeting will start after the *mataji puja*. By 11.00 there are about seventy-five women and forty men by the shrine. Members of the project team try to converse with 'farmers'. They are ignored. Ravi, a Community Organiser (CO), tries to break the exclusion by playing *kabbadi* with a group of boys. Men laugh at him, and the village Patel reprimands the boys for disturbing *mataji's puja*. Some of the team are worried that no PRA is happening, and expecting the worship to conclude, begin to assemble their own paraphernalia and try to get people interested in making a map of the village on the ground. 'Why are you doing this?' a man asks, 'You push off!' 'With whose permission are you here?' questions another.

The *puja* continues. It feels as though the goddess is expressing some community resistance to us development interlopers, under the quiet influence of the village Patel. There are rumours. Mansulbhai's son tells us that people have heard that the project is planning to build a factory, after all the Madhya Pradesh mining corporation was recently in the area carrying out a survey and talking about 'a 5-year plan' for rock phosphate. 'Your company makes fertiliser; people fear you are going to grab our lands,' he says. A migrant (nephew of the Patel) has returned from Surat with a story of a development organisation that started forestry work and took over people's land. We learn later that a disgruntled forest guard, suspicious of the project's impact on his own livelihood, supplied the idea. Villagers begin to prepare food by the shrine. The project team are frustrated; feel they have failed. 'We had to do PRA, it was a big need for us,' one later admits.

The Sarpanch arrives on a scooter from another village. Mansulbhai calls the team leader Rajesh and explains: 'See, villagers think you are going to grab their land. Yes, yes [he continues] we thought you are going to grab the land'. Rajesh: 'No. I wouldn't lie, here in front of a *puja* to *mataji*. I can show you some of our kind of work somewhere else.' The atmosphere is tense. A group of men gather at a distance. One asks again with what permission we are doing these things. The Patel leads the stand-off and Mansulbhai will not challenge it. 'It is your responsibility,' he says to the Sarpanch, 'you see them go.' The Sarpanch tells us to leave, warns that there might be violence if we do not leave immediately. We pack up and leave. The goddess continues to hold the community's attention.

In the evening in the roadside village of Janpur where the COs stay, a teacher comes to their house, 'What happened in Bharola? People say you were beaten up badly there!' Next day, the COs return to the village to try to patch things up and organise an 'exposure' visit to another NGO to explain their type of work. The Patel refuses to let people go. 'I know you have put a case against me,' he says, 'and you will take me to the police station.' It was the village Patwari who met the Patel and said that IBRFP people had registered a case with the police to say that they were beaten up in Bharola. Perhaps the rumour comes from a moneylender in Janpur keen to stir up trouble. The COs try to bring reason through the Block Development Officer (BDO) in Meghnagar town. He has already heard about 'the beating' and is convinced that the project workers are Naxalites. Later that evening two police constables turn up at the COs' residence and call them to the police station. In two days, they are explaining themselves to the Sub-Divisional Magistrate in the presence of the BDO, the Sarpanch and others. The project has become everybody's worst fear: to villagers it is a land-grabbing corporation; to the local authorities its workers are anti-government activists without mandate to work in the area.

For a brief moment, in Bharola, we development workers had the reverse experience of what it was like to be *looked at*, 'to apprehend oneself as the unknown object of unknown appraisals – in particular, of value judgements' (Sartre, *Being and nothingness*, cited in Francis 2001: 81). Not all PRA encounters were as problematic, or as revealing. During the same days, project staff working in the village of Kalpura across the border in Rajasthan accomplished a satisfyingly complete set of PRA mapping, modelling, matrix ranking, seasonality and 'transect' exercises and used the maps and charts to define (and even budget) project interventions addressing local problems of soil erosion and deforestation. But it was soon clear that many common issues lurked behind the apparent successes as well the obvious failures of PRA.

For instance, Bharola taught us that many development ghosts haunted the Bhil landscape and that PRA's esoteric accoutrements, its powders, pens and paper could summon the spectre of the loss of land rights from dam construction and flooded valleys, land acquisition for industry or the eviction of forest-land encroachers; while its land transects, mapping, and the language of forestry and water resources development were more clearly dangerous. Historical experience had taught Bhil villagers that outsiders proclaiming they were there to help adivasis develop came with hidden interests of their own. Conceding trust to outsiders depended upon grasping their motivations,[3] but the project team's assumed informality and their rhetoric of participation or joint planning amounted to a devious refusal to state their intentions plainly, equating them with the area's proselytising Christian missionaries (accusations of mission being a potent local idiom of mistrust). 'Previously you came as "brothers" [i.e. missionaries], now you come as development workers', said some. 'Today you are sitting on the ground, tomorrow you will be sitting on our heads', commented one woman in Bharola.

On the day we chose for our PRA, the goddess arrived in the village demanding devotion, 'cleaner' dress and purer dietary codes. Through her cult, Bhils would tactically adopt the values of upper-caste outsiders as a means to escape a marginality imposed by the exploitation and objectifications of these same outsiders. Would project PRAs similarly provide a means by which Bhil villagers would reconceptualise themselves in outsiders' terms in order to acquire the fruits of development? Was the tension in Bharola a ritually expressed resistance to such outside developer effects, orchestrated by the village *patel* (headman), who set himself against the younger broker-leader (Mansulbhai) and local government representative (*sarpanch*) both of whom saw opportunities rather than threats in forging links with external resource-bearing agencies? (IBRFP had placed trust in these brokers, mistaking them for authoritative representatives of villager opinion.) Perhaps the goddess invoked the sentiment that PRA (the *sine qua non* of participation) would after all be an instrument of development planning over which people would have no control. Was she right?

Experience insists that we set aside extravagant claims that participatory approaches will release villagers' knowledge so as to transform top down bureaucratic planning or reverse hierarchies of power in development (Chambers 1997). The relationship between knowledge and agency (cognitive change and behavioural change) is such that the articulation of 'local knowledge' (perhaps through PRA) is shaped by relationships of power rather than transforming them (cf. Green 2000); although this is not to say that people are passive victims of external designs. If the power of techniques of participation to emancipate is exaggerated, so too is the power of bureaucratic planning to impose. Instead we need a view of knowledge (whether labelled 'local' or 'expert-professional') as relational – produced through complex interactions between project development workers and Bhil villagers (and among them) (Pottier 2003: 2–4). This chapter explores the 'participatory planning' work that took this project from a design fiction to a set of plans and actions after 1992, in terms of such interactions, the knowledge they produced and manipulated, and the multiple meanings, tactics and cross-purposes involved. Its concern is with *how* rather than *what* is known (Pottier 2003: 2–4). My first focus is on Community Organisers (COs) in 'the field'. These are the project's 'street level bureaucrats' (Lipsky 1980, cf. Jackson 1997) left to negotiate the relationship between the project and its villager-beneficiaries in the awkward moments that follow community planning dramas, when the jeeps carrying away important senior people have become a distant rumble and cloud of dust. How did these fieldworkers interpret the IBRFP project model to Bhil villagers and establish their own status and professional identity? How did their efforts to relate, to solicit local knowledge, to involve people, to enlist cooperation or to broker deals intersect with Bhil society? How did they contend with the complex political life of places such as Bharola; and what struggles characterised the negotiation of the new IBRFP project 'in the field'? My second focus is on the processes of power through which external development agendas came to speak through local voices in this international participatory project; and my third is on the collaborations and compromises that practical action brought. My intention is not to criticise the efforts of this project team, but rather to point to some of the more significant and widely relevant insights that skilful project workers acquired and upon which they built in adapting their practice.

'VILLAGE ENTRY': NEGOTIATING PROJECT–VILLAGE RELATIONS

The fear and suspicions revealed in the tension between the *puja* and the PRA were mutual. Project staff were mostly middle-class and urban-educated caste-Hindus. They shared class characteristics with senior government officers at district level; and while their models of tribal poverty came from an enlightened discourse of participatory development, they were not immune to the stereotypes of locally dominant non-tribal groups (Chapter 3).[4] Many who were anxious about their move to remote adivasi villages, and worried about language, discomfort, poverty and isolation, easily objectified their feelings of otherness and insecurity in terms of prevailing representations of Bhil wildness and criminality, shared by their own disapproving families who wondered by what madness their young (especially unmarried women) were staying in such dangerous places where they were so vulnerable. And Bhil villagers too, wondered at how the parents of unmarried women could permit such a thing. The very presence of these development workers marked them out as other; an otherness experienced most intensely by young women workers who individually recall being shaken by witnessing events such as the death of a sick Bhil infant, or the brutal treatment of a bride.

However, unlike their colonial administrator, missionary or anthropologist antecedents (cf. Padel 2000), IBRFP staff could not shore up their own professional identities against representations of Bhil savagery and backwardness. The participatory framework questioned their status as knowledgeable specialists, just as it made Bhil farmers experts. Many fieldworkers did not know how to position themselves. They were confused about their identity and the purpose of the project. Some, often women, worked to resolve mutual otherness through personal relations across cultural boundaries. They stayed with Bhil families, brought foodstuffs to cook and share, participated in ceremonies, walked between scattered hamlets, sat on *charpoys* talking about anything. '[Bhil] women used to laugh at us a lot', Priya recalls, 'they thought our job was to walk from place to place, so when we visited they would ask, "Have you walked enough now?"' Like others she was struck by the willingness of Bhil villagers to relate closely to her, regardless of the schemes she felt that she had to deliver. She was surprised that when her parents came to the village to take her back home, her Bhil hosts came forward to insist to her mother, 'You don't worry: she is your daughter; she is our daughter also.'

But others felt an urgent need to *do* or deliver something that would help to resolve their own ambiguity and otherness. As Jagdish (male CO) put it:

> It is difficult to understand people's needs. I am not a Bhil, even if I read many books still it is difficult to understand Bhils, so I realised at that time something should be started from myself, otherwise I have nothing to do here.

Scarcely had the PRA *rangoli* powders and chalk faded from under the *mahua* tree or the schoolroom floor than project villages were bustling with what came to be called 'entry-point activities' – crop trials, tree nurseries, medical camps, informal schools, well deepening, hand-pump repair – and trucks full of men and women were taken on exposure and training visits. Project workers became problem solvers, suppliers of products (wells, credit, schools), influential people with connections (to IBRFP, government schemes), experts or advocates (for instance intervening to secure wages withheld from migrant labourers by labour contractors).[5] The delivery of activities mediated the social distance, uncertainty and ignorance experienced by staff. Like fieldworkers elsewhere (Arce and Long 1992) they found the acceptability of their presence in villages was largely based upon the benefits they could, or promised to, deliver. In some places COs used activities to address specific suspicions: chickpea trials convinced leaders in one village that the project's primary interest was not dam construction and the flooding of their valley; in another, visits to agricultural research centres dispelled the fear of proselytism. If they quelled anxieties, these initiatives also created demand for a constant stream of new activities and commitments. It had become difficult to relate to Bhil villagers or to sustain community discussions in the absence of inputs or events, all fuelled by a project-wide anxiety to 'keep up momentum'.

Influential knowledge, prominent beneficiaries

With the compulsion to be active, fieldworkers needed to enrol beneficiaries. '[We] were extremely vulnerable', one worker recalls, 'not just being outsiders but having to get things going; [we] needed people along with us.' But the connections that COs forged in Bhil villages through their technologies, stipends or subsidies, were highly selective. The headmen, office holders and members of leading lineages through whom fieldworkers had negotiated entry and 'built their presence in the villages' quickly presented themselves as lead beneficiaries. It was impossible to resist. After all, at this stage, project fieldworkers needed participants more urgently than village leaders needed the project; and it was easier for village elites to target the project, than for the project to target an invisible poor (cf. Kumar and Corbridge 2002). Bhil village elites worked to win project staff over to their agendas, and unwittingly the project provided them with the necessary tools. One of these was PRA.

With hindsight it was clear that early PRAs were under the control of the key village leaders whose interests featured prominently in the perspectives and needs identified. PRAs took place on their land, by their houses, in public spaces and social contexts over which they held sway. The successful Kalpura PRA was dominated by members of the Nagji patrilineage, effectively excluding smaller matrilocal groups from social maps, genealogies and the definition of community problems (Mosse and Mehta 1993). In another village, where staff thought they had found an indigenous informal space for the PRA by linking it to a *bhajan* (devotional singing) event, they inadvertently marked it out as the province of an elite group of *bhagat* Bhils.

Through PRAs men of influence could mobilise participation in a way that won public support for private interests, which they had the capital of authority to represent as *community* needs. The conventions of the PRA – group tasks leading to plenary presentations, generalisation and consensus, summed up as 'we think ... we want ...' – suppressed conflicting views, presented silence as consensus and provided those in authority with 'officialising strategies' to 'transmute "egoistic", private, particular interests into ... disinterested, collective, publicly avowable, legitimate interests' (Bourdieu 1977: 40). For example, it soon became clear that the persisting community need for check dams and irrigation probably reflected the interests of men of influence who held privileged valley bottom land;[6] they knew that much was at stake in controlling the flow of information at a moment of 'crisis', when the community was called to deliver collective knowledge and judgement to important strangers (which is why such 'complex' schemes were put off or deferred by lengthy technical and community negotiations). Occasionally, community priorities could be unravelled to reveal private concerns, as when the community need for education was shown to conceal the desire of a village Sarpanch for a contract to put up the school building and have it located adjacent to his house so as to benefit from the hand pump which would come with it. Had this private desire been better encoded in a *project* priority (i.e. agricultural development) it would have been better concealed and more effectively met.

These were perhaps only the most obvious forms of local domination that sensitive field staff identified. There were other scarcely noticed ways in which knowledge expressed social relations. First, that which the project documented as local agricultural knowledge or technology preferences was neither neutral nor general, but always spoken from a particular social position, for example in terms of access to land, labour, reputation, cattle, credit or gender-specific interests (cf. Chapter 3). Second, differentiated local opinion on technology or farming practice (preferred crop choices, tree species, agronomic methods or understanding of pest control) might also be saying things about the relations between people (for instance between men and women, cf. Fairhead, in Pottier 2003: 5). It might express conflict, make claims, or achieve exclusion in relation to the control of resources. In such contexts, silence and concealment of know-how could also be tactical (Novellino 2003). The prominence of the perspectives of the better resourced, together with the project's desire to introduce new technologies and programmes, could suppress the concerns of the poorest while exaggerating the potential benefits of project interventions.

Third, PRAs privileged a certain *type* of knowledge, that which was explicit, codified, recognised as such and expressible in language to outsiders as rules, norms, or 'indigenous theories': 'this is why we do this ... this is what this means'. Of such assertions, Bloch suggests 'we should be suspicious and ask what kind of *peculiar* knowledge is this which can take such explicit linguistic form?' (1991: 193–4). Agricultural knowledge that was non-linguistic, expressed as practical fluency or which could not be codified so as to be represented apart from practice (in words, charts or maps) remained quite literally missing from the picture. PRA charts themselves also concealed multiple meanings. On paper a tree was a tree, but in the social world the tree (or its removal) might also (depending upon who we speak to) be a symbolic statement about land tenure or gender relations, or a sign of resistance to agricultural intervention by the state (Pottier 1991: 9, see Mosse 1994).

The effects of dominance and exclusion were amplified by the fact that early PRAs were conducted when staff were inexperienced, within short time-frames, at a point when the project was negotiating its presence in Bhil villages. But above all it was the *public* nature of PRA events that made them subject to bias. They took place in public spaces (schools, temples), in the presence of local authority or outsiders and they involved recorded discussion directed towards community action with future implications. The open-endedness of PRA-based planning, its definitions of need, programme activity and 'target group', also made it subject to the effects of local power. As Christoplos, writing on rural development in Vietnam notes, 'by leaving open the definition of the poor farmer, the most significant variable in the planning process, participatory projects become tools for various actors (even the poor themselves) in the political arena' (1995: 2).[7]

Village big-men were also skilled manipulators of the project's small 'entry-point activities'. A few opportunists grabbed project resources, pilfered tree saplings or seeds, or withdrew from sharing agreements, but most contrived compliance with project norms. When COs emphasised that it was the poor who should benefit, they made sure that it was *their* poor (their family or clients) who did so. Understanding the significance of such strategies and the power dynamics of Bhil villages was of paramount importance to COs in order to negotiate the presence and work of the project, and to protect their own reputations as fieldworkers. In workshops they began to talk of the manner in which participation in new activities was not only shaped by relations of power, but would also *reveal* locally significant networks of influence. As the profiles of 'active' and 'non-active' villagers were listed on flip-charts in workshops, it became clear that, in the main, the 'active' were the better-endowed members of village society. Correspondingly, participation and access to the project and its activities was itself a sign of social prominence and status within Bhil villages, linked to other social resources such as clan membership, political office, participation in exchange networks, and the ability to speak well and forcefully (which was already strongly associated with leadership among Bhils, McCurdy 1964: 412, in Weisgrau 1997: 141). So the project offered new arenas (e.g. PRAs) and *symbolic* resources that could be used to enhance reputations and pursue individual mobility. Staff themselves began to endow wealthier individuals with qualities – as knowledgeable, open, innovative, organised, cooperative, clear sighted and able to speak for others. Fieldworkers needed such people to be seen to be effective. Indeed, by selecting those who already possessed the characteristics the project aimed to create – the educated, independent, solvent, modernising peasants – a measure of success was guaranteed (Li 1999: 309). Bhil social practice and staff discourse converged in making prominence in project activities an idiom of power and status, while allowing the better-off to qualify as 'poor' beneficiaries. The poorest, by contrast, were unwilling participants, they lacked knowledge or clarity, were irresponsible and pessimistic, pursued immediate benefits, were spoken for by others. Unable to navigate the links between their immediate needs and wider goals and so engage with external policy objectives, they lacked what Appadurai (2004) calls 'the capacity to aspire'. The poor would be high-risk and unrewardingly hard work. And so too would women.

Silencing women

Official project policy strongly emphasised the involvement of women. 'During donor visits it was gender, gender, gender', recalls Lakshmi, 'there was pressure; we were told that you *have* to involve women, but after the dust settled, there was the whole issue of how do you involve them and in what?' A striking fact of initial project PRAs was how difficult was to involve women. Their participation had been minimal. Depending of course upon age, marital status or wealth, women were constrained both *practically* by the structure of their work roles, which made it difficult for them to be present collectively, continuously and at central places (away from field and home) and *socially* by ideologies of gender (and practices of veiling) which did not acknowledge women's perspectives or give legitimacy to their expression in public – except where they affirmed conventional domestic roles (childcare, health, home-based activities) and kept the appearance of male control. If they spoke, women's voices were guided by male priorities and prevented from expressing difference or dissent. Of course, women's restricted mobility, poor schooling and low self-esteem (among other facts of gender inequality) restricted their knowledge base and ability critically to examine alternative options; but even where they had clear interests and reasoned views, say on trees, the arrangement of field bunds, grass species for vegetative bunding or on the preferred way to organise labour, they were socially prevented from expressing views on such 'public' matters.

The methods of PRA too – schoolish charts, maps and diagrams – marked the exercises as the province of men, biased to their kinds of models and unable to represent the concerns of women or engage their interest.[8] It appeared that women were 'muted' in their ability to express needs and desires through formal PRA events. Their characteristic 'inarticulateness' derived not only from a 'systematic hierarchization' that condemned women's interventions and knowledge to the unofficial, the private and the domestic (Bourdieu, 1977: 41), but also from a lack of fit between their ideas and experiences and the modes of public expression available (linguistic or non-linguistic). Women had to re-encode their needs and desires to make them understood (Ardener 1978: 21). Female staff working with women were implicated in this 'inarticulateness'. They found it more difficult to establish themselves as experts, or to translate their relationships (with women) into coherent demands or project activities. Having limited experience of the development system, Bhil women did not seem to know how to shape their expectations. They too lacked the 'capacity to aspire'. On the one hand, they imagined big infrastructure developments, irrigation schemes, hospitals and the like; but on the other, their expectations were individual and personal; 'a notion', as one female CO put it, 'that somehow or other I, as a woman, can support them, and maybe their children'. The mutual enrolment of project and participants was more complex in the case of women. Bhil women were not responding to the subtle signals and templates that project workers were conveying about how to be a development beneficiary, or translating their desires into readable form. Sometimes even our own ideas about women's social exclusion further silenced women's voices. As Bina Desai (2004) notes, when an agricultural worker says of a woman wearing *ghungat* (veiled) that 'she did not speak', when in fact she spoke and answered questions at the meeting she attended, he preconceives idioms of exclusion so as to silence an articulate woman.

At first, project workers responded to women's exclusion by promoting activities that were culturally defined as 'women's' – those relating to domestic roles: health camps, crèches, ball-bearings for grain grinders (*chakkis*) or smokeless stoves – in order to signal, in a practical way, their interest in working with women. Although this brought women to meetings, many COs realised that the rate of enrolment of women as 'participants' (independent of their husbands) would be set by the slower pace of relationship building with individual households, and changes in their self-esteem, and self-perception.

Aware of the biases towards elites or against women in project encounters (PRAs and others), project workers also changed the context, timing and techniques of PRA to make them less public (at home rather than in the schoolroom), more variable, and tried to incorporate practical modes of learning through demonstration (Mosse et al. 1994). Some COs also began paying attention to story telling or women's songs (cf. Raheja and Gold 1994). PRAs were complemented by more individual, in-depth profiles of families in different 'wealth rank' categories, which took us into the dynamics of debt and migration, labour and brideprice, and also by various training, 'exposure visits' and 'awareness raising' activities. In time, the presence of the project, its activities, trainings and especially its women's 'self-help' groups, created mutually reinforcing project–community spaces in which to bend gendered restrictions, identify shared gender interests and constitute a new gender-inclusive public in which the presence of women and their voices was normalised; what Foucault called 'heterotopian spaces' permitting different norms of social performances (Foucault 1986, cited in Jones 2000). Indeed, at a certain point, the very formal and public nature of the PRA that had excluded women, also gave their knowledge a new visibility and social recognition, as did women's visits to agricultural research centres. The problem was that village planning and project decision making were not geared to women's slowly increasing familiarity with PRA and other project discourse. Exclusion from the consensus became a matter of timing and not technique (see Chapter 6). Public events moved on, and fieldworkers had to contend with more immediate threats to their initiatives.

Developing fieldworker strategies

It was not too long before villagers' suspicions again emerged from the initial scramble for project activities. For several village big-men the limited material or symbolic rewards to be had from the project's early activities – a few seeds or tree saplings – were far outweighed by the dangers it posed. Those who exercised local power through the delivery of high-subsidy government schemes or public assets (wells, roads, buildings or electricity connections) realised that young, educated urbanite workers speaking of 'awareness raising' were a serious threat to their style of leadership and their links to rent-seeking junior state officials. These development workers provided information on a multitude of state schemes or citizen entitlements, and in their wake rarely sighted government officials – extension workers, doctors, vets, district collectors – made their way to uncomfortably remote tribal villages. Such knowledge and social connections were not welcomed by village elites whose power was based on the monopoly of such things, and it was always possible that the presence of the project would divert personally profitable state schemes away from their villages. From these concerns emanated further rumours of proselytism, or more direct attempts to obstruct the project. For example, in late 1992, the *tadvi* (village head) of Vanpur village, opened the door of his village to the project; but six months later when it became clear to him that the project activities, including its popular credit scheme, would threaten his own position and lucrative moneylending and land mortgaging business, he engineered the withdrawal of his dependants from the scheme, forbade his son to become a signatory of the new bank account and made his daughter-in-law resign from running the project-initiated crèche.

IBRFP COs had to learn how to bypass such obstructive leaders and yet win authoritative backing for their ventures. So, when resisted by the *tadvi*, COs in Vanpur village turned for support to his brother's son, Hurji, who opposed his uncle. This young man had the backing of his father, a man of stature in the community, who could not, however, himself openly come into conflict with his brother the *tadvi*. Hurji, together with a group of younger men including his cousins, could then offer support to the project, lead its new credit groups and thereby achieve a prominence in village affairs that would otherwise be denied them. Finding ways around village power and factions in order to enrol participants on schemes was a preoccupation of many COs with whom I sat in the early years of the project. Their diaries and notebooks contained sketches of the networks of influence and conflict in the villages in which they worked – social knowledge and 'social maps' that would never have found a place among the consensual charts of the public PRA (see Mosse 1995). Strategies began to emerge as people exchanged experiences. Strategies, for example, which left formal structures intact, and found informal contexts for innovation, where new ventures could be tried without risk of disrupting more formal social relations, where leaders could observe and change their attitude to the project without losing face. 'We have to get the programme away from manipulating leadership by shifting our attention to independent hamlets and clans', some said; 'or work with returned migrants, or shift from the older to the younger generation for support; from village leaders to their sons or nephews', others proposed.

The practical effect of such fieldworker strategies was to bring certain villagers to prominence as trained providers of programme-related skills and services, for example in forest nursery maintenance and tree-planting, grafting fruit trees, laying contours for soil and water conservation, or record keeping. Since it was the young or the educated or women (rather than a conventional elite) who in this way acquired fluency in 'project knowledge' and an ability to translate between villagers and the project, new patterns of brokerage and leadership emerged in some villages. These roles – deliberately multiplied to avoid village gate-keeping – were later formulated as policy – a growing number of Bhil men and women being honoured with the project title of *jankar* ('knowledgeable person'). After the third year, part-stipended *jankars* played a key role in all aspects of the project: in planning and implementation, in leading farmer groups and in contacting new villages, initiating planning and extending activities to them. Each activity generated its own skilled intermediaries (poultry *jankars*, flour mill *jankars*, meetings *jankars* ...), and the growing project information system brought new prominence to literate Bhil youth. Indeed, low literacy and the opacity of project systems gave considerable power to these mediators, record keepers and group leaders. By 1998 there was an army of some 1,300 *jankars* including an upper tier of 'cluster' and 'master' *jankars* taking on broader responsibilities. *Jankars* were privileged subjects for training – Balaji of Chitrapur village counted 304 'trainings' that he had received in his eight-year association with the project! – and capable IBRFP ambassadors, frequently speaking with authenticity on its behalf and participating in donor reviews and evaluation studies.[9] Indeed, although the title *jankar* was intended to imply local knowledge and skills, what it particularly signified was a privileged relationship with the project; a loyalty rewarded with education, opportunities and resources. Indeed, the rewards of privileged links to the project encouraged honesty and mostly precluded 'rent seeking' or plundering of group funds. In many ways the early dilemmas and anxieties of relating had been resolved through *jankar* mediation. And for the individuals concerned, being a *jankar* provided the opportunity to cross the boundary between the recipients and the deliverers of development. It is no slur on the sincerity and importance of their contribution to project work to point out that *jankars* well understood the economics of aspiration that mean that 'it is better to deliver development than to be its target' (Pigg 1997: 173), and might change their dress so as to signify where they now belonged (Gupta 1997: 330).

Situating project Community Organisers (COs)

The precarious legitimacy of IBRFP fieldworkers in relation to the village and local bureaucracy added to the practical problems of ill-health, long hours, risky two-wheeler travel (and frequent, sometimes serious, accidents), and the responsibility for new ventures and for carrying and dispersing money. To organise activities effectively, to recruit Bhil participants and to maintain their own credibility and status, field staff needed connections and networks beyond the village, as well as trustworthy *jankars* within them. They needed links to local revenue officers, foresters, agricultural extension or health workers, as well to the project office – friends in the Taluk town, in its government offices, in banks and among traders and suppliers, people of their own cultural class, to whom they would turn for emotional comfort and companionship as well as for more instrumental needs.[10] COs' residences in market villages might be lower-status places within the project hierarchy, but they had to become significant centres and official spaces locally, marked by the presence of files and ledgers, maps and wall charts. Field staff were not equally competent in establishing themselves in this way. 'You see', a fieldworker explained as our jeep clattered along the south Rajasthan roads:

> … some COs built their networks in the village, in the Block Office, in the Project Office. They had an intuitive sense of how to deal with this particular person; a heightened sense of how you manage a situation, a smartness. But others lacked this talent and would fail to connect. If they went to the revenue office, for example, they would fail to get the revenue map from the *talati*.

The relationships in 'the field' with kin, neighbours, officials and colleagues were gendered in ways that made the task of women COs enormously harder. The resistance that female staff faced from their own families was matched by pressure from male colleagues. While direct harassment was rare, the inability or unwillingness of staff (men and women) to acknowledge the distinctive capabilities and roles of women fieldworkers, and the normalisation of male working models in performance measurement, put women under invisible pressure. Late night meetings (especially where the boundary between office and residence was blurred), travel alone or with young men, all involved the negotiation of social disapproval, insinuation, embarrassment, criticism and sometimes overt harassment (problems common to many rural projects). Women COs repeatedly faced aggression, not in the Bhil villages in which they worked, but in public places (e.g. on roads from male drivers when travelling by moped or motorbike), or in their small-town neighbourhoods; and not just from men, but also from other women, most intensely from the wives of their male colleagues. Sometimes intimidation and harassment arose as a form of social censure on their departure from gender roles, but at other times single women workers were simply the easiest target for moneylenders and other local brokers resentful of the growing profile of the project among their dependent Bhil clients. This, for example, is how Priya (ex-CO) explains her experience of theft, open intimidation by neighbours and false accusations made against her to the police in the village where she stayed.

Women workers faced a double trial. They were required to work in ways that challenged stereotypes and established new norms of gender behaviour, while at the same time maintaining behaviour that would allow them to command respect within the community. They paid a high but invisible personal price in fulfilling their roles. This was painfully brought to attention after the death in childbirth (through no direct fault of the project) of one woman CO unable to limit the demands of her work while pregnant.

WHO SETS THE AGENDA?

So, the first stage of the IBRFP project involved complex village-level negotiations over knowledge and identity. Community Organisers' overt strategies to maintain their professional status and to secure participation in project schemes were matched by those of village elites to capture benefits, to resist or coopt the project. In the process some were excluded. The question remains: who set the wider development agenda, how were programme choices and decisions *actually* made, how was power asserted within this international aid project?

Participatory rhetoric demanded planning at the community level, by community members, and location-specific development plans. But despite our self-representation as passive facilitators of such processes, we project workers retained the power to direct and shape. We owned the research tools, chose the topics, recorded the information, abstracted and summarised according to our criteria of relevance. Hardly surprising, then, that development choices and the legitimising 'local knowledge' derived from PRAs or village meetings reflected and endorsed an external analysis of problems and solutions.[11] Thus, although farmers in these upland villages were most concerned with maintaining soil fertility, and emphasised the importance of cattle and fodder, and gave priority to capturing water in valleys for irrigation (Chapter 3), village planning exercises (PRAs etc.) invariably focused on soil erosion as a cause of declining productivity and the need for physical soil and water conservation (SWC) works along with improved crop varieties. 'When they do PRA the first thing that farmers ask for is water and irrigation', commented a consultant colleague, 'and the project always turns that around to SWC.' And as one CO illustrated:

> In Panipur [village] people were constantly talking about two lift irrigations from this river ... which we didn't understand, we didn't hear ... What could we offer – talk about bunds, field bunds, talk about trees, talk about crop varieties, that's it. [People] were frustrated because they were not getting what they wanted, but [they] understood what we can offer, at least in the short term: trees and field bund; so gradually they started talking like that, 'You see I have fields where I would like to make bunds', and all this.

In retrospect it is clear that what Bhil farmers initially sought from the project was not community conservation (of soil or trees), but support for capital investment to enhance individual household endowments of land and water (e.g. through wells, lift irrigation). Interventions that limited access to resources, or increased conflict over them, by enclosing the forest, reducing grazing or fuel-wood collection (and which conveyed the urban perception that adivasis are responsible for the environmental destruction) were not favoured, but agreed to as a condition for, or in the hope of, delivery of key investments; that is, as part of an implicit contract between the project and villagers (Weisgrau 1997: 190–1). As Weisgrau, working in south Rajasthan, suggests (an NGO) programme concern with conservation 'is not always consistent with the Bhil belief in the regenerative powers of the earth's resources'; that 'the earth will take care of us', grass and trees will regenerate and new sources of water will be found, perhaps by the inspired mediation of the Bopa priest (1997: 190–1). But, by concurring with the soil erosion discourse and the need for physical SWC works (contour bunds, gully plugs, etc.) Bhil farmers were able to meet their urgent and immediate need for off-season wage labour.[12]

Many staff and consultants later felt that, with erratic rainfall and undulating topography, water harvesting (rather than soil conservation) should have been 'the number one priority', and that Bhil villagers had been sold short. Others acknowledged that productivity and farming system concerns had diverted attention from the central importance of wage labour migration, debt and dependency in Bhil livelihoods. Perhaps the way IBRFP problems and programmes were framed was overly influenced by the presence of a plant breeder and soil scientist on the original consultancy team, and the absence of a livestock or water resources specialist, although that is not the only factor. Priorities were also driven by social development preoccupations, and by project exigencies. Attention to farmer priorities for water resources was marginalised by my – the *participation expert's* – own value-laden judgements about inequitable benefits, or complexity (technical or social), or capital intensiveness, local capacity or the demands of collective management, while SWC was favoured for spending budgets, spreading benefits, providing wages and getting money into savings groups (see Chapters 5 and 6). SWC itself gave first priority to work in the valleys ('*nalla* plugs'), which offered quicker, more dramatic and visible results, while avoiding land of the upper hills cultivated by the poorest under contested tenure as illegal 'encroachments' (anxiety over which might anyway lead to self-exclusion) (cf. Baviskar 2004).[13]

In practice, however, project staff did not need to *impose* their views. Bhil villagers increasingly anticipated and complied with outsiders' points of view in their self-presentation. In their local histories drawn up in PRA 'timelines' villagers proclaimed themselves fitting subjects of development. On the one hand, such histories emphasised needs arising from deforestation and erosion, and on the other, they signalled openness to modern technology. In these 'timelines', the past was marked by ecological decline, while present and future time was measured in terms of the arrival of technology in villages: for example, 1988 – the first diesel pump; 1990 – the first use of urea; 1992 – first bicycle; then radio, flour mill, TV.[14] There were stories of 'social progress' too – the end of buffalo sacrifices to *mataji*, the first use of shirts or tiled roofs, the first '10th pass' student or the first government job; histories of becoming modern to which the project was invited to contribute its benefits and technologies. Bhil narratives of impoverishment and improvement coexisted. By the end of this book it will be clear that just as the former (stories of the loss of forest, soil, grazing and rising debt) were drawn into project planning to justify interventions, so the latter (narratives of progress that placed isolation, food scarcity, forced labour [*veth*] and dependence on forest gathering as things of the past, and modern changes or even rising migrant incomes as harbingers of the new good times) would be drawn into evaluations and impact assessments as a record of project achievements (see Chapter 9).

In constructing their 'needs' and technology preferences, villagers made their own interpretations of the project's intentions. Take the case of trees: initial PRA 'matrix rankings', which focused on the actual *uses* of trees, identified a wide range of species and multiple uses for them,[15] but when village-level nurseries were set up and farmers (women and men) were asked about their needs and the species to be raised, there was an overwhelming preference for one particular species – eucalyptus.[16] Actual uses were even reinterpreted in terms of 'needs' expressed in the light of project deliverables. Some villagers, for example, indicated preference for eucalyptus as timber for housing when, in fact, they had little or no experience of using the species for this purpose. It happened that the village nursery programme at the time (1992–3) was sponsored by the State Forest Department, which was perceived as strongly favouring eucalyptus (the most commonly planted tree under 'social forestry'). Nine years later, in April 2001, the second year of a severe drought, these choices were viewed in a different light. As I stood beside her plot of eucalypts swaying in the evening breeze, Chittiraben told me, 'at that time we only asked for *nilgiri* (eucalyptus), now I heard [in an NGO workshop] each tree takes 10,000 litres of water from the soil; all the wells nearby have dried-up'.[17]

So, villager needs and identities were shaped by perceptions (or misperceptions) of what the project was able to deliver.[18] The need for eucalyptus was, like the desire for SWC, a low-risk community strategy for securing known benefits in the short term (mostly cash or wages), which might have been jeopardised by some more complex and differentiated statement of preferences. Farmers might use a wide range of trees and manage soil fertility in complex ways, but in negotiating with external agents, perceptions about what technology is *available*, and which demands are *legitimate* and will secure a relationship to the project as patron were more pressing. And these were shaped by the project's own activities. So, after a project-organised visit to the Krishi Vigyan Kendra (agriculture science centre) women begin to prioritise the planting of subabul and lemon, which the visit emphasised. Clearly, Bhil villagers did not view technology as separate from their relationship with the project patron (cf. Burghart 1993); so its adoption could signify their status as appropriate clients. Villagers were so firmly and imperceptibly enrolled onto external definitions of need, and so adept at translating their interests into those of outsiders, that the exceptions – women's talk of hospitals, or personal problems – were out of place. When, after reflecting seriously on their problems, people of Chotipur village concluded that what they really needed was a pistol with a permit to arm themselves against raiders to whom they regularly lost cattle and household property, the suggestion was laughable to project outsiders.[19]

LOCAL KNOWLEDGE OR PLANNING KNOWLEDGE?

The 'local knowledge' so important to our model of participatory planning (the outputs of PRAs, village plans, etc.) turned out, then, to be a rather unusual type of knowledge produced through project activities and negotiated across opposing views (of women/men, villagers/staff, social/technical) within villages and the project team. It was strongly shaped by dominant local interests *and* by project objectives; into it were woven the analyses of consultants, scientists or government officers; it matched programme priorities, but offered a simplified view of livelihoods and landscapes rationalised in terms of project models;[20] it was knowledge *for* action not *about* livelihoods strongly conditioned by perceptions of project deliverables, and shaped by the desire for concrete benefits in the short term and relationships of patronage in longer term.[21] Ultimately, 'local knowledge' was a collaboratively produced normative construct bargained between IBRFP staff and Bhil villagers that obscured diverging interests and manoeuvres (within project team and villages alike). In practice, what became prized as IBRFP's 'participatory planning process' (PPP) was not a process of participatory learning based on local knowledge, but rather a process through which Bhil farmers acquired a new kind of *planning knowledge* and learned how to manipulate it.

Amidst the templates, charts, statistics, rational planning frameworks, diagnoses and prescriptions, and printed workplans, all geared to producing information and rationalising decisions for an external agency, it would not be surprising to discover that Bhil villagers were unaware that these exercises were all about privileging *their* knowledge (cf. Fiedrich 2002: 93–5). Indeed, techniques of PPP (PRA graphics and the like) did not reveal so much as *modify* farmers' knowledge so that it led to desired conclusions/solutions (SWC, improved seeds, etc.), which were already present *before* the problem analysis began (2002: 93–5). The PPP's effect was not to expose diverse farmer practices, but to reconfigure and funnel them into the general prescription; in a way, to isolate agricultural knowledge from the knowers and their practical and social context.[22] For example, matrix-ranking isolated crops, trees and other technology from the grid of obligations and constraints (of labour, debt, dependency, relations with *sahukars*), thereby introducing a 'fantasy of consumer choice' (2002: 99). In the same way participatory crop trials involved appraisal of seed characteristics independent of inputs, crop–land–water relations or the status of the cultivator (see Chapter 6). In the end, villagers spoke through PRAs as we wanted them to speak. They were equipped to produce knowledge that the project needed. Participatory planning tools (PRA, Community Problem Analysis, strategic planning and village workplans, etc.) were disciplinary exercises in right thinking; techniques through which outsiders controlled the knowledge that others possessed (2002: 66, 82–9). But they were also symbolic enactments indicating the transformation of marginal tribals into development beneficiaries and bringing them into a relationship with the project. Participatory planning 'processed' the needs and visions of Bhil communities into project schemes, while concealing the political effects and the agency of the project outsiders.[23]

At the very least, PPP demonstrates the contradiction that people's 'agency can only be accomplished through imported structures for participation' (Green 2000: 70). Bhil farmers *became* indigenous experts through complying and collaborating with project systems. As Green argues, participatory techniques both assert and deny local agency because they *control* agency (2000). Farmer practice is honoured, but also discredited in relation to the superior models of knowing and rational decision making introduced by educated well-dressed outsiders, guided by foreign 'participation experts' (like myself) and reflecting currently favoured donor policy. So, when (from 1998) ODA/DFID emphasised a 'sustainable rural livelihoods' framework with its 'pentagon of capitals' (see Chapter 7), these were soon found scratched on the ground in its projects' inaccessible tribal villages, as well as firmly entrenched in fieldworkers' minds as the means to discriminate real from false needs, between villagers 'with vision' and those needing 'proper guidance'. In the words of one IBRFP worker:

> Sometimes in any village if the vision is not clear [they] say, 'You give only one big scheme [i.e. irrigation] [and] you go.' And this kind of stress is created. But if you follow all our process and first you clear

the vision of the community and then you conduct PRAs, and after that we sensitively do a CPA, then after the CPA then the emphasis is on the farming system ... I think [at] that time they understand the 'livelihood capitals' very well. If they understand the natural capital, if they understand the physical capital, they understand about the social capital, they understand what human capital [is], they understand about the financial capital. If they understand very well, then vision [is] built at that time they will plan very very well.

Participatory planning may be a means to advance top-down perspectives, but there is always potential for cooption (or at least compliance) from below (White 1996: 14). Local 'planning knowledge' was the means by which project staff *and* villagers (in the first instance only men of influence, but later a wider cross-section of people) colluded in translating idiosyncratic local interests (in wage labour, wells, pumps, housing support or loans) into legitimate demands. Villagers could also get their own ideas for schemes inserted into programme packages. Flour mills, grocery shops or other innovations would be picked up by project staff and in a few months every village would have one. Interests from top-down and bottom-up may not have matched, but there was a shared interest in a concrete plan of action which suppressed difference. Compromise allowed both sides to benefit: villagers gained sanction for activities in their neighbourhoods; and field staff, by delivering desirable goods and schemes, won support from locals who agreed to 'participate', attend meetings, train as volunteers, host visitors, save and make contributions, and in other ways validate both the wider project and staff performance within it.

But there was something more than the tactical acquiescence of villagers in external representations of their livelihood for practical reasons. Perhaps, as Novellina suggests, participatory techniques had a *confessional* dimension, in which Bhil farmers admitted inadequate, environmentally destructive practices and the need for improvement and imported models of agriculture, forestry or soil conservation (2003: 286–7). It is also true that, through the project's modernising conventions of PRA, through visits to centres of scientific agriculture and by adopting new technologies, Bhils sought to present themselves as the rational planners, progressive and worthy beneficiaries they understood they were expected to be (cf. Fiedrich 2002: 89–96). By adopting the conventions and technologies of outsiders they were aligning themselves with cultural practices through which alliances could be forged with benevolent members of the dominant class. And the significance of that is that this is precisely the logic that lies behind various Bhil reform movements, and the *devi* cults in particular (Hardiman 1987a: 164). Indeed, Baviskar, writing about the same 1992 *mata* phenomenon, comments that it was not so much about adopting caste Hindu practices or (as Hardiman suggests) a democratisation of upper-caste values, but 'a carefully considered contingent capitulation to dominant ideology' (pers. comm. and 1995: 97–103). The cult of the PRA and the cult of the *devi* had more in common than we realised. In both Bhils contended with outsider evaluations of them, drawing on these tactically to represent themselves and their social aspirations. I will take up this theme again in Chapter 9.

EXTERNAL IMPOSITIONS

Whatever the rhetoric, the reality is that people participate in agency programmes and not the other way round. Inequality in planning negotiations is scarcely concealable. In IBRFP, 'local knowledge' was part of the project's exercise of power in *constraining* as well as enabling 'self-determined change'. It was project outsiders who needed 'local knowledge' about livelihoods, and often used it to bargain with villagers, to challenge their claims on the project, to reject as well as accept villager proposals, to negotiate subsidy levels, savings, cost recovery or resource sharing arrangements and to allocate labour benefits or gender roles on project works. The polarity set up between extractive and participatory modes of learning obscures the fact that, once produced, information will be used in various ways in a project system, including to privilege certain subordinate perspectives within communities.

Project workers also used 'local knowledge' to negotiate the participatory approach with sceptical stakeholders – the ODA, technical consultants or senior management.[24] The fact that 'PRA-type' information had been set as a new scientific standard by donors and other agencies did not, in itself, democratise power in programme decision making, but it did widen the range of interests that could gain legitimacy by being labelled 'local needs'. In this sense, participatory approaches and methods served to represent external interests *as* local needs, dominant analyses *as* community concerns, and in doing so helped to conceal the agency of external actors.

Despite IBRFP's strong emphasis on its PPP, several programme choices were entirely unrelated to this process. PRA charts and diagrams were regarded as little more than attractive wall decorations, making public statements about participatory intentions, providing, as one staff member put it, 'a licence' that labels any activity participatory. PRA symbolised good decision making without influencing it. The simplistic assumption that better access to local perspectives will ensure that programme decisions are more participatory is only too obviously blind to the institutional realities of rural development, and the needs of project organisations like IBRFP in their own right.

First, in the project's early stages activity choices had less to do with planning and problem analysis and more to do with the pragmatic need to forge relationships with villagers and manage their petitioning. Second, as will become clear in Chapter 5, priorities were influenced by the wider institutional setting of the project and its need to maintain relationships with government, state auditors, senior management, research institutions or donor advisers, each with their own agenda that required the introduction of a stream of sometimes useful but not infrequently flawed or inappropriate schemes such as certain new winter crops, compost pits, mushroom cultivation, bio-fertiliser, women's handicraft, first-aid kits or animal-drawn farm machinery,[25] all presented as 'local needs'. Local planning was a type of policy making in which, as noted in Chapter 2, designs and schemes are significant less for *what* they were than for *who* they brought together (Latour 1996: 119).

In the immediate aftermath of the bungled PRA in Bharola in 1992, for example, staff enrolled Bhil farmers on the district collector's favoured new winter crop programme in order to secure credibility with district officials. Embarrassment followed the discovery that the seeds promoted (varieties of sunflower, wheat and chickpea) required irrigation, were expensive and that most villagers were barred defaulters from the cooperatives through which they were supplied. Field staff immediately inaugurated a face-saving seed-credit scheme in villages with little clue as to who was benefiting or whether seed loans were recoverable. One mistaken judgement followed another. When, at the end of the season, the project planned bulk sales of the 'marketable surplus' of chickpea through a local cooperative to maximise farm profits, it overlooked what women were telling fieldworkers about such cash crops being their household savings account, sold in small quantities in local markets throughout the year as need arose. The project's long and troubled attempt to promote mushroom growing, for which one CO commented, 'there is now only archaeological evidence', also had a lot to do with keeping in with the enthusiasms of a district collector.

Third, the project was a site for other institutions and agendas contending for influence within wider policy or research arenas. Our own consultancy operation was one such. IBRFP was also the ideal field site for a range of Indian and UK-based research programmes, especially the ODA's centrally funded research in plant sciences and forestry. The conception of the Bhil uplands and similar agricultural environments as 'complex and diverse' appeared mistakenly to justify a multiplication of experimental ideas, technologies and interventions to expand poor farmers' choices. [26] Meanwhile, changes in the nature of the aid programme (during the 1990s, see Chapter 9) made such sites increasingly scarce and intensified the pressure on field-based projects such as IBRFP to host research, to accept research-based technology or provide field sites to test it. The research–project link was a battlefield: UK research managers complained about the 'lack of response from bilateral programmes in taking up the results from the research programmes' (interview), while project workers complained that 'villages are like laboratories for other people's ideas'. Even if expanding technology options *per se* offered little to poor Bhil farmers facing tight socio-economic constraints with very little room for manoeuvre, compromises and accommodations of technology were a means to establish and increase the project's reputation (cf. Latour 1996: 99). Finally, as will be explained in the next chapter, development choices were also profoundly shaped by IBRFP's organisational systems and procedures, its budget categories, time-frames and targets into which field staff had to translate local demands. Irrigation schemes that villagers desired were expensive, risky, technically complex and required high-level sanction; SWC was low-risk, and spent the budget.[27]

It would be a mistake, however, to view participatory planning systems such as IBRFP's *merely* as instruments of project manipulation and villager compliance, having no effect of their own; or as producing only decontextualised, manipulated knowledge and a growth of ignorance and miscommunication, rather than 'a growth of knowledge and social innovation' (Rew 1994, cited in Pottier 2003: 11). For Bhil villagers, the experience of 'modern' rational planning, of representing problems and possibilities apart from structural constraints, could be liberating in a certain way (cf. Fiedrich 2002: 99). For sure, Bhil farmers were not going to acquire new practical expertise through PRA encounters, but in communicating to outsiders they might reflect on their practices in new ways. As Bloch suggests, the 'unpacking' of non-linguistic expertise and 'putting it into words' (or diagrams) was *un*likely to add to the practical efficiency of a familiar operation: in fact, quite the reverse. But linguistic (and other kinds of) explicitness might be associated with, and allow for, innovation (1991: 193). The process of translating an individual, often fragmentary, experience of a difficulty into the collective awareness of a problem with a view to change, and from this to a programme of action would require new understandings, skills and institutional arrangements, all of which involved external intervention to identify the limits of existing knowledge and systems of problem solving. Much more than PRAs, this would involve techniques of animation, awareness raising, non-formal education or problem solving (cf. Davis-Case 1989).

CONCLUSION

By the end of 1995 a highly committed project team had sensitively built relationships with people in a handful of the poorest adivasi villages in a remote corner of western India. Slowly over three years they earned a remarkable level of local trust and credibility, by helping farmers identify and test improved rice and maize varieties for poor upland soils with few inputs, providing them with credit, initiating low-cost soil and water conservation work, deepening wells, providing tree seedlings, vegetable seeds and improved breeds of goats and chickens, and mediating external connections. Through constantly meeting, sitting, discussing, explaining ideas, conducting PRAs and CPAs, taking men and women to distant research centres or bringing government experts and administrators to their doorsteps, they exposed Bhil villagers to new technologies, ideas and ways of thinking. Daily they collided with the unfamiliar contours of Bhil society and understood them a little better, responding flexibly to a complex social and institutional environment, learning a lot as they groped for successful interventions, sometimes drawing on *ad hoc* interventions based on 'off the shelf' development ideas or government schemes. Villagers would themselves readily contrast IBRFP with earlier experiences of missionaries: here were outsiders who respected their worldview and lifestyle and with whom they gladly did business.[28]

For a British bilateral aid project in the early 1990s, this was an entirely new way of working. This is not to say the approach was politically radical. Like most forms of 'participatory' development, the project was determinedly isolated from wider fields of social and political action (Green 2000), and distanced itself both from established political institutions and from politically active unions, NGOs and social movements (for instance the nearby Narmada Bachao Andolan protest against dam construction), despite individual connections. Its actions did not derive from a wider political economic analysis of tribal underdevelopment and exploitation. And its conception of 'empowerment' was mostly limited to 'having a place, a voice, being represented within an administrative or management system' (James 1999: 14) – power *to*, rather than power *over* (Nelson and Wright 1995). The policy concept of 'participation' worked to transmute broad political issues into more local and technical concerns, while masking the actions and power of the project system (staff, consultants, donor, etc.) within local arenas. Still, over the next three years field staff continued to refine their practice of 'participatory planning' in the light of experience. They remained the core competence of this project, developing and negotiating long-term (five-year) and seasonal plans with communities. For some this would be a slow, complex and reflective process; for others something accomplished through a brief period of PRAs and exposure visits to other project villages (or video shows) which consolidated 'local needs' around available programmes followed by village meetings to negotiate responsibilities and contributions, to appoint *jankars* and produce resolutions on schemes to be forwarded to the project office. Either way, as the next chapter will show, project staff had to contend with increasing pressure from organisational relationships, and from above, which made their 'participation' task ever more difficult. I turn now to take a closer look at project organisation as a system of relationships.

5
Implementation: Regime and Relationships

Models of project cycle management construct the 'implementation phase' as a domain of the routine, a world of rule-following subordinates that falls between the main acts: the optimism of design and the judgement of impact (cf. Quarles van Ufford 1988a). My purpose is to challenge such a policy-centred view. When introducing the book I made the proposition that 'development interventions are not driven by official policy, but by the exigencies of organisations and the need to maintain relationships'. The point draws on the post-Weber organisational theory of Mintzberg (1979) and the work of Quarles van Ufford (1988a), which recognises that 'the scope for control in professional organisations such as development bureaucracies is limited, and even decreases as they become larger' (1988a: 26). A donor has little hegemony, and at most its policies have the capacity to shape rules and codes for others' behaviour within a loose domain; something Latham (cited in Eyben 2003: 9) refers to as 'social sovereignty'. Within agencies themselves, organisational disjuncture and social segregation limit the control and knowledge of upper over lower levels in the system, such that the shape of a project organisation can be imagined as an hour glass: a thin bottleneck limits the capacity for influence of policy directors and advisers over an operational core (Quarles van Ufford 1988a). Plans legitimise and ensure access to funds, but implementation is not generated by policy intention (1988a: 26). Bureaucracy itself is not an instrument of policy, Quarles van Ufford goes on to point out, because 'bureaucracy is an *independent* generator of ideas, goals and interests' (1988b: 77, citing Vroom). That is to say, the work of organisations is more immediately shaped by their own 'system goals' – those of organisational maintenance and survival – than by the formal policy goals of the minister (1988b, citing Mintzberg 1979).[1]

This chapter looks at the project system as a set of relationships at the level of office (PMU) and organisation (KCBL), and at the way in which the maintenance of relationships meant that the practices of 'implementation' were shaped less and less by formal goals and more and more by the 'system goals' of the organisation, namely to preserve its rules and procedures, its systems of rank and administrative order, and its relationships of patronage. Indeed 'implementation' consolidated an internal project order while reproducing the class relationship between project staff and Bhil villagers as management and labour, patron and clients. The chapter will, then, link micro-organisational processes to macro-effects, which as Heyman suggests, requires that we 'tack between internal work struggles and external work accomplishments, seeking the power results' (1995: 265). But there is a paradox. While systems of administrative control organise work routines, policy ideas provide a means to rationalise action and form part of the complex thought processes (judgements, classifications) that staff have about each other, about managers or villagers. Chapter 6 will turn to this 'thought-work' – the 'partially routinised manufacture of thoughts' (Heyman 1995: 263) – as a key aspect of development organisations. Neither chapter intends to judge practices against norms: to evaluate.

THE OFFICE – AN ARENA OF COMPETING IDEAS AND GROUPS

At first, the ambiguity surrounding the idea of participatory development generated considerable uncertainty about how to 'operationalise' it among IBRFP staff. There was a differentiation of views and professional identities that revealed the project as an arena in which people with different responsibilities, tasks and different constructions of reality competed for power (Quarles van Ufford 1988b: 83, following Lammers 1983). In fact, different ideas, approaches, professions or development backgrounds provided the principles of social structure in the project team, where personal pasts (of class, caste, gender, religion or region) were 'bracketed' out in the organisational present (Heaton 2001: 141).

Because of the lack of clarity on the project's participatory strategy, an office politics quickly emerged around competing views and approaches. While some (technical and administrative staff) desired clear-cut and immediate technical and market innovations, and wanted to move rapidly to implement larger-scale SWC, forestry or irrigation programmes in order to meet expectations from above (from bosses) and below (from farmers); others were firmly against ill-considered interventions in complex livelihood systems about which project staff knew little. An activity like SWC, they said, raised many unanswered questions: who had been consulted; how would new contour bunds affect existing land use; what were the costs/benefits for seasonal migrants; would there be cost recovery for maintenance; how should labour benefits be allocated; who would supervise, keep records and make wage payments, at what rate, to households or to individuals (women or men); and how would these issues be negotiated with communities? Work on forestry or irrigation raised yet more complicated issues around collective action, women's access and equity. As Ravi, a former CO, perceptively recalls:

> ... about one and a half years into the project there was a tremendous pressure from [the] top saying we need action, and then the middle-level staff – the support group [technical and social science specialists] – did not come up with a solid idea to the management ... rather they took two different stands and divided into two different groups – one is pro-action and one is slow action kind of thing.

Such tensions, surely common in hybrid project teams made up of different disciplines and development cultures, brought to life contradictions already written into the project design (Chapter 2). Widely divergent interpretations of 'participation' circulated the office. Crop specialists wanted to *consult* farmers (using PRA and focus groups) on the desirable traits of improved varieties grown in supervised crop trials on their fields. SWC and forestry specialists wanted *collective agreements* on land treatment and implementation modalities. 'Social' specialists wanted *capacity building* for long-term change in relations with moneylenders, the market and the state. Different views of the task implied disagreements over time and progress. When some proclaimed, 'We have demonstrated the participatory approach, we can now move on to implementing our major physical programmes', others shouted, 'No! No! You don't understand, you have no experience, we have hardly started, there is a long way to go!' As Latour comments in relation to technology projects:

> The frontier between 'the bulk of the work' and 'fine-tuning the details' remains in flux for a long time; its position is the object of intense negotiation. To simplify its task, every group tends to think that its own role is most important, and that the next group in the chain just needs to concern itself with the *technical details*, or to apply the principles which the first group has defined. (Latour 1996: 67)

These differences of opinion resonated with deeper social divides within the project office; between, on the one hand, technical and administrative staff grounded in the result-oriented practices of fertiliser marketing, and on the other, non-technical social specialists with NGO backgrounds. This distinction overlapped that between KBCL and non-KBCL staff, permanent and fixed-term contracts of employment, a compliant or a critical orientation to management. Then, into this arena of dispute, visiting consultants and donor advisers projected their own disciplinary and philosophical divisions, which mirrored and amplified the project team's. When some of us congratulated IBRFP on the identification of an improved variety, or on SWC works, others agitated that this didn't count for much if the seed supply and distribution was not managed by farmers, or if the project's hidden subsidies resulted in dependence. While some of us used arguments about the 'social complexity' of interventions to resist the management's implementation imperatives, others countered that the work (e.g. SWC) could not wait for detailed social analysis: 'information is for long-term fine-tuning', one said, farmer skills would be acquired in the course of implementation.[2]

Staff and consultants were mutually enrolled on each others' agendas. During donor or consultant 'missions' staff could speak with the authority of field experience in support of my position in arguments with consultant colleagues over designs or plans, just as I, as an outsider expert, could present the dissenting views of fieldworkers who were constrained in what they could say by their position in the organisation's hierarchy. As Lakshmi, a 'social' field specialist recalls:

> There were differences between consultants and there were tensions; and it was funny because it reflected the whole politics of the project team. We had technical specialists and social specialists, [and] our strengths vis-a-vis the technical people came from what – you know – what you or B [another consultant] would say; that's where we would have more say, and we could use that as a kind of negotiating thing. I mean who is going to listen to Lakshmi [laughing]. It is easier, you know, having David Mosse ... you and B were the ones who dealt with difficult things, so you were also a troublemaker!

But while staff allied themselves with external consultants during the heightened negotiations of 'missions', they quickly shored up relations with management after the foreigners had left.

The project's development strategies were never independent of the politics of team relationships. The fate of ideas, the outcome of debates and the effectiveness of action that resulted, depended crucially upon the emergence of networks (cf. Long 1992: 23). IBRFP consultants' reports and recommendations, for example, were presented as independent, professional technical documents, but they were never treated as such; or if they were, they would sink without trace. Ideas had to be forged through relationships; and those consultants who arrived late, or who did not build internal coalitions around their ideas (maybe around themes of gender or equity, or the promotion of fodder species), or could not get staff with sufficient status to associate with them, found their ideas, however pertinent, falling through the cracks of the organisation and fading with their own departure.[3] In practice, expertise is relational; a truth that is acknowledged when consultants later complain that 'there was a failure of the project to engage with our reports', or when team members speak of ideas being given 'a political colour'. One put it this way: 'If I got hold of David's report and made suggestions, it was taken that I'm David's person and I'm trying to push things.' So, in the project team as much as in Bhil villages, technical knowledge was an expression of social relations.

So, the project office was a complex community of ideas and of people. Village-based Community Organisers, least secure in their jobs, had to read and engage with this community carefully in order to win notice, gain reputation and promotion. Of course they had to build alliances and give importance to key seniors when in town. But they also had to win legitimacy by developing appropriate professional styles as fieldworkers. As he reflected on his work as a CO, Krishnan concluded that there were two such styles. First, there were individuals from the region; fluent in the vernacular, with experience of working with local NGOs and familiar with a target-oriented programme delivery. They sought support from office managers and technical specialists anxious for visible progress and measuring fieldworker efficiency in terms of the uptake of physical schemes. They largely ignored the social and gender specialists installed as guardians of the ODA's policy agenda. As Krishnan put it:

> … they didn't have much of [an] understanding about what the Project Document is talking about and what ODA consultants are talking about, y'know, the process, [and] they were not much worried and not much stressed; 'yaa, we have done it all in our previous jobs … we'll use it, let

them speak; whatever David Mosse can, let him speak as much as he can, we'll do as per our idea' [laughter].

Second, there were non-locals, qualified from professional institutions and competent in English who 'had a better understanding of the process' and stressed the ODA's normative participatory model, 'thinking, "this is the kind of approach we should follow" '. They sought support from the projects' social specialists and consultants who would regard their talent for speaking participatory principles, for researching and reflecting. Of course these identities were, to a degree, socially pre-determined (by class background) rather than freely chosen, although polarised by competition for the scarce resource of reputation in the project, and the need to protect against criticism – whether accusations of 'top-down' implementation and ignoring the process, or of making the search for 'process' an excuse for inaction, poor performance and nil results. Either way, given the ambiguities of participatory development goals, without supporters COs would be exposed and vulnerable. The maintenance of relationships was crucial.

Now, during the first years of the project a preoccupation with the internal negotiation of development ideas and professional identities made it hard to generate project-wide consensus on meaningful action, even while everyone felt they were learning a lot. (Some felt that 'people created conflicts in order to learn'.) 'Participation' generated a certain confusion and frustration captured by one former CO:

> We were all the time kneading the dough ... to make a softer chapatti, but we never had the chapatti [laughs]; we kept kneading, confusing ourselves, confusing villagers and we never really knew how to make a better chapatti ... [there was a] lack of strategic guidance. We had very experienced people like [names] but the project couldn't use them ... it is a system constraint ... the system [was] set up to work well but something [was] blocking the process ... the cogs [were] not engaging.

This was a new project whose strategies, guidelines and procedures were weakly developed and much contested; so too was its organisational hierarchy. Senior people did not have an unrestricted power over fieldworkers. 'Bottom-up' principles, competing agendas and accountabilities, and the constant interference of outsiders gave fieldworkers *de facto* autonomy to develop their own operational interpretation of both villager needs and project goals, and their own strategies of intervention in both arenas.[4] Moreover, senior people depended upon them for knowledge, contacts and actions in order to secure the outputs for which they would, in turn, be held accountable. Added to this, the project manager allowed a relatively open, self-critical process to operate within the team.[5] He knew that he was not a figure conducting an orchestra of development inputs and ideas following the master score scripted by the donor, but rather master of a ship at sea subject to a cacophony of conflicting information about coordinates, readings of the weather and sightings of land, defending itself against a suspicious and mutinous crew subject to outside incitement.

CONSOLIDATING A REGIME OF IMPLEMENTATION

From the project's third year (1994–5) a decisive shift was under way from the uncertainties, tensions and conflicts of negotiating a 'participatory process' for planning, to the certainties of programme action; or as one former CO put it:

> Initially we thought if we do the process then [the] outcome will come automatically … [later] we became action-oriented: physical targets, SWC, tree programmes, well deepening, irrigation projects, lift irrigation, *pucca* wells, crop programmes on a large scale in all villages … [we thought] the process was in-built, like in a computer: you do things and [the] process is carrying on inside … automatically.

'Implementation' changed project relations and brought new accountabilities. An organisational emphasis on activities, targets and spending resulted in a clarification of hierarchy. This was inevitable. Meetings became more programme-focused, guidelines were formalised, tasks more narrowly defined and staff induction periods shortened.[6] The project was increasingly organised, conceptualised and reported around its 'sectoral programmes' (in crops, trees, SWC, etc.), each supported by an overseas consultant working with a counterpart 'Field Specialist', a set of guidelines (based on earlier experimentation) and a project-wide budget. The pressures of procedure and technical reporting reduced time for specialists to interact. Disciplinary perspectives were amplified. For example, the project SWC Field Specialists, trained in agricultural engineering, gave status to *engineering* approaches to soil/water management and physical structures, to the exclusion of agronomic or biological approaches involving crop regimes, trees or grasses. These were the responsibility of Crops Specialists and Foresters respectively. An organisational emphasis on maintaining role clarity and professional identities diverted attention from the complexity of Bhil farmers' concerns.

The implementation regime and its accounting system demanded a huge quantum of information and statistics in the form of farm data, payment sheets and consolidated reports. This not only preoccupied fieldworkers with record keeping, measurement and inspection of works, but also brought into existence a 'sub-hierarchy' of posts – trained village 'volunteers' (*jankars*), 'Master *Jankars*', specialist SWC Community Organisers, Assistant Field Specialists, Field Specialists – constituting, for example, an 'SWC team' with its own system of classification and documentary practices.[7] To this textual discipline of reporting was added the temporal discipline of schedules and deadlines (Heaton 2001).

When the growing pragmatism reduced complex social issues into matters of implementation delays, it became harder for cross-sector staff with responsibilities for gender or equity to define their roles or protect their space. Some key 'social specialists' left the project, complaining, as one put it, of 'a great threat to [my] functional responsibility to take care of the process approach'.[8] The effect was to remove an intermediary level in the staff team, to unify the project's structure of authority, to reward compliance over challenging criticism, and to reduce the room for negotiating and contesting strategies. The balance of responsibility and power in the project team shifted towards key technical specialists and *their* concept of 'participation' – the introduction of new key technologies and review through focus groups – became generalised.

These changes altered significantly the way village fieldworkers experienced their roles and relationships, and their sense of professionalism and autonomy. As Bhil villages became more perfectly 'project places', operational procedures substituted for the negotiation of identities. The professional and the personal became more separate. People no longer spoke of integrated village-specific strategies and had less time to debate alternatives with different groups in a village. With pre-defined programme categories, budgets and targets, there was hardly any need to translate local concerns. As a programme develops a set of workable interventions, the logic of planning inevitably becomes from solutions *to* problems, regardless of the quality of the 'participatory process'. Bottom-up and top-down dovetail imperceptibly. There was also less time, or need felt, to reflect on the programme as a whole, or for deepening knowledge on the dynamics of rural livelihoods and power structures. As Bhil villages became more 'manageable', differences and inequalities within and between them were increasingly under-perceived.[9] It was more efficient to work with, than against, local brokers and elites. COs also spoke to me of a narrowing of their role as programme responsibility shifted to the project office's technical specialists (in crops, engineering or forestry); and the more villagers 'shrewdly reconise[d] that the range of things on which summary decisions in meetings can be solicited increases in direct relation to the rank of the … officer present' (Sivaramakrishnan 2000: 443), the more some COs felt marginalised as go-betweens or 'field assistants': specialists made the presentations to visiting donor teams, and technically trained village *jankars* reported directly to them, 'like STD line'. COs merely put up individual activity proposals (for a well deepening here, SWC there) to project HQ, mobilised villager labour and arranged village resolutions on modalities (cost/sharing etc.) to fit with programme requirements and allocations. Some became de-motivated. 'There was no incentive to do village planning', one commented, 'at review meetings nobody asks what [you] did in the month, missions go only to a few active COs' places. We closed our minds … [were] least bothered about activities, [only] perks and salaries, TA [travel allowance] bills.'

Now, not all COs experienced this tension between their village-level work and the wider implementation logic in the same way or to the same degree (or would express it); and overall their position was not comparable to field staff in standard top-down development programmes. They built on a different foundation of village work. But still, staff faced growing pressure to meet implementation targets, not only set from above but also demanded from below.

'There were targets for like wells, targets for SWC … for say seed distribution under FAMPAR, and nursery raising,' said Jagdish reflecting on a changing working environment. 'Each CO was assessed on targets; they started asking, "How much seeds and fertiliser are COs distributing?" and then my villagers started to compare themselves with other villages. In my villages only one truck of fertiliser had come, in other villages three or five trucks … '

Fieldworkers found that activities and expenditure against targets were now the key measures of their performance. Monthly meetings would often focus on the quantitative record of physical activities, driven by the demands of the upwardly oriented Monthly Progress Report (MPR). In 2001, following a harsh DFID review of Phase II, target-orientation was so intense that the calculated ratio of programme expenditure achieved in relation to CO costs (salary plus travel claims) was referred to in staff performance assessments. Mutual surveillance and competition between staff only re-emphasised quantified output: 'if one CO is doing ten wells, a second will say, "I will do fifteen" ' (CO interview). The pressure to perform against targets was not always experienced as a bad thing. Quantified outputs allowed fieldworkers to demonstrate to bosses, officials *and* to villagers that they were accountable; and this helped explain motivation and build trust (see note 3, Chapter 4). COs adapted by reducing the time spent on uncertain community processes that were invisible as output and which invited arbitrary judgements on their performance. Like other 'street-level bureaucrats' they sought ways to reduce the complexity and uncertainty of their task, and to limit the demands and expectations of them (Goetz 1996, Lipsky 1980). They used their networks for efficient delivery and to advance their careers in the organisation, aspiring to move from field to office and on to higher managerial posts.

Social goals were also translated into quantifiable outputs, reported as the number of PRAs, meetings, groups or women present. Early uncertainty about the meaning of 'involving women' was resolved in the operational interpretation of the gender objective as 'equal participation of men and women in project meetings and activities'. Female COs emphasised getting women to formal meetings so that records could show (as indeed they did) that their attendance was not significantly lower than men's. By 1996 data also showed that women comprised between a quarter and two-thirds of participants in most activities, 26 per cent of all trained volunteers (opening new public roles to them), 35 per cent of participants in exposure visits, and 43 per cent in training sessions;[10] and that their share of employment on project works (where they received equal wages) was between 43 and 50 per cent (Shah 1995). Clearly the emphasis on producing statistics had its positive effects; but then a numerical record of attendance was far easier to generate than evidence of women's influence over programme choices or design (see Chapter 6). It was also easier to show increasing levels of women's participation by initiating a range of 'add-on' women's programmes – handicrafts, kitchen gardens, food preparation, smokeless stoves – than to change the way major land-based activities were done.[11]

Under pressure to get things done, project staff also took on more of the organisation of activities *themselves*, brokering deals with suppliers, arranging delivery, making payments and keeping records; or used *jankars* as intermediaries to do things for them.[12] Ordinary villagers began to retreat from temporary planning/decision making positions to the more familiar role of passive beneficiary, strategising to maximise short term benefits from wages and subsidies. As Bhils were incorporated into programme work as low-status project workers, foremen or wage labourers, staff and beneficiaries began to differentiate as management and labour (or patron and client), reproducing the class-based divisions of society at large (cf. Luthra 2003). Social hierarchies challenged in early planning became reasserted at implementation. For example, Ravi pointed out that when, in 1994, he (a CO) began to pay wages for soil and water conservation work being implemented in villages, the honorary suffix to his name used by villagers changed from – *bhai* (brother) to – *sahib* (sir). Handling money conferred power, and where male staff took on the role of wage payments, gender inequalities within the field team were also seen to be reinforced.[13]

Without intending it, field staff found themselves acting as local patrons and benefactors. Rather than making subsidies redundant by transferring skills, they had become the means to acquire subsidies. They were figures from whom villagers sought to curry favour ('not with money but with some good works, or *subji, makai* [small gifts of produce]' one CO said), and towards whose schemes villagers' desires would bend. The fact was that implementation norms invariably introduced subsides in some form in order to facilitate delivery: improved seeds and other technology were supplied on credit; the project covered transport costs, organised purchase or buy-back. In the case of assets like improved wells or compost pits, farmers' contributions were demanded, but in labour rather than cash (even where farmers were quite used to making cash investments for such assets). Better-off villagers ensured privileged access to these subsidies in ways that field staff were less and less aware of.

As risk-averse upwardly accountable fieldworkers were constrained to take on more responsibility for executing programmes, Bhil villagers discarded the disciplines of participation endeavouring to make themselves project employees and clients. They refused to extend their systems of reciprocal labour exchange (*hamo*) used for land clearing or house building to project work such as SWC. Self-help, low subsidies, local contributions, project withdrawal or cost-recovery were anyway hardly self-evident ideals to villagers accustomed to maximising gains from high-subsidy state programmes. The very mention of recovery could evoke the fearful memory of revenue officials imposing repayment demands for 'bunding work' executed by the state decades earlier. Although they were now familiar with the official rhetoric of 'people's participation' (*jansahbhagita*), in common parlance 'participation', *bhagidari*, implied simply that a contribution (of money or labour) had to be made; and the extent and nature of villagers' *bhagidari* (contribution) was a matter for negotiation and agreement with outsider patrons.[14]

The implementation regime gave the select cadre of trained *jankars* an influence that grew steadily as the project covered more and more villages. *Jankars* became the project's field-level representatives, mediating relationships with staff and filtering benefits within their own villages. They monitored and supervised physical works and often regarded themselves as project employees (if not private contractors, Baviskar 2004) with the power to assess work and sanction payment. Some staff viewed this as a significant shift from their earlier and intended role. As one senior person said to me:

> ... we rather skewed the potential of *jankars* as real agents of a more indigenous type of development ... they became the delivery mechanism which is away from the original thinking ... I was living with those people, those *jankars*, sitting with them for eight, ten hours in those meetings and I know that in many places people have come up with their own way of doing things. But [we had] our made-up guidelines ready ... when you have your guidelines with you, your own deadlines to meet, your fund management issues, these are strong restrictions ... you don't give space ... [*Jankars*] are vulnerable ... in front of a range of people from outside ... they see things from those outside perspectives ... they should have remained in their own domain and come forward with their own way of doing things.

At least the role of *jankar* encouraged some women to adopt new public roles; but here too, management insistence on a target of equal numbers of male and female *jankars* could have the effect of generating a range of gender-typed subordinate assistant roles or gave women prestigious roles (such as running a flour mill) that were taken over by their male kin.

Of course villagers were not simply passive recipients of project patronage, and *jankars* were no mere project lackeys. *Jankars* strategised along with villagers to modify the way in which programmes were delivered. In the case of SWC, for instance, they worked to increase wages through the choice of structure (stone rather than earth bunds) and by maximising bund length;[15] they ignored contours and used bunds to mark field boundaries and shore up ownership claims; they ignored 'watershed principles', prioritising 'gully plugs', *nallah* bunds and terraces at the bottom of slopes which gave the immediate reward of new rice fields, over work in the unproductive upper slopes (where official attention to forest 'encroachments' had to be evaded, Baviskar 2004), and even used bunds to divert water from the maize-growing hillside to their lowland *nallahs* and rice fields (Smith 1998). The UK consultant complained that 'early hopes that SWC as implemented by the project-trained *jankars* would be based on a modicum of soil science have been unfounded' and elsewhere that 'The quality of work by some farmers [is] so poor that they should not have been paid.'[16]

The fact remains, however, that villagers themselves had little control over project processes or budgets. Rather than implementing their own 'village development plan', they found that components of it (individual schemes and subsidies) would be delivered on an item-by-item basis (instead of in logically related bundles)[17] by an administrative system that was unknown and unpredictable.

Poisoned goats and purchasing committees

In IBRFP's sister KBCL project in eastern India, goats were supplied to village groups to distribute in pairs to their members who would rear and repay a kid. While reviewing the project in 1999 I heard stories of goats dying. Goats do, of course die, but project goats seemed to be dying more than others (a look at state-level Monthly Progress Reports showed mortality among goats ranging from 20–30 per cent to an alarming 80–90 per cent). In one village seven recently delivered goats had died, many, I was informed, because they had poisoned themselves by eating toxic plants. 'Don't all goats occasionally poison themselves in this way?' 'No', answered a Santal woman who had lost two project goats, 'our country goats know to avoid poisonous plants, they grow up here.' But the project's purchasing procedures would not allow villagers to buy local goats. Purchases under the goatry programme had to be done centrally by a Purchasing Committee which included the Accounts Officer and COs. Goats had to be bought in batches from the market and delivered to villages. These goats were 'alien' to the local environment. They were also hungry as more land was under crops during the monsoon.

Sanctioning procedures involved powerful but distant decision makers, taking anything from six weeks to a year. Goods and services (seeds, goats, pumps, tractor hire or stones for SWC bunding) were delivered by the project using standard unit costs and following centrally managed procurement. Often the system worked against villagers' interests. Wage payments could be held up for months by bureaucratic accounting procedures: field measurements and payment sheets prepared by *jankars*, checked by COs and verified by qualified engineers and approved by KBCL accountants in New Delhi. Time can also erode trust (Desai 2004). Fixed guidelines displaced people's designs and reduced learning. 'We became slaves to our guidelines, and we stopped experimenting', commented Raju. Privileging budgetary and bureaucratic reality can produce unfortunate results (see Box).

The project organisation's systems and procedures, and its pressure to meet targets and disburse underspent budgets, also influenced the programme *choices* that were made in the first place. There was a systematic preference for familiar and conventional programmes over complex or risky initiatives where approval might be uncertain or delayed (e.g. lift irrigation schemes); a preference for capital items relatively easily delivered without collective action (e.g. wells, pumps), and for work that offered rapid, dramatic and visible results quickly securing local support (e.g. SWC on valley land rather than on the 'encroached' upper hills). Standardisation and a disincentive (among staff *and* villagers) to diversify or innovate locally created deep and reinforcing grooves. Everyone already knew what villagers' problems were and what worked, and the project controlled a fairly fixed menu of technologies and activities. As noted earlier, PRAs became largely symbolic. Staff now knew how to write them up; how to move swiftly to expenditure. There was 'no need to reinvent the wheel every time'; and new entrants to the project team quickly realised that they should not question what was known and what had been done for years. As the logic of implementation pushed practice towards standardisation, it was virtually impossible to ensure that 'participatory planning' involved local problem solving, or even choosing between alternatives. In fact, the 'quality' of the 'participatory process' mattered less and less. Regardless, the process would quickly unfold into an activity calendar drawn on the ground with villagers scheduling the implementation (over five years) of items with budget allocations and successfully executed elsewhere.

Village work plans could roll off the office printer with only the village or hamlet name changed (and inadvertently, not even that).

Two clarifications: first, I do not wish to imply that overall IBRFP's programme choices were mistaken or irrelevant to villagers' needs; they were not. Indeed, by comparison with earlier government schemes, IBRFP interventions were better designed and implemented, better targeted, involved reduced subsidies and probably had a better chance of long-term sustainability. My point is that the shifts that hardened status hierarchies within the organisation and between staff and villager clients also locked its learning into the timeless rigidity of organisational rules and generalised schemes. There was strong convergence that confirmed preoccupations, narrowed options or restricted information flows (while nonetheless advertising villager consent and consensus). The interactive experience of a 'first generation' of fieldwork that framed choices became frozen into budgets and approval systems with an in-built resistance to change. 'Slowly, slowly', one senior member of staff admitted, 'we began to get away from that interactive process'. In consequence, there was less and less ability to adapt project strategies to the dynamics of rural poverty or the different needs of farmers, migrants, forest gatherers or wage labourers. The danger was, of course, that the system would fail to capture diversity or detect elite manipulation, limiting the chances that minority interests would find their way into project budgets. Opportunities would be missed, impact would be limited.

Second, this shift from a system that was open and interactive to one that was relatively closed and controllable, was not *intentional* but an instrumental effect scarcely perceived by project actors themselves (staff or villagers), and even less by outsiders. Indeed, as villagers shaped their 'needs' and priorities to match the project's schemes and administrative realities – validating imposed schemes with local knowledge and requesting only what is most easily delivered – the project's institutional interests became *built into* community perspectives, and project decisions became perfectly participatory. As I argued in Chapter 4, if villages ended up ventriloquising the project design needs, it was partly because artful and risk-averse villagers asked for what they knew they would get, *and* partly because the development agencies involved were able through their planning instruments to project their own various institutional needs on to rural communities' local knowledge. Either way, a fundamental disjuncture between village realities and project systems, between participation and delivery systems was hidden from view.

VILLAGE 'GROUPS': RATIONALISING RELATIONS WITH VILLAGER CLIENTS

Development agencies commonly simplify or rationalise their interface with beneficiary communities through the promotion of groups of various kinds. The IBRFP project was no exception. Indeed, 'Self-Help Groups' (SHG) were increasingly important to its *modus operandi*. The project based its SHGs on existing units of Bhil social organisation by encouraging membership of small (20–25 members) *falia*- (and lineage-) based groups to meet, record savings, rotate project-financed credit funds and operate grain banks, flour mills, shops or other enterprises. These *falia* groups soon provided the primary interface between the project and people, offering a 'single channel', the means to consult with people, to address questions of participation or equity (i.e. 'decisions by the group in favour of all') and in other ways enabling the project to 'extract itself from the business of micro-managing development' (Manor 2002). For members themselves, meetings at appointed times were for negotiating with project workers. Reproduced in all villages, groups provided IBRFP with a useful simplification of Bhil social reality, rendering it more amenable to systematic recording and quantification, but, equally, concealing inequality, exclusion and the complex local politics of clan conflict, credit dependency or land disputes that had earlier preoccupied field staff.[18] Most importantly, groups were a central part of the project's system for making investments, delivering inputs, administering activities and accounting for finances.[19]

Villagers came to view IBRFP as an 'only-through-groups-project' and widely took SHG membership to be a precondition for access to project benefits. Soon, the new villages that project staff contacted were already organised into sets of groups in anticipation. Less experienced field staff hardly needed to look beyond these groups in their interactions with villagers. By February 2001, there were over a thousand self-constituted lineage-residential groups, named, and with a stable recorded membership of around 80 per cent of the households, constituting a 'database-able' representation of Bhil society.

Now, these groups were formalised as part of a vertical relationship with the project, the emphasis being on internal solidarity rather than wider alliances. Horizontal links to other groups through federations, or to NGOs, panchayat institutions, cooperatives or banks – which were feared because the rigidity of their repayment demands – were typically weak and slow to emerge; this was hardly surprising given the importance of the project as a source of improved seed and credit (see Chapter 9). These groups became part of IBRFP's activity management machinery: *first*, by undertaking SWC, well deepening, forestry nurseries and other physical works, or providing points for the distribution of improved seeds on credit; and *second*, by receiving large, diverse and repeated investments allowing the accumulation of capital and assets (pumps, threshers, flour mills, shops, etc.), and continuously diversifying enterprise activities in Bhil villages. Since groups were often under the control of their leader/*jankars* (whose names they initially adopted) they also formed part of *their* networks of patronage. (Later project staff insisted that groups take their names instead from national leaders such as Nehru or Gandhi.)

Initially, the project promoted SHGs as savings and credit institutions. Nothing symbolised the transformation from tribal 'hand-to-mouth' underdevelopment better than the 'moral discipline' of saving. But individual savings remained at a very low level (2–5 rupees per month), they were often intermittent and contributed a very small part of the total group funds.[20] It appeared that villagers perceived the savings entered into their passbooks at regular meetings not so much as accumulating independent capital as a certificate of their status as project clients, and a guarantee of entitlement especially, in the short term, to waged work on project schemes. Where necessary, it made sense to borrow to keep up passbook payments; but when labour-generating schemes ended, savings would fall off sharply. The project itself did not emphasise the slow accumulation of independent savings, but rapidly built group funds (i) by making grants for rotating cultivation loans (for seeds and fertilisers),[21] (ii) by linking groups to employment generation schemes and paying a portion of wages (e.g. for SWC work) into savings accounts, and (iii) by making capital contributions to *group*-owned enterprises (such as poultry, seed distribution, pump-hire, village shops or handicrafts). In the latter supply-driven arrangement, the capital contribution expected from participating groups was minimal; and since the approach was to kick-start an economic activity with a one-off grant, there was always also an incentive for group members to propose new activities in order to secure further project resources. Indeed, an ever expanding range of activities and investments (pumps, wells, compost pits, grain banks, flour mills, bio-gas plants) was needed to sustain group processes and increase the fund. Critics pointed out that capital investment in existing economic activities (poultry, goat rearing, grain milling) added little to their scale or profitability, and that in the case of new enterprises, project support distorted incentives for taking up marginally viable and questionably sustainable activities.[22] In effect, the project was complicit in encouraging farmer groups to multiply grant-generating activities and protected these against failure. Meanwhile SHG group funds accumulated tens or sometimes hundreds of thousands of rupees.

It is significant, however, that most groups did not routinely disburse their funds to members as loans for individual needs, businesses or brideprice, although this is precisely what happened in the indigenous financial institution of *chandla* (Chapter 3). Why did so much income (at least from the better-off households) find its way into *chandla* payments, and so little into SHG savings accounts? Why, when group funds had accumulated considerable capital, was so little rotated as credit? The answer may be to do with the different relationship between money and social obligation in the two systems. In *chandla*, money directly reproduced social obligations (payments simultaneously met and generated obligation) through personal networks. In *chandla*, money is obligation; it is 'hot', constantly circulating, generating more obligation and more money within particular social networks.[23] It is the social network and its accumulated obligation that offers a failsafe insurance arrangement for those in the circle. Voluntary savings into a project-supported group fund involved no such obligations, and borrowing only weak ones.

The only means to generate security through SHGs was through financial *accumulation* and perpetuating a relationship with the project. Groups did indeed maximise the accumulation of funds (and assets) from the project as a form of social security, and insurance against uncertainty or enterprise failure. For large parts of the year these 'cold' funds simply sat as unutilised capital in bank accounts.[24] Of course there were exceptions, Self-Help Groups that expanded their financial services, routinely circulated funds among members to meet a widening range of credit needs and generated income from interest payments, significantly, several women's groups among them. But the majority adopted conservative strategies perpetuating themselves as clients of the project (rather than operating with autonomy), maximising the acquisition of further grants, assets and project-initiated enterprises. These may have been economically marginal, but they sustained a relationship between project patrons and adivasi client groups. Indeed, the range of activities of an SHG (and the size of its fund) was a measure of the intensity of engagement and the strength of the group–project relationship. 'Passive groups' were those without activities. Arguably, for villagers, IBRFP money in their group accounts represented a project interest in them, and was a guarantee of continuity in the relationship. As such it was not available to generate other obligations within the community through lending. The fact that project money (an external gift, a public resource) was not *able* to generate obligation (in the way that private money could) was evident from very poor repayment rates.[25] If lent, project funds would/could not be recovered, and their dissipation might threaten the relationship with project patrons: patrons could lose their interest, villagers their reputation as trustworthy clients and custodians; or, worse, dangerous obligations could be created – patronage could turn into claims on land or labour.[26] This strategic use of external financial resources is consistent with Wood's (2003) argument that poor people facing chronic insecurity prioritise the maintenance of relationships with people (patrons or projects) having better access to resources and offering social protection in the short term, even though this limits their capacity for longer-term economic mobility.

It is unsurprising that Bhil villagers with a long history of economic insecurity and exploitation, living in a region of underdeveloped markets and currently experiencing the loss of protective patronage (as *sahukars* turn to increasingly exploitative economic relations, see Chapter 3), sought to secure and protect relations with new patrons rather than to strive for autonomy through independent enterprise, or that they adopted the risk-reducing strategy of maximising material benefits in the short term (for example, from wages or wells). And who is to say that wanting patronage and resources from the project is less a sign of empowerment than wanting to manage your own resources (Fiedrich 2002: 65)? At the same time, from the project side, organisational conservatism encouraged relations of patronage with Bhil groups. The upward accountability of staff and the demands of external audit produced procedures for programme delivery that made it impossible to treat villagers as autonomous partners or to delegate the managerial aspects of the programme to them (i.e. locally unintelligible accounting systems would not allow the transfer of funds or authority over budgets – for SWC or other works – to self-managing farmer groups). Staff themselves commonly did not believe that adivasis were able to manage their financial affairs: 'If we give money to them they will just eat it up,' said one project specialist. And where they were not involved in financial management, it was difficult for Bhil villagers to take on other planning and monitoring functions, or to retain plans, records and the like. Indeed, project systems worked to minimise administrative risk associated with Bhil farmers developing their own way of doing things, making their own decisions, taking their own risks and making their own mistakes. In practice, what IBRFP needed was reliable clients not autonomous partners.[27]

Despite the spread of organisational patronage and control, the persistence of donor-promoted participatory ideals still generated tension in the project. At the very least, the ideals of participation and the obligations of patronage, or even those of a good employer, were in conflict. The confusion of goals that this produced is evident when a consultant colleague of mine writes: 'the problem with [such] regular payments [to labourers on SWC works] is that it begins to appear that that the project is employing people rather than empowering them'.[28] Field staff were anyway not entirely enrolled into the organisational hierarchy, and the project was not simply 'a status system calibrated according to proximity to the head office or higher managerial levels' (Goetz 1996). Some fieldworkers continued to carve out spaces for autonomous action and dissent. They 'tried to escape' from the pressure of targets, refused programmes pushed from above (e.g. mushroom production),[29] appealed to participatory principles and accused their colleagues of 'hardly bothering with the poor' or 'compromising professionalism' with a culture of gift and favour in their relations with villagers.

RELATIONS ACROSS AN INSTITUTIONAL INTERFACE: BROKERAGE AND CORPORATE PHILANTHROPY

It would also be a simplification to portray project management as relentlessly driven by targets and downward delivery. The project had a dual accountability, *both* to senior KBCL management for quantified results and accounted finances, *and* to the ODA donor for implementing a participatory development model (and in fact also, third, to the Government of India). While senior KBCL managers, now driven more by the system goals of organisation maintenance than by explicit marketing concerns (Chapter 2), acted to further incorporate the project into its organisational culture, the project management had to work relentlessly at the interface with the main organisation (KBCL) in order to protect IBRFP's identity and room for manoeuvre.

IBRFP was a small experimental unit within a large marketing corporation. Running the project involved devoting considerable management energy to maintaining relationships upwards with senior KBCL marketing and accounts managers, Board members and bureaucrats, constantly translating the project into *their* terms. This was necessary in order to get things done – since these people had the power of sanction over resources (and careers) and used it[30] – and also to create a buffer to protect the development project from more direct control from above. First, a 'plans–targets–outputs' *representation* of the project had to be sustained, and a quantitative record of achievements supplied. The Monthly/Quarterly Progress Reports concealed the contingencies of development in a programme-wise inventory and cumulative account of deliverables: 'during the quarter 43 spray pumps, 855 water sanitation kits, 45 First Aid Boxes and 70 store bins were allocated to different groups', 'a cumulative total of 246 PRAs in 103 villages, 7,466 meetings involving 53,966 women and 96,352 men'.[31]

Second, project procedures – budgeting, sanctioning and expenditure, fund flows and accounting, recruitment and promotion – had to be given the *appearance* of KBCL regularity. Officialising improvised practice required a paper trail from Bhil villages to Delhi, as well as constant personal mediation to persuade, cajole and maintain relations with the guardians of 'proper channels' and 'due procedure'. Sometimes procedures prevailed (schemes were delayed, goats were poisoned), but often they could be worked around. Courtesy calls, waiting on approval in Delhi, visits with prestigious foreigners, the hosting of senior visits to the project, cards, gifts, even trips to London – were all necessary to 'facilitate the process', to deal with the grinding lethargy of programme approval or to influence change in the system. Such transactions simultaneously reiterated rank and the order of things as viewed from behind the Delhi managers' desk and served to cut down to size the foreign-fertilised 'tall poppies' of the project.

Above all, managing relations across the boundaries of organisational culture required skilful mediators, multilingual in the discourse of village, project office, corporate bureaucracy and donor policy and able to translate between different rationalities and expectations. Success as a manager-broker meant having the type of personality able to identify the needs of others, to self-efface, to defer to or honour another, to know what is appropriate, to feel that institutional relationships are important enough to sustain the many small investments (visits, gifts, deference …) and personal costs required; to have a marketing instinct, 'to be a blade of grass blowing in the wind' listening to what the powerful forces want and delivering.[32] In IBRFP, this was a role skilfully played by the project manager. He was held personally responsible for the achievement of targets and compliance with institutional procedures by his bosses and Board members, but at the same time had to protect the project from the implications of KBCL systems in order to satisfy the donor concern with participation. In Board meetings, for example, he had to deliver an account of the project in terms of targets and achievements, but then write up the minutes of these meetings so as not to give legitimacy to expectations incompatible with project goals. As we passed time on a night train to Dahod, reflecting on the project's history and the fulcrum role of the project manager, it became clear to me that the mediating demands on him were intensely personal, that the loyalties and honour that shaped relationships with staff and bosses were deeply felt (and so therefore were the betrayals when they occurred). Reflecting wearily on the costs of his buffering role, he commented, 'I have now developed the resistance, [the] shock absorbing capacity.'

In any organisation, a manager who is held personally responsible for the delivery of targets and is expected to respond to arbitrary requests (for information, hosting VIP visits, etc.) has little choice but to demand the same from his staff in the field. The KBCL organisational culture brought to bear a pervasive system of vertical control, patronage, and the granting or withdrawal of favour, which demanded loyalty and personal accountability for success, while generating a pervasive fear of failure. 'We always appreciate *our* successes', commented one senior member of the team, 'but failure is always seen as the failure of an individual … it is a cultural thing'. It militated against experimentation, innovation or learning, by perpetuating insecurity and reliance on systems. Indeed result-orientation and fear of failure were institutionalised in the project as part of the wider hierarchical but personalised organisational culture.[33]

Just as IBRFP field staff needed consultants to express their own dissenting agendas to their bosses, so too did the project manager. Indeed the project manger was able to negotiate with his seniors (and therefore across boundaries of rank and status) because foreign consultants could speak on his behalf, although always in the name of (donor) policy. The consultancy team leader, in particular, was a key broker, mediating the difficult relationships between the donor patron and the client project agency (ODA/DFID and KBCL), between different advisers within DFID, as well as between the project manager and his own bosses and the Board. Such brokering requires the fostering of close and trusting relationships between key individuals in different parts of the system – between consultants, advisers, project manager and directors. It also involves an ability to exploit ambiguous insider/outsider positions to create space and give actors in organisations a room for manoeuvre that is formally denied. The broker/mediator is a person of constantly shifting size and institutional position. A person who can speak at one moment for DFID, or even the government of the UK, at another for the project, its manager, the consultant team; at yet another moment he speaks as a rural economist, a project worker, or 'JL' the individual speaks as himself, expresses a passing comment, as Latour puts it:

> ... solely in the name of his own imagination. Someone else, or his own unconscious, may even speak for him. Depending upon his relative size he may capture everyone's attention for ten years, or that of just one person for a mere instant. He may be called Mr. Large or Mr. Small. Actors [Latour continues] come in varying sizes. They do not have an essence that has been fixed once and for all. They can speak in everyone's name, or no one's; it all depends ... Variation in the relative size, in the representativeness of the actors ... characterises all members of a technological project ... In a project's history, the suspense derives from the swelling or shrinking of the relative size of its actors. (1996: 44–5)

It goes without saying that development projects generally are never simply 'implemented' by single-sized actors through formal structures of responsibility; they not only require (and bring into existence) a range of unscripted inter-institutional broker roles, but also need extensive informal networks of support, built personally through relations of trust and maintained through an out-of-sight 'economy of favours and obligations' existing at the margins of legitimacy (or maybe in some cases legality). Ultimately it is not policy consensus, rational planning or bureaucratic procedures that make projects like IBRFP run. It is personalities, brokering skills and the channels of influence of individual mediators, buffers and filters. As Scott puts it, 'formal order ... is always and to some considerable degree parasitic on informal processes, which the formal scheme does not recognize, without which it could not exist, and which it alone cannot create or maintain' (1998: 310). The more innovative or institutionally complex a project, the more dependent it is upon the '*metis*'[34] of those dealers and brokers operating the informal space between agencies. In IBRFP, the ODA/DFID (and its consultant advisers) set up a project which, because of its conflicting agendas and cultures, was in many respects truly *unmanageable* and singularly dependent upon unacknowledged informal processes and relations to function.[35] A state-of-the-art participatory development project within a fertiliser marketing organisation required virtuoso brokers, long chains of translation and extensive networks of support.

Maintaining relationships upwards and translating the project into KBCL terms also exposed it to the wider political logic and culture of an Indian farmer cooperative marketing agency. Central to this was dramatisation of the role of KBCL as a patron, and tribal villagers as clients and consumers of KBCL's corporate philanthropy. Senior KBCL managers supervising the project knew that trust built clients and customers: 'If I don't know you I don't trust your technology.'[36] Indeed, they emphasised 'rapport' with villagers over technical design or development strategy. Field staff were exhorted to develop goodwill and close relations with villagers, 'to be their family, to help with marriages, pay for the wood [at] funerals, to give money and sort out problems'.[37]

Unlike the project's donor advisers or consultants, KBCL managers did not suppress the idiom of the gift. Gifts 'make you closer', and involve the logic of clientship rather than entitlement (cf. Li 1999: 309–10). But more significantly, the idiom of the charitable gift permits a development activity to be understood in a way that allows the giver a role; gives status and honour to the donor/benefactor, while conferring obligation on the client/beneficiary. The project was full of occasions for KBCL ritualised public gifting – the inauguration of check dams, the public distribution of seeds, school books or medical kits. At these and other occasions senior visitors (including foreign donors and consultants) were honoured and garlanded, sweets were distributed; there were tribal dances and even gunfire and the arrangement of fine curries to feast a senior official. Such celebrations were important for field staff too, since their own position and effectiveness was enhanced in the eyes of villagers by dramatising the status of the visiting officers to whom they were linked – powerful managers, bosses, foreign consultants/advisers or political figures. To the extent that these occasions could also be viewed as lavish acts of *hospitality* laid on by the Bhil beneficiaries, they may also have served to counterbalance the oppressive power of unreciprocated gifts (Eyben 2003: 10, drawing on Herzfeld 1992).

For project staff, the sense of ceremony and ritual that erupted into project implementation had to do with an idea of development that was *relational* rather than rational; it was about maintaining relationships with villagers and seniors. To *technical* donors and consultants (including myself), however, such celebrations of status and rank, gift and gratitude, made little sense, and were singularly inappropriate in a participatory development project. Indeed, late in the year 2000, under circumstances of increased donor pressure and surveillance (see Chapter 8), it was necessary for project management to circulate a memo stating that there should be 'no sweets or … gun firing … [and] the pompous garlanding, sweet distribution etc, has to be stopped during the visit of our officials and other delegates'.[38]

Now, the culture of corporate philanthropy celebrates the transforming role, as well as the status, of the giver. While donors and consultants constantly effaced their own role and endlessly stressed villager agency during their visits, senior KBCL managers accepted (and expected) attributions of personal agency during field encounters. When, for example, a KBCL Director recalls his visits to 'the field' he interposes himself as an agent of tribal development. First, he tells me the story of an old Bhil woman he met once. She used to go house to house, begging for food and visiting neighbours until, that is, a problem with her legs made her housebound. Unable to go out and meet people she became lonely. And so:

> …my wife called the CO and gave him money and told him to buy lots of bangles and take them to the old woman's house. She was told to sell these bangles at the same rate as in the market. With the proceeds more bangles would be bought; losses would be covered. Now most of the time there are people with her. She is no longer lonely.

Next, he recalls confronting a farmer sceptical about a new crop variety:

> I ask the farmer how much he gets from his plot of land; he says Rs 12,000 worth of crop. I say, 'I will give you Rs 12,000 so you will lose nothing. Now you let me show you what to do on this land.' The experimental plot is planted with new seeds and fertiliser, all done my way. This plot produces overflowing measures of grain which tastes and

grinds the same [as the old variety]. The farmer is left exclaiming, 'with this land I got so much of produce!'

Finally, the Director is walking around a village when he comes across a forest patch that had to be protected. 'When I saw the trees come[ing] up I took a promise from the people, I got the people to pledge not to cut the trees, [and the] people threw down their axes in front of me ... '.

There are a few points to make. The first is that here the Director, like other senior officials, fulfils corporate expectations about the behaviour of managers, revealing the 'shopfloor' style of KBCL management, which (mistakenly) connects autonomous action by senior managers with effective outcomes (Ouroussoff 2001: 44). The senior man by-passes intermediary authority, and even tries to catch field staff out by asking villagers separately about a particular visit or action. The second point is that the narrative reveals a form of populism which, like the wider political strategy, creates (or recalls) events that symbolise and allow the accrediting of success as a personal struggle on behalf of the poor (Gupta 1998: 76). Third, in the Director's narrative, development is relational not technical. It comes to tribal people as a personal *gift* from a high status ('royal') personage, as a *challenge* or involves a *pledge* from the people.[39] For the Director, project work in remote tribal villages stands in continuity with personal voluntarism. He likens it to his work with the Rotary Club and the patronage of religious figures and ashrams. The Director's actions in the field emphasise the personal rather than the organisational. Villagers throw down their hatchets as a pledge; the project manager later presents two of these to his boss, varnished and mounted on a shield – a personal development trophy that now hangs on a staircase in a Delhi suburb.[40]

Of course a project system such as IBRFP is no less a matter of relationships for European donor advisers and consultants than for Indian agencies and beneficiaries; but the relational is suppressed rather than dramatised, just as the technical is emphasised. DFID also operated within the logic of the gift (in relation to KBCL itself). The donor and we its consultant representatives were complicit in celebrations of the gift. These, significantly, concealed a more complex economic reality in which those honoured as donors (DFID officials, consultants, ourselves) were proportionately the far greater beneficiaries of aid money in a project system that 'redistributed' at least 25 per cent of funds to UK institutions and consultants.[41] In this sense, the idiom of the gift is a public fiction that gets around the harsh facts of power and economic asymmetries (Baviskar pers. comm.).

CONCLUSIONS

The broader argument of this chapter has been that the implementation practices of development are shaped by an organisation's system goals rather than by the formal goals of policy. In this case, the IBRFP project came under pressure to conform to KBCL's systems and procedures, to respect its hierarchy, observe its rules, to deliver progress in its terms (that is as quantified outputs) and to produce a patron–client relationship between the project and its Bhil beneficiaries, however inconsistent these demands might be with participatory development as conceived by the project, the donor and its consultants.[42]

In fact, both project workers *and* Bhil villagers consented to an authorised model of participatory development while making of it something quite different from what was intended (cf. de Certeau 1984: xiii), conspiring to reproduce relations of patronage. While KBCL's system goals produced 'hidden transcripts' that preserved organisational systems and incorporated Bhil farmers as clients, people themselves refused the discipline of self-help and sought continuing patronage, forming groups, adopting technology or maintaining demonstration plots in order to keep up the relationship with project patrons. This is not surprising. For one thing, as noted in Chapter 3, economic survival for Bhil communities has always depended upon forming alliances with those with better access to resources – *sahukars, rajputs* and today NGOs and their projects (Weisgrau 1997: 93). For another, the project functioned in a wider political context of development as patronage. The competitive environment of adivasi districts in which NGOs or departments try to secure clients for their programmes, is infused with notions of territoriality, loyalty and obligation. Conflicts between development patrons over claims to a given village, or responsibility for the existence of particular 'groups', are common (cf. Rew and Rew 2003). Moreover, Weisgrau argues that NGOs 'share structural features with traditional elites'; a fact that is marked in certain cultural acts (1997: 93). When a south Rajasthan NGO hosts a Bhil Gavri dance-drama in the name of fostering local cultural tradition, the performance enacts a relationship of patronage and obligation modelled on that between Bhils and their *sahukar* creditors, *rajput* overlords or affines, for whom they perform (1997: 194–6).

As systems of patronage, projects also provide resources for individuals, and help to advance political careers through contacts and organisational skills. Their activities help redefine and extend restricted Bhil social networks, for example, through inter-village meetings, and so contribute more generally to local party political processes (Weisgrau 1997: 108, 125). And of course it is important to stress that a project like IBRFP does not only have local clients and beneficiaries. Organised internally as a nested system of patronage, the project directs the flow of aid resources into training, research budgets, travel, new jobs or contracts. It provides a means for staff social mobility, career advancement and the acquisition or reproduction middle-class lifestyles. Indeed it is the expectation not only of project workers and managers, but also trainers, consultants, UK universities and others to profit from the flow of aid in projects.

Viewed from an individual's perspective, project implementation is not only (or primarily) about executing policy, or even putting schemes in place, but a matter of sustaining a set of relationships that secure a person's identity and status, and which are a precondition for action at every level. Effective relationships are necessary to win support, sanction the flow of resources, build reputations, trust and reliability; to fend off the arbitrary judgement. And because an aid project is a 'long chain of organisation' with loosely integrated parts in which different levels (field:office, project:boardroom, agency: donor, donor:consultant) operate with a high degree of *autonomy*, defining and redefining policy in terms of separate rationales and clienteles (Quarles van Ufford 1988a), these relationships involve acts of translation and brokerage. Stability in the world of action does not come from coherent policy, but from effective relationships. Indeed the urgent demands they make – for personal loyalty and favour, for compliance with routines and procedures, or with systems of rank and deference – appear to set aside the official model. 'All day long we are in relationships,' the project manager says as we continue our journey though the night to Dahod, 'even if we go in the train compartment we need relationships or our bags will be stolen ... you need to build the systems and structure which will make the programmes and policies by making people close to you ...' Perhaps because he is a marketing man, he understood something fundamental about the aid and development process. When viewed within the project as a system of relationships, villagers, project workers, managers or donor consultants appear as political actors with a sophisticated understanding of dynamic interests within their organisations and wider society. Given this, the current vogue of criticising participatory development as 'depoliticised' pays undue attention to official representations (which do downgrade the political), and too little to practice.

6
Consultant Knowledge

In his book on the Vietnam war (*The Perfect War*) James W. Gibson highlights a striking contrast between the 'warrior's knowledge' expressed in the memoirs, novels or plays of the soldiers in the battlefield, and the accounts of the managers of the 'techno-war'. While warriors write of relationships and social encounters, the war managers provide rationalising narratives of official strategy. The fieldworkers and unit managers are the project's warriors whose informal narratives informed the previous two chapters. Like the warriors', this is a 'fragmented knowledge falling below the threshold of "scienticity" ... in that such stories or accounts do not follow the social and intellectual rules governing who can be a serious thinker and the correct form for serious ideas and important facts' (Gibson 1986: 462). This 'warrior knowledge' – of relationships and conflicts – does not speak in the language of higher policy, and does not influence conventional assessments of progress (positive or negative). This is marginalised, silenced, subjugated, even dangerous knowledge (cf. 1986: 462). It does not generate data or offer explanations (1986: 464) or make authoritative judgements. In contrast, there is the knowledge of the project's generals and strategists, its consultants and advisers. This is policy knowledge, contained in official reports, available at privileged bureaucratic sites (in head office or donor office) expressed in development models and project frameworks. It is the focus of official meetings, 'missions' and reviews. It expresses rational intention and generates explicit strategy; it makes judgements of success and gives authorised meaning to events as the outcome of intentions. It provides knowledge of the project as a generalised technical system that can be discussed in wider conferences, or take published form (cf. Gibson 1986).

A conventional project story would follow the project cycle logic; it would begin with the generals – with plans and designs – and then move on to discuss their implementation and outcomes. In these chapters I reverse this logic by moving *from* practice *to* rationalising theory, from the operational world of the project warriors (Chapter 5) to the conceptual world of the generals – consultants, advisers and policy model makers (this chapter); from the world of relations to the world of ideas. Of course, contrary to what Gibson's analysis implies, development workers at every level participate in both worlds: they experience relationships and produce representations. But my point will be that once the project was established as a set of actions and relationships, conceptual work did not *precede* or direct action but followed it, providing an authoritative framework of interpretation, or a 'second-order rationalization of politically and economically ordered work routines' (Heyman 1995: 265).

I will explore the relationship between work routines and policy models through the roles and writing of expatriate consultants. These were not members of short-term teams assembled for rapid project design or evaluation missions (Stirrat 2000, Wood 1998), but long-term project associates and representatives of the donor; part insiders, part outsiders, whose inputs were organised around key programmes in which they (we) were specialists – crop technology, soil and water conservation, forestry and local institutional development,[1] and the cross-cutting issues of participation and gender. Over many years, we developed a closer and more informal working relationship with project staff than most consultancy teams; and the trust we gained gave us unusual access to the internal workings of the project. But the knowledge that we consultants developed was still based on a view from afar. Grammig (2002) suggests that (foreign) expertise necessarily implies cultural distance and ignorance of the local in order to establish a privileged 'universal' point of view.[2] Certainly consultants had a fragmented experience of the project, disengaged from the day-to-day routines and the pressing demands of relationship building. Their knowledge of the project derived from short visits after long journeys, sleepless passage through airports, on overnight trains, within busy itineraries that connected thinking about the project to other intellectual endeavours – research, teaching, policy advice, conferences or consultancies in other places for other clients. Precisely because they had no place in the project organisation, consultant perceptions were shaped by unusually structured visits and information flows: meetings with managers, the core team and field staff dutifully assembled to represent experience and events; short visits to particular villages in the company of staff in the habit of interpreting (both language and events) to foreigners; meetings with village groups and walks across the 'treated' landscape; training workshops; appointments with senior officials and evening reviews at the guest house or dinner with dignitaries. These were also part of varied strategies that project staff adopted for handling foreign experts and keeping distance. Distance could allow project staff, on occasion, to reject expert knowledge by labelling it Western, although it also meant that foreign experts could challenge technology promoted by local staff as 'nationalist'.

For consultants the project is a stimulating place for thought and analysis, discussion and debate, which potentially links project practice to current conceptual preoccupations (theories, policy or experimental designs). For the project team, such visits are non-routine moments of heightened negotiation (Chapter 5). But the consultant reports that result, written on laptops in the sanctuary of a guesthouse in the company of strong tea, clattering fans and air-conditioners, adopt a genre that requires the disembedding of knowledge from such project politics, and its translation into normative rules and models. The structured report (sectioned into strategy, progress, recommendations) restricts and bounds a surfeit of information on events and a multiplicity of opinions. It provides order, emphasises the systematic, the rule or principle; it uses technical language to arrive at a diagnosis, it makes a prescription and, most importantly, interprets for higher policy. So, consultants undertake a kind of 'thought-work' intended to guide the behaviour of staff who have wills and motivations of their own (Heyman 1995: 263), and to provide coherent interpretations of events for bureaucrats. The outcome of this work is a huge number of visit reports, progress reports, annual reports. Sometimes these are written to convince, sometimes to encourage, sometimes to critique or to promote the project or the professional reputations of their expert authors.

In turning attention to consultants, then, we shift from the maintenance of relations within the project and with Bhil society or KBCL management, to the mediation of relations with the donor, the ODA/DFID. Consultants mediate at the interface between project operations and donor policy, interpreting each to the other. In relation to the project, they are outside experts expected to clarify policy, to train, demonstrate or guide staff in advancing specific programmes. In relation to the donor, 'insider' consultants establish significance, deliver expert judgement and report progress. Over time, as a project progresses, a consultant's power decreases in relation to a project, but increases in relation to the donor. Consultants have great influence over new projects derived from their ability to interpret donor policy and to formulate legitimate strategies and approaches; but this influence declines as project routines become established and take over. Correspondingly, the influence of consultants in relation to the donor increases along with their capacity to interpret increasingly complex and illegible project practice for distant donor advisers.[3] Indeed, between 1990 and 1998, the pattern of IBRFP consultant work shifted gradually from the interpretation of donor policy for the project, to the interpretation of project practice for the donor. By the end of the first phase of IBRFP (1998), members of our consultancy team universally expressed frustration at their inability to have any influence over project practice;[4] but at the same time our capacity to produce project models of great clarity for the donor (and beyond) was never greater. Over time the nature of our reports changed too: they contained less and less of the politics of organisation, and more and more of the logics of programme and policy. The less influence they had, the more repetitive they became, reiterating the same observations, the same questions and the same recommendations – articulating an increasingly timeless abstract project model.[5]

Writing now with hindsight and oriented towards the later stages of our thought-work, I draw the conclusion that outside experts significantly failed to determine project practice, while succeeding in generating policy theory out of it.[6] But, as I will show, the contribution varied between individuals, disciplines and programmes, producing distinct scenarios. Before turning to these, I want to make a few points about the role of information in establishing domains of consultant expertise.

BEING EXPERT

> Using information, asking for information, and justifying decisions in terms of information have all come to be significant ways in which we symbolize that the process is legitimate, that we are good decision makers, and that our organizations are well managed. (Feldman and March 1981: 178, in Alvesson 1993: 50)

In order to assert professional standing as technical experts and to justify particular recommendations to IBRFP, in the early months and years of the project consultants felt they had to develop a professional overview of the domain in which they had expertise, whether crop production, forestry, livestock, social organisation or gender relations. We repeatedly insisted that the project was dangerously ill-informed in this or that area and was in need of additional research or data collection for 'proper planning'. The SWC consultant needed runoff data, the irrigation consultant needed data on 'the water holding capacity and infiltration characteristics of the soils',[7] the forester needed data on 'the ecology of the species being managed', the livestock consultant needed 'a livestock recording calendar designed to allow input:output analysis',[8] and the social development consultant (myself) insisted on a quantum of 'social data' including household resource flows or migration data that everyone considered excessive.

We each demanded our own stream of information – specialised PRAs, formats for data collection and activity monitoring – to feed into our own particular management models, insisting, as one put it, 'that project staff should collect information and data in a systematic way, and guidelines should be prepared on the data required and the format in which it [sic] should be collected and presented'.[9] Indeed, consultant reports were invariably accompanied by data collection formats with instructions for field staff (often feeding into external research interests), and suggestions about how the project could reorganise its staff, activities or information management to better suit a particular expert's needs. Data were necessary to develop generalised intervention models. The forestry consultant, for example, calculated that it would take 87.6 tonnes of air-dried wood each year to substitute for the 3.6 Gj energy that an average household obtained from burning dung.[10] 'Arriving at this figure,' he wrote, 'one can now very easily estimate the number of trees needed to supply the required amount of fuel wood, and the management regime needed to produce those trees.'[11]

There was a desire to reach some sort of closure on our understanding of agro-ecological and socio-economic realities, and to generate a 'comprehensive information base', a model or simulation (in text, tables, maps or GIS). Indeed in 1994 a UK researcher was commissioned to review farming systems information, identify gaps and develop a 'model report' on a properly researched village – a Bhil community legible to outsiders (cf. Scott 1998).

If the need for project insiders was to *relate*, the need for outsiders was to *know* (or to relate through knowledge). For outsiders, distanced from the everyday processes of the project, acquiring and deploying knowledge was a means to agency within the project that involved a sort of simulation maintained by data. Information was the primary medium of consultant–staff interaction. Visits were organised around information-generating meetings, workshops or village visits. Demanding information or putting in place segments of the project to meet information needs was a way of managing relationships with the project. Of course information was also a matter of legitimation, 'symbolis[ing] reason, reliability, security, even intelligence' (Feldman and March 1981). As such it helped manage our professional relations with colleagues or donor advisers – well-researched villages were testimony to consultant expertise – and to negotiate intervention models with project staff. And information helped us deal with our own uncertainty, and the anxiety of responsibility for change. But most consultants' information systems remained separate from the project's operational system, which did not generate an *internal* demand for the knowledge that consultants considered important. There was little respect for empirical research of marginal concern to practice, and accommodating external demands for data was a low priority, especially when these did not comply with existing operational hierarchies. In consequence, few systems of information gathering set up with external support were sustained, and several technical programme posts remained unfilled.

We may have failed to put in place our respective professional knowledge regimes, but our efforts had the powerful effect of establishing the programme and disciplinary divides which structured the project. Our separate guidelines, standards and routines, data sets and schedules, formats to be maintained, technical skills required, training programmes (and so forth) contributed directly to the lack of integration about which we later complained. On the one hand we wanted separate systems. We insisted, to take a forestry example, that villages should be skilled 'out-planters' supplied by 'nursery raisers', advised by 'trees *jankars*' (nursery or out-planting), monitored by Community Organisers, trained and evaluated by State Field Specialists (Trees), overseen by the 'Project Field Specialist';[12] each with specified responsibilities, tasks and targets, which together comprised a smooth running tree-making, moving and planting machinery that would support the flow of forestry material from seeds in nurseries to protected trees on the land – slowly but surely greening the landscape. On the other hand, we complained, as one put it, that 'it's either seeds, or it's bunds or it's trees; we don't seem to have people who can go out and talk to farmers and discuss problems holistically … it's become too departmentalised'. It was our own disciplinary boundaries that were reproduced in the project structure and that drove the programme approach.

This was a general problem, but the way in which consultants engaged with the project and the effects that they had varied between programmes. I want to turn now to some different consultant narratives in order to give a sense of the debates that surrounded various IBRFP programmes and the models that consultant knowledge generated. I will begin with the crops programme, which will illustrate a consultant-led research-oriented technical initiative with a strong externally generated model operated successfully at the margins of the project's operational system. Second, soil and water conservation (SWC) will offer, by contrast, a programme embedded in project systems and hierarchies and resistant to consultant advice. Third, I will look at how consultant inputs into group development and participatory planning produced powerful representations, sustained regardless of practice; and finally I will consider work on gender where the consultants' critical analysis and normative models managed neither to influence practices nor to establish themselves as authoritative within the project system.

THE CROPS PROGRAMME – PVS / PPB

The crops programme was different from others in IBRFP in that a strong external technical lead gave it the flavour of an international research project. At the core of the programme were new experimental methods for the collaborative development of improved cultivars by farmers and scientists (at state agricultural universities) that would lead to the official release of varieties with higher yields and reduced risk for low-input marginal areas. But the programme was only partly oriented towards Bhil livelihoods. It was also, through its scientific publications, directed at the Indian and international research community, government and donor advisers. Here its aim was to establish scientific recognition for a new type of data – participatory farmer evaluations – which would reveal the systematic bias against marginal upland areas in existing systems for technology development, and show how this could be overcome (Chapter 2).

The programme involved the innovative ideas of 'participatory varietal selection' (PVS) and 'participatory plant breeding' (PPB) brought by consultant John Witcombe from plant breeding experience at ICRISAT and developed with project staff.[13] These methods, now well documented and replicated in other programmes worldwide, make farmers rather than state systems the arbiters of new crop technologies and where they might be grown (Joshi and Witcombe 1995, 1996, Witcombe et al. 1998, 1999). The basic idea was to identify (and later breed) improved varieties of maize, chickpea, black gram and pigeon pea that matched farmer preferences, and then test them through farmer participatory trials.[14] In 'introductory trials' selected farmers were guided to experiment systematically with new varieties. Their judgements and criteria – yield, taste, price, storage, etc. – were recorded. In 'adaptive trials' successful varieties were sold at commercial rates to a wider range of farmers, and spread farmer-to-farmer without aggressive extension and input packages.[15]

The expatriate consultant provided the experimental designs and used an international reputation to negotiate shifts in scientific practice among collaborating Indian scientists, and further afield; but in his own narrative it is the cultivars that are the *dramatis personae*. First, there is Kalinga III, the most successful of five upland rice varieties tested (in 1992–3), which yielded more and matured earlier than local rice varieties and was especially adapted to poorer land with low inputs. For these and other qualities[16] farmers (government agencies and NGOs) were keen to buy this seed from the project. Next was ICCV2 a variety of chickpea (a crop grown in the post-monsoon *rabi* season), then TPU-4 black gram; others followed.

With a few exceptions (certain maize and black gram varieties), the advantages of improved seeds over the local 'land-race' varieties were significant. Moreover, insofar as the aim was to promote an alternative experimental research method, it was the improvements over officially recommended crops (rather than those farmers actually grew) that really mattered. Certainly in 1994 the consultant could conclude that 'the project approach of ignoring the official release recommendations when choosing varieties has been amply rewarded … all of the [officially] released material recommended for these states performed poorly in the low-input, low-fertility, drought stressed environments of the project area' (Joshi and Witcombe 1995: 7). Benefits for Bhil farmers, however, depended upon significant improvements in the yield of the main local staple, maize, 'the one that was most difficult to crack' (Consultant). Since existing maize research had produced nothing relevant for rainfed uplands, after 1996 Witcombe developed a breeding scheme for crosses between high-yielding maize varieties and local land-races uniquely adapted to local conditions, carried out at the project's research farm. Farmers selected the parent material, grew the early generations, selected the best plants from their own fields, and evaluated the new lines (through PVS). This method of participatory plant breeding (PPB) produced the maize variety GDRM-187. It was a major success, both in that it was highly preferred by farmers for its greater yield, earliness, pest resistance and grain quality, and in that it entered the state system (in Gujarat) and was officially released (in 2000) and so entered formal production and distribution.

In the crops programme, then, external expertise developed a technical model (PVS/PPB) with its own domain of knowledge and practice (crop trials, seed handed out in villages) and its own outcomes – improved crop varieties.[17] The model was 'context-free' in two ways. First, crop trials were 'a synthetic product originating with the research team' (Gatter 1993) whose experimental design presumed that agriculture was a technical enterprise in which individual elements (varieties) could be isolated from wider crop, land and agrarian relations (Appadurai 1990, Gatter 1993). The 'knowledge products' of PVS were detached from actors, the farmers, in that the characteristics they possessed were regarded as genetic and general rather than contextual; and in this sense their advantages were not dependent upon landholding, crop management, inputs, labour or credit relations, or linkage to markets.[18] Removing context in this way allowed project economists to apply their own generalising models to make predictions about the economic gains from overall yield increases, and to say, for instance, that Kalinga III 'alone will pay for the project'.[19] Indeed, as a scientific method, the PVS/PPB approach of using farmer evaluations in breeding, testing and popularising new varieties was a huge success and a major advance on prevailing regulatory frameworks, with wide implications for policy and bureaucratic practice. [20]

The second way in which the crop technical model was context-free, and a reason for its stability and success, was its independence from the operational routines of the wider IBRFP project. Improved seeds were developed and handed out, which did not depend upon ground action in every village, on the creation of self-sustaining institutions or the resolution of complex collective action problems (but see comment on seed supply below). As a sophisticated form of market research – albeit focused on the subsistence needs of marginal farmers and drawing on their capacities to experiment – PVS was even broadly consistent with the rationale of the wider marketing agency. Significantly, the consultant's project narrative (in reports and publications) reveals a scientific interlocutor relatively uncritical of project systems (compared to social development consultants), who reserves critical judgement for external state systems.

In reality, seeds and the crop programme had a context in both ways. Improved seeds would not solve problems of crop production on their own. As Yapa (1996) points out, seeds are not just material things, but 'the embodiment of a nexus of interacting relations (social and ecological ...)'.[21] By decontextualising, the PVS/PPB model underplayed the significance of changes needed in seed supply, agronomic practices, dependency and credit relations, and generalised and so exaggerated the potential development gains from new varieties (see Chapter 9). As one staff member put it:

> ... varietal selection was not enough, the challenge was yet to come, the challenge was in crop management, crop husbandry ... and the livestock–crops–trees interface [where] every farm is unique [and] where the blanket approach never works ... and we suddenly stopped.

Then there was the question of seed supply. The advantages of higher-yielding maize varieties would be diluted through cross-pollination, so every three years or so farmers had to buy new seed. Once varieties were officially released, they could be promoted through the state extension system. But this took time. Meanwhile, the project had to supply farmers with improved seeds. Initially the supply of new seeds on credit along with fertiliser to farmer groups worked because of its compatibility with a system geared to strengthening links with client farmer groups (see Chapter 5); but this could not meet rising demand for seed from farmers, government or NGOs. Similar limitations were associated with the few (five) Bhil farmer groups with winter season irrigation that were promoted as decentralised 'seed production centres' and trained in seed processing, tagging and bagging.[22] Unlike crop trials (PVS/PPB), these other matters required engagement of the wider project system or implied staff action in every village. But the wider project system could resist external influence and innovation. Agronomic innovations such as growing under-storey horsegram with maize, proved difficult to get under way; and despite its expertise in marketing, the KBCL bureaucracy was unwilling to risk marketing seeds that Bhil farmers preferred, but which had not been officially 'released' and were only 'truthfully labelled'.

So, a consultant-driven technology development model operated successfully within a separate knowledge and institutional domain and spread its knowledge products well outside the project boundaries, but once contextualised in the project, once the benefits of new technology depended upon project systems, or demanded changes in well-oiled mechanisms (i.e. the case of improving agronomy or seed supply), they were vulnerable to institutional inertia, resistance or rupture. Inadequately institutionalised, crops consultant knowledge was constrained to be a generalising experimental science speaking outwards to a wider community. By contrast, the influence of soil and water consultant knowledge was restricted because experts were 'locked in' to prevailing operational systems rather than locked out of them.[23]

SOIL AND WATER CONSERVATION – LOCKING EXPERTS IN

The technical purpose of the SWC programme was to halt erosion, excessive runoff and the loss of nutrients that led to decline in crop yields, and to improve infiltration through better-managed pasture and tree resources.[24] This aside, by 1994 SWC had in practice become the engine that drove the project: it disbursed development budgets, met quantitative targets, provided labour benefits, sustained farmer groups (through contributions from wages), supported a cadre of *jankars*, and reproduced professional identities (of engineers) and a hierarchy of posts at the level of the project office (cf. Chapter 5). Fulfilment of these ends determined the technical options and procedures that were adopted and formalised in practical guidelines. The focus was on physical SWC structures on private land (maximising disbursements, wages, etc.). Planning was to tight deadlines through rapid surveying techniques in which project engineers and village *jankars* made judgements about work on individual holdings, aggregated into SWC budgets. Work was quickly executed by employing otherwise migrant villagers (at more or less local wage-rates) to dig SWC structures on their own land, and as skilled workers and supervisors.[25] The project also paid for transport and other costs (grass seedlings, tree saplings, wire for gabion structures, etc.) as well as making a contribution to future maintenance.[26] Meanwhile, staff ensured financial accountability upwards by paying wages and keeping records themselves (Chapter 5).

This implementation machinery was fairly immune to external expert influence. Instead, our own normative discourse of participatory SWC developed in critical reaction to practice, as follows. First of all, as the soil scientist consultant reiterated, SWC should involve a broad 'land husbandry' approach, including biological and agronomic as well as physical measures. This 'holistic approach' should involve a range of low-cost approaches including planting fodder grasses, green manuring mulching and other vegetative methods to improve infiltration, water-holding capacity and the organic content of the soil. It required dialogue with farmers on a case-by-case basis, small trials, persuasion and extension. It also involved planting trees and grasses on the upper slopes of common property and the resolution of complex issues of ownership and maintenance.

Next, there was the question of subsidies.[27] In principle, we agreed, farmers should not be paid to make improvements on their own land. Subsidies were known to result in poor quality work, to enforce external dependencies, to reduce incentives for innovating low-cost methods or for maintaining SWC structures. Subsidies undermined sustainability and in any case were economically unjustified on private land. Indeed, our soil scientist claimed that:

> ... [the] early indications are that SWC could have a payback period of less than 5 years in most cases ... because present farmers can change their cropping patterns, in particular more rice can be grown; [and] rice both has a greater value per unit weight and yields more per unit area.[28]

Drawing on recent NGO work,[29] we argued that farmers should take loans for land improvement and repay into their group funds, creating a resource for future maintenance and the development of common lands. On upper slopes, of course, the full payback period would be more than an individual lifetime,[30] and the benefits of SWC (and the costs of land degradation) would largely be for future generations. Returns would also be social rather than individual, and some benefits would accrue to land users downstream (Smith 1998). For these reasons, subsidies would be justified in certain circumstances. Perhaps, some of us argued, there should be differentiated subsidies, depending upon the type of land and ownership. Logically, we reasoned, subsidies undermined participation, but practically they were necessary to get work done. Even if subsidies of some kind were inevitable, it was essential that villagers through their groups, rather than the project through its field staff, actually manage the process. Villagers should develop SWC plans, control the finances, pay wages, employ *jankars* and build up funds for future maintenance. Is it sustainable? we asked of project initiatives; what motivates farmers – land husbandry or labour wages? These were stimulating debates that whiled away long journeys and sociable evenings with project staff, or were performed in meetings. Through critical commentary on practice we framed and refined our participatory model. Indeed, this was a model that arose out of negotiations, disputes and contested practice; it was not given at the outset. But unlike the crops programme, this consultant discourse, did not have its own domain of practice. It had rather little practical effect, did not lead to managerial decisions. Indeed the project manager had the political sense to absent himself from meetings which he realised could lead to decisions and commitments that he knew well he would be unable to put into practice. In relation to local institution development, to which I now turn, consultant thought was also constrained to focus on the normative decontextualised model. In this case, it is my own thought-work as the expatriate specialist (between 1990 and 1998) that I have to explain.

LOCAL INSTITUTIONAL DEVELOPMENT

I began my work as the consultant advising on project strategy for 'local institutions' with a dilemma. Even in 1990 everyone knew that local organisations were a precondition for successful and sustainable rural development,[31] but the little local history I had gleaned indicated that these were part of the problem not the solution. The adivasi experience of externally promoted associations, whether dairy cooperatives, women's or youth groups or NGO-promoted village development societies was one of bureaucratic control, poor representation of the weak, or management failure and collapse. These 'societies' (*mandals*) and their self-serving leaders were part of many a village history of development failure that I listened to in early visits to Bhil villages (see Mosse 1996b). So my guidance to the project was vague: the model I proposed was the absence of a model; or the need for 'location-specific strategies' leading to a diversity of organisations for different purposes (for artisans, women's credit rotation, irrigation cooperatives, etc.) at different stages, depending upon patterns of leadership, settlement, kinship or seasonal migration. I offered what I took as guiding principles: 'move gradually from small, simple, single-task groups to larger complex institutions; build on existing affinities; be careful in promoting leaders; allow people to evolve their own rules and structures' (etc.).

This exercise in cautious rational planning was curtailed by rapidly unfolding events. The project system demanded operational rules not abstract principles. Staff had found their own blueprint and, borrowing from neighbouring NGOs and former employers, began promoting community-wide 'Village Development Societies' (VDSs) (as well as a few activity groups around wells, irrigation pumps or tree nurseries). My original dilemma was not so much resolved as illustrated. VDSs were an imposed technology, transferring 'urban' procedures (registers, records), and meeting outsiders' administrative needs.[32] They were dominated by elites and by men, they institutionalised unequal access to project benefits and were soon collapsing. Expressing such concerns was the second phase of my work. The third was to formulate an alternative institutional model. Project experience had made the dilemma a little clearer to me. It was this: farmer organisations are essential for sustainable rural development, but collective action is costly to people (i.e. it has heavy transaction costs) and institutions are prone to failure. There were, I reasoned, two ways out of this dilemma, both aiming to reduce the costs of collective action. The first – reduce the size and social diversity of the group – was already anticipated in the fragmentation of VDSs themselves. After two years, these were breaking up into smaller, more socially inclusive kin- or hamlet-(*falia*) based groups with which field staff had begun to work.[33] The second way out of the dilemma – restrict the tasks that institutions undertake, specifically to the management of common *finances* – was borrowed from currently favoured policy models, and especially the new (mid-1990s) centrality given to savings and credit as the basis for local institutional development (cf. Fernandez 1993, 1995).[34] So the model was elaborated as follows:

> IBRFP farmer institutions would be kin/hamlet-based micro-finance institutions (MFIs), defining rules for themselves, rotating credit funds, financed by savings or bank loans and lending to members for a range of consumption or productive purposes (including profitable valley-bottom SWC work). Groups would gradually free their members from the usury of moneylenders and promote individual enterprise; but they would not themselves aim to accumulate assets or run group enterprises. By starting out handling their *own* savings, group trust and management and accounting skills would develop gradually. Additional (project) finance would be made available only on the basis of carefully assessed competence. Effective groups would be able to handle project SWC funds and recover costs from profitable valley bottom work (i.e. new rice fields) into maintenance funds.[35]

Let me make a few comments on this example of consultant 'thought-work'. First, it was, at one level, a retrospective rationalisation of practice linked to a legitimising micro-finance policy model.

Second, the model was produced and intended to be read as a critical commentary on the project's patronage-investment approach (see Chapter 5); and was an attempt to shift the project's operational regime from 'programme delivery' to people's 'capacity building'. If self-managed farmers' groups (rather than SWC bunds) became the regulating centre of the project, the pace of investment or the scale of programme activities would be determined by the *capacity* of these groups (i.e. the people) to manage them. Group strength (measured against specified performance criteria and indices of 'group maturity') rather than physical or expenditure targets would be the yardstick of success. Training priorities, time-allocation, decision making, staff incentives would (or should) all be affected. And the many formats, steps and stages, and the lists of indicators contained in my reports made the point that a capacity building approach required attention and resources that were incompatible with business as usual.

Third, the institutional model was thoroughly modernist. On the one hand, it deployed the managerialist language of linear progressions, inputs and outcomes. This was largely so as to mobilise support from colleagues, donor advisers and project staff in a failed effort to influence management. To a degree, then, the model was framed by the politics of project relationships. On the other hand, it brought a conception of organisation and money management that was quite different from that which prevailed in Bhil villages. In the micro-finance (MFI) model, SHGs were organised by explicit rules of attendance, regular savings, keeping accounts and records (etc.) emphasising self-discipline and the proper use of loans. Indeed, I regarded such money management activities as a training ground for skills in the management of scarce resources in other domains – soils, trees, crops. The groups' financial transactions (framed by assumptions of the modern cash economy) were governed by the arithmetic of savings, loans, interest rates and fund availability, and aimed to promote enterprise among risk-taking individuals accountable to the group (cf. Fiedrich 2002). However, their logic departed from Bhil institutions such as *chandla* or *notra*, in which, it will be recalled, money transactions served the purpose of developing enduring social relationships and where it was obligation rather than money that accumulated; in networks rather than bank accounts. My SHG-MFI model, then, involved a socially disembedded conception of money (and management) relatively free of the burden of social obligation. At the same time, it attributed group processes (membership, regular meetings, record keeping, etc.) with almost automatic powers of transformation, empowerment and capacity building – based on the idea of participation in a public realm of rule-bound debate and interaction (implicitly drawing on Paulo Freire or Jürgen Habermas) (Fiedrich 2002: 65). The importance placed on group membership, saving and fund rotation as the source of security, and a neo-liberal emphasis on individual (or collective) responsibility (and rejection of dependency as the refusal of responsibility, cf. Dean and Taylor-Gooby 1992, cited in Dahl 2001: 21), concealed or denied the importance of social protection and relations of patronage, obligation or even employment for both Bhil villagers and the project. But as Weisgrau notes, for Bhil women in NGO *samitis* (groups), the difference between being 'members' of a *samiti* and 'workers' for wages is subtle and does not seem relevant (1997: 166).

The social effects of the imposition of this external logic of group processes will be judged in Chapter 9. For now I have to admit that, apart from being incompatible with project–villager relations based on patronage, and under-supported by my own weak networks within the project team, many of my proposals were (in hindsight) quite unrealistic in operational terms. Some, like the 20-page 'group appraisal format' were simply impractical (and largely rhetorical); others (substituting group capacity for expenditure targets) were politically impossible given IBRFP's entrenched operational regime. Although impossible to acknowledge at the time, from a certain point of view, this consultant's policy model (forged as an instrument of organisational politics between 1995 and 1997) was not only unimplementable, but also never seriously intended to be implemented. I was not producing plans for action at all but rather working to prise apart the ideal and the actual (cf. Mitchell 2002). The model's purpose was, then, to institute a framework of *interpretation*, a standard for judgement that legitimised one set of practices (promoting farmer self-management) while de-legitimising another (developing relations of patronage). In framing the model, like other consultants, I was 'speaking' more upwards to the arbiters of success and failure (donor advisers), than downwards to project actors.

The final phase of my consultant inputs (1996–8) was indeed preoccupied with the assessment of project institutions against the policy norms that I had put in place. As already explained in Chapter 5, measured against the standards of the new MFI model, IBRFP's groups were very poor performers. They had low saving, poor recovery and fund rotation, and a propensity to multiply questionable group activities rather than lending for individual enterprise. My reports particularly complained of the weak financial management capacities of the groups (poor book-keeping and dependence on staff) *in relation to* the large size of their funds (mostly derived from project investments rather than member savings). However, judged from a point of view in which securing social protection and stable patron–client relations is central, the very features that defined group failure – dependence, accumulating funds, multiple collective enterprises – were the markers of effectiveness, just as a really good SWC programme was one that spent budgets, gave employment, pump-primed groups and sustained relationships.

As our policy models of participatory SWC or MFIs gained coherence, they not only provided a basis on which to judge practices, but also concealed the logic behind those practices. The more sense the generals made to themselves in terms of their plans and strategies, and the more judgemental they became, the more ignorant they were of the rationality of the project's warriors and unit commanders and their Bhil collaborators, who were happy to let the red-faced generals blather on about participation.[36] But while consultants were operationally marginal, they produced powerful representations; and while these representations emerged from contested practice they became representations apart from practice, objectified as prior to and shaping action (cf. Mitchell 2002, passim). To show this I turn again to project debates on participatory planning.

THE PARTICIPATORY PLANNING PROCESS

As IBRFP's social development consultant advising on 'participatory planning', in the early years I worried about the weak analysis of local problems, the imposition of ideas, concession to the logistics of government schemes or outside researchers, or just the confusion of smoke and mirrors that lay behind the thin practice of PRA. This concern with a shift away from the process of reflection and learning under the imperatives of implementation was shared by many staff members. Through a series of workshops and reports, we (the project team) argued for and developed a systematic sequence of procedures regarded as necessary to produce a proper participatory village work plan: 'PRA → critical review of PRA → Community Problem Analysis (CPA) → development and negotiation of village work plans → agreed implementation plan → issue-focused awareness and skill training' (Mosse et al. 1994, Sodhi et al. 1993). This was 'a logical flow of steps for achieving participation of the people, identifying and deciding their respective needs in a collective way'.[37] It set a standard that would prevent exclusion, ensure careful consultation and analysis of community problems (avoiding the instant mirroring of project design and community responses), appraise, prioritise and phase options for intervention according to their complexity or the need for collective action, and equip villagers to take control of the process.

But this 'participatory' framework was profoundly contradictory. What counted as 'proper participation' was defined by those other than the Bhil participants, and the assessments of risk, responsibility, complexity or community competence were external and, for example, managed to suppress villagers' priority for water resources. Like the model of group development, the framework and its managerial language of control ('strategic planning', 'key steps', 'systematic application', 'formal decision making', 'consistency across village clusters' and the like) had more to do with external consultant (my) efforts to assert influence over project management and disorderly practice.

Unsurprisingly, the effect of this participation discourse was neither to transfer planning power to Bhil communities (see Chapter 4), nor to organise and clarify practice. Indeed, its notion of 'process' involved a string of mixed messages (about action/inaction) that contributed to confusion, unclear expectations, frustration and delay; opening up an impractical space that was quickly filled by standard interventions, guidelines and procedures rather than community capabilities. But what the participation discourse did do was to put in place a powerful normative schema through which practice could be *represented* and interpreted by staff and by outsiders. In this scheme, planning was an ordered sequence of learning and action in which communities were the objects of transformation effected by the techniques and routine sequences of the project (PRA, CPA, training, etc.), and through which they (Bhil villagers) acquired capacities for self-knowledge and self-help. Soon our reports and conversations began to speak in the language and sequences of the model. Instead of complicated interactions shaped by relations of patronage and power (Chapter 4), engagements between project and villages became moments in a linear progression from 'entry point' to 'withdrawal'. Even critical documentation confirmed a model in which events were interpreted in terms of progression from suspicion and subsidies to community control. So, in conceptualising the process of participation in order to regulate it, we provided a framework which allowed a dangerously chaotic situation shot through with power to be understood and communicated as a manageable sequence of procedures to be completed (meetings, PRAs, work plans), and which could be easily monitored by senior officers and taken to demonstrate community consensus, consent and inclusion (Chhotray 2004). Again, consultant thought-work (as in SWC and group development) provided both critical commentary on institutionalised project practice *and* the means to establish validating policy models (for participatory natural resource development, micro-finance or planning) apart from practice. However, in the case of gender analysis, to which I finally turn, the consultant critique of project practice failed to produce or sustain an authorised abstract representation.

GENDER ANALYSIS

ODA consultants working on gender issues (always an irregular and contentious presence, and Indian rather than expatriate) had an important role in defining and defending a 'gender strategy' for the project. These consultants had a dual focus, first on gender as an aspect of programme development, and second on gender relations within the project team. Even more than in other cases their work depended upon developing internal networks and coalitions at village and project level in support of ideas and principles. But these networks were always fragile and the ideas often met personal and institutional resistance, which is one reason why the gender strategy never achieved the status of a robust project representation. There was no IBRFP gender brochure.

A typical statement of IBRFP gender objectives was: '(i) enabling women to define their own needs and priorities in farming system development and strategies to address these, and (ii) enabling women to gain control over important livelihood resources'. As with other consultant models, the gender strategy developed from critical reflection on practice. To begin with, consultants noted that IBRFP's operational emphasis on 'equal participation of women' (meaning number and presence) concealed the more complex issue of the *nature* of women's participation in the project; and did not necessarily signal any change in gender relations – in which inequality derived not from women's lack of participation (in farm activities or expertise) but from the social construction of this participation (see Chapter 3).[38] Consultants asked *which* women (in terms of kinship, clan or class) participated and spoke for others, *how* were they present (e.g. in PRAs) or *what* differences were muted? Women, they wrote in their reports, were mostly present as unskilled labour (e.g. in SWC works), but excluded from key areas of programme decision making;[39] even in designated 'women's activities', staff spoke with men while women filled the polybags and did the weeding. Project interactions amplified the gender hierarchies of Bhil society, consultants claimed.[40] Despite staff knowledge of women's roles and interests in agriculture, even in areas of women's expertise (seed management, fodder, household finance or credit) men were at the fore. It was men not women to whom improved seeds were distributed, and who managed the crop trials (although women's opinions were solicited in evaluating new varieties). The credit and input supply scheme was organised with men and through groups they controlled. Men were sought out by experts with new technologies (for crops or cattle breeds), by scientists, bank managers or local officials. Moreover, consultants challenged, the technologies offered to women – stoves, grinders, mills, vegetable seeds – emphasised their domestic roles; and the lower-profile of these household technologies within the project as a whole confirmed the generally low social status of the domestic domain (Crewe and Harrison 1998: 101).

There were many efforts (some consultant-inspired) to make women and their concerns more central; but time and target-bound planning and activity schedules made it hard to sustain them. By the time women's groups had begun rotating savings we noted, the project's input supply credit was already organised around groups controlled by men: women saved but men took the credit. In planning a lift irrigation scheme in one village a modified design was put forward in view of women's concern about access to drinking water, but was later abandoned on the grounds that it over-complicated the scheme. Indeed, 'gender issues' (and their consultants) only added unwanted complexity to staff under pressure.

From the project's first experience of PRAs, gender consultants proposed ways in which women's perspectives could better be articulated. They worked to conceptualise the gendered nature of roles, interests and responsibilities within the Bhil farming systems to show how the benefits and costs (e.g. additional labour) of project schemes and technologies could be different for men and women. They suggested identifying the 'areas of influence' and room for manoeuvre that women had for non-confrontational strategies that recognised and strengthened women's expertise, decision making and managerial roles.[41] They argued forcefully that in the absence of decisive action, innovation, new technology and outside expertise would place project initiatives firmly within a male domain. This would not only exclude women, but also undermine their existing roles, expertise and influence. But how could project staff, bound by the logics and social order of the project implementation regime, deal with such ideas in practice? What procedure would direct project management and decision making to gender concerns? One idea was that every proposed project activity would be subject to a formal 'gender appraisal' prior to approval. This would identify the areas of strategic importance to women in relation to each activity, the possible impacts and ways of enhancing women's positive involvement, the support needed to achieve this and the basis for monitoring gender impacts in terms of practical (e.g. workloads) and strategic (e.g. bargaining power) interests (Moser and Levy 1986).

This consultant thought-work also involved its own socially disembedded models. Its bargaining model of gender relations and empowerment brought instrumental rationality to the fore, and already presumed the autonomy which was the desired outcome for women actors. In the analysis, women's roles appear as contractual, or a matter of choice or negotiation. The actor and the act are separated (work exists before it is gendered) in a way that may not correspond to social experience (Fiedrich 2002). More practically 'gender appraisal' never found its institutional context. Despite repeated consultant insistence, it never became part of the IBRFP routine; neither did the recommended service rules, procedures and structures of support for female staff (dealing with harassment etc.). The project was not lacking in gender workshops and trainings at different levels, but the systems that gender consultants (and project counterparts) tried to establish for working with women conspicuously failed to compete with programme specialisation and delivery routines.

My point is that gender models not only failed to become practice, they also failed to become part of the project's self-representation, in the way that other models (PPP, MFIs, PVS/PPB) had. The reasons are neither surprising nor hard to find. Normative models survive where they find support within organisations, or where they help address demands on organisations from outside (from donors or senior managers). In IBRFP there were neither internal support nor external demand for anything but the simplest notion of gender equity – the presence of women. Moreover, gender consultants, being especially sceptical of management intentions to address gender, were unwilling to prepare materials that 'would not be speaking any truth and more of falsehoods' as one put it. Over time, the demand for gender consultants dwindled, visits were erratic and then ceased entirely. Within the project, gender concerns remained marginal to the principal lines of control, responsibility for them was fragmented, given to a series of short-term local consultants or specialists. None was able or willing to hold a post that was so sidelined within the organisational structure for long, and as the team segregated into disciplinary specialists under pressure to deliver, the space for gender as an issue was further reduced.[42] But, perhaps more important, as with our work on 'groups', consultant models themselves misconceived the nature of changes in gender relations that *were* occurring as a result of project interventions, a point taken up in Chapter 9.

CONCLUSIONS

The different experiences of a plant breeder, a soil scientist, an anthropologist or a gender sociologist in relation to the project are interesting in themselves (those of the forester, livestock specialist, engineer or economist tell other stories), but I want to close by drawing out some general points. The effect of international consultants working on the ODA's IBRFP project was two-fold. First, they put in place specialist disciplinary domains which defined the project's 'deliverables' (crop technology, SWC, groups). Disciplinary divisions were built into project routines and the professional ambitions of staff – as agriculturalists, engineers or foresters – in ways that made it harder to work across programmes, and which failed adequately to correspond to the livelihoods needs of farmers. For instance, external expertise under-emphasised the critical area of livestock-fodder, and there was a corresponding project-level failure to recruit specialists in this area.[43] Second, we consultants variously perfected models, for participatory technology development (PVS/PPB), SWC, group formation, or participatory planning. These models involved a kind of generalising knowledge disembedded from context – crops from agrarian relations, soil from labour, money from social obligation, SHGs from patronage and social protection. Now, with the exception of PVS/PPB, these models did not precede and direct action, but emerged through critical reflection on practice (i.e. the routines and contingencies of the project's operating system). Consultants and their staff counterparts lacked the capacity (alliances or networks of influence) to change behaviour or to translate ideas from an international development discourse into local practice. Instead our 'thought-work' – reflections, strategies – provided the 'second-order rationalisations' that helped shape the way in which project practice was represented and communicated 'upwards' to donor advisers, government officials, colleagues and others, as well as 'downwards' to fieldworkers. Indeed, consultants were valued, not for their ability to redefine practice, or to tinker with operational rules, but for their conceptual work, which helped managers rationalise and stabilise authorised representations of events; our ability to produce the models, metaphors or worldviews that could be 'sold upwards as rationales for resource requests and downwards as justifications for orders' (Heyman 1995: 269). Better models meant better translation of practices into higher policy, and better links to the donor, which would enhance the reputation of both project and consultants.[44]

The same models, metaphors and worldviews filtered down through the system, not as direct instructions for action, but as templates for thinking and talking about events, reporting or communicating to outsiders, and as self-representation and project identity; ensuring that, for staff, the legitimacy of their own roles and that of the project were interlinked.[45] These representations became second nature. This I discovered when listening at length to staff speaking about the objectives of the project and their role in achieving them (and also when staff views were captured in written responses).[46] Almost everyone had a strong vision of development as *self-reliance* – 'the development of villagers by villagers using their own resources and not dependent upon anybody', as one CO characteristically put it;[47] and they presented their own role as catalysts, trainers or guides: 'our contribution is quite less … No! my contribution is nothing, because I am only [a] factilitator and mobilise the community [who] have the main power through making groups.' Putting statements together, a coherent overall narrative emerges:

The people in this area have problems of degraded forests, soil erosion, low productivity, a lack of improved agricultural technology. They lack sufficient food grain and employment and so migrate for long periods. Fundamentally, people lack awareness; they are illiterate, ignorant and innocent. They do not know about government schemes, they hesitate to meet officials and lack faith in others. We want to see increased production through integrated farming systems development: improved varieties and SWC, improved pasture and forest, and more off-farm income generation. There will be sustained self-help groups, trained *jankars* both men and women. We will make people aware, they will have linkage to government services and schemes. They will be self-reliant, confident and skilled, able to fulfil their needs at the local level without outside help. Our role is to facilitate, motivate, to train and guide. Problems can be solved by building capacity among the community.

This authorised model, the one that is consistent with the project rationale, reiterated in donor documents and consultant reports emphasising community capacity building, self-reliance and integrated farming systems development, is the one that dominates. (Significantly the representation demonstrates that the 'gender agenda' failed to achieve the status of a legitimising narrative within the project system: staff showed a limited ability to articulate gender elements of poverty and project objectives in an unprompted way.)[48] There is no place here for relationships of employment or patronage, subsidies and schemes, budgets and targets; no place either for Bhils seeing their future in terms of relations with 'outsiders', social protection, getting jobs, migrant incomes or individual mobility through party politics. As they imposed boundaries on Bhil communities (Li 1997), IBRFP staff internalised a role for themselves – as facilitators of community self-help – that contradicted the necessary preoccupation with programme delivery (revealed in 'back stage' stories). In fact, a season-wise time-allocation exercise completed by groups of COs showed that most of their time (up to 80 per cent, depending upon season) was actually devoted to activity implementation (purchasing, monitoring, travel, record keeping) rather than the provision of knowledge and skills to communities; and broader development goals disappeared entirely when COs turned their attention to performance assessment and spoke of their individual performance being measured in terms such as 'implementing work as per the monthly plan', or 'the timely submission of monthly reports'.

What is the relationship between development workers' actions and their legitimising theory or strategy? Well, as Latour reminds us, 'actors don't have *strategy*; they get their battle plans, contradictory ones, from other actors … actors offer each other a version of their own necessities, and from this they deduce the strategies they ascribe to each other' (1996: 162–3). But all actors are also social scientists providing themselves with theories to stabilise this 'inter-definition of the actors' (1996: 180), to unify, simplify and make coherent, so that given interpretations become 'realised' (1996: 172). We consultants were actors like others, but we used our power and networks (into donor or academic communities) to authorise our own unifying meta-narratives and make them the stories that others actors must tell themselves about strategy (cf . Latour 1996: 164). The project then systematised these models into training manuals and brochures, providing official representations of practices that were in fact generated by a hidden operational logic. These were necessary in order to put back together the worldview of project staff that was constantly fragmented by the everyday contradictions of practice.

Of course, we consultants also had to stabilise our own theory of what we are about – in terms of prevailing development discourses, through research, project reports and statistics, through village studies, economic analyses and 'end-of-project-reports'. These were what Latour calls 'valorimeters' that ensured the translation of one point of view into another and were the means to generalise interpretations, 'to make incommensurable frames of reference once again commensurable and translatable' (1996: 180–1). That was our job: to sustain and stabilise an interpretation, to reproduce the 'idea of the project' and its logical connections between objectives and activities.[49]

As we collaborated with project staff over years we produced designs, recommendations, inspiring and motivating models of how things should be done. Perhaps such over-ambition produces project failure (Kumar and Corbridge 2002). Certainly our legitimising representations systematically diverted attention away from the institutional politics, relationships and the operational rules of practice, and therefore we purveyed development fictions and fantasies. The imperative to create coherence, the 'drive to reach closure' (Ellerman 2002: 289) is dangerous. But there is a dilemma, for without policy models it is hard to mobilise political and institutional support for change. The empirical judgement of whether policy goals can nonetheless produce desirable effects will have to wait until Chapter 9. In the next chapter I will look at the *power* and in Chapter 8 at the *dangers* of policy coherence.

7

The Social Production
of Development Success

In a brilliant analysis of the politics of technology development focusing on 'Aramis', the prestigious but aborted Parisian rapid transport system project, Bruno Latour reminds us that all projects begin as systems of signs, texts and language, and that the relationship between these and objects and events is uncertain. 'Depending upon the informant and period,' he writes, 'the project may shift from idea to reality or from reality to idea ... This is something Plato didn't anticipate. Depending on events, the same project goes back into the heaven of ideas or takes on more and more down-to-earth reality' (1996: 67–8).

The reality of a development project too is always in question, and remains so even during execution. This is what makes it a *project* rather than a part of ordinary life (1996: 76). It is always possible to ask, 'Is anything happening? ... Is it sustainable? ... Can it be replicated?' And there is the same circularity: if signs become actions/objects through implementation, the move is also back into text. This we saw in the work of expatriate consultants, which turned project actions back into stable normative models.[1]

Moreover, a development project cannot in any definitive way proclaim its own reality; this is always contingent upon outside judgements. Project reality has to be determined through the interpretive work of experts who discern meaning from events by connecting them to policy ideas and texts – logframes, project documents (and vice versa). Indeed, a project does not exist independent of our (expert) opinion of it (Latour 1996: 76). When authorised observers – reviewers, evaluators – construct stories that affirm that a project has genuine participants, functioning programmes, has been implemented on schedule, is sustainable, replicable or has achieved an impact, it acquires reality. Alternatively, with reports of 'nothing happening', 'negligible progress', that institutions are unsustainable or defunct, a project loses reality. But there are no objective meters here, only interpretations; only more of less acceptable stories (Phillips and Edwards 2000), and these are, of course, always a means to particular ends – in the extreme, project termination or extension. This makes constructing a project story highly contentious. Disagreements arise over *who* is qualified to construct knowledge about a project (which experts, insiders or outsiders) and *how* it is to be done (methodology) (2000). These are heightened moments in the assertion and resistance of power between donor and recipient, although in the end there is usually a shared need for an 'acceptable story' (2000) that mediates differences and buries contradictions in order to sustain relationships and the flow of resources. In spite of formal demands for objectivity and independence, experts are charged with producing, and themselves intentionally construct, the evaluation story as a 'shared commodity' (2000: 57). And since a project gains reality and becomes successful with the unity of points of view, its managers have to resolve disagreements among experts on effectiveness, or economic viability or sustainability, and work towards a consistency of interpretation. There is also a circle here. Success itself unifies, just as failure fragments into the dynamics of blame (Latour 1996: 76).

Project evaluations are actually just one moment in a wider and more routine process of making meaning and framing interpretations. It is this rather than evaluation *per se* that is the focus of this chapter. As mentioned in this book's introduction, my concern is not whether, but *how* a project is successful (and later unsuccessful); how success is made and *managed*. This departs from usual 'M and E' (monitoring and evaluation) concerns, which focus on appropriate definitions of success or measures of progress and achievement. It is true that the new politics of development has spawned a variety in methods, including participatory monitoring and evaluation, which (more in principle that practice) acknowledge multiple criteria of 'success'. But the focus is still on measures and meters of performance, albeit judged from different points of view. My point will be that development success is not merely a question of measures of performance; it is also about how particular interpretations are made and sustained *socially*. It is not just about what a project does, but also how and to whom it speaks, who can be made to believe in it.

So I will ask how IBRFP was made successful (in the next chapter I will turn to failure). Success, I will argue, depended upon (i) establishing a compelling interpretation of events, (ii) sustaining this as a key representation (through model building, reporting and field visits), and (iii) enrolling a wider network of supporters and their agendas, whether donor advisers, researchers, government officials or regional NGOs, and linking them to the success of the project. Later parts of the chapter turn to the costs and crises of IBRFP's particular regime of success: the loss and recovery of reputation. In short, the chapter addresses my third proposition (see p. 17): that all development projects (not just this one) work to maintain themselves as coherent policy ideas – as systems of representations – as well as operational systems.

MAKING A SUCCESS OF PARTICIPATION

Despite the fact that the logic of IBRFP practice routinely contradicted the official models (Chapters 5 and 6), the project was constrained to promote the view that its activities resulted from the implementation of policy. Even though (in key respects) its practices departed from principles of participatory development, IBRFP became an exemplar of this mode of development. When most shaped by the inflexible demands of programme delivery, the project was winning a wide acclaim for its *participatory* processes and the sophistication of its methods that brought a fairly constant stream of Indian and international visitors. How was such unambiguous success produced from complex contingent practice?

First, this was good marketing and a convergence of the development agenda of participation and the self-promotional goals of a fertiliser company. The project effectively turned participation into a commodity (loosely speaking), which, like urea, could be bagged with the company label on it. This was made possible by the high profile accorded to this as a participatory project by the donor, and by a rising demand for skills in participatory approaches and a package of methods (mostly PRA) by large-scale government programmes,[2] and by the project's ability to deliver these. Through skilful public relations the project succeeded in establishing 'participation' as a commodity, and itself as the primary source or supplier, which enabled the wider organisation to reap the rewards of high-profile visibility and reputation. The work that consultants like myself did in documenting and systematising 'participatory processes' (Chapter 6) inadvertently helped in this commodification and the 'marketing' of a complex relationship between IBRFP staff and Bhil villagers as a set of techniques, flow-charts and formats reproduced and printed as guidelines. These could then be transacted as gifts to senior managers or state officials with whom relationships had to be built. As I travel with the project manager to meet the Chief Minister's Adviser in

Bhopal, there between us on the back seat of his Ambassador car sit a pile of packages gift wrapped in tissue paper. These are summary manuals, among them the IBRFP Participatory Planning Approach for Livelihood Enhancement 'presenting the processes practised by the IBRFP', a gift for the senior officer.[3]

Second, the ambiguity of the master metaphor – 'participation' – itself facilitated the production of success. As the idea of 'participation' became embedded simultaneously as normative model (Chapter 6) and standard techniques (Chapter 5), a cumulative record of the routine – PRAs, attendance at village meetings, trainings, work plans, or crop trials – not only provided an unassailable quantitative record of the project's participatory performance, allowing the project to claim success in ways that did not depend upon field-level verification, but also 'promoted the impression of radical change [awareness, or empowerment] without threatening the basic project of controlled and orderly manipulation of change' (Porter 1995: 64). The polysemy of 'participation' allowed, for example, farmers' contribution (itself a product of tactical accounting, see Chapter 6, note 25) to imply 'empowerment'. So in various ways the narrow technical practice of 'participation' invoked the impression of dramatic social change by symbolising local agency and concealing that of outsiders.

But well promoted 'participatory' events/actions were insufficient. Success depended upon the efficient and timely execution of high-quality programmes in measurable quantities that held the attention of outside observers, political bosses and paymasters, as well as securing continued participation from villagers. After five years over 1,500 km of contour trenches and earth and stone bunds had been constructed, 2 million tree seedlings planted. The technical quality of forestry and soil conservation works was high,[4] and staff could point to concrete benefits from SWC, such as the replacement of lowland maize with higher-value rice, improved moisture retention or increased yields of the winter crop. PVS had identified varieties that improved yields (Kalinga III rice by 46 per cent), tested and popularised through farmer-to-farmer spread. Village Forest Committees (under the Forest Department's Joint Forest Management Scheme) allowed regeneration of areas of denuded teak forest and increased the availability of fodder in villages. Hundreds of wells had been deepened, pump-sets distributed and *jankars* trained. The project could boast the delivery of a great range of additional innovations, including improved poultry and goat breeds, bio-fertiliser, kitchen gardening, fruit orchards, compost pits, sprinkler and drip irrigation, 'farmer-friendly' equipment (from iron ploughs to maize shellers and wheeled hoes), and a variety of group-run (and individual) income-generating activities (e.g. grain banks, grocery shops, envelope making, sun-hemp crafts, mushroom cultivation and many more). Investments in 'human capital' through health and education programmes, village schools, adult literacy, first-aid and water-purification kits, along with hand-pumps, community halls and houses for the destitute added to the wide range of activities to which visitors would be introduced.

The delivery of these programmes was, however, far too important to be left to *participatory* (i.e. farmer-managed) processes;[5] hence the strong vertical control of activities and implementation backed by systems of reward and punishment (Chapter 5). Indeed, staff who tried to be *too participatory* – spending too much time investigating needs or women's perspectives, or insisting on the slow build-up of capital and skills in village groups – would be seen as under-performing by both project and community. 'When I tried to escape from the pressure of targets that compromised the process,' explained Jagdish, 'it put a question on my performance; it harmed me.' Resented by the project as poor implementers and by villagers as weak patrons, some field staff resigned from the project, their frustration palpable in our conversations. A few went on to establish their own NGOs locally only to face similar pressures later on.

Here was a contradiction: high-profile publicised (or marketed) 'participation processes' on the one hand, vertical control over programme delivery on the other. It is a contradiction that must characterise all participatory interventions faced with inexorable pressure from the wider market for development success, in which both participatory goals *and* their denial in practice are necessary to manage reputations. This led fieldworkers to take control of natural resources development, just as, in another project, 'in order to present [an income-generation programme] as a successful micro-enterprise the staff ... sacrifice pedagogical goals of passing on skills that would enable their clients to succeed in the private sector beyond the NGO' (Luthra 2003: 251). But the point is that this sort of contradiction is easily concealed.

Ultimately, what secured the rising reputation of the project (in 1994–6) was neither a series of trivial participatory events (PRAs etc.) nor even the delivery of quality physical programmes. Rather, success depended upon the donor-supported (and consultant-elaborated) *theory* that linked participation/farmer control on the one hand,

and better, more effective/sustainable programmes on the other. When interpreted through the assumptions of the project model, a landscape of well laid-out SWC bunds, woodlots, wells and pump-sets, as well as field trials and adopted new technologies, not to mention hundreds of SHGs with an expanding range of group activities, is read, not only by visitors but by staff and management themselves, as demonstrating the success of ODA goals of people's participation and farmer-managed development, regardless of the complex actuality of practice. The point is that a validating project model (theory or policy) establishes precisely the causal link between participatory processes and efficient implementation that is absent (or difficult to establish) in practice.[6]

SUSTAINING A REPRESENTATION

Put simply, IBRFP development activities were brought about through a complex set of social, institutional and political relations informed by 'hidden transcripts', but the project was constrained to believe and promote the view that these activities were the result of the implementation of an official participatory approach (its 'public transcript', Scott 1990b). There is no suggestion of duplicity. As I made clear in Chapter 6, interpreting and presenting events through the official model was a habit (of mine too). Project designs become thickly woven into representations of professional practice, identity or the habitus of staff. Neither do I suggest that maintaining representations is all that the project did, that it was in some sense ephemeral; nor that the IBRFP project is in any way exceptional here. Participatory models and ideals of self-reliance are often more part of the way projects work as systems of representations, oriented upwards and outwards to wider policy goals and institutions that secure reputation and funding (or even inwards as self-representation), than part of their operational systems (Mosse 2003a).

This was a successful aid project because it sustained a coherent policy idea, a model offering a significant interpretation of events. Now considerable work is needed to sustain such a system of representations beyond the immediate project. Indeed, from its third year, project management (including consultants) was increasingly oriented towards managing the inevitable but profound internal contradiction between participation and patronage, precisely *through* development and communication of its project model. How was this done?

First, considerable effort went into articulating an integrated project model that could explain events as the outcome of participatory planning, technology development and the promotion of farmer groups, drawing on the consultant work discussed in Chapter 6. Consultant reports, manuals, workshop, seminar and promotional videos all reaffirmed the model. By the third year (1995), the model had become so important that in a revised logical framework it was restated as *the* key Purpose of the project, which was now the establishment of a 'replicable, participatory and sustainable farming systems development *approach*' – that is, a model (rather than sustainable increases in production etc.). Emphasising this, the project developed a 'replication programme' and a 'dissemination strategy' as key Outputs. Affirming the project as a replicable model enhanced its appeal in donor circles, especially given the ODA's commitment to policy influence through projects. As a simulation, the model allowed the contingencies of social and institutional setting to be ignored (Fairhead 2000: 101). So the project could become an exemplar or 'archetypal application' of donor policy. Indeed, further, the articulation of donor policy itself depended upon its exemplar projects, which provided official visitors with the skills in interpretation necessary to frame and sustain policy, for example, on participatory development within the agency (cf. Fine 2002, referring to Kuhn 1962).

Inevitably perhaps, managers of successful projects find an emphasis on dissemination more rewarding than struggling with the contradictions of implementation (although, of course, they have to do both). In several cases the IBRFP project was very successful in selling its model, particularly in the technical crops area. Dissemination involved the production of manuals, national/regional seminars and workshops, audio-visual productions, training for NGOs and GOs on the now systematised 'participatory approach', a bi-annual promotional pamphlet (*maitri*, or 'friendship'), and several films with catchy titles such as 'Seeds of Progress' or 'Beyond 2000', which 'bagged' the Fertiliser Association of India award.

As one perceptive staff member explained, these materials not only stabilised external interpretations of the project, they also had internal effects, disciplining the thinking and information production of project employees:

> You make a film, and you make a poster, and you design a brochure ... these are all silent gestures, as a manager you do not have to say certain

things in certain ways, you act so as to communicate … If I ask a person to design a specific folder [brochure] in a specific manner, in a certain set language, using certain flowery words, I do not just communicate that I want a very nice looking folder, I communicate that I need things to be in this particular way, so things [i.e. statements, data, representations] beyond that brochure would take the same shape as the brochures; and that is what happens.

More generally, the models that secured the rising reputation of the project externally, and that were summarised in slogans, charts, wall-hangings, banners or photo displays in the project offices, were also a means to build internal coherence among a diverse project team. Senior staff and managers worked hard (through meetings, events, displays) to foster a project culture and identity around its approach so as to hold staff together, to encourage loyalty, counter staff turnover and contend with the *de facto* contingency of staff action.

Whether driven externally or internally, the incentive to produce coherent representations blurs the boundary between the normative and the descriptive, so that project planning manuals become cited and reproduced in project or donor texts as project experience. Of course this reproduces rather than resolves project contradictions.

A second means to affirm and adapt models and representations in order to manage relationships upwards with ODA patrons (among others) was project reporting (assisted by consultants). The descriptions of events in project reports were heavily laden with reference to prior design. Although the progress reports of the initial years (1992–4) emphasised field experience and future plans, those of later years were solidly structured by work plans and the categories of the project's cause–effect model, its logical framework. This imposed a highly selective, technical and deductive grid onto unruly practices and events, demanding information on the accomplishment of predetermined schedules and outputs, or at best lessons learned. Progress reports helped donor advisers interpret 'the field' *in terms of* current policy assumptions, satisfying an ever more demanding audit culture of the donor, but leading to closure and organisational ignorance.[7] The critical writing of consultants (Chapter 6) itself inducted project staff into the art of representing events in terms of normative models, removing contingency, history (and politics) and pushing towards the timelessness of a policy idea. Reports, briefing papers, Aide Memoires, terms of reference, all helped to provide an enduring map of the territory, lending stability to knowledge about the project, affirming its models and creating the comforting illusion that the project implemented policy and was successful because it was well designed (cf. Latour 1996: 78). Of course the interpretive power of project reports depended upon how they were read too; that is, the standing of the particular policies they expressed and the status of their advocates inside the donor agency. In this regard, the IBRFP project model was strengthened in the mid-1990s by the rising status and power of Social Development Advisers within the ODA (in relation to technical advisers) whose perspectives it expressed.

Third, visits to the project, especially visits by donor personnel, were occasions to *explicate* the assumptions of the project model. In the mid-1990s the ODA's Annual Review Missions (ARMs) were the most focused of the many visits by donor advisers, senior managers or research teams. These were 'rituals of verification' (Power 1997). Weeks ahead, project staff and consultants would be redirecting their energies to preparing a representation of actions and events to anticipate and guide the ARM's concerns, using the numbered paragraphs of recommendations from the previous year's report as their guide, and in various ways making project effects visible. Equally detailed would be attention to the comforts and luxuries of VIP visitors accommodated to the highest possible standard.

The review visit transforms the space and suspends the routines of office and village. The interpretive possibilities of such 'missions' are deliberately constrained by consultant reports, briefing packs, staff presentations linking the approach to outputs; and by short, highly structured and closely accompanied visits to remote tribal villages, village meetings and planted questions. In the selected villages everyday life gives way to project time, space and aesthetics. The village is organised to resemble the project text so as to be pleasingly read by outsiders: the presence of completed PRA maps on the ground and of smartly bunded landscapes, wood lots, and colourful groups of women, provide the simultaneous presence of the village plan and its execution. For a moment the village is not a public space, but property of the project (cf. Heaton 2001: 92) which provides access and interpretation to visitors who, in conversation with villagers, are utterly incapable of anything but assenting to the explanations offered; so long, that is, as the evident command of the project over its villager clients is overlooked. Indeed, the other ordering is hierarchical. The visit's meetings give spatial expression to the ranked arrangements of the project: visitors and senior managers on chairs and charpoys, field staff in attendance, villagers seated on the ground, women shuffling hurriedly to the edge or off the mat (*dhurrie*) spread out for the meeting (cf. Weisgrau 1997: 163). The project displays the power to summon, the people are present on command 'showing evidence of deference and gratitude' and readied for interrogation (Li 1999: 307). The ordering of time, and the endless waiting of villagers for the arrival of the VIP's motorcade itself signifies hierarchies of power. Altogether less obvious is the ordering of expression – who speaks, who is silent and what is said – evident only at moments of transgression; the embarrassment surrounding the inappropriate question, comment or translation.

These are paradoxical rituals in which the power of the donor over the project is publicly acknowledged but practically denied. Visitors are honoured but controlled; powerful outsiders turned into gullible spectators. As one CO recalled such visits:

> Villagers came together, fifty to a hundred or two hundred; a great drama. Women welcoming visitors with *tilak*. So all consultants and visitors were very happy, enjoying these things and [they] forgot to ask questions. Then we show a few things, the meetings register, savings in the [group] fund ... one PRA model on the ground. Some *jankars*, experts in how to present things [and] updated a few days earlier on how to speak, will present.

The more influential the visitors, the more formal, structured and shorter the visit and the more impenetrable the displayed public face of project rationality. These highly stylised public appearances, in which senior aid administrators engage staff and beneficiaries to 'collect feedback' are like secular durbars (Sivaramakrishnan 2000: 441); but they also implicitly allude to the insecurity of control of the donor over the project, senior over junior, in everyday project life (Heaton 2001: 218). Their mimicry of the donor's rational process allows slippage which also speaks of disavowal (Bhabha 1994, in Heaton 2001: 221).

Now, visitor ignorance of project practices is *not* individual but institutional. When, at the end, the donor visit wraps itself up in text, the individual doubt, the personal scepticism, the private wonder at what it is *really* all about, fuelled by glimpses of project politics that erupt in the interstices of the structured visit, all disappear. The ARM's official Aide Memoire provides an authorised interpretation of achievements against goals, affirms progress and promise, comments on efficiency and economic returns, or on the speed and scale of project implementation. It recommends some adjustment in priorities: there is need to 'reduce entry-time to new villages', 'streamline financial decision-making', 'plan expansion', and to set targets and milestones of achievement. Overall, the ARM affirms the project model and underlines the categories within which practice is to be represented.

The review mission has been an occasion to engage in expert debate and policy reflection, rather than to examine actual practices in any critical detail. And ODA staff visiting from Delhi or London were never short of expert advice arising from current preoccupations whether these were organic farming, or salinity problems, or livestock surveys, or labour saving technology. The 1995 ARM contained a remarkable 84 separate recommendations.[8] Each visit leaves a trail of ideas, a few offering genuine inspiration and insight but many of scant relevance to practice.[9] Visitors to IBRFP were given a rich experience obligingly tailored to their particular interests: they were allowed to give expert advice, taken to otherwise wholly inaccessible tribal villages and honoured. For some, the visit to the project provided an occasion for expert diagnosis, for others a moment in which to affirm broad aid policy goals. IBRFP colourfully brought together at a local level, the ODA's policy concern with dryland agriculture and food security, a focus on the poorest parts of India, participation and the credibility that came from direct links to the grassroots; all rare indeed. As a senior adviser put it:

> … it was a good day out. The project demonstrated to senior people the type of development that they felt comfortable with: something remote, something rural, finding happy communities benefiting; a bit like sitting on a loo seat that you know has been sustainably logged. Things about which our rhetoric was strong but reality relatively unrealised.

As much as anything, then, visits helped to secure project success. Visitors remained ignorant of the contradictions of the project, or unable to criticise the dominant interpretations offered. The more the project's reputation grew, the more and higher-status the visitors. To a steady stream of donor advisers were added 'scientific visitors', NGOs and international experts. Very few senior ODA administrators were not taken to this flagship project. Prestige visitors included the ODA's Permanent Secretary, British MPs and the British High Commissioner to India. At one point, during a royal visit to India, there were rumours of plans for a helipad in one of the project's most celebrated villages and a visit by Prince Philip. At a ceremony in Delhi, the project manager was given the accolade of an honorary MBE. Against a history of aid project failure, the IBRFP was a shining jewel of participatory poverty-focused development in the British aid crown.

CONTEXTUALISING THE PROJECT

As will become clear in the next chapter, such success is not a necessary outcome. Project staff never have full control over outsider interpretations; things could always go wrong, villagers or the ARM might not perform their roles. Success is not guaranteed but *produced* through processes requiring constant joint work. Indeed, through their writing, hosting and promotion, IBRFP staff not only worked to stabilise particular frameworks of interpretation, but also to secure these socially by actively recruiting and enrolling a range of supporting actors who will 'decide to connect the fate of a project with the fate of the small or large ambitions they represent' (Latour 1996: 137). This work that sustains or revives a project (in his case the Parisian rapid transport system) Latour describes as 'contextualisation':

> ... [the project] nearly becomes a pile of paper covered over by the drab surfaces of closed files ... But then something happens: the work of contextualisation starts up and is so successful, so sprightly, that Aramis ... has become a political slogan, a reference in so many speeches and in so many newspaper articles that it has a life of its own; it can't be stopped ... Contextualisation is fabricated and negotiated like everything else: by tying bigger and bigger pots and pans, more and more of them, to the project's tail. When it stirs it is going to stir up all of France. It makes enough commotion to wake up a minister. (1996: 142–3)

IBRFP was contextualised in the interests and agendas of the UK donor and development professionals through writing and visits, but its staff also summoned large crowds of Bhils for organised public displays that connected the project to wider national audiences and agendas. The calendar of national celebrations, for example, enabled the project to speak to the broad Indian government agenda of tribal development and nation building. Republic Day and Independence Day celebrations in Bhil villages were occasions when the project drew official and public attention to its interventions and the social transformation of marginal tribals into modern Indian citizens that they effected. Considerable efforts went into the organisation of these occasions at which, as the Progress Reports record, 'project function-aries explained the importance and meaning of [the] national anthem and tricolour and the importance of Independence [or Republic] Day'. Poor tribal people 'celebrated with patriotic and devotional songs', while village women conducted the flag-hoisting ceremonies.[10] In 2001 the project made elaborate preparations for some 7,000 Bhils to celebrate Republic Day in villages (in Gujarat) 'where people were totally unaware about this great day'.[11]

These spectacles, which include cultural and sporting programmes with prize-giving, locate popular national identity within a 'narrative that is simultaneously about progress and about the cultural specificity of Indianness' (Skaria 2003). In the project setting they are enactments which, on the one hand, reveal the 'marginality' of adivasis – 'laggards who will be made modern by the unfolding narrative of the nation' (2003) – and, on the other, dramatise their incorporation through project-led development. As an MPR states, the aim was to make 'the community aware about this propitious day' to demonstrate 'a deep sense of patriotism', to 'help us build rapport and close interaction with the tribal community' and jointly to take the 'path of fighting [the] evils of illiteracy, inequality and poverty'.[12]

Linking its activities to these national events as well as international ones such as the International Women's Day or Health Week was a way in which the project created a public for its work of developing tribals. These were dramas performed for an audience of government officials, teachers, politicians, senior managers and other VIP outsiders with whom the project needed to maintain relationships and establish its nationalist credentials, and who were publicly honoured through chairing or prize-giving. Perhaps the most ubiquitous symbol of project success, and an essential element in the preparation for any dignitary's visit, was the 'demonstration PRA', a public symbolic enactment of the transformation of marginal tribals into modern development beneficiaries by the project (see Chapter 4).

These events (as well as outsider visits) simultaneously dramatise underdeveloped backwardness and project success. They draw attention to aspects of IBRFP's work which create (or simulate) authentically local places and local people. PRAs, PVS trials, Self-Help Groups are all 'technologies' for the production of locality, community or indigenousness (cf. Appadurai 1997). They demonstrated fulfilment of 'a desire not only for a certain kind of development practice, but also a desire for a certain kind of "traditional" person [or place] to be first the object and then the product of development efforts' (Pigg 1997: 260). The best exemplars of such transformation were the project *jankars*. So, when in 1995 Independence Day was celebrated as '*Jankars* Day' 'men and women *jankars* from all fields were brought to the dais' where they were acknowledged, appreciated and honoured in front of the KBCL Marketing Director, District Collector, DFO, Additional DDO and 'a large crowd of villagers'. Here they pledged to take up the challenge of community development.[13] Now, because *jankars* were already selected from among the more progressive members of their villages, social differences *within* the community could be presented as progress achieved by means of project action (or individual mobility represented as social change, Weisgrau 1997: 189). Promoting success depended upon the manipulation of 'standard narratives of backwardness and isolation' and (as noted earlier) selection of those already in possession of characteristics that the project aimed to produce (Li 1999: 309); thus considerably amplifying the effect of IBRFP programmes.

Bhil women were especially potent public metonyms of the transforming relationship between the project and its tribal clients: for example, Sakkaben the 'quiet and shy woman ... mute observer', who through contact with the project set up a women's group and then contested and won a panchayat election, or Samudiben who demanded that her savings group make its records public, both of whom were featured in project MPRs.[14] And 'new horizons [were] brought to the light', noted the August MPR in 1998, 'when Veronica Ben (*jankar*) of Itawa village was selected as one of the district representative[s] to update the Chief Minister about the overall progress of the Watershed programme in the district'. A tribal woman speaks to the Chief Minister, and in doing so, the role of KBCL in nation-building at the tribal periphery is celebrated.

In project representations – reports, photographs, brochures – there is indeed a 'feminisation of the beneficiary' (Heaton 2001: 184–5). It is women who best give public expression to development success. They are beneficiaries *par excellence*. Celayne Heaton, working with NGOs in Nepal, suggests further that a public focus on women allows project workers to reconcile the requirement to maintain good relations with beneficiaries while asserting their need for 'development'. Making women the prime targets, the ones who need developing, allows men to deny their negative beneficiary status. At the very least, there is a dilemma: the more development interventions emphasise women and women's needs, the more women become the signifiers of underdevelopment (2001: 185). The dilemma is even more pointed when, in IBRFP, women are the vehicles for displays intended to enrol supporters and shore up success.

So as well as donor officials and KBCL managers, the project had to enrol Government of India bureaucrats responsible for the project, officers of the local administration, agricultural scientists and regional NGOs, among others. Each brought a variety of agendas concerning marketing, research, district development or nationalism to which the project had to relate. Every opportunity was taken to cement relationships with the local administration by implementing government schemes, acting as a nodal agency, or providing 'master trainers' in 'participatory techniques' in a variety of programmes.[15] Increasingly, village *jankars* were called on to represent the project, undertaking PRAs or trainings for the District Collector and so enhancing their status and that of the project. The project's need to extend its connections, and KBCL's marketing imperative, combined well with the ODA's desire to 'replicate the model' (partly to justify high project costs, inflated by expatriate consultant fees).[16] So the project would stretch and amplify the significance of its own links to meet the donor agenda. For example, in December 1996, the MPR reported a six-day training on aspects of PRA with ten scientists from the Indian Grassland and Fodder Research Institute (IGFRI) as 'a milestone achievement for the project [that] reflects the adoption of the project approaches by a national-level institute and the influence on the policy of the same'.[17]

There were of course many explicit reasons to forge connections: in order to facilitate programme work, to acquire necessary expertise, to learn and exchange information or, as ODA administrators would put it, to 'manage the environment'. But the project's investment in 'linkage' far exceeded these pragmatic demands. Staff continuously transacted symbols of project success, from elaborate public ceremonies to the simplest items: gift-wrapped manuals, publications, cards, brochures and photograph albums. As an indicator of the importance attached to 'contextualisation', as much as 20–30 per cent of the space in MPRs came to be devoted to reporting 'links' and visitors (often justified under the ODA rubric of 'dissemination' and 'replication').[18]

In order to understand the imperative to connect, to link or network, it is necessary to appreciate the fragility and uncertainty of meaning in development practice, the hidden contradictions and the unreliability of judgements; the fact, ultimately, that 'development success' is not objectively verifiable but socially produced. It is an institutional process not an objective fact. It is something that is not known in itself, but only by the relationships that emerge around its presence (cf. Harper 2003: 277). Searching out friends and allies was not just a natural part of KBCL's marketing culture. The project needed strong institutional links and extended networks to build its reputation; but, more than this, project existence and survival depended upon maintaining a widening circle of individuals and institutions who would underpin the project as a 'system of representations', provide its context and constitute a reliable interpretive community, a group of 'believers'. Indeed, in a development project as in a magico-religious system, judgements and belief are managed through social relationships: relationships of trust imply belief, they affect judgement (Harper 2003: 277, Pigg 1996). Of course it was not always possible to enrol collaborators. IBRFP's networks were selective and avoided critical or competitive organisations. Networks grew along the lines of power – upwards to suppliers and benefactors (government, researchers), or downwards to dependent agencies (small NGOs). Links with peers, with established, experienced NGOs or those set up by ex-staff, those who could exclude themselves from the community of believers, were typically weak (see Chapter 10).

Maintaining even selective networks and legitimising representations requires considerable work by skilful brokers who read the meaning of the project in the different institutional languages of its stakeholder supporters and so sustain long chains of translation (Latour 1996). And this is why project designs need ambiguity and have to be porous to different agendas (Chapter 2). For projects 'there's no *inertia*, no *irreversibility*; there is no *autonomy* to keep them alive'; no respite from the work of creating interest and making real (1996: 86, emphasis in original). As it progressed, IBRFP agitated more people and agendas, it acquired more actors, and actors of greater stature (cf. 1996: 127). The bigger the network and the more diverse the interests tied up in it, the more stable the project and its policy model, and so the more assured its 'success'. IBRFP had robust networks, an extensive interpretive community which gave it an uncommon resilience. Nobody assumed that participation was easy or the project faultless. Critical writing on the project, including my own, could be routinely included in information packs, raising eyebrows, but mostly adding extra endorsement to the model by demonstrating openness to criticism. As interest spread and the project became the destination of field placements, the subject of masters theses and PhD proposals, this wider interest in the project could itself simultaneously symbolise success, 'spread-effects' and 'wider dissemination'.

HIDDEN COSTS IN A REGIME OF SUCCESS: GATECRASHERS AND DISSENTERS

The more that the success of the project was tied up with its new allies and participants, the more room they took up (Latour 1996: 127). The more people that were invited to the party, the more energy was expended attending to their needs, and the more their needs shaped the project. The District Collector favoured mushroom growing and needed a *rabi* seeds programme for the district (Chapter 4). He also required an implementing agency for his watershed and women's development programmes. ODA advisers, consultants and researchers, KBCL managers, government officers or politicians made other demands and had other ideas for the project to materialise (Chapter 4), and their information needs had now to be met.[19] The effort required to manage links and relations began seriously to compete for attention with programme work in villages. External commitments (reporting, training, dissemination and the satisfaction of officials) made demands on staff that were always more urgent than routine work in the field. This only increased pressure for strong managerial control over the delivery of standard, high-profile visible activities.

By the late 1990s, IBRFP's field team responded to the pressure of success with a new division of labour. 'Some were high performance COs – good at spending money, [others] were good 'cos of linking with government: [A] had good presentation skills; [B] had good local rapport ...' (former CO). Senior staff and managers were increasingly committed outside. Some staff began to talk of 'over-linkage'; others of 'visitor-driven programme[s] with showcase package model villages' . Still others spoke perceptively of the stunted development and halted learning of the project arising from 'trying to capitalise relationships on each and every step, which takes you to those favoured steps only, again and again'. The combination of external orientation ('contextualisation') and internal routinisation deprived the project of the rich learning and field adaptation that could have been its hallmark. Even the most senior, committed and loyal staff admitted that project systems and the swell of praise inhibited experimentation, innovation and learning from farmer knowledge of SWC methods, fodder species or the crops–fodder–livestock complex.

The project's regime of success also fostered doubts and corroded ideals among field staff. A system in which the rewards for managing representations appear to be greater than those for facilitating community development, surrounds purpose with uncertainty. This easily turns to the kind of frustration and resentment that was palpable in my interviews with former field staff, whose testimony questioned both the validity of project representations and the success of the model. On the manipulation of project data one says:

> Look. those 'quantitative' things. I mean, like, I was there. I developed a format. And then half of them used to come [back from the villages], half of them I used to cook, right ... And they never ask what I am doing ... So [management] thought [the] job was probably more to market the project, because that was giving a lot of incentives. Marketing the project rather than working in the project ...

Some questioned whether they really had lessons to disseminate, or whether they were just regurgitating participatory theory ('from some IIED book') in the guise of experience. But, above all, these fieldworkers were self-critical and had a sense of having failed villagers, of having been seduced by 'success'. 'We put our legs on villagers to come up ourselves; we learned, we experimented with different things, but at what cost?' asked one. Another asserted:

> ... complacency, complacency! I do 5 metres of field bunding and I get so much of reward ... we were in the air, forgetting about the people ... Everybody liked that fame ... our age and maturity. [We thought], fine this is great, our project is talked about so much, our project is covered by TV crews, television networks and there are lots of papers about our project ... and plenty of visitors ... and also we learned the technique of how to satisfy the visitors ... you talk about participatory process, you know community problem analysis, this diagram and all this. And during this two years or three years ... we built such a nice rapport with the villagers, you know, because of our initial training or whatever, our sensitivity, our orientation and we all sat in their kitchens, we even know how much cowdung cake was used [for the fire] ... [they didn't criticise us] ... You have to go back to the culture of these people. They are tribals, very good people in their heart. You know, their self-respect [is] so high, they would not beg. So, what they want – a simple smile a pat on their back from a pant-shirt walla like [me] is a great honour

for them. Y'know they don't need any other promise or commitment from you …

Although such statements from ex-staff have their own specific social context (and while, as Chapter 9 will show, they are not an accurate reflection of the overall significance of project interventions) they do capture an unease, anxiety and 'false atmosphere' that is palpable in any regime of success oriented towards external expectations. Nonetheless the confessional tone over-dramatises the role of field staff and underestimates the active collusion of Bhil villagers in building the project reputation. Villagers concur in representations of their needs, help meet targets, agree to 'participate', to attend meetings, to train as volunteers or to save; they are willing to host visitors, monitor missions or evaluation studies, and in other ways validate both the wider project and staff performance within it, in order to gain access to benefits that *are* important to them – wage-labour, low-interest credit, agro-inputs, pumps or tree nurseries – and, above all, to retain locally influential patrons and benefactors.

In the regime of success, such doubts and dissension from below are scattered and isolated, buried in personal experience, while:

> … enthusiasms come together on high … [E]very time someone up above asks somebody down below for an opinion … the person up above gets an opinion that's more positive than the one the person below really holds because the people down below revise their opinions so that they'll jibe with what they think the people above really want. (Latour 1996: 154, 160)

There are intermediaries (to further paraphrase and adapt Latour) who transform the fieldworkers' doubts into near certainties, so decision makers (managers and donors) think the project is technically viable as well as politically opportune: 'and the same intermediaries transform the decision makers' fears into near-certainties, into orders given to the [field staff]. So the [field staff] think [IBRFP] has political support … Everyone is unanimous about [IBRFP], but, as in a poker game, nobody thinks that the others are bluffing' (1996: 160).

MID-TERM REVIEW – A CRISIS OF REPRESENTATION

The apparently secure foundation of project success was first jolted early in 1996, not by muted internal dissension and fieldworker anxiety, but by IBRFP's external Mid-Term Review (MTR), and the 'independent study' which preceded it (Shah et al. 1996). This study (by a team jointly assembled by the project and donor) was striking in its refusal to accept the validity of the prevailing criteria of success, namely the concept of 'participation' itself, or to accept the assumptions of the model that more participation equals better programmes and impact. Indeed, the report criticised the project for having *too much* participation and too little impact.

The study team met a confident and articulate project staff preoccupied with sustaining a model of participation. They would speak of little else. When asked to prioritise project goals and purpose, 'participation' received the highest score; their time was devoted to 'participatory process'; participation was normative principle, guide for action, and framework of meaning and interpretation. But these outside evaluators were not predisposed to be drawn into the project's discursive regime. With the polite understatement of the genre, their report pointed to the narrow programme focus that had resulted from application of a routine, technique-driven 'participation package', and which had failed to generate new information, problems or solutions. In particular, they indicated that a preoccupation with 'participation' had become isolated from concern with people's livelihoods, and had actually produced programmes that were technically weak, unimaginative, with limited coverage given the project's resources, and which ignored important elements of Bhil livelihoods, namely water resources and seasonal labour migration. It was they who raised the question of 'What measure of women's empowerment does quantified equality of presence actually provide?'

The evaluators had broken ranks with the project's interpretive community, and questioned the assumptions of the model. Suddenly, extravagant claims about the impact of PRA training (above), or statements that 'village meetings have been the core activity during the month'[20] exposed the project. The project did not, in fact, have a model that worked or could be replicated. And worse, it was guilty of purveying participation illusions. The report cynically noted that:

> ... being accountable for generating measurable impacts is far tougher than being accountable for faithfully using a hazy, intangible, almost ephemeral, participatory planning process [PPP]. For the same reasons, GOs and NGOs may be strongly attracted to adopt IBRFP's PPP approach, especially if they can find funders to support them without having to show concrete livelihood impacts. (Shah et al. 1996)

We rose to defend ourselves. I wrote to the study team leader in February 1996 to insist that they were wrong to oppose 'participation/ process' and 'livelihoods/impact'; surely the separation of the two indicated too *little* participation, not too much. While their analysis perceived a disjuncture between representations (participation process leading to livelihood changes) and operations (routine techniques producing little impact), I clung to the 'implementable model' and wanted to make it better, more sophisticated. They were right; I was wrong. Other members of the consultant and project team took exception to other conclusions of the study: that the yield benefits from improved varieties were marginal; that SWC was principally viewed by people as an employment-generation scheme; that the trees programme had yet to deliver benefits and over-emphasised eucalyptus; in short, that the economic impact of programmes was rather insignificant. Some vigorously contested the study's research methods and data – particularly its sampling procedure (see Chapter 9). But still, the evaluation had unsettled certainty and shown the nature of project effects and the causal links of the model to be contestable. If the celebrated 'participatory planning process' could be seen as ephemeral, and if the yield increase of the most successful new variety Kalinga III could be portrayed as either 46 per cent or 6 per cent, depending upon method and assumptions,[21] then strong networks of support to stabilise the interpretation were more important than ever.

Now, such studies rarely if ever give grounds for donor disenchantment in projects that find support for other political or administrative reasons, and the project had survived critical commentary before. However, on this occasion, the official ODA Project Review Mission (1996) which followed the evaluation study did not limit itself to the usual concerns of implementation efficiency, speed and expansion, but sustained the challenge to the master metaphor, participation. The IBRFP project, designed on an early-1990s wave of criticism of top-down technology-driven state programmes, now had to answer awkward questions about the transaction costs of participation, how much participation was needed, whether the project would ever leave, or what was the evidence of impact? The participatory approach had to be justified against an alternative 'investment approach'. Why had a project so secure in success suddenly become vulnerable? Well one thing is sure, it was not because ODA advisers had acquired a new capacity to penetrate the reality of project practice. Rather, it was because they were asking different questions. The external (ODA) policy environment was changing. How?

In 1995 the administrative centre of the ODA's India aid programme was decentralised from Victoria Street (London) to the vacated Polish embassy building in leafy diplomatic south Delhi, and reconstituted as the Development Co-operation Office Delhi (DCOD) with satellite Field Management Offices for different sectors (health, education, forestry, etc.) and a cadre of Indian Project Officers. The move brought senior management closer to the complex institutional reality of the ODA's field programmes, their many stakeholders and processes. On the one hand, this justified extended project design phases, partner dialogue and flexible process approaches. On the other hand, it brought a new managerialism to project processes which required that ODA staff be equipped with new tools and models to manage this complexity and turn it to the rational purposes of the aid programme (e.g. Logical Framework Analysis, Stakeholder Analysis, Impact Assessment, Gender Appraisal). In particular, there was a more analytical approach to project design, and demand for clarity about the causal relationship between donor-supported activities and the now more clearly articulated poverty-reduction goals[22] (cf. Shepherd et al. 2000). In short, ODA management wanted not more reality but better models, and to this end a US management consultancy 'Team Technologies' was contracted to train ODA staff and project teams in model making using the patented logical framework-based TeamUp™ method (see Chapter 2).

The ODA's move to Delhi also brought new ambitions. The rubric of 'value-for-money' that justified high expatriate costs demanded (i) the transformation of a diffuse collection of isolated projects into a rational and integrated programme, (ii) expansion and replication of successful rural development models on a scale 'capable of attracting the attention ... of district, state and national politicians, administrators, technocrats and businessmen responsible ... ',[23] and (iii) the use of these to influence Indian government policy. No project could be justified in and of itself. Projects like IBRFP had to expand, replicate and 'be capable of wider influence to justify their costs'.[24] But they also had to deliver. The new aid management regime unfolding in Delhi in 1995–7 demanded information on the impact of aid projects on poverty, which could no longer be left to *ex-post* evaluations. Spurred by a UK government spending review that required information on how ODA was achieving its objectives, and informed by work on impact indicators and participatory monitoring by IDS Sussex, Action Aid and GTZ, as well as ODA's own Evaluation Department, 'impact assessment' became a 'movement' within the organisation. New questions were asked about the socio-economic *effects* of projects like IBRFP accustomed to accounting for expenditure or programme activities. At the same time, the presence of greater numbers of 'cross-cutting' social development and institutional advisers was prising open the black box of participation and its assumptions about sustainability or gender equity.

So, when the ODA review team – unusually led by the administrative head of the India aid programme – arrived in IBRFP's Dahod office in April 1996, they were concerned more with *premise* than progress or promise. IBRFP and its model of participatory farming systems development was something of a test case for the application of new policy and aid management theory. Cost-efficiency, impact, agency withdrawal, policy influence, scaling-up and replicability; these were the terms that shaped conversations and filtered the experience of visits to Bhil villages. Above all, it was not the *practice* of the project that the ODA team was scrutinising, but its *theory*. The ODA's interest was in the project as a coherent rationalising policy idea, not in the events and relationships of practice (the 'operational system'). If this was a project crisis, it was a *crisis of representation* in which participation was no longer an adequate metaphor for the development process. The project was vulnerable to 'failure' not because of its practice, but because a new (ODA) policy environment made it harder for the project to articulate with the preoccupations and ambitions of its donor supporters and interlocutors. Indeed, the ODA review team did not ask the project to change what it did, but to modify its *theory* in order to bring it into line with new 1995–6 thinking on matters such as impact assessment, project cycle management or value-for-money. The Review Team insisted that the project revise its logframe, changing its Purpose from 'a participatory *approach* ... ', to 'sustainable improvements in livelihoods ... ', and that it 'clarify the instrumentality between process and benefits ... ' (i.e. produce an 'impact model' to explain the relationship between what the project was doing and the changes in people's lives).

REFRAMING IBRFP: RETURN TO 'THE HEAVEN OF IDEAS'

The project never did clarify the instrumentality of its model, instead it focused on demonstrating impact through a series of detailed impact assessment studies that included economic surveys of crops and SWC, forestry and irrigation, and eight detailed village case studies undertaken between 1996 and 1998. There was, in addition, a study of seasonal labour migration which I coordinated in 1996–7 (Mosse et al. 2002). Some of the empirical findings of these studies (which I co-coordinated) are discussed in Chapter 9, but the point to emphasise here is that while their stated aim was to reveal the impact of the project model on tribal livelihoods, their immediate purpose and practical effect was to model rural livelihoods so as to show how project interventions (realigned within a new policy framework) would improve them; that is, to clarify and justify a new development model rather than demonstrate its effects.[25] After all, this was the most urgent need for project survival, or as Quarles van Ufford suggests, showing the need for further action is always politically more important than demonstrating results (1988a: 25).

At the time, IBRFP studies paralleled (perhaps even anticipated) the ODA's new London-based policy work on rural development which brought a shift away from both the productivity-focused idea of improving rainfed farming and the natural resources-focused concept of watershed development towards the people-focused concept of sustainable rural livelihoods, centring on the multiple livelihood options and strategies of the poor (Carney 1998, Scoones 1998).[26] ODA staff considered that the approach to rural development in India had 'focused too much on the promotion of natural capital (FS and forestry) at the expense of other issues important for people's needs',[27] when it was clear that, as the chief livelihoods adviser put it, 'the forests weren't really separate from the rice paddies, and they weren't separate from carrying bricks in urban areas'.[28] At the same time, the concept of rural livelihoods also served institutional ends by helping DFID managers resolve disciplinary conflicts between natural resources and social development advisers. At any rate, by 1999, 'rural livelihoods' had taken root in DFID as the new way of 'thinking about setting objectives in development'[29] and the way of reorganising (and renaming) old natural resources departments and advisers in London and Delhi. But as early as 1996 our (IBRFP) studies were already responding to gathering expectations of the policy shift. They produced a dynamic and socially differentiated 'model of change' showing that the synergies of project action (physical and institutional) had meaning and impact in the context not only of low crop yields, eroded land or deforested hills, but also of deficit-induced debt and dependence and the vulnerabilities of seasonal migration, disease or drought (see Chapter 9).

These studies ensured that Bhil livelihoods and the project model were *both* conceptualised in a way that tracked shifts in the ODA/DFID's policy. They were not oriented to changing project practice. Indeed, there is nothing to suggest that the new sustainable rural livelihood framework actually improved the scope for social analysis or open-ended planning at the village level (cf. Rew and Rew 2003). Rather, timely analytical work between 1997 and 1998 'recontextualised' the project by reconnecting its model of development to new trends emerging from London, making IBRFP once again an exemplar and an effective container for ODA/DFID policy.[30] The crisis of representation was resolved; for now, the project would not be allowed to fail. In fact our studies were part of a collaborative effort by the project staff, consultants and ODA/DFID advisers to rebuild project success that had another intention, namely the justification of funding for a much expanded £27 million Second Phase, a seven-year project working not in 75 but 275 'core' villages, whose purpose will have been achieved by the year 2005 if the 'livelihoods of 675,000 poor rural people in selected areas of western India [are] sustainably enhanced and [the] technologies and approaches used [are] widely disseminated'.[31] It would spread its effects to an additional 1,050 villages including 550 adjacent 'dissemination' villages benefiting from transferred technologies and have an entire component devoted to 'disseminating project technologies and approaches through partnerships' with government, NGOs and other organisations.[32] The administrative discourse of the 'project cycle' had again allowed the recovery of optimism: failure was relegated to the past, hope reserved for the future (Quarles von Ufford and Roth 2003). As we withdrew from the contingencies and relationships of practice and reproduced IBRFP as a sophisticated rational project design presented in conferences, in papers, in brochures, pamphlets and handouts, the project retreated back into text, returning to 'the heaven of ideas'.

CONCLUSION

So the general argument is that development projects are 'successful' not because they turn design into reality, but because they sustain policy models offering a significant interpretation of events. They are *made* successful by social processes that disperse project agency (Li 1999: 304), forge and maintain networks of support, and create a public audience for their work of social transformation. Project staff work hard to maintain representations even while, to varying degrees, they are aware of and uneasy about the contradictions that underlie growing coherence. Likewise the work of consultant and donor staff suppresses what is in fact growing frustration with the effects of IBRFP-KBCL's operational systems (delays, administrative lethargy, unfilled posts, the failure to devolve financial or personnel decision making powers, and their negative impact on staff morale) in a primary effort to secure the project as theory and representation.[33] In other words, policy models do not generate practices, they are sustained *by* them. Development proceeds not only (or primarily) from policy to practice, but also from practice to policy. Correspondingly, project failure is not the failure to turn designs into reality; but the consequence of a certain disarticulation between practices, their rationalising models and overarching policy frameworks. Failure is not a failure to implement the plan, but a *failure of interpretation*. As I have shown, such failures are corrected by conceptual rather than practical work; and here evaluation and impact studies have a key role. In IBRFP, our studies were not a means to discover the facts of project operations, but an exercise establishing *ex post facto* rationality and consistency with (new) policy.[34] The information they generated did not help 'to manage decision making, but to account for it to the ministry' (Quarles van Ufford 1988b: 90). Specifically, what these studies did *not* do was to investigate the operational system and social relationships that produced project outcomes. They could not distinguish impacts from efficient vertical delivery and patronage from those of farmer-led development. The relationship between participatory policy and livelihood impacts was no clearer, and inherent contradictions were evaded.

The IBRFP project, remodelled in preparation for its new phase emerged bigger and more beautiful. According to the fifth and final Annual Review of Phase I (December 1998)

> The project ... approach can now clearly be seen as a resounding success. The mission was impressed with the breadth and variety of activities and the competence of their execution. Our eyes were opened wide by the capacity of the village professionals (Jankars) and by their potential to contribute to project expansion and influence. Out of the confidence the project has helped create, village communities are becoming self determining and Self Help Groups (SHGs) are becoming entrepreneurial and developing new business skills ... Core staff are now very experienced and maintain that four years with the project is worth 20 years elsewhere.

Their enthusiasm, breadth of knowledge, empathy with villagers and *esprit de corps* are impressive.[35]

Those who joined the DFID–India team during 1997 and 1998 describe IBRFP as 'absolutely cutting edge, the coalface ... The message [was] that, as far as DFID, not just DFID India, and development in general [was concerned] this was where it was all happening' (DFID Adviser, Delhi). IBRFP was the 'jewel in the crown'. It comprised a set of highly innovative, successful and replicable components – the innovation of participatory varietal selection, the power of groups, the system of *jankars* – which cohered into a whole, and which had to be part of any future DFID rural development initiative.

But two years later, in December 2000, the DFID Annual Review (the first of IBRFP Phase II) wrote one of the most critical reports ever written on a project. In the previous 20 months, the project progress in implementation was judged to be 'very disappointing' or 'negligible'. Only 8 per cent of the budget had been spent.

> ... as yet, few villages have work plans and almost no development activities have been undertaken ... [the project] has yet to develop and implement a strategy to influence the policies and programmes of government and other organisations ... [there is] weak management at all levels of the organisation [and] the failure to address the urgent needs of drought-affected people in the region showed management to be out of touch and ineffective ...

The project was given four months to demonstrate that it could overcome its problems, but if it failed to meet milestones set following the 'mission', its funds would be substantially reduced, re-channelled or even possibly the project permanently closed down. What on earth had happened? How had success turned so dramatically to failure? This is the subject of the next chapter.

8
Aid Policy and Project Failure

> Projects do not fail, they are failed. Maybe policy fails projects (as in terminates them). Failure is manufactured not inherent. (Latour 1996: 35–6)

Development success depends upon socially sustained interpretations, which Chapter 7 shows are also vulnerable to the effects of policy change. But when at one moment a project appears as the most successful DFID project of all time, and at another sits on development's 'death row', we have to examine changes not just in frameworks of interpretation but also in the alliances, the mediators, the chains of translations, interests and agendas that are tied up in a project and ask what happened to them. In this chapter, it will become clear that major policy change involves the rupture of the relationships that make a development project function and secure its reputation. If 'success' depends upon extending networks and enrolling more and bigger people and their interests, failure is produced by the cascading effect of individuals disconnecting the fate of their ambitions from the fate of a project: a form of 'decontextualisation' in which a project has fewer and fewer pots and pans tied to its tail; it makes a smaller noise and awakens fewer people of less importance (Latour 1996: 137). The failure in interpretation is a social failure. At a certain point (which will be explained) IBRFP began to lose support, and as this happened it began to lose reality, so that an Annual Review could conclude that nothing was happening, the landscape was empty, Bhil villagers' needs were not being met and the project was invisible to District Collectors, even its hold on its own staff was tenuous; it had no capacity.

So, this chapter will examine the interlinked shifts that produced IBRFP 'failure' in 1999 and 2000. Some of the problems faced by the project arose directly or indirectly from the drive to policy coherence that came with the formulation of its Phase II; some derived from changes in a broader DFID policy environment brought by the UK Labour government in 1997 and interpreted through its staff working in Delhi. I will deal with each of these in turn, moving from the project itself to the wider policy environment. In this way I hope to exemplify and address wider questions concerning the relationship between policy and practice in development, and explore some of the issues and contradictions of current British aid policy in India, and the effects of policy change. We will view IBRFP, then, as one element in a shifting aid world, part of the contradictory impulses that donor aid workers have to manage.[1]

POLICY COHERENCE AND INSTITUTIONAL INCOHERENCE

Those British and Indian staff who sat in Delhi attending to DFID's ambitions and working to reinstate IBRFP as a viable design at the start of its Phase II were involved in a purified assertion of donor policy over institutions and relations that was to have damaging effects.

First of all, re-framing the project as a policy-driven technical discourse overlooked complex questions of institutional capacity and gave currency to a grossly simplified view of 'up-scaling', 'mainstreaming', 'fast-tracking' and 'replication'. A huge burden was placed on a complex and shaky system: the project had to create a new organisational structure (see below), to quadruple the size of its operations, recruit and train well over a hundred new staff including senior fertiliser men who knew little about rural development, fast-track its process (reduce village entry time), while retaining its intense focus on participation, 'cutting its costs' by transferring tasks to trained village *jankars* and framing an 'exit-strategy'.[2] The same ODA advisers who had asked the project to question and rethink its core model, now demanded that it disseminate its *proven* approach and technologies, replicate its (otherwise over-expensive) model, exert policy influence (over systems of rural development or crop certification), increase 'linkage' to the structures of government (including local panchayat raj) as well as to NGOs, the private commercial sector, markets, banks and research institutes, and 'become a laboratory [that] ... will generate ideas, technologies and approaches of value to the rest of the [aid] portfolio and provide a dynamic centre for demonstration, training and learning'.[3] The paper ambitions of policy knew few bounds, and little of the new contradictions they were writing into the project system, which would unfold in time. Sustaining itself as a new and sophisticated system of representations, while the criteria of failure multiplied, would be demanding indeed.

Second, and more seriously, the new ODA-orchestrated policy consensus significantly overlooked the unstated interests, hierarchical relations and culture of the project agency KBCL. Or rather these were pathologised as a problem to be contained in the new phase. 'Overall progress', noted the Phase II project document, had been 'constrained by the need to follow the management systems and procedures of the mainline KBCL organisation' which were unsuited to an innovative process project working with poor farmers in a remote area.[4] So when approving the Phase II project, DFID expected KBCL to significantly change its institutional arrangements so as to increase the autonomy of the project, by creating either a separate Division or a separate legal entity, a Trust, to manage the project independent from prevailing KBCL structures and systems. Partly because of its own anxiety about taking on long-term liability for a large number of new staff, KBCL did indeed form a separate Trust with a governing Board composed of ex-officio KBCL directors, Indian government and DFID representatives and independent (NGO/academic) members, and the project manager as member secretary. But this donor-encouraged effort to weaken the link between the project and the mainline KBCL immediately unleashed highly disruptive attempts to grasp back control and security, both by senior KBCL management and project staff.

For some time, ODA/DFID advisers had been trying to weaken the central bureaucratic control of KBCL over the project. So it was not hard to see how some in KBCL would view the formation of an autonomous Trust in April 1999 as a challenge to their authority over the project. It was not surprising, therefore, that KBCL senior managers/directors attempted to assert *de facto* control over an institution, the formal control of which was slipping from their grasp. KBCL formed a minority of trustees on the Board, and the structure of the Trust meant that its control over the project was no longer possible through the carefully articulated hierarchical relationships and brokerage which had earlier allowed the translation of project goals and KBCL system goals into one another. In the transition to Phase II, these relations were disrupted, not least by the departure of one of the key senior brokers, the KBCL Marketing Director. The loss of this 'cover' exposed the project (and especially its manager) to the unmediated attention of KBCL top bosses. The formal structures of the Trust provided little protection against their informal action.

One instance of this was a rash of politically mediated *sifarishi* appointments (staff with 'recommendations'). These were one way for KBCL managers to influence the project through their kinsmen or those of their political bosses, and so to reincorporate the project into the cultural mainstream of the organisation (as well to forge their own personal and political alliances). In the interpretation of many in the project, one of the key objectives of KBCL bosses was to use senior appointments in the project team to mount a challenge to the project manager for fear that, backed by DFID, he would assert his own personal control over the new Trust. A quite remarkable series of appointments, transfers, allegations of impropriety and the manipulation of factions was involved here, playing on latent networks of caste, on staff aspirations and insecurities. Among the mutinous factions were a group of 16 of the most experienced staff (with the project for 6–7 years) who had filed a court case against KBCL for unfair dismissal at the end of the project's first phase to demand the right to permanent employment. This was a disgruntled group, alienated by personal insecurities released in the transition to the Trust and complaining of arbitrary treatment, of penalties, and appraisals designed to pressurise them into giving up their case against KBCL. They were easily aligned against the project manager who they mistakenly viewed as the source of their problems.

This 'carnival of division', reminiscent of an election campaign, presents a striking contrast to the 'rituals of unity' evident during donor review missions, and so highly praised not long before as the project's impressive *esprit de corps*.[5] Such contests for control over new institutions, especially where they involve high-profile avenues to status or access to resources, are familiar to anthropologists of South Asia (as well as to project field staff observing the politics around Self-Help Groups in Bhil villages) (cf. Mosse 2003b: 276–87). Mines and Gourishankar have argued that in India leadership is characteristically exerted through institutions. The Indian 'big-man' is an '*institutional* big-man' defined by the institutions which he controls and which establish publicly his credibility as a trustworthy individual and a generous and altruistic benefactor of the public good (1990: 762). The wide range of institutions through which leadership is enacted include temples, charities, schools, loan societies, self-help groups, political parties, labour unions or NGOs. Arguably, individuals *need* institutions to head in order to become or remain leaders (1990: 764). In this sense, the Trust represented a symbolic resource over which KBCL bosses needed to regain control; or at least they (and some project staff) intended to prevent the project manager from becoming an 'institutional big-man' through control over the Trust. Equally familiar to those who work with donor-funded projects is the anxiety of staff who are on short-term contracts linked to external funding (Ahmad 2002), a fact which has a powerful influence on incentives, and on the way projects are managed and represented.

But perhaps less obvious is the fact that it was the imposed rationalities of donor policy that released this institutional disorder. Among the effects of the project's transition was disruption of the very systems which ordinarily produced coherence (results, success, support and internal solidarity) from the contingencies of practice by reliably translating between the field of action on the one hand, and the system goals of KBCL or the policy models of DFID on the other. This translation allowed a degree of project autonomy (from organisational hierarchy or the demands of policy) and was necessary to ensuring security of employment. The Phase II project lost more than key individuals who brokered upward links within the KBCL hierarchy. It also lost the key DFID senior adviser who had advocated the project within the donor agency, and when the University of Wales lost the consultancy contract to W.S. Atkins International Ltd, the project lost its original consultant team too. In other words, the apparent chaos of the project was in part a product of the disruption of the wider social systems that mediated and stabilised interpretations. From another point of view the 'carnival of division' was a display of institutional *resistance* to an unmediated imposition of a donor policy agenda.

The fact that the new Trust became a battlefield for control, and the fact that a body of highly experienced and skilled staff sought employment futures through litigation, signals the failure to manage project-cycle-induced uncertainty. The breakdown of the informal relations of the project's operational system seriously disturbed the fragile securities of employees and made the project manager a victim of the logics and cultural politics of institutional leadership. There were several months of personal (dis)stress before a modicum of stability was reasserted, although the litigious staff lost their case and their jobs, and KBCL retained control over the project manager, subjecting him to a committee of inquiry which two years later led to his temporary suspension and eventual resignation. Brokers at institutional interfaces are as vulnerable as they are necessary in aid projects.

DFID's textually mediated process of change was incapable of capturing the real uncertainties and social disruptions that it generated; and even if individuals (e.g. advisers) had relevant knowledge, the official discourse (e.g. of Review Missions) refused an institutional analysis, resorting instead to diagnostic simplifications such as 'weak management' which neglected to draw DFID's own decision making and its effects into the frame. In fact, DFID construed the complex effects of a change in the relationship between donor patron and project client as operational failure. But in reality, project operations and field practices – what project staff actually did – changed little in the shift from success to failure.

CONTINUITY OF FIELD PRACTICE

The DFID mission to determine the fate of the IBRFP project in May 2001 was preceded by an 'Independent Review' of the project's 'capacity to implement participatory rural development'. I undertook that review along with Supriya Akerkar. It was not an easy exercise, to hold discussions with people anxiously facing the prospect of the humiliating loss of careers and reputations. Reactions to DFID's ultimatum (which was taken utterly seriously) were complex. Of course there was the extreme desire to please and to display achievements, but also an embarrassment and vulnerability, which gave us an uncomfortable power; our every need anticipated, our every expression keenly observed for signs of destiny. But we knew these people well, we had worked with many of them over ten years. Supriya had been a member of the project team in the early years, and I had an association from the beginning. As we talked with specialists in offices over tea, or with fieldworkers in small hot rooms, or walked once again across the rolling Bhil landscape, or bumped along in jeeps, or sat with exhausted and harassed managers late into the night over a beer, we were able to detect multiple strands of feeling.

Here was a project that had lost its interpretive community and its context, whose networks were in tatters. Among senior staff this left a sense of confusion and betrayal; betrayal by the donor and its brokers who had so consistently supported and promoted the project, but turned their back on it during a difficult transition. There was a feeling that DFID had abandoned the ideal of partnership, refused to take responsibility for changes that they had insisted upon, had denied the project understanding and ignored the process. DFID staff had participated in Board meetings and were not ignorant of events, but they had failed to contextualise; their judgements had become arbitrary.

As we travelled among the parched Bhil villages in the company of project staff in the burning heat of April (2001) after a year of failed monsoons, it occurred to us that the practical performance of the project had been misjudged. There were complex but intelligible reasons why spending and physical works had been slow up to the previous December besides the organisational problems, and it was hard to see how more could have been expected. With the threat of closure, and in order to address DFID criticism, staff had accelerated the delivery of 'drought relief' works, including SWC, well deepening, hand-pump repair/installation, veterinary camps and group credit, which they argued had helped to alleviate the drought-induced problems of unemployment, labour migration, low grain stocks, fodder and drinking water scarcity or cattle disease; a view that in some places villagers endorsed. But in fact, the anxiety to show progress forced unrealistic claims. For example, the 183 project 'grain banks' were certainly not going to solve problems of food shortage. Many were not sustainable, and even as a relief measure the grain 'bank' made a small contribution, perhaps feeding a family for one month or so. In reality the scale of the drought problem was well beyond the reach of the project, which (as an agent for long-term development) was probably ill-advised to introduce itself in new areas by responding to demands for *ad hoc* relief through accelerating its development work.[6] But in this, as in other areas of their work, the project staff were unable to negotiate the possible. They felt under intense pressure to comply with donor demands. And compliance pays dividends: condemned in December (2000) for failing to 'respond to the urgent needs of communities severely affected by the drought', seven months later the project was being held up as a model of 'drought proofing' to be documented, presented in seminars, filmed, sung about in villages and held up to government.[7] How fickle are the interpretations of development!

In 2000–1 donor pressure for results had the immediate effect of amplifying the well-established contradictions of participatory development, turning the project into a target-oriented spending machine and reinforcing vertical control over programme delivery. Internal relations of command and control were strengthened. Project managers took 'weak management' to mean field-level inefficiency and issued stringent instructions down the line to speed up activities. The opportunity costs of participation (let alone the strategic integrations of sustainable livelihoods) were as great as ever. Field staff were informed of their 'dismal performance' (often measured in terms of levels of expenditure in their villages). Employees were reviewed fortnightly; many were put on probation, transferred or threatened with dismissal. Since insubordination was equated with inefficiency, the gang of 'court case' staff became scapegoats for poor project performance. When they boycotted performance appraisals they were sacked.

In the throes of a crisis, the project bureaucracy reaffirmed its structure. Operational staff were segregated into programme-sector teams to maximise delivery of outputs in the short term; senior management worked to reinstate the project's identity, its systems of representations and networks of support. Indeed the crisis of transition increased the energy and efforts put into the production of a new array of strategy papers and pamphlets, publications, pictures and public ceremonies expressing the new model of sustainable rural livelihoods. Once again, the project etched the Bhil landscape with contour bunds, tree pits, gabion structures and wells; and once again a powerful representational machinery allowed these to be read as sustainable livelihood impacts. Project contradictions were not only concealed but also reproduced among staff. Supriya and I were again struck by the sharp distinction between, on the one hand, a confident articulation of the project narrative of participatory development and sustainable livelihoods by staff, and, on the other, their account of the everyday practical world of programme delivery (see Chapter 6).

There was, in all, a remarkable continuity of project practice. The dramatic shift from star status to near closure (from an agriculture to a livelihoods project) was not accompanied by any change in what was actually going on in project offices and Bhil villages. Field staff were as hardworking, sincere and talented as ever; skilled in the art of negotiating project contradictions and community relations, and were increasingly joined in this by a cadre of village *jankars*. Participatory planning was no less compromised by the exigencies of programme delivery, and client farmer groups continued to contradict the policy model of micro-finance institutions (Chapter 6).[8] The issues we raised in our April 2001 report were no different from those in reports of 1998, '96 or '94. Despite changes in its model and its institutional arrangements, the project reproduced enough of its procedures, its culture of accountability, marketing and patronage to ensure that its particular way of doing things persisted. Since these were not the result of policy design, they were not changed by it either. The project raised similar problems and similar hopes. Meaningful engagements between villagers and the project still produced important local benefits even under conditions of severe drought. In short, I was as puzzled by the project's recent 'failure' as I had by been by its earlier 'success'.

A quite fundamental change *had* occurred though, not in the field practices, but in the DFID policy that the project was required to affirm in order to exist. A new policy environment, beyond the shift to 'sustainable rural livelihoods', made the ruptures of transition (from Phase I to Phase II) potentially lethal. As the brokering networks that sustained project reality by linking it to higher policy came apart, IBRFP fell into the policy shadows. It slipped from the present (or future) into the past. IBRFP became an archive, perhaps no more than a usable symbol (e.g. of DFID's past experience in dryland India) in negotiations within the wider policy game and in relation to newer and bigger programmes.[9] It is necessary now to shift to the perspective of this wider aid policy environment in order to understand how the IBRFP lost its validating framework, its interpretive community and its capacity to translate between policy and practice.

A NEW DFID POLICY ENVIRONMENT IN INDIA

Shortly after coming to power in 1997 the new Labour government set out the agenda for its Department for International Development in a White Paper (DFID 1997). Perhaps for the first time British overseas aid was given a coherent policy and a single overriding objective, namely the reduction of world poverty. Why a firm policy shift towards the reduction of poverty should threaten a project with an intense focus on the poor in some of the world's poorest districts is not immediately obvious. It was not, in fact, DFID's broad policy objective, but the strategies chosen to achieve it that challenged IBRFP, and in particular the new conception of development 'partnerships' with aid recipient countries.

In the early 1990s, DFID (then the ODA) sought influence though designing projects outside the state framework 'to demonstrate innovative, sustainable and replicable approaches'.[10] As a Delhi-based adviser put it, 'it didn't matter how much you spent within the bubble. It worked, you reduced poverty and all you had to do was to make lots more bubbles.' The 1997 White Paper was critical of this proliferation of small projects and of the chaotic marketplace of aid flows which had resulted in a 'Balkanisation of the Third World', making it virtually impossible for countries to generate comprehensive pro-poor national plans and discouraging of reforms to improve government effectiveness (DFID 2000: 94; Quarles van Ufford 1988a: 27). The White Paper announced (*inter alia*) a move 'away from supporting specific projects to providing resources more strategically in support of sector-wide programmes or the economy as a whole' (DFID 2000: 38).[11] The new policy language set up an opposition between 'projects' and 'partnerships', placing the former in the category of the neo-colonial (unequal or paternalistic), while stressing the equity (government-to-government) of the latter (Dahl 2001: 15–17).[12]

In India this meant a decisive shift away from ring-fenced donor or parastatal project structures (such as IBRFP) and (back) to working within state systems. India was home to half a billion of the world's poorest people and development efforts here would be crucial to realising DFID's commitment to the international development target of 'a reduction of by one-half in the proportion of people living in extreme poverty by 2015' (OECD 1996). Only government had the resources to allow work of a sufficient scale and continuity to have any meaningful impact. Total development assistance to India amounted to as little as 1 per cent of the GDP. DFID aid projects were 'spots on a canvas' whose impact on poverty was further limited by the lack of convergence between sectors, while DFID's larger capital projects in the energy sector (coal and power), which had been used to allocate under-spent aid budgets, had tenuous links to poverty reduction (Shepherd et al. 2000). After 1997 it became an article of faith that the best opportunity for aid to have a large and sustainable impact on poverty was through partnerships with government that gave 'donors a role in policy dialogue and capacity building' (India: Country Strategy Paper, DFID 1999: 9).[13]

The change in direction was supported by two critical reviews of DFID's India aid programme; one focused on poverty-reduction strategies (Shepherd et al. 2000), the other on approaches to participation and partnership (INTRAC 1998). Both studies endorsed the view that 'high impact aid' demanded increased participation of 'secondary stakeholders' (government departments, rather than just local beneficiaries) with stronger 'ownership' of DFID initiatives and a shift away from a narrow preoccupation with accountability for efficient disbursement of public money through micro-managed demonstration projects, and towards higher-level partnership based on shared goals and responsibility. So, by 1999 there had been a fundamental change in aid strategy from producing replicable models to policy influence within state systems.[14]

A policy environment shaped by new Labour and the 'post-Washington Consensus' notion of the virtuous state ensured that aid to India would expand through funding government programmes.[15]

In a speech in Delhi in March 1999, the Minister Clare Short declared, 'Donors must end the old competition to put their flags on a series of projects. Instead we need shared commitments to government-led programmes investing in long-term development.'[16] In the rural sector, the most immediate opportunities for this were offered by large-scale watershed development programmes under the progressive and participatory 'National Watershed Guidelines'.[17] This huge national programme – now a significant Government of India framework for bringing together rural development inputs – offered an opportunity to 'mainstream' participatory natural resources work. The new aim of using DFID finance to achieve policy influence and incremental quality improvements in state programmes was signalled by giving watershed programmes in Orissa and Andhra Pradesh (AP) the title of 'rural livelihoods projects' and by expanding beyond land-based investments to financial services for micro-enterprise, especially for the landless poor (see Turton 2000a).[18]

However, even as they came on-stream in 1999, these livelihood initiatives – which after all still involved project models and structures – were already marginal to an increasingly influential view articulated by staff interviewed in Delhi (in 2001) that state governments (not projects) were the key agents of development, and that DFID should not focus on funding specific (state) programmes, but instead make increasing resources available (in the short term through budgetary support) to assist selected governments (of Orissa, Andhra Pradesh, Madhya Pradesh, West Bengal) to develop their own overall strategies for poverty reduction; or in various ways (as a condition) finance the cost of fiscal, governance or pro-poor reforms that would make these strategies sustainable in the long run. These reforms might include disinvesting from the loss-making power sector, cutting the civil service to free up resources, decentralisation and anti-corruption measures. Assistance would go into these areas and into systems of financial accounting and social impact monitoring (DFID 2000). DFID's approach supported and encouraged a trend among other development agencies, including the IMF, the World Bank and the Asian Development Bank, who now linked concessional finance to Poverty Reduction Strategies (PRS, the reformed 1980s structural adjustment policies) and with whom DFID worked in tandem in their Indian state-level partnerships.[19] So, DFID's interventions would be planned at the state level in the context of 'overall development goals and fiscal priorities' (DFID 1999: 14) and would involve dialogue at the highest (ministerial) level. Instead of grants approved on the basis of project models (theorised inputs in relation to impacts) and paid against milestones of achievement, budgetary assistance would be provided to partner states on the basis of demonstrable commitment and past performance (on the reform agenda), and outcomes would be known through state-level poverty monitoring by systems improved with donor technical assistance.[20]

The point is not that general budgetary support was viewed as an exclusive paradigm for development assistance – it was not – but that there was a strong view among DFID staff that there had to be a move 'upstream' to achieving more effective policies, and a disengagement from the micro-managed project.[21] Even though partnerships with the state might involve a 'long-term up-hill battle over the basic understanding of poverty', and even though the shift from project models to the wider systems involved greater risks (the government system might be a 'leaky bucket' into which to pour money [Delhi-based advisers]) this was the only way to have a larger impact.

As you would expect, the new policy had its critics. Some advisers felt subject to a centrally defined agenda that suppressed alternative approaches, muted conflicts and made the donor community increasingly self-referential (cf. Eyben 2003: 26). Others worried about a concomitant loss of local contact and a growing ignorance of field realities. 'You have an awful lot of people now operating in DFID in India', one told me:

> ... who never go to a village, never talk to anyone apart from senior government people ... Projects feel that people in Delhi are making decisions without them ... and if [DFID] people are not able to talk from knowledge, from operating on the ground, then you lose the respect of your partners.[22]

Certainly some Indian project managers I spoke to experienced the retreat of DFID upstream not as a transfer of ownership and power, but as the removal of support critical to negotiating a difficult reform agenda within their own departments.[23] With the loss of projects and their models (i.e. theories that linked aid inputs to outcomes), yet other advisers worried that it would be difficult to target activities to the poor, to attribute development effects, or to be accountable. There was a lot to negotiate. As one adviser noted, it's a lot easier to match DFID and state government agendas if you take 75 per cent of the state population to be 'poor', than if you take the figure as 12 per cent. Of course, it was equally possible that broader non-project partnerships with state governments would make DFID accountable for *too much*. As I write DFID has become embroiled in controversy over the government of Andhra Pradesh's rural development policy and its emphasis on commercialising agriculture and the promotion of biotechnology. As a financing partner of the Andhra Pradesh (AP) state, DFID has faced high-profile criticism in the UK media and parliament.[24]

Perhaps unsurprisingly, changes in donor *practices* were neither as rapid nor as radical as was the language of policy. Like their project fieldworker counterparts, donor agency officers articulated powerful policy representations that were not a good guide to their actual doings. In 2001, the management of projects and programmes remained the administrative core of DFID in India. Moreover, the language of partnership and policy dialogue concealed a divergence of perspectives between DFID and its Indian government partners. When interviewed in September 2001, many senior Indian bureaucrats 'used to projectizing their requirements' still viewed 'dialogue' with donors in terms of concrete funding and technical expertise rather than as a strategic policy process. Defying the donor's self-representation, they attributed limited significance to external (donor) agencies, and dismissed the idea of 'policy influence'. The senior Indian officials I spoke with (in Andhra Pradesh and Madhya Pradesh) located the roots of current policy reform firmly within indigenous political change, and spoke assertively of space within the state system being *given to* donors in areas of mutual agreement by strong governments.[25] In the view of one senior government officer (and DFID programme manager) the critical change was not that *donors* had decided to move from projects to partnerships with the state, but that a progressive state (AP) had developed a new capacity to operate in 'project mode'; that is to recruit flexibly, to invest in young professionals, to innovate around guidelines or collaborate with local NGOs. So, the new policy of state-level partnerships throws up yet other links in development's chain of translation, other interfaces for normative and ideological negotiation across different agendas and interests, geared towards different publics – British and Indian (Quarles van Ufford 1988a: 22, 25). Down below, policy is fractured by political contingencies: government officers are frustrated by a donor weakness for fashionable models and partial solutions;[26] and donor staff by the whims of shifting senior Indian government postings which disrupt carefully negotiated partnership and dialogue. But up above, powerful representations of coherent and shared policy conceal such disjuncture and the autonomy of different levels of practice (donor, state or project).

The fact that policy changes, and changes rapidly, has the effect of making the chains of translation in development more complex and harder to negotiate. From 1997 the pace of change in DFID began to accelerate. By 2000, parastatal projects like IBRFP were no longer the cutting edge that they had been during the previous five years but rather, as one DFID manager put it, 'first-generation' projects. The second generation were state watershed programmes, and the third generation state-level partnerships. Each generation was briefer than the previous one. As the cycle of policy fashion became shorter than the life of individual projects, it became increasingly difficult for these projects to secure themselves and their success on articulations of policy. This aspect of a crisis in development is evident when a senior DFID adviser speaks of the 'new rural livelihood' projects as having 'seen us through a particularly difficult transition ... ', but in the next sentence of 'language from around this office which says [we] really don't want to have very much to do with these *old projects* ... ' . Projects which are just beginning in operational terms (in year one of ten), are middle-aged or senile as policy representations. The relation between intention and outcome has become so uncertain that the same adviser commented: 'I think it is going to be difficult actually in the next couple of years to think about any kind of initiative at all, because things seem to be moving so quickly, and the ground seems to be moving under our feet, as it were ... '.

Such aid workers inhabit a purified world of discourse, disengaged from 'field' realities, unfettered by the contradictions of implementation. They are part of the aid agency as a representation-manufacturing machine. The increasing illegibility of implementation to donors is another aspect of a 'hidden crisis' (Quarles van Ufford 1988a) (see Chapter 10). But for projects, the inability to secure themselves and their legitimacy on rapidly shifting policy constructions is threatening in a more concrete way.

A PROJECT ON DEATH ROW?

IBRFP Phase II was designed as a state-of-the art rural development project, but by the time the intergovernment agreement was signed in April 1999, the project's legitimacy was at best tenuous. The new policy environment was hostile to 'enclave' projects with 'parallel structures'. There was no longer place for the 'replicable model', and the new politics of scale withdrew legitimacy from a time-consuming downstream micro-managed project.[27] IBRFP exemplified the type of proliferating small programme criticised in DFID's second White Paper as tying up valuable administrative capacity in developing countries (DFID 2000: 94). It was 'over-designed, over-resourced' and therefore of marginal relevance to government (DFID adviser). For an aid bureaucracy which had become more institutionally literate, innovative projects were no longer the way to influence policy. Project approaches were not transferable and the very idea of replication was suspect. Indeed, many in DFID hardly cared to discriminate between success and failure of projects. The new upstream view was that 'traditional' projects were by definition successful within their bubbles, but that was not the most relevant feature of them. Success had itself become irrelevant. Or perhaps we should say that project 'success' was no longer about performance but about institutional *location*, and IBRFP was in the wrong place.

Because it was outside the mainstream government system (a cooperative under the Ministry of Fertilisers) the project was judged unable to exert the wider influence needed to justify its high costs (Shepherd et al. 2000: 100). Because it 'focussed on direct development outcomes rather than influencing the policy and institutional environment',[28] and because it was a multi-state project falling beyond DFID's 'focus states', IBRFP did not fit naturally within the new India country strategy. Although the project had 'knowledge products' such as Participatory Varietal Selection, 'the seed sub-sector into which these fed was itself in need of serious overhaul; engagement with it would be a prerequisite for influence' (2000: 100). Few recalled that less than a decade earlier British aid had turned down a proposal to work with the state government Department of Agriculture in favour of the parastatal KBCL – the new hope for development assistance that was at the time bogged down in inflexible, unresponsive state bureaucracy.

Almost all DFID-India staff I spoke with in 2001 placed the project at the margins of current policy. It had 'fallen from grace', and some were asking 'Why are we doing this? this is a waste of time.' There were moments when advisers appeared able to open some policy space for the project, for example when in 1998–9 it was able to nestle as a source of innovations and lessons within a package of DFID livelihood projects supporting the Government of India's watershed programme, crowned by a training, monitoring and evaluation support programme with the central Ministry of Rural Development[29]

– 'something so upstream you couldn't get further upstream', as one adviser involved put it. But at other times, for instance when negotiations over this keystone project failed and the rural livelihoods sectoral programme collapsed (along with all sectoral programmes), IBRFP had little policy space and there was 'a serious question about whether the project should continue' (DFID adviser). Many in DFID were unwilling to look to IBRFP for lessons (except for how *not* to do things). The project was given the *passé* 'rainfed farming' badge and excluded from the new club of 'livelihoods projects'. It bore new policy labels of exclusion: development enclave, replicable model, parallel structure, sectoral, niche, downstream, small, micro-managed project. IBRFP had become the flared trousers of the late 1990s DFID wardrobe. Its public appearance in London (January 2001) was not in the policy high street, DFID's Victoria Street headquarters, but in old world St James' Palace in the eclectic company of a sustainable agriculture conference hosted by Prince Charles.[30]

Policy shifts do not just alter the fashionableness of development approaches; they also rearrange relationships and the allocation of power in organisations. DFID was changing from being a centre from which expertise was sent out to support projects, to a machinery for policy thought. With the shift from projects to policy-related grants technical advisers lost profile and position as their client networks overseas disappeared. In Delhi, DFID's agenda involved closure of the independent sector-based field management offices set up in 1995 (Chapter 7) and a move to centrally located state teams (for Orissa, Madhya Pradesh [MP], AP, etc.). In the new configuration, key technical advisers (the principal advocates and protectors of projects) lost power to administrator programme managers. The former lost administrative roles and had to jostle for a place on state discussion forums or even travel itineraries. The displacement of technical advisers also weakened the project's link to natural science research programmes and cut off another arena of attention and support.

Such organisational change had a profound effect on the systems that earlier sustained the success of the IBRFP project by linking it to policy. The project was associated with old structures; it fell within the old fiefdoms of ODA sector advisers. It carried the imprint of an earlier regime. Projects have personalities in the corridors of aid agencies, and with the loss of its senior adviser in India, the IBRFP had little defence against the harsh wind of new policy. New policy brought new advisers, unable to recognise the project's symbolic capital of history, and saying 'I wouldn't have started from here … '

Life can be uncertain for a project which has outlived the policy regime that it served, and continues precariously at the margins of legitimacy. Project brokers had to fight to protect their corner. IBRFP's survival depended first upon special support arrangements to provide cover and buffers, and second upon key initiatives to reconnect the project to new policy imperatives. The first involved handing DFID 'field management' responsibility to the lead project consultant who (as Project Adviser) was about the only person who *could* broker the increasingly difficult link between project and policy. The second involved some subtle re-framing of priorities and representations so as to move the downstream project 'upstream by bringing it within the compass of our work with our partner state of MP'.[31] The project would have to find new significance and new supporters in relation to DFID's present interest in state policies; success would be in terms of 'upward linkage' and 'policy influence'. Taking their cue from DFID missions, project progress reports quickly started giving their greatest emphasis to relations with government at central, state, district and local (panchayat) level, rather than village-level practices; and the project found that it could plausibly present an array of links, promotional connections or contracting for the government as 'influencing policy'. Consultancy services too (my own included) were used to draw IBRFP out of the 'project enclave' and enable it to speak to the wider agendas of DFID (and other donors) and the Government of MP.[32] Connecting to niche interests within DFID was another possibility, although the best example of this – the initiative to support and organise adivasi migrant labour under DFID's rubric of 'rights-based approaches' (Mosse 2002, 2003c) – has proved difficult to negotiate within the conservative patronage-oriented culture of KBCL.

Negotiating policy change is made harder by the fact that donors in general, and DFID in particular, are not good at communicating their policy processes, and projects like IBRFP are not well placed to read policy changes. We have already seen how project staff could feel themselves subject to arbitrary judgements and viewed DFID's 'upstreaming' as the denial of donor responsibility. When the DFID Project Adviser addressed the Trust's board meeting in July 2000, policy change was issued rather as a gale warning.

> DFID is also changing with the changed world and is now giving more emphasis to the strategies, policies and partnership with government. The Rainfed Farming Project [has] to perform well in order to continue receiving support [and] must develop stronger links with government.

This was aid conditionality sharp-ended at the project level. Within a year the IBRFP had been compelled to move its headquarters (and staff) to the DFID partner state capital, Bhopal. Paradoxically, the more higher policy insisted on a shift away from clientalist relationships between DFID and its projects (cf. Eyben 2003), the more DFID asserted the power of patronage over IBRFP in order to force compliance with the new aid agenda.

As the new policy model and project practice were translated into one another, new contradictions unfurled. IBRFP was expected to exert strategic influence over state policy and practice. However, district administrations under pressure to meet targets and disburse developments funds tended to view the project, not as a source of innovations, but as a good implementation partner for state schemes.[33] What impressed them as both rare and important was not the project's development model but its operational efficiencies, its logistical capacity and its accountable delivery system.[34] And it is true that, with a couple of notable exceptions (PVS or the jankar system), it was not obvious that the project had innovations to pass on. Indeed, it illustrated many of the same problems constraining government systems: the pressure of quantitative delivery or expenditure targets, weak field-level interdisciplinary convergence, shifting priorities or problems retaining qualified staff. However, there was great pressure on IBRFP from donor and senior management to *appear* to be linking to and influencing the state in fulfilment of policy goals. This pushed the project more and more into the role of development contractor or client of government (the only kind of relationship available), which ironically actually closed off the possibility of broader policy dialogue, without either extending the reach of the project, or addressing government constraints.[35] Other tensions threatened to emerge around the promotion of independent people's associations (Self-Help Groups and their federations) and a new policy insistence that rural activities be undertaken through the elected institutions of local government (panchayat raj).[36] Suffice it to say that sustaining a new set of policy representations instituted a new set of contradictions, which were well-concealed because the notion of 'governance' or policy influence involved just as much exploitable ambiguity as did participation. Reconnecting the project to the new policy model did not add to efficiencies of field practice, quite the reverse; but it did rescue IBRFP from 'death row'. And, on the whole, IBRFP has been rehabilitated within DFID-India's aid portfolio. A few cans again rattle when the project moves; District Collectors, officials in Bhopal or DFID administrators stir.

CONCLUSIONS

The extraordinarily turbulent transitions from 1998 to 2001 that brought IBRFP to the brink of closure and collapse occurred, not coincidentally, with the move to more coherent and centrally determined DFID policy. Ironically, DFID's new language of partnership and dialogue came along with assertions of power that ignored, overrode and ruptured the complex instrumental relations of brokerage that had sustained project success in the previous five years. In such circumstances Abdelrahman and Apthorpe suggest that the donor 'dispossesses the local partner of its own results-oriented integrity' (2002: 47). The implication is not that policy change is bad. In fact, new policy creates new relationships and makes new connections between people, and that is part of its value; and frameworks that focus on global institutions and state policy are obviously key to the progressive repositioning of bilateral donors. But rapid policy change and assertions of coherence with little regard for its institutional effects is a worrying characteristic of aid agencies today.[37]

We have seen how when policy changes a project's conception of development problems, goals and organisational identity, and signs of success and failure are reconstituted in order to ensure continued support (Quarles van Ufford 1988a: 22). And earlier chapters pointed to the fact that this work on policy representations is autonomous from operational work. As Quarles van Ufford puts it, 'the organisational need for control [of implementation] is not great, as long as the top is able to convince its sponsors that policy is well implemented, or that more funds are needed because of grave development problems' (1988a: 25). Of course, consultants and advisers in the wider organisation (DFID) are firmly part of this process. They share an interest in maintaining new policy representations which provide a 'rallying force' (1988a: 25) in support for their own ideas, work and positions, and in demonstrating the need for further action, which ensures an inbuilt stimulus in development policy for a series of new approaches and a succession of new starts (1988a: 25). And the more autonomous from practice (the more 'upstream'), the freer policy change is to serve its own organisational purposes (1988a: 25). At each point in the chain of organisation the orientation is firmly *upwards*.

Let me underline two conclusions. First, despite the autonomy of policy process from actions, policy change has critical effects on organisations that have to articulate with dominant representations to retain legitimacy. Second, when policy changes rapidly – faster even than the life of a project or programme – the disjuncture between representations and practices increases. Development agencies are forced into a reactive mode, orienting their energies to preserving themselves as *systems of representations* – using whatever resources are available to achieve this end (research, consultancy, links with government). The demands of policy also create a state of institutional anxiety as managers have to represent 'success' across a range of fields over which they have no control (e.g. influencing the state), which in turn directs practical efforts towards organisational maintenance. If 'successful' projects are those that resemble donor policy models, then development agencies are made better at managing their upwardly oriented representations, while directing their practical efforts to system goals and preserving identity, neither of which improve the chances of learning or effectiveness in poverty-reducing change.

I suggest further that strong policy convergence can amplify the negative effects of rapid policy change. The more coherent the policy consensus (or the more politically important the idea of convergence) and the less it tolerates dissension or permits counter-models to persist or emerge, the greater the pressure on development agencies to appear to comply. As donors impose central agendas and ensure that practices are rendered coherent in terms of a *single* overarching framework, making themselves the privileged source of de-politicised, de-contextualised and universalist policy ideas, they not only institute standard approaches, inter-project uniformity and obscure the value of difference, innovation or experimentation (Shepherd et al. 2000: 22, 28), but also further reduce organisational effectiveness.

Given that DFID's India policy is part of a wider *convergence* of aid policy internationally under the 'inclusive liberalism' of the Poverty Reduction Strategy (PRS) process or Comprehensive Development Frameworks (CDF), there is an argument to be made about the risks and costs of unified aid frameworks applicable at the global level (Craig and Porter 2003).[38] This is not the place to put such an argument, but it may be useful to recognise the parallels when, for example, Craig and Porter identify the following as risks arising from PRS policy convergence: (1) that because sustaining agreements involves considerable institutional effort or 'compliance costs', aid recipient states become over-oriented to 'determining the technical and institutional framework for links to global markets and international aid transfers' (2003: 53–4, 66); (2) that this upward orientation displaces local accountability and resources generation; or (3) that a technical, juridical and disciplinary framework results in a 'much depleted capacity to engage practically ... [with the] local political economic manifestations of poverty or with the highly contingent ways that new opportunities might be turned to good effect' (2003: 66).[39]

The 'power effects of donorship' are far-reaching indeed (Slater and Bell 2002: 350). Despite proclamations of partnership, power inequalities are reproduced in the making and execution of policy, in the 'dependent leadership' (in projects or countries), in the language of education, tutelage or trusteeship, in the displacement of alternative visions and in the rules of partnership. But in the end it is important also to remember that the arrogance of policy is that it under-recognises its own autonomy from events, and therefore overstates the importance of its pronouncements.[40] In fact, the naked exercise of donor power is moderated by the structurally determined weakness of donor management in relation to operational work, by the ambiguity of development goals which allow reinterpretation, by the constant need for negotiations across institutional interfaces and by the fact that, in the end, donor agencies need recipients to spend their budgets. In consequence, rather less than is imagined changes when projects are recalibrated to the current policy models. Recipient agencies 'defy the control of donors by giving the appearance of obeying the rules of aid exchanges without actually putting them in to practice' (Crewe and Harrison 1998: 89). There is disjuncture and autonomy of different levels in the 'chain of organisation'. Each level has to accommodate the other, but operates with autonomy. This works against integration and the effectiveness of 'bullying or benevolent' donors (Quarles van Ufford 1988a: 19). It also makes the effects or impacts of aid unpredictable. It is to these that I want now to turn.

9
Aspirations for Development

The previous two chapters present the idea that 'success' and 'failure' are policy-oriented judgements that preoccupy the narratives of project and donor, but obscure the underlying operations and relations of development. This chapter shows that the socio-economic effects of a project system are also obscured by its policy models. Here I leave the upstream world that negotiates policy and legitimacy, and return to the social experience of being a beneficiary of the IBRFP project. What did project action mean to Bhil villagers; what local interpretations are hidden behind the externally oriented language of 'impact'?

In addressing the question I will draw on a series of village studies undertaken over two years (1996–8).[1] Partly, it is the failure of these to fulfil their intended purpose of demonstrating project impact that makes them useful. Tracing the links between project inputs, outputs and synergistic impacts, or even measuring change in complex and fluctuating livelihoods in the absence of a baseline, proved impossible. Instead, these village studies concerned themselves with recording villagers' *perceptions* of changes during the project's first years (1992 to 1997–8). Of course, the way in which villagers spoke to their interlocutors was not independent of external ideas and interests. This research had the purpose of vindicating the role of project actors (or policy design) and to a degree appropriated Bhil experience for this external cause (cf. Hardiman 1987a: 9). The information generated was also shaped by complex local agendas of hope, expectations or 'a history of failed negotiations with the project' (Phillips and Edwards 2000: 59). But still, as a record of changes that Bhil men and women wished to convey to outsiders it says something about their experience of being beneficiaries under the IBRFP project.

NARRATIVES OF CHANGE – POSITIVE AND NEGATIVE

Given IBRFP's preoccupation with the negotiation of policy representations, it was a relief to discover that overwhelmingly the Bhil villagers affected spoke well of the project and considered that they had benefited from its actions over five years. Through interviews, PRAs or groups discussions they obligingly endorsed the project's own model of change, asserting that they were becoming better off. Mostly this did not mean increased cash inflows, but rather reduced outflows for food grain in the lean season or to service debt. Better crop yields, new fodder sources, improved livestock and home-grown vegetables all increased *food security*. And this was what people valued most. 'We used to buy grains for eight months', people in one village recalled, '[and] bring food grain to the house on bullock carts … after *holi*, no one used to be in the village.'[2] Now, many concurred, there was food grain for an extra three or four months and fewer people left for migration.

Explaining the changes, researchers were shown how new stone SWC bunds checked soil erosion and prevented crops being washed away; how they retained moisture and increased both the intensity and the area of cultivation: maize replacing millets on the slopes, and rice being newly grown in the valleys or behind the new structures. Those who received engines to pump water from rivers or from deepened wells spoke of a new winter (*rabi*) harvest of wheat or chickpea; and SWC and early-maturing varieties had even made this possible for those without irrigation. Indeed, in some villages as many as half said they now grew a winter crop of wheat. New higher yielding, sweeter tasting, drought tolerant (early harvesting) or better selling rice, maize and chickpea seeds were a boon (and after only four to five years it was too early to assess their full impact).[3] They were carefully saved and passed on to neighbours and kin. Stories of experiments and farmer success multiplied and spread to adjacent villages, and the seed (sold or given) followed quickly. When the project supplied seed to local shopkeepers and traders, the new varieties spread to more distant villages. As the popularity of the rice variety Kalinga III grew, traders began to charge a premium.[4] By 1997, about half the seed sown in project villagers was of improved varieties (without however displacing local varieties or reducing biodiversity, Witcombe et al. 1999).

Villagers spoke too of the benefits of fodder and fuel from trees and forests protected under JFM (Joint Forest Management). 'We used to have to buy fodder after [March], now it lasts until [July]', said a group in one village, 'we got 600 bundles of grass from the JFM and about 500 from grass on the [SWC] bunds; in addition to this we [have more] paddy and wheat husk … and straw';[5] and in another, field staff reckoned that by harvesting, storing and selling surplus fodder from 200 hectares of protected forest (at peak prices), households earned on average Rs 3,000. More fodder, villagers said, increased cattle herds, allowing the wealthier to shift from small to larger livestock – from browsers (goats) to grazers (cows, bullocks and, most indicative of new wealth, buffalos)[6] – while the poor kept more goats of improved breeds, especially where women's groups ran share schemes.

For a few people the increase in income came from sales of fodder or livestock, and a few households could pay off debts through the sale of surplus grain or cash crops such as black gram and chickpea. For the majority, however, the main source of income benefits was waged labour on project works. Whether in the form of increased wages, improved livestock or food security, the project was a source of benefits that were perceived as extremely significant in economic terms. This was confirmed by a self-confessedly rough-estimate economic analysis of a sample of reported net income gains which judged that after five good monsoon years (1992–7) overall combined net incomes had increased by a third, mostly from increased *rabi* season cultivation.[7]

Running against this endorsement of project impact warmly conveyed by a majority to investigating staff, there were counter-currents, of complexity, anxiety and disappointment. Some viewed SWC works as offering no more than temporary wage employment, or resented the loss of land to bunds.[8] Some worried about the rising costs of cultivation following project inputs of seed and fertiliser, or even the ecological effects of the latter. The very fact that fragmented landholdings and a shortage of cattle for manure had made fertiliser more critical to meeting subsistence, led some farmers to speak of a new 'addiction' of the land to fertiliser after the project arrived,[9] or to complain of the 'hardening' and 'drying' effects of prolonged fertiliser use.[10] One village study argued that the increased availability of inorganic fertiliser had wider effects on crop–cattle–land relationships, contributing to a 'shift in the equilibrium point of livestock in the system'.[11]

Opinion on new seeds was not universally positive either. Farmers who habitually home-saved seed were not keen on expensive seeds that had to be purchased, even on credit. Improved seeds only did well in particular soil/moisture conditions and yields varied greatly across farmers' fields.[12] Moreover, the anticipated positive synergies of seeds and SWC did not appear. Rather, disappointment was increased by the fact that while the project promoted pump irrigation and engineered field terraces and *nallah* plugs specifically to maximise water retention, the crop varieties that it promoted were suited to dry conditions, poor-quality stony soils and unbunded fields.[13] This meant that in heavy monsoon years or on flat 'bunded' land, the new seeds performed poorly (except in the winter season),[14] and when planted in drought years or on poor sloping land their advantages over local varieties were not always perceived.[15] The experience of uncertain or marginal benefits occasionally bred scepticism towards the new technology, especially among women.[16] 'I don't know or understand the new varieties, [or] the practices they require', commented one, 'we don't know the intervals between weeding. I am worried that ... we will lose the yield.'[17] Monsoon variation in particular meant that while the crops consultant expected Kalinga III to become the dominant variety in two years, it had not, despite its significant (46 per cent) yield advantage.[18]

In Chapter 6, I suggested that 'context-free' technical models (i.e. Participatory Varietal Selection – PVS, Participatory Plant Breeding – PPB) resulted in products (improved varieties) that were expected to produce economically significant incremental benefits by replacing local varieties, offering big financial returns to project investment. It was clear, however, that the dramatic aggregate economic gains from plant breeding in the long term could disappear in the short term and locally with monsoon fluctuations; as could the seeds' generalised advantages (drought resistance, yield, etc.) once the new technologies were re-embedded in the complex micro-environments, networks of obligation, family relations or market connections that constituted Bhil cultivation practices. Here, they were treated as a small situation-specific addition to available options for cropping. The benefits of technology development refused the general application; they produced a small ripple not a big splash.[19] In IBRFP, new hope lies with the PPB-developed maize variety GDRM-187 which not only emerged as 'highly preferred' in PVS trials and was already generating excitement in certain project villages in 1997, but was later also officially released for cultivation in upland areas of Gujarat state (Witcombe et al. 2003). However, the early maturity, better grain quality and yield advantage (16–29 per cent) that GDRM-187 showed over local varieties in trials will only result in sustained adoption and livelihood benefits if the contextual demands of ecology, seed supply, drought, deficit or debt permit expression of these characteristics.[20]

The early project years of 1993–8 had been a time of rising incomes and many marriages, but things changed during the drought years of

1999 and 2000. The advantages of improved varieties or SWC were effectively eliminated. The core livelihood hardships of depleted grain stocks, scarcity of fodder and drinking water, cattle disease, unemployment and labour migration intensified hugely. They were mitigated only by waged employment provided by ongoing project work (SWC, well deepening, hand-pump installation), together with small loans from group funds and grain banks to meet their members' urgent need for food, fodder or medicine.

The only lasting resource development benefit that villagers would point to was fodder from some of the better-established joint forest management (JFM) schemes, which, in some cases, had saved their herds. But even in good years, not all villagers described a virtuous spiral of increased fodder (from JFM or better crops) leading to more cattle, more manure and increased soil fertility. Some explained how more fodder from the JFM schemes did not compensate for the accompanying restriction on grazing and the rigorous enclosure of forests; or how free grazing in the village was lost as cropping intensified and fallows reduced; or again, how a shortage of labour to harvest grass from forest plots meant that labour-poor households faced a new fodder crisis. The costs of restricted grazing led some individuals to withdraw from JFM schemes, and in one case the *sarpanch* advised closure of the whole scheme.[21] Sometimes cattle numbers declined as cultivation intensified since, in relative terms, the costs (in labour) of keeping surplus livestock for manure or milk had increased.[22]

Never far from people's minds was the fact that the changes that increased production (especially irrigated *rabi* crops, JFM and vegetable growing) also increased workloads; and since many of the additional activities were culturally defined as women's tasks (weeding, tending trees or vegetables, applying fertilisers), the additional burden mostly fell on them. Some complained that:

> ... now [with JFM] we have to cut fodder and bring it to the animals instead of grazing [them]
> ... [because] we are not allowed to enter the JFM area [there is less fuel-wood and] we have to burn cowdung cakes and chickpea sticks ...[23]
> ... [whereas] before the JFM men used to go to Rajasthan ... in *halmo* groups and harvest grass.[24]

Soil conservation structures brought additional weeding, and lift irrigation schemes increased the demands on women's labour to such an extent that people had begun to demand higher brideprice from families with irrigation.[25] Women in small households, with few to share the work, sometimes concluded that from the project they 'had greater workloads without receiving personal benefit'.[26] This is not to say that women did not value labour-saving technologies such as threshers or rice-mills[27] or nearby water sources (wells, hand-pumps, ponds), but that such initiatives rarely produced a net reduction in workloads or altered the gender inequalities. As a young woman from Bijori village explained:

> … we used to get up an hour earlier to grind the flour; now we take the grain to the electric mill in the next village [but] I don't see a real change, especially where there is just one woman in the house and all the children are small and cannot help. When the daughters grow up, then maybe it will be better, otherwise no change. We still spend the same amount of time cutting fodder; we still go to the jungle and bring wood. The only difference is that now we have to hide from the guards; there is no less weeding to do, still the same number of weeds grow. In fact the only difference is that there is more rice growing than before, due to SWC work there is also more maize now, so we have more weeding to do.[28]

For women, project benefits came at a cost; as one put it 'when the tree nursery is so time-consuming the fruits will be too precious to eat!'

Research confirmed the judgement of field staff that access to project benefits was uneven across the community (Chapter 4), although we should remember that in these Bhil villages there is often little, in absolute terms, to distinguish between the 'poor' and the 'better off'. These are unstable categories mistakenly reified by the use of rather flawed 'wealth rank' methodologies.[29] Still, it is certain that the principal economic gains from project activities accrued to households in proportion to the land they possessed (quality as well as quantity). Families with more land benefited most from new seeds or SWC, planted more trees (in many villages tree ownership among the poorest had not increased at all); and the beneficiaries of lift irrigation schemes, wells, check dams and pump-sets were those who already owned the best fertile land at the bottom of the watershed. Wealth in labour and the ability to invest time were also important in order to benefit from seed trials, deepened wells, collected fodder or waged labour. Smaller (younger) households were unable to realise their entitlement to fodder shares under JFM. Moreover, some villages' forest protection committees (VFCs) were constituted so as to exclude a minority belonging to lower-status clans or marginal settlements from fodder and other benefits, and in others, JFM initiatives amplified intra- and inter-hamlet conflicts over grazing, or were themselves hampered by clan, factional or party political conflicts (Singh 1998). However, these are common problems in JFM and one study which included VFCs in both project and non-project villages showed that the former were more inclusive and less conflictual than the latter (1998).

The better educated gained privileged access to project resources as *jankars*, for example, being able to influence the siting of wells and bunds or obtain a greater share of seeds or loans; while the poorest, especially as absent migrants, were socially excluded from benefits and unable even to defend their entitlements (e.g. to fodder). Those with least land contributed most of the unskilled labour for project schemes, and by accepting lower 'participatory' wages effectively subsidised land improvements for the better off; while through compulsory deductions from their wages, they made disproportionate contributions to common funds. This was one of several ways in which inequity was built into the project's participatory mechanisms. The wider politics of 'success' ensured that fieldworkers and managers hard-pressed to meet targets, spend budgets and produce signs of progress were willing to accept the better off as their target group (self-presented as the poor). After all, these made for easier/better participants, they were more cooperative and aware; they possessed the prerequisites of participation – *land* for new seeds; *time* for meetings; *labour* for project activities; and they were rich in 'the capacity to aspire' (Appadurai 2004), that is to connect their needs to wider goals and external policy objectives. The poorest were hard work and non-compliant, their land resisted the new technologies, they lacked time or labour to realise new entitlements to water, forest resources, credit or employment as members of user groups; and as non-members or migrants they disappeared from view altogether. Few staff could afford the risks of pursuing them. As already noted, it is not uncommon for agency staff to select those people who already possess the characteristics that a project aims to create – the educated, the organised, the innovators, independent, solvent, modernising peasants; that way a measure of success is guaranteed (Li 1999).

The survey of changes in net income (mentioned above) found no evidence of an equalising effect of the project, suggesting instead that the poor and the 'better off' not only benefited to different degrees, but also in different ways. Richer families gained most, and mostly from increased agricultural incomes (especially from irrigation and winter season crops); poorer families gained least, and primarily from wage labour. And largely because of the nature of IBRFP activities, during the project years the gap between the very poorest (including long-term migrants) and others widened.[30]

Significantly, unlike the gender inequality of workloads, the economic inequity of benefits was not reflected in villager narratives. The poorest households may have received a smaller proportion of benefits; they may have been primarily incorporated into the project as labourers rather than farmers; and they may have subsidised improvements on their richer neighbours' fields, or contributed over the odds to common funds; but they were unwilling to acknowledge still less challenge such inequality publicly, not least because, while they may have gained least, they needed the project most. That is to say, the security offered by more stable cropping, wage labour and, as we will see, low-cost credit, were disproportionately important to the poorest households.

Where resentment fermented was where benefits failed to measure up to expectations; where villagers were caught in the crossed wires of patronage and participation, disappointed when expected wells or bullocks failed to arrive, 'cheated' when wages were docked as group fund contributions, frustrated by mistaken measurements and lost records, or angered when payments were delayed (sometimes by as much as seven months). An exasperated women in one village said, 'we made proposals for smokeless *chulas* [stoves] ... for a goat rearing project, and for a sewing machine. Nothing happened and we have lost faith that this project will ever benefit women.'[31] In another village, a local newspaper reporter wrote, that 'the Patel was so angry [because of unpaid wages] that he said he would shoot anyone who came to the village from the project!'[32]

CREDIT AND FARMER GROUPS

We were rather surprised to find that in every village people insisted that the most important gains from the project were from the new Self-Help Groups. The first aspect of this was the provision of seasonal credit at low cost through groups without collateral silver or the need for brokers (initially advanced in kind as seed and fertiliser by the project). Universally, this was viewed as a more significant agricultural benefit than either SWC or improved seeds; and the reason was that group credit allowed the *timely* purchase of seeds and fertiliser. Some explained:

> We used to buy seed on credit and repay in kind ... if we borrowed 20 kg we had to repay 40 kg, now we repay only 25 kg to the seed bank ... we used to have to borrow cash from the moneylender ... when I borrowed Rs 500 I had to repay Rs 750, so I feel I am gaining by Rs 250 and getting the urea on time ... We have more money in our hands now, so we feel richer ... Now we use [the IBRFP group] more frequently than any other source of credit.[33]

Some farmers held that timely sowing and increased fertiliser use (evident in all study villages) was responsible for a 20–25 per cent increase in maize yields. There is no doubt that the uptake of improved seeds itself was influenced by their (exclusive) availability from SHGs on credit in villages (and especially where only improved seed was available in this way).[34] Indeed, sometimes this was stated as the main motivation for adopting new seeds.[35]

In reality, group loans were relatively small, certainly in relation to villagers' overall credit needs (representing as little as 3–10 per cent of household borrowing),[36] or in relation to the amount of money that could be raised through *chandlas*, and were unlikely to reduce household debt significantly. In any case, it was unusual for group loans to substitute for other sources of credit. Indeed, people explained how membership of fund-holding groups – symbolised by the passbook – actually increased access to *sahukar* (moneylender) credit at lower interest by providing a sort of collateral substitute: 'We just show our passbooks.'[37] What was important for the poorest (often excluded from credit entirely) was that groups provided the means to acquire purchased inputs such as fertiliser for the first time. Almost all villagers (80 per cent) were members of groups because they could provide flexible and unmediated access to cultivation loans *when needed* without lengthy negotiation. Taking into account the interest payments, the gifts of liquor, cash or chicken to loan brokers, lost wages and the compulsion to sell crops early at low prices to repay the loan (and so borrow again for food at the end of the season), it would cost well over Rs 350 to secure a seasonal loan of Rs 500 from a moneylender, but only Rs 25 from the group.

Moreover, project SHGs also offered cheaper bulk purchased fertiliser, transport and flexible repayment. But more than this, for the poor, SHGs offered freedom from the social burden of dependence upon moneylenders precisely in situations where they were most vulnerable – that is, when in urgent need of critical cultivation inputs, when the power of usurers over them was most keenly felt. Villagers sought freedom from harassment for repayment, freedom to decide when to sell their crops and above all freedom from anxiety of protracted loan negotiations that critically delayed inputs and reduced yields.[38] Time, as much as land, water or labour, is an agricultural resource scarce among the poor (cf. Appadurai 1990: 210): 'we can't afford to waste even half an hour in the monsoon season', emphasised one farmer.[39] Perhaps it would be easier to appreciate the impact of development projects on the poor and on women if analysed in terms of *time* as a critical resource, rather than income or production. In the IBRFP project, while group credit gave farmers control over time, other technical changes reduced control over, and increased competition for, time.[40]

For all of the above reasons, even though they received a smaller proportion of available group credit, the perception of benefit was skewed towards the poorest Bhil households who were most at risk (from loss), who had fewer alternatives and who depended upon group loans to the greatest degree. Better-off households built security by investing in networks of social obligation, realised as capital through *chandlas* or *notras* – but for the poor, who lacked such networks, membership of an IBRFP-backed group afforded a substitute security (and reduced vulnerability) by way of credit to meet urgent cultivation, food or emergency (e.g. medical) needs, not to mention entitlement to work on project schemes. At best, group membership would reduce a little the everyday dependence on usurious *sahukars*, which was probably a precondition for income gains from agriculture or enterprise of any kind. Now, if for poorer households, group membership was important because it could reduce exploitative dependence, (a) by providing substitute social networks, and (b) by bringing people into a relationship with project benefactors, for the better off it was the latter that was the principal benefit. Regardless of the success or otherwise of the groups as farmer-managed micro-finance institutions, they were perceived as the most important change because they stood for access to a range of other project benefits, whether wages, seeds or credit.

Of course, despite their importance to farm livelihoods, credit groups cannot be viewed as an unqualified good. We know that only a minority of groups realised their potential as credit institutions. Many showed low levels of trust, poor fund circulation or independent management (Chapter 6). Some faced leadership problems or manipulation by moneylender *jankars*. In some cases, dominant group members were themselves moneylenders, on-lending group credit to poorer households. Some folded, or their credit activities had to be suspended owing to non-repayment, returning villagers to the moneylenders.[41] Without doubt many offered opportunities for control and patronage by a village elite, and occasionally their presence made dealings with external *sahukars* more difficult rather than easier. A few feared that the availability of cash would itself make farming more cash dependent: 'We have money in the hand and [we] spend more.'

MEETINGS AND MODERNITY

The project Self-Help Groups, however, had a significance beyond the economic benefits they offered. Like most project 'impacts', including those related to agriculture already described, the effect and social significance of SHGs derived not from project inputs *per se* (still less from project designs) but from the infusion of project activities and relationships into existing regionally specific processes of change. As such villagers' perception of SHGs requires interpretation.

The groups were almost universally described by their members as strongly cohesive and supportive. Villagers emphasised the collective accomplishment of tasks like the bulk buying of fertiliser, or said things like, 'If someone's roof needs repairing urgently before the monsoon, group members will offer help without asking for liquor.'[42] Villagers pointed as well to the sociality of meetings, discussions and planning, when members of scattered households (especially women) come together. Group events were experienced as fun/entertaining, and the commitment of time required not burdensome. This unity and cooperation is contrasted with an earlier time of disputes and family quarrels.[43] It is not obvious how such proclamations of unity should be interpreted; after all, mostly these were not new associations but formed out of strongly cohesive structures of lineage and *falia* (hamlet). First, and perhaps least plausibly, it is possible that such 'unity' is a mask for divisions, or even that project patronage so concentrates power in Bhil hamlets that factional conflict is suppressed. But this is unlikely given that there were many cases in which groups promoted new political leadership challenging existing elites (see p. 88 for one case). Second, group membership and declarations of unity are perhaps intended to demonstrate the presence of effective community (invisible as kinship) to outsiders, most immediately to project patrons (i.e. IBRFP), but then more widely to government, NGOs or even *sahukars*. Today, evidence of group cohesion, idealised in wider development circles, brings symbolic and material gains in itself. Community in this sense is a sought-after 'commodity' that group members can offer for 'sale' to would-be patrons or scheme-implementing bureaucrats (Fiedrich 2002: 174) or use to deter would-be exploiters.

The third possibility is that expressions of unity indicate the presence of an alternative mode of collective action in Bhil villages. In this regard it is significant that, along with the celebration of group unity, there was a parallel commentary on the decline of other forms of reciprocal exchange and social obligation: the *halmo* system of labour exchange with liquor or food was being replaced by hiring wage labour; livestock were being sold for cash rather than consumed, gifted or sacrificed in fulfilment of social or religious obligations; and SHGs themselves offered freedom not only from *sahukars*, but also from the terrible pressures of *chandla*, whose obligations extracted forced payments or threatened social isolation.[44] It begins to look as if SHGs were institutions allowing a form of cooperation and mutual support that was independent of burdensome social obligations, and in which voluntary savings and project subsidies substituted for social obligation. This was especially attractive to the poor with weak social networks.[45]

SHGs not only forged new types of collective action, they also offered a cultural critique of old ones. The discipline of meetings and savings was opposed to lavish spending on festivals, animal sacrifices or brideprice. The order of schedules, ledgers, minuted resolutions, rules and fines especially repudiated disorderly collective action mediated by *daru* (distilled liquor). Interestingly, abandoning alcohol was often ranked as the most significant change brought about by the project. Alcohol was connected to ill-health, debt, social conflict and, most seriously for women, with domestic violence. In fact, women directly linked the social discipline of group processes with reduced domestic violence (and, relatedly, the reduced need to return to their natal homes to escape abuse). So, an interesting question is raised here about the relationship between new and existing forms of social capital. The promotion of SHGs appeared to displace and morally de-legitimise social capital mediated by alcohol. Was this a problem? It depends on who you ask. Certainly for women, and those with weak networks (e.g. of *chandla*), SHGs were a modern form of association offering freedom from the burden of mutual obligation and alcohol-related domestic violence, as well as links to project patrons.[46]

The decline in alcohol and abuse was important because it was central to women's physical and emotional well-being; but its centrality to Bhil villagers' 'change narratives' may also be related to the wider issues of identity and modernity with which it resonated. After all, alcohol has long been a core symbol of Bhil underdevelopment, and renouncing *daru* a Brahmanic virtue and idiom of progress and modernity – for example, in numerous *devi* cults, and in Gandhian and other social and religious reform movements (cf. Hardiman 1987a). The IBRFP project as a whole, but its SHG groups in particular, were contexts in which Bhils learned 'to see themselves as they understand others to be seeing [and judging] them' (Pigg 1996: 180), where they had to contend with 'cosmopolitan criticism (on radio, in offices, when they travel as "hicks" to the city)' (1996: 180), and where they complied with outsiders' constructions of progress and civility. Hardly surprising, then, that their narratives of change deal in the currency of stereotypes and negative adivasi self-images, and key symbols and processes of improvement:

> Five years ago I was sick often and used to drink a lot. Since the project started I have stopped drinking and am healthy, this is because of exposure visits.
> [We] are not wearing torn clothes any more, there is a great change in life, especially because of the meetings. Now men sit together and discuss and help to solve each other's problems, regardless of clan …
> Some men in the village have started to wear trousers or shorts instead of *lungis*; they have started to sit together for group meetings and have learned new things.[47]

Through meetings (commonly in the presence of field staff) villagers not only make decisions, pass resolutions and petition the project, they also make themselves modern in a specific way. As noted in relation to PRA timelines (Chapter 4), project staff and Bhil villagers together construct the project – and especially its Self-Help Groups – as a modernising force, and in doing so look back on a tribal life of isolation, fear, ignorance, conflict, alcoholism and domestic

violence. The project provides the context in which outsiders
bringing new structures and routines (groups, meetings, formats),
new leadership and new rules, broker aspirations of modernity
among marginal adivasis. In IBRFP, technologies too, whether seeds,
urea, SWC or diesel pumps, were a medium through which adivasis
– culturally different and of 'another time' – became modern and
co-temporaneous with project agents.[48] Elsewhere, missionaries and
Christian conversion have played this role, or Hindu nationalists
or Gandhian social reformers (Karlsson 1999, 2000), each today in
dangerous competition and conflict with the other. Each offers a new
economy in social life, release from ritual and social obligations (and
expenses), a new order and orientation and a 'better' way of being.
Adivasi development and religious change (or conversion) are often
idioms of each other; and in both the renunciation of alcohol is a
prime marker in the adivasi story of modernisation.

CULTURE, CONSUMPTION AND CONNECTIONS

While participatory development attempts to reverse or bury the
misleading dichotomies of tradition/modernity or indigenous/
scientific, they 'thrive in the world we aim to describe and interpret'
(Pigg 1996: 176), for the particular reason that these are cultural
distinctions of progress *produced* (or performed) in the context of
forging relationships with outsiders. Bhil endorsements of distinctions
between rational order (e.g. of meetings) and tribal disorder (e.g. of
daru) – or more generally between a modern puritan middle-class
lifestyle of thrift, account keeping and cleanliness, and customary
tribal backwardness – served tactically to maintain a relationship with
the project patron. Ironically, the development practices through
which IBRFP workers most clearly establish and advertise their dealing
with the apparently authentic (but actually simulated) 'local' and
'indigenous' – PRA, PVS, SHGs – are precisely those which for Bhils
are avenues to the modern. The point is that, despite our ideals of
participation, in development poor people become 'empowered' not
in themselves, but through relationships with outsiders having better
access to resources; and not through the validation of their existing
knowledge and actions, but by seeking out and acknowledging the
superiority of modern technology and lifestyles, and by aligning
themselves with dominant cultural forms (cf. Fiedrich 2002). Here
IBRFP fits into an historical pattern. As Hardiman writes of the pre-
Independence Devi cults among Bhils, 'assimilation to dominant

values ... provided a meeting point between the adivasis and certain progressive members of the dominant classes ...' eventually linking them to the wider nationalist movement (1987a: 164).

In project villages, people also commented on the fact they had begun to consume differently. 'Everyone in my family has developed city tastes, like potato', says one man; 'earlier they used to eat wild food, now they don't like to eat this stuff.'[49] The renunciation of *daru*, bathing regularly, wearing dhotis, eating rice or potatoes, planting improved varieties (or adopting other signs of a modern lifestyle modelled for them by project workers) – these are behavioural norms and patterns of consumption that are important because they facilitate and signal alliances and new routes to power. Here objects (and practices) are given meaning and value because, as Douglas and Isherwood argue, they allow households that possess them greater 'discretion in interaction with outsiders and hence greater ability to maintain desired social relationships' (1978). Correspondingly, 'to be poor is to be poorly connected through things to other people, to fail to mount the necessary rituals of consumption' (Fardon 1999: 139, citing Douglas and Isherwood 1978). Orientation to 'modern' patterns of consumption (or practices, or beliefs) also implies social differentiation according to lifestyle; new distinctions and new exclusions, that 'introduce a kind of marbeling of cosmopolitan status into village life' (Pigg 1996: 173, cf. Bourdieu 1984). This was noted in relation to the status claims of reformed Bhagat Bhils, expressed in diet, dress styles and education (Chapter 3). And here IBRFP has its own social (as well as economic) effects by modelling and differentiating access to high-status consumption patterns. It is significant that, in the context of the increased importance of consumables – soap, tea, fertiliser, cloth – better-off households spoke of project benefits in terms of greater interaction with the market (selling surplus and spending on consumables), but poorer households spoke of benefits in terms of going to the market *less* and a reduced need to borrow or to purchase food-grain for survival.[50]

Villagers and staff also expressed the project's social effects in terms of increased 'confidence' and 'awareness', terms which mostly referred to the acquisition of a facility to deal with outsiders and their institutions (banks, government administration), engendered through external visits or training and symbolised by the bank passbook. In every group interview, villagers contrasted the present with a former fear of strangers and intimidation by officials (e.g. forest and police) 'coming to take things away from or cheat [us]'.[51] Old brokers (*sahukars* or headmen) are displaced when the formerly distant figures of the District Collector or bank employee are brought within the sphere of personal contact. The project may have established its own brokers and intermediaries, especially *jankars*, but it still had the effect of making outside authorities a little less separate and 'other' (Klenk 2003). 'I had never seen the Collector', said one man, 'until Ajay [CO] brought him to the village walking by foot in the rain.'

The project not only makes parts of the state's development apparatus accessible to Bhil villagers, it also makes remote adivasi villages legible to the state (Scott 1998). Villages make a new appearance on the administrative map, in the circuits of extension officers or health workers, or at the monthly meetings at the district headquarters. Village teachers drawing salaries but working in far-away non-tribal places reappear; the schools are no longer empty, and older people rather than children are seen herding livestock.[52] Health and veterinary camps take place way beyond the metalled road, the Forestry Department begins a JFM, and the Collector pours more and more schemes into remote villages through the IBRFP funnel. The Bhils are a little less 'wild'. As a forest officer put it, they are now 'getting on the line', coming on track; they are listening now, and are more articulate.

There is an influential line of critical writing that views such development effects as a repressive extension of state control at the fringes, where new services serve to govern (Ferguson 1994: 253), or argues that for tribals 'remoteness tends to be the best insurance against poverty' (Padel 2000: 289). However, project villagers' narratives suggest that what is involved here is a curtailment rather than an extension of bureaucratic power; increased respect from officials and greater independence from their arbitrary demands (at least while under project protection). A Bhil woman, for example, tells a project worker how she stood up to a Forest Department worker falsely accusing her of building her house with pilfered timber, and how she now refuses the expected gifts of *daru*, goat or chickens to officers from the cooperative, police or Forest Department. An increased demand for accountability (in the presence of the project) applies equally within villages, allowing project-trained *jankars* to contest local elections and displace established broker-leaders 'who do not know anything'.

Outsiders' narratives of tribal development and progress are most powerfully expressed and displayed in relation to women: present, unveiled, knowledgeable and speaking to, even arguing with, outsiders (see Chapter 7). In interviews Bhil women themselves speak of mobility not only in the context of the project and its trainings and 'exposure visits', but also more routinely to the market. Women spoke of their knowledge of fertiliser, of bank accounts and of no longer being cheated. They also reported 'taking more care of their appearance'. 'Women are more fashionable ... they have changed the type of blouses they wear and the cut of the skirt', comments one village study.[53] But above all, women spoke of a civilising of their menfolk, and a new optimism and motivation instilled in *them*. In the first place, women spoke of the reduction in drinking and violence, but then also of the change from a time of apathy when men 'saw no way to improve their situation and would drink and fall asleep during the day, leaving women to do routine agricultural tasks'.[54]

The improvement of *men* was a women's project concealed behind the official language of the empowerment and upliftment of women. For the most part, Bhil women did not seek a realignment or renegotiation of gender roles; nor was autonomy or the demonstration of independence – paraded so visibly by the project – particularly important to women who already knew how to exert influence where they needed to.[55] As Fiedrich, working in rural Uganda, concluded, the issue for women was not male dominance, but male weakness; the problem of men as failed providers (2002: 141). And so women try to make men 'more rather than less central to their lives', try to secure their respect, make them approximate more closely the ideal of a good husband, and so achieve domestic unity and status in the community (2002: 141).

The ability to comment on the behaviour of their men was perhaps something new; and the existence of women's groups certainly proved significant in negotiating greater permissiveness from husbands in this and other regards. Women's groups did provide a means for women to express opinions and interests in public (and so contribute to village development plans); they offered arenas for more independent financial decision-making or income generation. Through the mechanism of compulsory savings women also gained more control over income from their wage labour, and some had access to loans in their own name for the first time. However, the new room for manoeuvre for women was heavily circumscribed. It was not the majority but only a few key women, often *jankars*, who expressed and brokered changes in gender relations. As one ordinary group member commented:

It was wonderful when Vacula Ben [the *jankar*] was here. She really made us understand things. [But] it is really difficult for us to talk to the men in that way; they cannot teach us the way she did. We have to hide our faces when we are talking to men … women can only learn from other women, men cannot teach them. It is definitely important to have female *jankars*.[56]

But even if they did not herald radical change women felt their groups gave them new opportunities to meet regularly as women outside normal working and kinship contexts, to give voice to issues or just 'to sit … talk, joke'.[57] In this sense groups were more important in changing relations *between women* than with men. 'Earlier we only had mother-in-laws in the groups', Priya told me, 'but later the younger generation also came and were recognised.' Finally, to reiterate, the project could not claim to have *produced* these and other social and lifestyle changes, but it did provide a context in which social aspirations could be expressed, whether these concerned gender relations, or a feeling for modernity or freedom.

BECOMING BETTER FARMERS OR LABOUR MIGRANTS?

Despite themselves exemplifying urban lifestyles, project staff intended to secure solid peasant identities among their Bhil beneficiaries, and consequently made the reduction in urban migration for wages a key indicator of project impact. Did the project reduce seasonal migration and affirm Bhil agriculturalist identities? It is rather difficult to answer the first part of this question, (i) because the 'impact assessment' studies were conducted after only five years of the project, and (ii) there was anyway much inter-year variation in the degree of migration. The evidence that we did generate from villagers presents a picture that is complex and difficult to interpret.

In several villages examined there was an *overall* decrease in the amount of migration between 1992 and 1996 in terms of the number of migrants and especially the *duration* of migration (from 6.5 to 4 months per year in one Jhabua village), which reversed a previous upwards trend. Commonly the decline in male migration was greater than female. Indeed, in some villages there was a slight increase in the number and duration of women migrating. As expected, reduction in migration was greater among better-off landed households; but then in some villages the reverse was true, notably in those with irrigated winter (*rabi*) cropping where levels of 'opportunistic' migration, determined by the availability of surplus household labour, were maintained or increased.

Localised decline in migration was primarily explained by the availability of wage labour on project works (SWC, forestry, etc.). The effect of the project on migration was therefore short term. Indeed, in the drought years of 1999–2000 labour migration from all villages soared, and in 2001–2 was kept high in some places by construction work opportunities in post-earthquake Kuchch. Only one programme – lift irrigation with its demand for labour for a second (*rabi*) crop, and offering an increase in income seriously able to offset migrant earnings – was likely to compete directly with (and so reduce) migration in the long term.

We have already seen that project benefits were skewed towards land- or labour-rich households. It also seemed that it was better-off men – those least in need of migrant earnings – who were able to limit their migration (and reduce the discomfort and expenditure involved) in order to participate in project activities and devote more time to their farms. Interestingly, the slight reduction in the migration of higher-status, articulate males contributed to a recorded *perception* that migration had reduced far more as a result of the project than it actually had. In several villages throughout the project area, survey data showed that the number of migrants had actually increased.[58] One Dahod (Gujarat) case study not only showed an increase in the number of migrants, but also revealed that most of this increase (87 per cent) derived from additional *women* migrating. Despite this, group interviews recorded the contrary view that labour migration from the village had *fallen*. Typically, they recorded the dominant views of household heads who had been substituted in migration by women or other socially less visible individuals.[59] Change in the *number* of migrants is not, however, a good measure of project effects, since although more people were migrating, they were leaving for shorter periods, working more flexibly and retaining more of the income earned. This was a more important positive change than a reduction in absolute levels of migration. However, villages did not share the project's zero-sum view of migration in relation to agriculture. Even though they sought every opportunity to earn wages locally and to increase agricultural income, redirecting their energy from migration to their land, in the end farming depended upon migrant earnings (for inputs, investment or debt management) just as 'cultivating' urban work relied on village networks (see Chapter 3). It was no longer a paradox, that people in one Dahod Bhil village could perceive themselves as becoming better off, while experiencing a five-fold increase in the number of migrating households.[60] Growing recognition of the irreversibility of seasonal labour migration to Bhil livelihood strategies, and the fact that, certainly for the poorest, project impacts were unlikely to reduce this, led to my involvement in recent IBRFP efforts to develop a programme to support adivasi migrants rather than to reduce their migration (Mosse 2002, 2003c).[61]

DISJUNCTURE BETWEEN DESIGN MODELS AND PROJECT EFFECTS

After five years the IBRFP project effects were complex and contradictory. What is significant is that they were so often at variance with the assumptions of the policy models which legitimised the project and in terms of which it was either praised as a success or condemned as failure. For one thing, the project's models under-emphasised the significance of cash incomes from seasonal labour migration to livelihoods and sought to promote farming systems' development as an *alternative* to migrant livelihoods. But the actual effect of the project was probably to deepen the interdependence of agriculture and labour migration by pushing a trend towards greater reliance on cash incomes. While IBRFP philosophy urged self-sufficiency, the project (further) opened the door to input agriculture, productive credit and cash cropping. New cultivation and new lifestyles demanded more spending on fertiliser, clothes, medicine, utensils, vegetables, oil, spices, garlic or mosquito spray, to draw from long lists through which villagers explained the rising cost of living. Brideprice too was inflating, and with it the demands of *chandla* and *notra*.[62]

Second, the project model emphasised the gains from natural resources *research* rather than extension (Shepherd et al. 2000). The approach of the crop programme specifically was to identify new crop technology that would of itself increase yields without the need for changed practices or additional inputs. It was breeding rather than agronomy based. But on farmers' fields in rainfed areas, it was the weakness of extension, or at least the (socially determined) constraints on input supply, including credit, that most seriously limited production. Where agricultural productivity increased in IBRFP villages, it was held to have less to do with improved technology (seeds and low-cost soil and water conservation), and more to do with new access to inputs of credit, fertiliser and irrigation premised on changed social relations and project patronage. In fact, the predicted high rates of return based on the spread of improved varieties had not been realised by the end of Phase I, although in 2001 hope remained for the maize variety GDRM-187.[63] (By then, however, the ODA–DFID had become more interested in the wider *policy* impact of the PVS crops programme in changing state institutions.)[64]

Third (and relatedly), while the participatory model was premised on an alternative low-cost, low-subsidy approach that promoted rainfed technology, low external inputs and self-sufficiency, the most tangible economic benefits derived from the *external* provision of subsidised inputs/credit, irrigation (LIS, wells, pumps and check dams) and employment. In other words, the reported increases in net income resulted from an extension of the classic irrigation–seed–fertiliser green revolution combination to rainfed areas (cf. Shepherd et al. 2000). As some commentators put it, the project model had underestimated the 'key poverty reducing components of rural growth – irrigation, livestock, high value crops, non-farm employment' (2000). Its no-subsidy, low external input approach was anyway misguided given the supply push policy environment (2000). Certainly the role of KBCL itself as an input supplier to Bhil farmers was from the start heavily circumscribed by the project's participatory model. This model also paid little attention to market development, in which KBCL could have had a role (cf. Shepherd et al. 2000).

Fourth, there was a contradiction between the model's emphasis on independently managed Self-Help Groups (SHGs) and the project's effect, which was to create dependent groups through patronage and investment. Perhaps the 'expectation that externally driven projects could result in sustainable local organisations was itself questionable' (2000). Perhaps, as the village studies strongly suggest, 'of greater importance are the short-term qualitative benefits which result from the *process* of organisational development' – self-confidence, better links to government agencies, reduced alcohol and violence or increased school enrolment; outcomes which feed into existing streams of socio-cultural change (2000).[65]

The project philosophy also expected collective economic and environmental benefits, but in many respects benefits were individualised. That is to say, the project contributed to personal mobility, individual accumulation or political agency. Such outcomes often fell outside the framework of evaluation altogether. Unspoken was the individual mobility through the accumulation of assets, or project employment via the role of *jankar*. The project will certainly also have facilitated the individual pursuit of political careers or local office (even the foundation of new NGOs) by enhancing negotiation skills, skills in organisation (e.g. mobilising for events/rallies) communication and leadership (cf. Weisgrau 1997: 174–85). Through personal networks and upward links forged via development projects, individuals quickly attract the interest of political leaders (1997: 174–85). Weisgrau suggests that two factors may have enhanced the rising level of Bhil political participation and at the same time strengthened the link between development projects and the political process such that good beneficiaries become political leaders. The first is political decentralisation, which has turned local panchayats into vehicles for adivasis to enter the arena of local government, and the second is the increasing penetration of Hindu nationalists into adivasi areas (1997: 8). With the latter comes the threat of communalised identities and violence, as witnessed in Gujarat in 2002.

The IBRFP project exists within a wider political economy and can be analysed along with similar projects in these terms (although this has not been my focus). Some might argue, for instance, that the project has unacknowledged structural effects; that 'by integrating rural peasants into the cash-based, commodity-based system of income generation [it was] ... acting as the agent[s] of the government, on behalf of the transnational capitalist system' (Kothari 1986, via Weisgrau 1997: 104); others, that it reproduced 'the statist discourse of development, modernisation and nationalism' denying its own politics behind an apolitical technocratic view of development (Kamat 2002, in Baviskar 2003); or even that it has some unspecified part in the rise of communal identity politics (e.g. through a regionalised modernisation agenda). All arguable points, although not ones that would add greatly to the ethnographic understanding of development. Certainly it would be hard to defend the radical credentials of the project. Indeed, no one would attempt to do so. The project's many self-maintaining connections (brokerage and translations) made it inherently conservative and structure-affirming in its effects, reconstituting rather than challenging relations of power, authority and patronage at every level – in Bhil villages, in the project team or within the corporate organisation, donor and beyond. Indeed this was critical to its mode of functioning.

But, while global relations of power and policy processes can be drawn into an understanding of the way in which this international development project came to operate in these Bhil villages and the effects that it had, their logic remains opaque to local actors (cf. Das 1995: 201–3). The point is that people transform, reshape or, in de Certeau's terms, 'consume' these wider process (including IBRFP schemes), even succumb to them (cf. Friedman 1993, in Das 1995: 201–3). Our own rationalisations and official models are also subverted, and our schemes put to local social ends. Perhaps our schemes underpin social rank, or are drawn into conflicts over resources of grazing, water, land, party affiliation or kinship divisions, maybe amplifying them (Weisgrau 1997). Our technical ambitions run aground on people's cultivation practices; our financial models are destroyed by their decision making. In a variety of ways, people discard the discipline of participation and self-help by making themselves clients, labourers or employees so as to secure continuing patronage, capital assets or wage labour. Unruly objects of development, these people strive to be modern when we want them to be indigenous, chaotic when we demand order; they present themselves as our clients and employees when we call them partners; dependent when we insist on their autonomy. They make a mockery of our models and our explanations. But still smile and work with us to hold our models together.

CONCLUSIONS: THE VEIL OF POLICY

What I hope this chapter has shown is that even though IBRFP's legimating models were contradicted, not only by the project's mode of operation but also by its socio-economic effects, the project *did* have a significant positive effect on the lives of many thousand adivasis in the villages of this western India region, albeit often in unscripted and unintended ways. Now this does not make IBRFP a shining example of 'participatory development'. To claim this, or to refute it, is to give priority to policy success or failure and to ignore how things actually happen. Indeed, an intense emphasis on current policy burdens projects with models ('participation' or 'governance') which may have little bearing on the actual reasons for the socio-economic effects they have.

Take the central project idea of *'enhancing community self-reliance through institutional development'*. As we have seen, this came to mean establishing self-help farmer groups capable of independently organising local development: managing financial and natural resources, supplying agro-inputs so that the project would withdraw its services from given villages and areas. This model, adopted by

NGOs throughout South Asia, became central to IBRFP's policy representation. But in this case it was an obscuring policy vision. Much to the frustration of many (including myself) this policy vision was never, could never have been, turned into reality. After all, the project's reputation, the performance of local field staff, the cultural processes of SHGs and technology adoption, the interests – indeed the core rationale – of the project from KBCL's *and* the Bhil villagers' point of view, were all based on the project's network of patronage and welfare, largesse and the delivery of agro-inputs and an expanding range of high-quality programmes, increasingly through village groups and *jankars*. To be sure, many of the project activities increased knowledge, skills and contacts; even released a 'spirit of experimentation' as one member of staff put it. But the whole venture required the retention and extension of project power not its transfer to people. This carefully controlled and intensively managed system was simply not going to be abandoned for the grave risks of allowing independent decisions and financial responsibility, local autonomy and the withdrawal of the project. Why would the KBCL project want to get rid of its best customers, and villagers a serviceable patron? Even assuming it wanted to promote farmer self-reliance, the project was part of an organisation whose hierarchy and system of accountability was not able to take the risks necessary to devolve power to communities. In fact, as Abraham and Platteau (2004) note, participatory approaches present a more generic dilemma. Enhancing community or demand-driven approaches requires a more intensive agency presence (time, personnel, resources). This both compromises the claimed strength and cost-efficiency of participatory approaches, and also means that agencies are pushed or drawn into patronage modes of work. This is especially so in agricultural development, which demands continuity and follow-up; in which project agents become suppliers of technology and market intermediaries (and this is one reason why NGOs hoping for autonomous development outcomes avoid agricultural development, Desai 2004).

While it was never internalised into project procedures, the group-based model of farmer self-reliance persisted. It was a key element in the project's Phase II, newly underscored by a DFID Sustainable Rural Livelihoods model, with the language of 'social capital'. The model was initially forged in the early 1990s (by myself among others) to underpin a key negotiating position in development policy arguments, and as a critique of dominating agrarian modernism and KBCL patronage. However, it bore little relationship to the institutional possibilities of this project structure, at this time, in this place. Examined critically, the self-reliance model was not only unimplementable but also involved a neo-orientalist de-legitimising of all forms of external dependence – subsidies, moneylenders, migration, agro-inputs or the marketing of commercial crops – as deviation from the primacy of local control and the protection of low-risk subsistence livelihoods. It ignored the project's own reality. IBRFP was not a hidden hand consolidating self-reliance by executing participatory development policy; it was a powerful external source of patronage interacting with regional and historical processes of change. For its Bhil beneficiary communities it was a means to access external resources, to articulate broader social ambitions and cultural re-evaluation as well as individual economic and political mobility.

10
Conclusions and Implications

So what can be concluded here about the relationship between aid policy and practice? Perhaps that projects can work, but not because they are well designed; that it is dangerous to impose policy prescriptions without taking institutional contexts into account; that policy change ruptures informal systems supporting projects; or that an upstream focus on policy increases ignorance of the instrumentalities and contingencies of aid.

Evidently, even in relatively small projects the relationship between policy models and development outcomes is complex and obscure. The intersection of the world of policy thought and the world of development practice is partial and socially managed. Policy discourse generates mobilising metaphors ('participation', 'partnership', 'governance') whose vagueness, ambiguity and lack of conceptual precision is *required* to conceal ideological differences so as to allow compromise and the enrolment of different interests, to distribute agency and to multiply the criteria of success within project systems (cf. Dahl 2001: 20, Li 1999). But ideas that make for 'good policy' – policy that legitimises and mobilises political and practical support – are not those that provide good guides to action. Good policy is unimplementable; it is metaphor not management[1] (although 'management' may be the most important development metaphor of all). Or perhaps, rather than unimplementable, we should say of policy design 'that it's "in contradiction" with other ideas [e.g., system goals] that they also want to keep' (Latour 1996: 92).

Correspondingly, policy models are poor guides to understanding events and the practices and effects of development actors, which are shaped by the relationships, interests and cultures of specific organisational settings. Of course this is common knowledge among reflective donor policy makers, who know how their own institutional relations and practices are concealed within the coherent policy papers they produce. But at other levels too – in donor policy groups, consultant teams, project offices, field staff meetings, PRAs or villager assemblies – a significant part of development *practice* involves the reproduction and stabilisation of policy models (often the same ones) which both conceal and provide authoritative interpretations of practice (one's own or other people's). Projects sustain policy by working to effect an artefactual separation between representations and reality (models and events, designs and effects, science and production, technology and nature) that 'allow reason to rule, and allow history to be arranged as the unfolding of a locationless [policy] logic' to which expertise is attached (Mitchell 2002: 15, 36). Project actors – including consultants and donor advisers – abstract from practice, silencing aspects of their own interventions and the wider politics of aid of which they are a part, to produce and protect policy models. By concealing its processes, and its social-historical context, the IBRFP sustained the notion that its success was good policy well executed. The disjuncture between policy and practice is not, therefore, an unfortunate gap to be bridged between intention and action; it is a necessity, actively maintained and reproduced.[2]

Policy models are, further, secured upon social networks that constitute interpretive communities for projects and programmes. These 'public transcripts' of development are sustained by the powerful *and* the subordinate, both of whose interests lead them to 'tactically conspire to misrepresent' (Scott 1990: 2). In development we cannot speak of policy controlling or disciplining, being resisted or subverted. Policy is an *end* rather than a cause; a result, often a fragile one, of social processes.

The IBRFP project 'worked' in two distinct senses: first, it established itself as an exemplar of policy, generating valid interpretations; and second, it had some positive local socio-economic effects. There is no necessary connection between the two. The project did not work *because* it turned policy into reality. Rather, it sustained policy models offering a significant interpretation of the situation. In the case of the crops and other PTD (Participatory Technology Development) programmes, the 'interpretations' offered (of the socio-ecology of Bhil farming) through the application of the PVS/PPB project model took the concrete form of new technologies such as improved seeds (Kalinga III, GDRM-187, etc.; that is to say a new relationship of patronage and input supply can be interpreted as improved technology). Like other interpretations, technologies were successfully disseminated, sold, adopted by the state or other projects, and used to account for (as much as produce) change elsewhere. In a sense, all development programmes work politically through interpretation and the creative capacity of policy to connect economic and historical processes of change to its normative schemes. This allows villagers and fieldworkers, as well as bureaucrats and government advisers, to collude in making privileged knowledge and technology (often outsiders' knowledge and technology) the authors of history; a kind of history whose causal chains lead back to managed budgets.

Does this make policy irrelevant? Not at all. Policy interpretations are far from superfluous to the concrete effects of development (and improved seeds are not superfluous to yield increases). Policy provides the context for action[3] and is crucial for a project like IBRFP to work in the second sense. Socio-economic benefits would not have arisen in project villages without the validating frameworks that connected project action to international policy goals, whether 'participatory development', 'sustainable rural livelihoods' or 'good governance' (or to Indian national and regional policy goals), so as to mobilise support and to draw assemblies of actors and new resources to places like Bhil western India; not forgetting that development policy also facilitates flows of resources to other beneficiaries – donor staff, consultants, training institutions, universities, academics, myself – even while it organises our attention away from them, and so reproduces relationships of power and privilege. Chapter 8 showed the potential resource implications of failing to connect to policy.

We can also look at the issue the other way around, and say that in order to 'work' policy models and programme designs have to be *transformed* in practice. They have to be translated into the different logic of the intentions, goals and ambitions of the many people and institutions they bring together. Locally, for example, participation is translated into patronage, new seeds into sources of credit. The first phase of IBRFP worked and deserved the praise that it received because its project management, consultant mediators and village workers skilfully translated between the incompatible logics of the donor policy process, KBCL's organisational interests and villagers' desires. For policy to succeed it is necessary, it seems, that it is *not* implemented, but that enough people, and people with enough power, are willing to believe that it is. Failures arise from inadequacy of translation and interpretation: from the inability to recruit local interests, or to connect actions/events to policy or to sustain politically viable models and representations.

COSTS AND RISKS OF MAINTAINING ORDER AND DISJUNCTURE

There are consequences and costs to the way projects like IBRFP work. First, a preoccupation with (project) models as determinants of 'success' and 'failure' means that a donor's knowledge of development is overly model-based or deductive, and allows little inductive understanding of contingencies and instrumentalities, or open-ended learning. Perhaps development thinking needs to make the same shift science studies have proposed, that is 'from a "representational idiom" [of science] that leaves us only with epistemology, and towards a "performative one", an ontology of processes' (Pickering 2002, in Desai 2004).

Second, because the emphasis on the preservation of policy models occurs within unequal relations of power, the orientation is always 'upwards' in international development. Even in 'bottom-up' projects, policy innovation comes from on top. This has several important consequences. Hierarchies of power ensure that Bhil villagers or IBRFP staff comply with donor policy theorising, they agree to shifting goals and do not stand up and hold the project or donor accountable for its ideas/representations (or the money spent). To ensure further funding and support, projects have to continue to reflect external agendas, to bear the stamp of the plan, rather than reflect their own organisational and social reality. Projects remain forever *projections*. Their actions and events never have meaning in themselves, but are constantly recalled or translated back into the policy text, from which they can never fully depart in order to become part of the everyday (cf. Latour 1996: 24). Hence the constant need for expert interpretation. So, for organisations as well as for local communities, empowerment or simply survival comes not through validation of their own knowledge, processes or cultures, but through orientation to the knowledge and narratives of more powerful players. Project managers bear a heavy policy agenda, while 'on Jhabua's [adivasi] villages falls the burden of being ecologically sustainable' (Baviskar forthcoming: 29).

When external (donor) policy provides the framework for interpreting effects, and when the real instrumentalities are ignored, Abdelrahman and Apthorpe refer to 'dispossession' of the local partner (2002). 'Dispossession' can be viewed as an effect of power at many levels within project systems such as DFID–IBRFP. It is most intensely experienced around moments of policy shift that bring a reconfiguration of meaning, arbitrary judgement and the risk of failure. As I noted in Chapter 8, when policy changes faster than the life of a programme, which is now normal, project agencies (such as IBRFP) become increasingly reactive, directing their energies to the upwardly oriented process of preserving themselves as systems of representations rather than towards action or learning.[4] These effects, I noted, are amplified by greater convergence and coherence of the policy of donors such as DFID.

The preservation of policy models, the subjugation of the politics and instrumentalities of development and the dispossession of a project agency can be illustrated with an example from the IBRFP project in which I am myself implicated. Towards the end of the first phase of the project (1997–8), I had become highly critical of the project's failure to promote participatory development and especially the weak and dependent nature of its farmer groups (see Chapter 6). Now, my own construction of 'failure' and the project's (and DFID's) construction of 'success' endorsed the same participatory model, privileging it over the reality of practice. In some respects at least, the policy model provided an unreliable interpretation and a misleading judgement (Chapter 9). Had I made a more pragmatic appraisal of project action – less shaped by ideological debates, neo-liberal ideas of individual responsibility and empowerment,[5] or (*mea culpa*) middle-class NGO intellectual distaste for Indian industrialist perspectives in general, let alone those of a fertiliser company – I would have seen not a failure of 'participation' but new avenues of non-state patronage, advantageous in a remote tribal area, extending input infrastructure (credit, fertiliser, improved seeds) or marketing possibilities. As we saw in Chapter 9, these occurred even as the project purveyed images of farmer-management or self-reliance (and now of 'state-linkage'), and was (is) represented as 'success' or 'failure' in terms of one or other policy idea. At the end of Phase I, the project benefits of patronage (new inputs, management subsidies), and mediated links to regional, national and international agricultural research agendas were highly significant. Arguably, they depended upon the permanent and expanding presence of the project organisation as a parastatal extension service, offering better technology and more affordable inputs to remote adivasi villages rather than autonomy and independence. This may or may not be 'participation' or 'sustainable development'; and it certainly failed to articulate currently dominant international development ideas of 'farmer-managed development', and therefore remained a subjugated project logic.

So, even if a project fails to articulate one or other preconceived model; if it fails to be 'fully participatory', or to adopt a genuine 'livelihoods approach', or to exert influence over 'governance', it can still have important livelihood effects. IBRFP was a partly successful 'participatory development' project. It might yet prove to be a viable 'livelihoods project'; or, who knows, even a 'governance project' as it stumbles along with a heavy policy baggage (multiplying its own internal contradictions) and maintains a complex 'system of representations' requiring skilled international consultants to articulate. But perhaps with less policy correctness it might have been a rainfed technology input supply and marketing agency in a national cooperative, building on an existing institution and its corporate values. Perhaps ... But as such, and if it failed to articulate policy, it would not have been a successful *development* project. Its power to assemble supporters and resources would have been diminished; and, moreover, it is most unlikely that it would have directed resources to the poorest subsistence farmers in a remote tribal region.

If one problem with the assertion of policy over practice is the subjugation of certain positive outcomes; a second is the perpetuation of false models, simplifications and development illusions. In the competitive market for success it is difficult for dependent agencies *not* to portray their actions as achievements in terms of currently favoured models. The cost of breaking ranks is high and public disputes over meaning and interpretation are rare. But, when they do occur, they are very informative. Let me illustrate. Imagine a meeting in September 2001. IBRFP staff have invited members of an NGO working in the same region to their office to talk about 'collaboration' – part of the DFID imperative to disseminate and replicate the current project model. The visiting NGO staff first ask IBRFP to explain their analysis of problems in the area. The project staff provide a coherent rendering of the project strategy: develop Self-Help Groups and commons management institutions like JFM groups, popularise improved varieties and withdraw after five to seven years to ensure sustainability of natural resources development work. There is a pause. Then a senior member of the NGO staff speaks:

> You know, after 30 years working in this area we are stuck. We face a real problem creating institutions around common resources: problems of tenure, encroachment; there are different interests ... What do we encounter on the ground? These solidarities are fairly weak. IBRFP has an assumption that collective action exists, it is an achievement, it is benefiting a large number of people. [You assume that] these solidarities [e.g. SHGs, JFM groups] exist ... [you] put a flag on them as village republics ... These are convenient assumptions. If we [NGOs] don't put forward simple ideas, we don't get resources [from donors]. But we say, even if you go five times, and make petitions, [you] can't even put a single tree on common ground without factional conflict. Each faction

has its *mandali* [group]. There are fallacies about what is possible for NGOs ... We do a disservice when we affirm false assumptions. We [IBRFP and the NGO] are occupying the same space, but we have completely different narratives. [We] also put in resources, but even then we are not able to make a dent on certain issues. Some things do not respond to resources. IBRFP has apparent success ... [but] greening is a seasonal thing. [We] do not have to advertise success, [our donors do not demand it]. What is worrying is if we fudge the basic reality.

The members of an experienced NGO deliberately place themselves outside IBRFP's interpretive community; they confront the model, defy the representation, disoblige the donor, resist dependence and refuse to 'overstate what is possible'. Their politics refuses collaboration across a chasm of meaning. IBRFP staff do not know how to respond. Later, when the visitors have left, over coffee a senior manager, entirely without irony, dismisses the NGO's points as 'wholly idealistic'. Not for the first time I have the sense that in development, experience and practice are compelled to return to stable policy representations even if these are deceiving blueprints proclaiming innovation.

BEYOND PROJECTS

Projects are no longer the favoured instruments of international aid; but the fact that development's knowledge workers have broader visions has not removed and may in fact have amplified the problems of order and disjuncture discussed in this book. First, many of the institutional effects at the project level find their equivalent at national and international levels, especially in the context of a new convergence of global policy around donor supported comprehensive national development frameworks, which are as weak on 'transmission mechanisms' as are projects (Craig and Porter 2003). Reform agendas, national 'participatory' approaches (e.g. Participatory Poverty Assessments or citizen consultations) or programmes of decentralisation (all part of state-donor partnerships) are policy commitments contradicted by institutional practice. For example, conditional grant arrangements involve 'hardwired' mechanisms (financial incentives, administrative procedures, budget-expenditure norms or disciplinary reporting) that direct investments to pre-defined ends within national poverty reduction strategies, or translate local needs into the categories of central planning in ways that underline upward accountability and orientation towards maximising the flow of resources from outside (Craig and Porter 2003). Equivalently, the *modus operandi* of decentralisation (in the absence of a strong and impartial state) often involves 'making accommodations with local strongmen rather than expanding democratic spaces' (Heller 2001, cited in Abraham and Platteau 2004).

Second, the policy-oriented staff of donor agencies like DFID are themselves increasingly removed from the contingencies of development. The hands-on expatriate-managed projects tied to donor-country expertise and exports have, quite rightly, all but disappeared, certainly from British aid. Unquestionably, development policy has become more postcolonial. But at the same time, as noted in Chapter 1, aid policy has become more managerial. Its ends – the quantified reduction of poverty or ill health – have narrowed, but its means have diversified to the management of more and more: financial and political systems and civil society. A unipolar global political order renews confidence in rational design and social engineering. It is an implication of the rise of global governance (Duffield 2001), and attended by a new 'economics imperialism' (Fine 2002). Today's 'high managerialism', precisely contrasts the 'high modernism' of the 1950s and 1960s models in which a broadly defined and radically future-oriented development end – the transition to modernity, or westernisation – was to be accomplished by the narrow means of technology-led growth (cf. Scott 1998). Indeed, the former goals of development (socio-political transformation) are now rationalised as its means (see Quarles van Ufford et al. 2003). The paradox is that 'high mangerialism' actually controls less and less (Quarles van Ufford et al. 2003: 9). It privileges policy over practice. Donor advisers and specialists are involved in a scramble 'upstream' away from the localised triviality of 'neo-colonial' projects and programmes and into the offices of regional or national planning (2003: 9) to work out 'shared commitments to government-led programmes investing in long-term development' (Clare Short, speech in New Delhi, March 1999). More than ever, international development is about generating consensus on approaches and framing models that link investment to outcomes, rather than implementation modalities (Quarles van Ufford et al. 2003: 9). Questions of implementation are somebody else's problem. With the move from projects, the chains of causality (and accountability) in development lengthen and fade. New policy ambitions demand that 'the black box separating inputs and outputs/ effects is drawn larger and larger' (2003: 9), expanding the shadowed work of development's many translators and brokers. As a result more of the everyday is hidden. The contingencies of interventions and the praxis of programmes 'disappear between the proclamations of high-level development partnerships, sector-wide approaches (etc.) on the one hand, and the national/regional statistical record of reduced poverty, illiteracy, morbidity (etc.) on the other' (2003: 9).

'Of course, aid organisations like DFID still have to disburse money – indeed foreign policy dictates that the aid budgets of nations that claim a standing should grow, but old models linking spending and results (projects and programmes) have lost credibility' (2003: 9–10). Old instruments of development, such as building infrastructure (which at least disbursed funds efficiently), now have to be connected to new policy goals. There is a constant need for new theory to disburse funds meaningfully, to link money to goals. 'This is the work of increased numbers of knowledge workers in aid agency head offices; producing policy papers which explain, justify and make coherent' (2003: 10). Increasingly it is the representational world that is managed; success and failure are matters of legitimacy and meaning.

To reiterate, the problem is not that policy is coherent, but that a policy machinery fabricates its separation from political economy and that it becomes isolated from the local or vernacular to which it is nonetheless materially connected through fund flows, information and in other ways. A preoccupation with the politics of the policy process – legitimisation, enrolling support and securing funds – produces ignorance of project effects. Ethnographic research has a contribution to make to knowledge about both the fabrications and the 'downstream effects' of policy. Certainly the rather sparse ethnographic literature that exists draws attention to ways in which managerialist policy discourse is far from politically neutral, and can produce social and political effects which fall outside the policy frameworks and the knowledge of agency staff. To cite just one recent example, David Abramson's study of the use of 'civil society' rhetoric by donor-supported Uzbek national NGOs shows how the policy model fostered 'a particular hegemony in which "civility" is symbolically opposed to accommodating an Islamic political culture' (1999: 247). Indeed, Islam as an organising framework for Uzbekistan was systematically ignored in ways that alienated the poorer components of society and could serve to intensify conflict between different social groups. 'Civil society' conveyed a pervasive anti-Islamic rhetoric and mistrust of Islam in the donor and development community as well as in the government; expressing and effecting a 'strong ideological link between transnational development and certain local interest groups' (Abramson 1999: 247).

LOCAL AUTONOMY AND COOPTION FROM BELOW

An implication of the privileging of policy over practice and the limited scope for control in development, is the autonomy that subordinates in development's chain of organisation (whether field staff, agency managers or others) can create for themselves and their fields of action. In de Certeau's terms, they consent to development models while making of them something different, escaping the power of the dominant order without leaving it, using their tactics to contend with the strategies of consultants and donor advisers (1984: xviii).[6] In short, policy is coopted from below.

Indeed, it is easy to assume too much about the direction of power in development. As Cooper and Packard (1997: 3) point out, 'locating power does not show that it is determinant or that a particular discourse is not appropriable for other purposes'.[7] Moreover, the universal technical-moral language of development implicitly draws on ideas of universal rights and global citizenship which provide a basis for popular mobilisation; a discourse of control may also be a discourse of entitlement in which to press claims on the state or international development agencies (1997: 4). This is, of course, equally the case with the discourse of participation. It is mere polemic to talk in an unqualified way of participation as 'the new tyranny' (Cook and Kothari 2001). Ideas of participation may serve 'top-down' interests such as legitimation or efficiency (i.e. cost-saving), but they also have enormous potential to enfranchise perspectives from below, or to offer the potential for inclusion, empowerment or leverage (White 1996).

And of course this is true of the IBRFP project too. In a multitude of ways the language of participation provided new visions, new potential to defend interests or demand accountability and to open up liberating spaces beyond the control of the project. Even the public rituals which objectified poor tribals within the project's nationalist dramas of social transformation (PRAs, public gatherings) were simultaneously 'dramas of inclusion ... allowing the poor to work their way into the public sphere and visible citizenship without open confrontation' (Appadurai 2004). In 2001, when project staff were contending with 'failure' and locked into the task of delivering against targets and articulating new donor policy models, village leaders and *jankars*, experienced in the ways of the project, sat and talked with us in strategic and long-term ways about their future. It was they rather than staff who were considering ways to link SHGs together into federations (*maha mandals*) to negotiate more effectively with the state over forestry resources or to deal with failing groups or corrupt leaders, to resolve conflicts or to search out support for new farm or forest-related enterprises – needs felt more acutely in the context of recent drought. It was clear that the effects of 'participation' could change over time. Initiatives in cooperative resource management might collapse and disappear, but they could also deepen into forms of political action (White 1996). Reflecting on such encounters and outcomes, the project becomes again an optimistic discourse of hope. These are ends that can be worked towards. The emancipatory intentions of policy and the aspirations and interests of the poor *can* be linked.

ANTHROPOLOGISTS IN DEVELOPMENT:
HOPE, POLITICS AND CRITICAL REFLECTION

Trying to reconcile optimism and scepticism in development Quarles van Ufford et al. distinguish between development as *hope*, development as *politics/administration* and development as *critical understanding* (2003). These, they show, are historical phases in post-war development, as well as distinct domains of knowledge and action. These three domains also help to differentiate my own ten-year interaction with the IBRFP project, which involved a moral, a strategic-administrative (i.e. political) as well as a critical aspect. Although these perspectives are co-present, the personal shifts in working within a project community tended to bring one or other frame to the fore at any particular moment. So, at the outset when we were formulating and negotiating the project, when new staff and supporters were being enrolled, the IBRFP project was for me (and my colleagues) a set of moral choices; a design of hope. Goals were also moral responsibilities (to focus on the needs of the poorest, of women, to promote democratic processes). Characteristically, hope involved the redefinition of the past and present in terms of an imagined future. But project formulation, design and textualisation were also contexts for political engagement (see Chapter 2). The project was about coalition building and influence; it aimed to challenge established and dominant forms of knowledge. The chapters of this book have shown how the work of implementation, especially, was shaped by administrative and political agency. For me, this in turn gave rise to a need for a critical understanding of the project processes themselves; a perspective which gradually became more central to my own work over a ten-year period culminating in this book.[8]

There are obvious dangers in the assertion of one mode of thought/action over another. As this study has shown, hope's mobilising policy metaphors or the managerial optimism of the project cycle are poor guides to the administrative politics of project action; they have to be transformed in practice. But bureaucratic exigencies unleavened by the aspirations or visions of policy entrench existing structures of power and inequality of which practitioners remain ignorant without critical reflection. And the critical analytic 'hermeneutics of suspicion [of development interventions] leads to an impasse if it is not supplemented by a hermeneutics of recovery and reconstruction' (Quarles van Ufford et al. 2003: 17).

But in its different modes of hope, politics/administration and critical understanding development is 'a hetereogeneous field of action and imagination' (2003: 18). We cannot 'assume that the translation between different domains of development is always possible' – that policy can shape implementation, that research insights can influence policy. Incompatibility has to be expected and expectations of coherence avoided. One of the principal failings of recent debates on anthropology in, or of, development is the failure to acknowledge the heterogeneity of hope, politics and critical reflection. Instead the debate has reproduced the same institutionalised distinction between constructive engagement and disengaged critical analysis that results in the divergence of the careers of anthropologists as either development professionals (consultants, advisers, policy researchers), or as scholarly academics. While some of the latter accuse the former of contributing to the reinforcement of ethnocentric and dominating models in development, some of the former accuse the latter of elitist irrelevance driven by the intellectual trends of Northern academia. Caricatures of mercenary consultants or 'feeble forms of politically correct anthropology' (Grillo 1997) abound, seriously misrepresenting the varied spectrum of positions from which anthropologists work, and their individual capacity to combine engagement with policy and critical work (determined by things such as institutional affiliation – tenured academic or freelance consultant – market position, age/seniority, reputation with development agencies amongst others, cf. Wood 1998).[9]

Anthropologists *do* have a capacity to open up space for policy innovation, especially when linked by networks across institutional boundaries. But this capacity depends both upon developing close connections to agencies and the policy process, *and* upon independent critical reflection. If anthropologists become too close to the policy process this potential disappears. Consider, for example, the great increase in recruitment of anthropologists into Western development agencies that accompanied the rising profile of issues of poverty, participation or gender in the 1990s (Chapter 2). This gave rise to 'social development' as both a category of professional expertise and a pseudo-discipline in donor agencies such as DFID. The presence of this discipline was not easy to negotiate within donor agencies dominated by economic models or in developing country bureaucracies (where 'social development advisers' lacked technical counterparts, or sought substitutes among NGOs). Developing in the shadow of economics, social development promoted its own predictive, generalising concepts and methods, drawing anthropologists away from specialist regional analysis (cf. Bebbington et al. 2004, Mosse 1998a). Indeed, a tendency towards the universalisation of assumed processes of social change, rather than investigation of the actual context-specific process through which development outcomes are effected, made 'social development' more ideological than anthropological (as illustrated by my own work discussed in Chapter 6). The failure of social development to analyse political contexts (now increasingly recognised, cf. Eyben 2003) went along with assumptions about empowerment, self-improvement, natural collective action, a present- or project-bound analysis and an over-emphasis on social categories (women, the poor) rather than relationships between them (Green 2002: 62–4). Being confined, as it were, to the 'department of hope', limited the potential for innovation in development. This potential can perhaps be released by a critical-reflective turn amongst social development practitioners.

The assertion of distance from the concerns and institutional processes of development is also problematic for social anthropology as a discipline. Anthropologists working for development agencies in poor countries seldom need to be reminded that they work from positions of privilege within a 'regime of unequal international relations' (Cooper and Packard 1997: 5), across gradients of power as well as cultural difference. Unquestionably this presents its own problems and its own burdens. But what is more problematic for a reflective discipline is the failure to acknowledge that, as Little and

Painter put it, 'anthropology as a whole has helped produce and maintain, and continues to benefit from power relations on which development institutions and the discourses they generate rest'; and to place this moral burden on those who pursue particular career paths (1995: 605). It was, Burawoy reminds us, only the efforts of anthropologists to establish their own niche of expertise in the early 20th century that led anthropology as a discipline to professionalise itself with a focus on *dwelling* rather than travelling; but in doing so 'it overlooked the vast web of Empire, the multiple and asymmetrical connections between metropolis and colony that made focused field research possible [and ...] bracketed its own global underpinnings' (2001: 147). Perhaps, as Ferguson (1997) suggests, anthropological distance from development betrays an 'uncomfortable intimacy' of twinned discourses underpinned by the same grand themes of modernisation and globalisation (cf. Sivaramakrishnan and Agrawal 2003).

The ground of anthropological practice has changed fundamentally in the past two decades. The fact that anthropologists are no longer justified as value-free and objective observers, the source of politically neutral and authoritative scientific knowledge places anthropology back within historical relations of power. In relation to international development this provides opportunities, if not obligations, for engagement and self-critical reflection, for hope and critical understanding – neither of which is possible without close encounters with the administrative politics of development practice.

Notes

Note on documentary sources

Unfortunately there is no accessible or catalogued project archive that would allow unpublished documentation (memoranda, reports, studies, etc.) to be easily referenced. Key project documents – IBRFP project preparation and evaluation reports, annual reviews, consultancy reports and impact assessment village studies – were located with DFID (New Delhi/Project Adviser), the project head office (Delhi) and the University of Wales (Centres for Development Studies/Arid Zones Studies); in addition to these, progress reports, PRA reports, planning studies, process documentation, records of meetings and various *ad hoc* reports were in the project office (Dahod) or in more local state/cluster centres. I have of course accumulated my own archive of project materials

I INTRODUCTION: THE ETHNOGRAPHY OF POLICY AND PRACTICE

1. In this book I adopt a broad conception of 'policy' embracing global policy as well as strategies, models and designs which express this more locally. The justification for this is the strong interconnection that exists between project *designs* (causal theories, e.g. summarised in logical frameworks), policy *models* (frameworks and approaches, e.g. sustainable rural livelihoods) and the wider policy of a donor agency (e.g. participatory and poverty-focused development). So, while much of the book deals with policy as project designs, models and approaches, it will become clear (a) that these acquire form and win (or lose) legitimacy because they articulate (or fail to articulate) wider policy ambitions, and (b) that project exemplars are necessary to frame and sustain wider policy itself.

2. These targets include 'a reduction by one-half in the proportion of people living in extreme poverty by 2015, universal primary education in all countries by 2015, a reduction by two-thirds in infant and under-five mortality rates and by three-fourths in maternal mortality by 2015' (DFID 1997).

3. Following Duffield (2001) these may also be viewed as the preconditions for inclusion in the global economy. Correspondingly, social (and economic) exclusion is what defines 'the South' – increasingly the location, not just of poverty, but of conflict and instability, criminal activity, and terrorism. The international response to 'dangerous underdevelopment' is not globally inclusive economic development but 'global poor relief and riot control' (Duffield 2001: 7–8, citing Robert Cox).

4. On aid policy as a political project of strategic global governance, see Duffield (2001). It is significant that DFID's policy papers (DFID 1997, 2000) adopt the notion of *elimination* of poverty, which implies boundaries beyond which poverty (or ill-health) can vanish forever. Here, as Parkin

(1995) points out (with reference to medical thinking in East Africa), is a sort of 'black hole' solution to problems, which stands in contrast to the idea that poverty (or disease) is relational and requires constant counterwork; it is a managerial idea that does not easily fit with the concerns and options of people themselves.

5. Whether these are viewed as conspiratorial ends or unintended 'instrument effects' (Ferguson 1994) rather depends upon the theory of agency adopted.

6. See the writings of Agrawal (e.g. 1995), Gupta (1998), Li (1996, 2000), Mosse (1999), Moore (2000), Pigg (1992), Sundar (2000), which in various ways show how concern has shifted from advocating the authentically indigenous (or local or community etc.) in relation to the global-scientific, and towards exploration of the production of locality, indigenousness or community *through* development encounters.

7. To point out that development activities serve certain interests or have certain political *effects* is not to explain the motivations and meanings of those involved, or to undermine their ethic (cf. Crewe and Harrison 1998). The effect of things does not explain their properties. Sahlins (1999) takes to task the 'afterologists' – those new functionalists who would explain away culture as invented tradition whose truth is found in political utilities and instrumental effects; who indulge in 'explanation by way of elimination' – from whom we end up only knowing everything 'functionally, as devices of power ... not substantially or structurally' (1999: 404). Moreover, as Li notes (citing Friedman 1992), 'when anthropologists write, in their still authoritative voices, about "imagined communities" and "invented traditions"; they intervene in political struggles with major consequences for those whose certainties are thereby called into question' (Li 1996: 523).

8. Recent anthropological treatment of the state and bureaucracy also cautions against claims about the extension of 'bureaucratic power'. As Sivaramakrishnan (working on colonial forestry in Bengal) points out, policy intent is not to be mistaken for practical outcomes. The foresters' scientific working plans had to be reworked by local rights (1999: 244). Bureaucratic power is a fragile self-representation, sustainable only because of the unrecognised informal, compromises and processes – *metis* (Scott 1998) – that sustain practice. Uncritical ideas about the power and agency of 'the state' were earlier questioned by Abrams (1988) who drew a distinction between the 'idea of the state' as a unified source of intention and power, on the one hand, and the 'state-system' as a set of institutions of control, their personnel, practices and relationships, on the other (see Fuller and Harriss 2000). The idea (or ideology) of the state is a piece of 'symbolic capital' that supports the material power of the 'state-system'.

9. Pigg (1992, 1996) too shows how development narratives provide the conceptual distinctions (village/town; developed/underdeveloped; science/ superstition) which are actively deployed in defining place and social distinctions in a very particular way within hierarchical Nepali society.

10. As science and technology studies remind us, the actor networks that produce a development project are not confined to social relationships

but also involve *things*, technologies and other material resources, which constitute relationships. 'By themselves things don't act, but neither do humans' (Law 1994 in Steins 2001: 19; cf. Strum and Latour 1999, Winner 1999).

11. Latour's emphasis on translation and political acts of composition rests on the broader point that modernist ideas of the *a priori* unity of the social, or hidden social structure, have to be discarded. There is an affinity here with Stuart Hall's notion of 'articulation' which creates unities and cultural identities which are always provisional (Hall 1996).

12. Having written the final draft of this book I read Timothy Mitchell's important *Rule of Experts* (2002), which provides a parallel argument on a larger canvas. Mitchell examines the historical processes and new social practices that bifurcated the modern world into objects and ideas, reality and representation. The point is that modern development policy, which appears as rational abstraction separate from the social order it governs (as, for example, the law of property, the economy, capitalism), can be shown to be historically grounded in particular interests and events, contingencies, violence and exclusions. The apparent logic, universality and coherence of these ideas, and the expertise and rational design they call forth, are not inherent but produced through the messiness of contingent practice which succeeds in concealing social practice by effecting the separation of ideas and their objects. Policy does not precede and order practice, but is produced by it (see Chapter 6 this volume).

13. See *inter alia* Arce and Long (1992), Grammig (2002), Lipsky (1980), Long (1992, 2001), Long and Long (1992), Olivier de Sardan (forthcoming), Robertson (1984). Some of the collectives in this story – project agencies, marketing organisations, aid donors – are also social actors in the sense that they formulate and carry out decisions. Others such as 'the poor', tribal society, the state, NGOs, government, cannot legitimately be attributed with this quality of agency, even though these may comprise categories which are an important 'part of an individual's or organization's conceptual apparatus for processing the social world around them and upon which action takes place' (Long 1992: 23).

14. Burawoy, equivalently talks of an ethnography of the *production* of 'globalisation' as well as the experience of globalisation (2001: 150).

15. Jargon also disguises the relationships of development by creating 'the impression of the substitutability of people' (Kaufmann 1997).

16. While in the letter of their contracts development agencies often demand confidentiality or assert rights over knowledge produced, the capacity to assert such rights is seriously limited, and attempts to do so would often be more damaging than the independent publication of evidence or analysis. They would also have made it impossible to publish this book.

17. I will return to the role of anthropologists in development in Chapter 10.

18. The distinction between normative and pragmatic rules, deriving from F. Bailey, has been applied to development planning practices by Wood (1998).

19. In drawing a contrast between 'relativist' (or relationist) sociology and 'classical sociology', Latour (1996: 199) echoes earlier critics of anthropological authority (e.g. Pels and Nencel 1991), and of the anthropologist as decoder, cultural overseer who 'knows what everybody else is doing whether *they* know it or not' (Daniel 1994: 33), and in particular of the structuralist to whom society is a text to be read, and from which the '*real* meaning' of statements can be decoded 'regardless of whether they are acknowledged by its agents' (Asad 1986: 161).

20. The real danger, Latour suggests, is that people 'lose their recalcitrance by *complying*' (2000). He notes, by contrast, the contribution of feminism to new discoveries on gender, achieved by its effect of making potential interviewees more recalcitrant, more able to *object* to what was said about them (2000). The internet source (www.ensmp.fr/-latour/articles) from which this article was accessed does not give page references.

21. This book focuses on the policy idea of 'participation' in DFID, but another good example would be how 'social capital' (concept and quasi-causal model) has been promoted and shaped within the World Bank by those trying to forge the internal and external coalitions necessary to advance a 'social development' agenda in an economics-dominated organisation (see Bebbington et al. 2004).

22. Recent anthropology of development has devoted itself to critical analysis of development texts, their genre (Apthorpe 1996a, 1997, Gasper, 1996) or aesthetics (Stirrat 2000); the scientific knowledge they assert and the politics they conceal (Booth 1994, Chambers 1997, Sachs 1992); their construction of places and problems (Ferguson 1994); or the way they label the subjects of development (Wood 1985). Indeed, Arturo Escobar describes development 'a textually mediated discourse [that] substitutes for the actual relations and practices of the "beneficiaries", burying the latter's experience in the matrix that organizes the institution's representation' (1995).

23. Apthorpe argues that reading policy documents always requires more than the text; it needs 'a total picture of reason rules, responsibility, authority, community as well as just text' (1996a: 17), while Gardner and Lewis distinguish between: (a) documents (the outcome of social processes of persuasion and enrolment), (b) the beliefs, opinions or statements of individuals and (c) the activities undertaken (2000: 18).

24. A distinction borrowed from Baudrillard, via Hobart (1995). As Shore and Wright note, 'organisations exist in a constant state of organising'; they are concerned with the work of making 'fragmented activities appear coherent, so it can be claimed that an intention has been realised and a successful result achieved' (1997: 5).

25. I am sure that project managers the world over are aware of the power of representations. They are also aware that managing representations is a good deal easier that managing social order. (It is also striking how much published material of a donor such as DFID deals with recent policy, new designs manifesting the latest trends in development theory rather than the events and evaluations of existing projects.) But the very suggestion that projects are not about direct implementation with real effects is scandalous, far more so than criticisms of the imperfections of the model,

or even its unanticipated impacts. Similarly, the self-representation of policy as (rational) *decision making* is scandalised by the idea of 'policy as proposition, statement and style' (Gasper and Apthorpe 1996: 6) or, in contemporary British parlance, politics as 'spin'. The notion that public action (in development) is as much about communication as action should come as no surprise to those who read newspapers or listen to the radio in the UK.

26. The idea that development programmes involve consensus building around authoritative interpretations, fuelled by uncertainty and requiring networks of expert-supporters, finds a parallel in the world of global conventions (e.g. on the environment) which create knowledge-based 'epistemic communities' (Haas 1990, Watts 2001).

27. The idea that social practices *constitute* cultural norms or the score, rather than being generated by them, finds a parallel in post-structuralist critiques in anthropology (e.g. Bourdieu 1977).

28. Apthorpe's most recent work, focusing on SIDA's policy goal of 'local ownership' shows how development may succeed in practice despite its failure (or invisibility) as code or policy (Abdelrahman and Apthorpe 2002). The effects of enhanced 'local ownership' of programmes under SIDA's KTS (a technical cooperation modality) arose not from the principles emphasised by the donor, which were largely invisible or irrelevant to the partner organisations, but because the desired outcomes ('local ownership') were pre-selected for at the outset.

29. 'Poverty Reduction and Sustainable Development – The Challenge for Johannesberg', speech by the Rt Hon. Clare Short MP, Secretary of State for International Development, Development Policy Forum, QEII Conference Centre, London, 20 June 2002.

2   FRAMING A PARTICIPATORY DEVELOPMENT PROJECT

1. ODA India: Country Review Papers (1993, 1995), Lipton (1996: 503–4). During the 1980s India's share of UK bilateral aid fell in relation to that of other recipient countries. Overall, while UK financial allocations for aid remained stagnant, the share of bilateral aid fell as more money was directed into multilateral agencies (such as those of the European Union). In 1992/3 power, mining and infrastructure (railways, telecommunications, etc.) accounted for 38 per cent of the aid portfolio (54.6 per cent including ATP [Lipton 1996: 506]), health and education 11.8 per cent, and natural resources 5.4 per cent (ODA India: Country Review Paper 1993). ATP (Aid for Trade Provision) was a means to secure contracts for items from British firms that was scrapped by the Labour government in 1997.

2. ODA India: Country Strategy Papers (1993, 1995).

3. In the 1980s and until 1997 the British aid programme was managed by the ODA, part of the Foreign and Commonwealth Office. In May 1997, the new Labour government created a separate Department for International Development (DFID) with its own cabinet minister.

4. While ties to British exports were lifted in the interests of a poverty focus, there was at the same time another export boom which went uncriticised, namely the export of *expertise* or Technical Cooperation (TC) much of it for new poverty-oriented projects (i.e. specialists, volunteers, overseas training, research and especially consultants such as myself). TC increased as a proportion of bilateral aid disbursements to India from 8–10 per cent (1983–6) to 30–40 per cent (1989–93) (Lipton 1996: 511). In the IBRFP project, TC comprised 23 per cent of the ODA budgeted costs (excluding research) although by the end of Phase I (extended to 1999), 37 per cent of the original £3.8 million had been TC costs (Phase II PEC Submission). Worldwide in 1991–2, total TC accounted for more than half of British bilateral aid (Lipton 1996: 514). Critics point out that a shift from hardware to human skills may have enhanced poverty-reducing returns to aid, but the principal beneficiaries of the 'TC boom' were British consultants, trainers and the higher education system. This diverted funds away from core financial project aid, which in a country with as strong a skill base as India is hardly justified (Lipton 1996: 512–14). Given the typically weak links between consultants and Indian centres of knowledge production, British aid rested upon 'tied ignorance' more than expertise.

5. There was also a wider body of opinion which by the late 1980s was concerned that further gains from high inputs use (e.g. pesticide and fertiliser) were likely to be accompanied by high environmental costs, that capitalist agriculture produced not only winners but also losers – including a growing body of landless labourers, and that 'transfer-of-technology' approaches to extension were seriously weakened by inattention to farmer perspectives and indigenous knowledge (especially in the more extensive rainfed areas).

6. Comment by a senior ODA economist working on the India programme in the late 1980s; and a view expressed in a report advising against partnership with a state department for a new ODA agriculture project (Report of the ODNRI identification team visiting India for Proposed project 'Poverty alleviation in rainfed areas of Madhya Pradesh', July 1989).

7. Indian NGOs in Karnataka also used the media and high-profile controversies over international aid (e.g. to forestry) to negotiate a greater role for themselves in the state planning machinery, just as UK NGOs used the same controversies to enhance their own policy-influencing role.

8. Social Development Advisers were non-economic social scientists, initially mostly coming from the tradition of British social anthropology. In 1986 there were only two and a half Social Development Advisers for the worldwide programme (the 'half' was a trainee Associate Professional Officer post which I held in 1986–7). Five years previously there had been only one; but ten years later there were around 70 in a unit which had gone from being an adjunct to the Economic Service to an independent department with a network of professionals stretched across the global programme.

9. 'Side effects' such as displacement and forced resettlement following construction of dams, power plants or mining; the social consequences of mechanisation in agriculture (tractorisation) or fisheries (motorised vessels), to cite examples from my own work as an ODA social development adviser between 1985 and 1987.

10. ODA memo on Process Projects, November 1989. For further discussion on 'process' as method and metaphor in development see Mosse (1998a).

11. This formal proposal was itself the outcome of lengthy informal exchanges between ODA advisers and KBCL managers in which various enthusiasms were expressed as project ideas: fertiliser education, social forestry and cooperative strengthening among them. A number of years earlier, the ODA had provided capital aid (£42.9 million) towards KBCL's ammonia-urea fertiliser plant in Gujarat (in 1990, the world's largest cooperative unit producing 4,400 tonnes of urea per day), and had begun a successful initiative in participatory rainfed farming with the public sector Hindustan Fertiliser Company, as a follow-on to the discredited IBFEP project.

12. There were also those in the ODA who viewed a marketing agency as an effective agency for development. After all, at this time the market had become a 'master metaphor', providing a new definition of legitimacy and good policy; and results-oriented business had become a mode of organisational practice in development (Quarles van Ufford et al. 2003).

13. See note 4 above. This donor emphasis on equity *within* programmes (i.e. targeting) rather than between nations, contrasted an earlier era of decolonisation and national ownership (Nuijten and Gastel 2003). In India reliance on external expatriate consultants also arose from the refusal of the Government of India to allow resident TCOs (Technical Cooperation Officers) on projects.

14. The International Crops Research Institute for the Semi-Arid Tropics.

15. 'KBCL Rainfed Farming Project – Terms of Reference'. London, Overseas Department Administration.

16. My contribution to the IBRFP design borrowed extensively from other agencies, notably from Myrada (agro-ecological mapping/PRA), the Aga Khan Rural Support project (extension volunteers, Joint Forest Management – pioneered before an enabling government order issued by GoI in June 1990), the ODA/HFC (Hindustan Fertiliser Corporation) Eastern Rainfed Farming Project (field diaries, graduate Community Organisers) and more.

17. This analysis followed the World Bank funded National Agricultural Research Plan (NARP) in which problems and opportunities were defined by agro-ecological zones and Farming Situations on the basis of soil, physiography and climate (Balaguru et al. 1988, Raman and Balaguru 1988). This was used in the allocation of state resources, in defining research priorities and in official recommendations for cultivation regimes.

18. All examples drawn from the IBRFP Project Preparation Report 1990–91; Annex 5, 'Farming Systems in the Project Area', ODA/Centre for Development Studies, Swansea.

19. IBRFP Project Document, Overseas Development Administration, December 1992: 6.
20. Project Preparation Report, 1990–91; Annex 5, 'Farming Systems in the Project Area'.
21. Crewe and Harrison illustrate the way in which technology has little to do with hardware or expertise *per se*, but derives from 'the source and social context from which it emerged': 'When a [Sri Lankan] potter showed his brand new design for a sawdust-burning stove to a British engineer, the latter asked: "Do you make any other traditional stoves?" ' (1998: 103–4).
22. Project Preparation Report 1990–91; Annex 10, 'Plant Breeding, Farmer Choice and Seed Production'.
23. At one level, this was a 'social construction of technology' argument (Bijker and Pinch 1984), suggesting that technology has 'interpretive flexiblity'; that is to say the *working* of a technology has to be socially explained, it cannot be regarded as a matter of *intrinsic* superiority. Whether crop varieties are 'improved' depends upon whose views are solicited.
24. Far from being against science, the IBRFP design consensus chastised the Indian official agricultural research for being insufficiently scientific, for having its objectivity distorted by factors of institutional relations and power (careers, entrenched systems, competition). Only farmer judgements would be truly scientific. As Bina Desai (2004) points out, in both science and development discourse 'value is often attached to certain kinds of knowledge in a process of legitimation that tries to claim a distance from fields of power'; or Ludden: 'the more a text claims scientific status, the more it appears to lie outside of politics' (1994: 10, cited in Desai 2004). The argument for farmer participatory approaches in IBRFP is a case in point.
25. Such an analysis views the state as supporting class interests which benefit from the exploitation of tribal areas that constitute a sort of 'internal colonial frontier' and suffer from the systematic extraction of resources (forest, mineral or cheap labour), huge displacements from dams, industries and other big public projects which divert benefits elsewhere, and a systematic bias in the allocation of development resources towards the high-potential plains and urban industrial areas (Jones 1978). 'When for every rupee spent in tribal areas for tribal development and welfare at least four (and possibly more) rupees of resources are taken out, it is difficult to believe that there are serious policies to bring socio-economic development to the tribals' (Jones 1978: 51, cf. Corbridge and Harriss 2001, Gadgil and Guha 1995).
26. Project Preparation Report, 1990–91; Annex 6, 'Socio-economic Description of the Project Area'.
27. Four decades earlier there had been, on the face of it, a rather similar effort to combine the twin objectives of increasing productivity and promotion of village self-help in the 1950s Community Development (CD) programme. But for our design, this historical experience, itself influenced by Gandhian notions, seeded mistrust of both community and state as agents of rural development. Regarding the first, the CD

programme demonstrated how unequal access to new benefits would reinforce or amplify existing economic differentiation: technology and benefits were captured by larger affluent farmers, labour was displaced by mechanisation, infrastructure work benefited local trading elites but not the poor who were coerced into work; the close alliance of village-level workers with local elites facilitated their privileged access to subsidised inputs; cooperative efforts failed and new institutions (cooperatives and panchayats) were dominated by elites (Gaikwad 1981, Long 1977). On the second point (concerning the state), this vast national CD bureaucracy, which bequeathed the country its structure of sub-district development 'blocks' was, in L.C. Jain's phrase, 'grass without roots' (1985). A government machinery – inherited from the British and designed to 'resist political pressures rather than ... enable social forces to resolve political conflicts' (Jain 1985) – gradually undermined the functioning of the people's institutions (cooperatives, panchayats), and slowly transformed the CD programme into specialised sectoral anti-poverty programmes under direct departmental control (DPAP, IRDP, etc.), with the reduction/elimination of community involvement.

28. Though their design projects declare the identity of their beneficiaries (Sivaramakrishnan 2000: 437), but not always in singular or consistent ways.

29. See Porter (1995) for elaboration of the idea of master metaphors in development.

30. Recent work which posits polysemy and ambiguity as the specific characteristic of *local* knowledge, 'disambiguated' by scientific or policy discourses (Pottier 2003), offers an oversimplified conception of policy discourse as managerial and devoid of the sort of strategic ambiguity it clearly has.

31. Project Document, 1992, Annex 1 Project Framework.

32. Starting in just six village clusters, in early 2002 the Phase II project was working in 235 villages.

33. The 1992 ODA project document also included specific outputs relating to (a) supporting 'the role which women play in farming systems' and (b) linking to government agencies – for example to 'stimulate improved coordination of extension and research activities'. The first proved difficult to operationalise as an output (see Chapter 6), while the second did not become an operational priority until Phase II (see Chapter 8).

34. Collectively the team *could* not inscribe a broader political economic analysis of the causes of tribal underdevelopment into the project model, although individually they might want to. The analysis was constrained.

35. Project Document, 1992.

36. The logframe – especially its joint planning TeamUp version – proved an especially powerful instrument of such dominance in the ODA programme in India in the mid-1990s. 'TeamUp' was the ODA management's favoured means simultaneously to reassert singular rational input-output models *and* emphasise the participation of all project 'stakeholders'. Developed from the corporate world of the US, 'TeamUp' was in many ways singularly ill-matched to the cultural processes of aid project

negotiation in India, with its multiple organisations and agendas and the in-built need to preserve complexity and ambiguity in decision-making processes. According to one ODA adviser the TeamUp logframe was more 'a symbolic statement of aspirations than a practical management tool' (Internal ODA memo, Delhi, 21 Sept. 1994). And that indeed is precisely how it worked. ODA advisers and consultants were perfectly willing to invoke the rhetoric of the model and to use it strategically to invite collaboration while controlling events and outcomes. TeamUp was only subject to criticisms when, for example, senior members of a powerful Indian bureaucracy (the Forestry Department) were able to use it to derive 'a less satisfactory [project] design than ODA might wish for' (Internal ODA memo, Delhi, 21 Sept. 1994).

37. The innovatory participatory approach of IBRFP was portrayed as an extension of the project agency's (KBCL's) flexibility, client-orientation, freedom from bureaucracy and innovative organisational culture (see below). KBCL were informed that they had an historic chance to be 'market leaders' in rural development.

38. Fertiliser markets were regulated under the Essential Commodities Act.

39. C.E. McKone, Proposed ODA/KBCL Composite Dryland Development Project: Report of Visit to India, May 1989.

40. Interview with KBCL Junior Manager, Godhra, July 1990.

41. Composite Dryland Farming Project Proposal, KBCL, 1987; KBCL's Dryland Farming Project, draft note 1990; S. Kumar and A.A. Khan, Dryland Farming Project, Jhabua, KBCL Area Office, Indore, Madhya Pradesh, 1990.

42. KBCL was at the time negotiating a share of a large joint-sector fertiliser plant in Oman to supply the Indian market, and to take over an older state-owned plant in the eastern India region.

43. Baviskar (forthcoming) makes the interesting argument that a state government (of Madhya Pradesh) has itself promoted participatory development (its intensive 'watershed mission') to enhance the (poor) reputation of its administration vis-à-vis other states in order better to attract donor or central government funds.

44. Of course, there was no more unity of opinion on the new project within KBCL than in the ODA or in its consultancy team: a few emphasised fertiliser sales, others commercial opportunities, some image building and enhancing relations with government; and these opinions might be expressed to promote the project idea against detractors who regarded the project as a threat to personnel and financial order.

45. From 1998, KBCL's Chairman was a leading politician in Mulayam Singh Yadav's Samajwadi party which had a central part in extending this political agenda.

46. The number of project employees increased gradually from under 30 professional and administrative staff at the start of Phase I (with just 15 Community Organisers) to 172 in 2001 (including 71 COs) out of a full Phase II compliment of 257 people (IBRFP documents).

47. This team was so full of potential that the ODA invested heavily in orientation and training (in India and UK), so fragile that KBCL insisted that new staff sign a 'surety bond' as commitment to serve minimum number of years with the project.

48. A parallel suggested by reading Sutton (1999: 15ff).

3   TRIBAL LIVELIHOODS AND THE DEVELOPMENT FRONTIER

1. These were districts predominantly inhabited by groups categorised as Scheduled Tribes under Article 342 of the Indian Constitution, and eligible for certain concessions on that basis. While the majority of the population identified themselves as Bhil or closely related groups (Minas or Bhilalas), other *jatis* (castes, tribes) included Koli, Baria and Thakkar cultivators, Baniya, Jain and Bohra Muslim traders and moneylenders in larger commercial villages and towns, and low-caste (*dalit*) artisan and service castes (e.g. Chamars, Bhangis, Kotwals). The term 'tribal' here is a legal-administrative category; but since it still carries a cultural evolutionist idea of primitiveness (Hardiman 1987a: 15), I will mostly use the term applied by communities themselves, *adivasi*, not with its literal meaning – 'original inhabitants' – but as the adopted identity of people with a shared political and ecological history (see also Baviskar 1995).

2. See Padel (2000) for an excellent account of colonial writing on tribal society and the role of knowledge production in assertions of power and social control.

3. On the ambivalent political and economic relationship between Rajputs and Bhils see Baviskar (1995: 49–82), Deliège (1985), Skaria (1999) and Weisgrau (1997: 61–5).

4. Villagers today recall that Rajput princes took Bhil brides for their sons. IBRFP Mahunala village study.

5. See discussion by Deliège (1985: 34–6) and Weisgrau (1997: 58–66).

6. The Bhil Corps not only established order among the unruly Bhils, but proved them loyal subjects to the British during the Rebellion of 1857 (Sharma 1990: 11)

7. Anna Tsing comments on the role of 'primitives' in the (Indonesian) state discourse of development as 'icons of the archaic disorder that represents the limit and test of state order and development' (1993: 28, cited in Li 1999: 299). There is no dearth of instances worldwide of the use of irrigation, roads, forced settlement or plantations to regiment such people into ordered taxable communities (cf. Scott 1998). For the east Indian Konds, Felix Padel (2000) provides an interesting analysis of the legitimising colonial discourse around the master trope of human sacrifice. Like Skaria he argues that British rule changed the relations between Hindu and tribal society exposing the latter to new levels of exploitation (2000: 29), a history that cannot be ignored in relation to contemporary development initiatives.

8. IBRFP village studies: Jharola, Mahunala and Chatra Kunta villages, 1997.

9. An old Bhil man in a Dahod village recalled how he, like the adult males from every village, was compelled to do nearly a month's forest labour for the Baria king, unpaid and without food, mostly cutting trees and working in the royal sawmill. Every household also had to deliver specified amounts of green fodder to the royal cattle shed by bullock cart at their own expense (Tushaar Shah, fieldnotes for IBRFP Mid-Term Evaluation, August 1995).

10. For details on Bhil systems of debt bondage such as *sagri* see Vyas (1980) and Vyas and Chaudhary (1968), cited in Weisgrau (1997: 64).

11. The 1955 Rajasthan Tenancy Act, or the 1957 Land to the Tillers Act in Gujarat firmed up tenant rights and Section 73-A of the Bombay Land Revenue Code and subsequent land laws enacted in Gujarat, Madhya Pradesh and Rajasthan restricted the alienation of tribal land. Despite such legislation, disguised forms of debt mortgage in which land is effectively mortgaged to creditors and rented back on a share-crop basis, abound, as do informal systems of asset mortgage, tree tenure or the advanced sale of labour (see below).

12. Hardiman contrasts the relationship with *sahukars* with the more directly exploitative relationship of Bhils with Parsi landowners-cum-liquor dealers, which accounts for the frequent looting of liquor shops during Bhil uprisings (1987a: ch. 7).

13. The movement was violently suppressed in November 1913 when the British resident ordered the Bhil Corps to attack a gathering of Govindgiri's followers in Banswara and Dungarpur and upwards of 1,500 Bhils died (Weisgrau 1997: 39).

14. My information comes from press reports, and personal conversations in Baroda and Ahmedabad in April 2002 during the violence that erupted after an arson attack at Godhra killed Hindu activists in a train carriage. Lobo (2002) analyses the unprecedented gratuitous mob looting and arson against Muslims in the adivasi districts of east Gujarat as the result of a strategic Hindutvisation of adivasis in order to stall a dalit–adivasi–Muslim political alliance.

15. For example, the famous debate in the 1940s between Verrier Elwin who believed that the fragile culture of tribals should be protected, and G.S. Ghurye who argued for assimilation into the Indian mainstream (see Guha 1999: 157ff, Skaria 1999: 279).

16. When detained in a sub-district police station for half a day in 1993, I witnessed the raw edge of police violence against adivasi suspects – severe beating, electric shocks and the extortion of bribes from relatives.

17. These are not, it should be emphasised, the same as the official 'administrative' or Revenue Villages. Inter-hamlet ties often cut across official boundaries.

18. In south Rajasthan, Bhils formerly had a higher order unit of territorial organisation, the *pal*, constituted by a cluster of villages. (There were four Bhil *pals* in Banswara District.) These have now virtually disappeared as units of social organisation although they remain as units of exogamy and relevant in the settling of major disputes around rape or murder, or conflicts over inter-village grazing rights (Sjöblom 1999: 49).

19. The same names are found throughout the area. They are often names borrowed from former Rajput overlords (Deliège 1985). Clans themselves have little sociological significance. They are not corporate groups and unite only rarely, if at all, for ceremonial purposes. More relevant than clans are the local lineages which take clan names and make up the hamlets.

20. In one late-1970s five-village study in Banswara District, only 2 per cent of villagers knew the location of the Taluk panchayat office (Doshi 1978).

In general, the sphere of contacts and relations among Bhil communities is surprisingly restricted. Marriage circles typically include only 10–15 villages.

21. To indicate the scale of resources from which the poor were excluded, in 1985–6 alone, seven government agencies spent over Rs 686 million and employed 21,302 staff in Panchmahals district, which included Dahod (Bhatt 1989: 42). If distributed evenly among the district's 1,909 villages, each would receive over Rs 359,000 in the year and have 11 government employees in residence (1989: 42).

22. On processes of long-term economic differentiation in western India adivasi society see Breman (1974, 1985).

23. In the project area, in the early 1990s, at village and *taluk* levels panchayat membership was overwhelmingly adivasi, although president-ships at *taluk* level were sometimes held by non-adivasis. However, at district level power was more clearly in the hands of non-adivasis, largely because of the division of adivasis by party and faction, and the absence of a strong adivasi political identity in the region (in contrast to the eastern Jharkhand region). The next decade brought an increase in district positions held by adivasis, while panchayat reforms considerably increased the power of directly elected representatives in local government.

24. But as Baviskar (2004) notes:

    … closer examination of the provisions of the [relevant] Act [Panchayats (Extenion to Scheduled Areas) Act of 1996] shows critical lacunae and ambiguities. No financial powers are allocated to the gram sabhas; control over forests is still vested with the Forest Department; the gram sabha is powerless to stop land acquisition by the government. Thus what appears to be a far-reaching move towards making panchayats more accountable to the people they represent, may be greatly limited by its failure to specify powers and procedures for the gram sabha.

25. This pattern is consistent with Paul Brass's critique of the state and the cooption of politicians of the poor in India (1997, discussed in Corbridge and Harriss 2001: 202).

26. See Agarwal (1994) for an extended discussion of gender in relation to property rights.

27. The nature of the rights here is brought to light in an interesting case, which reverses the normal pattern of things. Mithaben is the sole inheritor of her father's land. She married a man from another village who came to live with her and cultivated land which still remained in her name. After 6–7 years Mithaben left to 'marry' another man. A dispute arose as the first husband demanded that Mithaben's family pay back the labour he had provided over 6–7 years (calculated at Rs 1,200 per year). The case illustrates the way in which marriage partnership is seen in part as a transaction focusing on labour. (Supriya Akerkar, 'Customary rights and status of Bhil tribal women in Rajasthan', mimeo, IBRFP, Dahod.)

28. Of course as much is true of non-adivasi women in the western region (see Raheja and Gold 1994).

29. Interview with women's group, Naganwat Choti village study, p. 50.

30. Maize comprises over 70 per cent of the cropped area.
31. Sjöblom (1999: 146) examined the domestic cycles and the sequential separation of cooking, grain storage, livestock and finally land in a south Rajasthan Bhil village, showing how an ideal ordered progression is contested by young men partitioning land early or women leaving their husbands.
32. For example, Jharola village study. Two points follow: first, the capacity of farmers to undertake soil and water conservation works to improve land fertility is often underestimated in project discourses – Sjöblom records one Bhil household having invested Rs 15,000 in labour over three weeks to enlarge a rice field and erect stone bunds (1999: 70); second, the movement of soil is not invariably viewed as erosion, especially where it creates fertile valley bottoms (1999: 69).
33. Naganwat Choti village study, p. 29.
34. PRAs (Participatory Rural Appraisals) and village studies, *passim*. Some spoke of returns on seed declining by half, and herd sizes of over 50 reduced to a couple of head of cattle. The perception of declining herds may be exaggerated in that large herds were formerly *jointly* owned (Sjöblom 1999: 110).
35. Small livestock, goats and chickens, are a more liquid form of asset providing a ready source of cash to meet medical expenses, to purchase seeds or to consume on social or ritual occasions.
36. During the 1990s check dams and lift irrigation schemes (which pump water uphill and then allow gravity flow to fields from storage structures) have been developed on a large scale in the area by the NGO NM Sadguru Water and Development Foundation.
37. The illegality of cultivation on Forest Department land allows junior forest officials to intimidate and seek bribes from insecure 'encroachers' (Baviskar 1995: 149–56, 2004).
38. 'Complex, diverse and risk-prone' (CDR) was a descriptive phrase first applied to marginal areas in the Brundtland Report of the World Commission on Environment and Development (Brundtland 1987). Thanks to John Witcombe for pointing this out to me.
39. John Witcombe, interview 4 June 2001.
40. The following paragraphs draw on observations made over several months, on interviews, PRAs and household profiles by Supriya Akerkar, IBRFP gender specialist (1982–3) (see her 'The role of women in farming systems, natural resource use and management', mimeo, IBRFP, Dahod) and also on the work of Mona Mehta, project consultant on gender (1992–5).
41. Women actually have to avoid contact with sick bullocks.
42. Children's labour is especially important in grazing and fodder collection.
43. Women also earn income through the sale of their labour and the collection and sale of forest produce and fuel-wood. Where income earning is not their *responsibility* they often have more control over the cash (e.g. from the sale of gathered fuel-wood).

44. A detailed profiling of work in selected households in one Bhil village by Shiney Varghese showed that, depending upon the economic position and dependency ratio of the family, between 53 and 68 per cent of labour days for all tasks were contributed by women (household profiles, Ratanmal village, IBRFP, 1995).

45. Officially promoted 'farmers' (*khedut, kisan*) groups are typically understood as *male* groups, while the activities of women's groups (*mahila samities*) do not emphasise their roles as farmers.

46. Marrying a second wife is a means to secure additional female labour, or children if the first marriage is childless. Also, in certain villages/clans there is a practice whereby families lacking adequate labour marry their young son to an older (adolescent) girl. The arrangement is usually detrimental to the girl who tends to run away after a couple of years out of frustration with the relationship and the burden of work. The boy's family then claims compensation from the girl's family and remarries their son. The girl cannot technically 'remarry' and will most likely go and live with another man, usually married.

47. Children provide considerable labour. They are active in cattle grazing, collecting water and wood and weeding, although their views on work are rarely sought. Boys interviewed in Bijori village said that grazing was their favourite job, while girls said they were afraid of the forest guards.

48. For example, if a person offered a *chandla* of Rs 100 on one occasion, and if the return chandla was Rs 125, the following one would have to increase by at least Rs 25, i.e., it would be a minimum of Rs 150. If through perpetual exchanges *chandla* payment reaches very high levels, individuals might agree to reduce the expectations. *Chandla*, an institution of east Gujarat Bhils, finds its equivalent in *notra*, but while a *chandla* can be (re-)called at any time, *notra* is restricted to marriages (Tushaar Shah, fieldnotes for IBRFP Mid-Term Evalution, August 1995).

49. Idiomatically male kin are needed to plough the land, and Sjöblom even suggests that 'agnates coming to rescue a woman in need of ploughing are not only temporarily assisting a woman, but ultimately saving the symbolic capital of men and, more generally, perpetuating male domination' (1999: 168).

50. Women's labour may be used and her jewellery sold or mortgaged to generate assets such as wells through which (male) owners can generate obligations by extending use rights to the women of kinsmen's houses.

51. Wealth ranking data from Jharola, Palasiapada and Naganwat Choti, 'Project impact on farming systems and livelihoods', Report to IBRFP, Dahod, January 1997: 25.

52. Credit cooperatives in the region have existed from the 1920s, and in 1934–5 there were 85 village cooperatives with 4,178 members in the 'Eastern Mahals' – that is Dahod and Jhalod taluks in east Gujarat (Shrikant 1967: 6, cited in Hardiman 1987b: 52).

53. Studies in the IBRFP project villages contradict the conclusions of one recent study on debt in Jhabua district (Amanullah and Sharma 1987) which reported a shift from private moneylenders to institutional sources of credit; and from credit for consumption to credit for production

(although it is unwise to attempt to distribute borrowing between two such uncertain categories, or to assume that borrowing for brideprice, *chandla*, housing or medical expenses is unproductive). Moneylenders interviewed in the Limkheda area in 1996 considered that there had been a 25–30 per cent increase in the demand for credit in the previous five years as a result of uncertain cultivation, a growing need for cash and the enhanced capacity to manage loans through migrant earnings (Jharola village study).

54. The lowering of grain prices after the government imposed price regulations in the late 1970s, encouraged *sahukars* to insist on repayments in cash rather than in grain (Jharola village study).

55. IBRFP PRA exercises, Nov. 1996, Jharola and Palasiapada village surveys. These figures should be treated with caution since details on indebtedness are notoriously hard to obtain, and information on the consequent mortgaging of assets even more so.

56. Jharola village study.

57. Project surveys, Lal (nd), see Breman (1985) and sources cited in Mosse et al. (2002).

58. One survey in Gujarat estimated forest produce as contributing 22.5 per cent of household earnings. The same survey identified 127 different species of medicinal plants (Lal nd).

59. Interview M. Mistry, September 1991. The rate for 100 bundles (5 kg or 8 hours picking) increased from Rs 11 to Rs 17, still low considering the prevailing retail *timru* rate of Rs 32 per kg.

60. In one survey as many as 40 per cent were almost entirely dependent on labouring of some kind (Lal nd).

61. These and other figures on seasonal labour migration from Bhil villages in the IBRFP project area come from a survey covering 2,588 households in 42 project villages covering the year 1995–6. For a fuller presentation of the results of this research, and further references on adivasi seasonal labour migration see Mosse et al. (2002).

62. Male migrants are recruited by their *mamas*, maternal uncles, or *behnois*, sisters' husbands.

63. Mosse et al. discusses the strategies, risks and careers of *mukkadams*, some of whom are moneylenders in villages, while some have settled in towns (2002: 72–3); see also Mosse (2002, 2003c).

64. Of course the two intersect. Newly formed households are smaller but also have fewer resources, poorer quality land and higher dependency ratios. They are forced into longer-term migration to acquire resources for houses, cattle and implements.

65. The complex and contradictory effects of unequal and individualised earning from migration on household entitlements, on marriage relations, on the division of households, on age and gender hierarchies, and women's roles and entitlements are discussed in Mosse et al. (2002: 81–3).

66. Even a medical doctor from one Dahod Bhil village and head of a Surat medical college regularly sends his *chandla* even if he cannot come for the ceremony (Tushaar Shah, fieldnotes for IBRFP Mid-Term Evaluation, August 1995).

4   THE GODDESS AND THE PRA: LOCAL KNOWLEDGE AND PLANNING

1. Pseudonym.
2. Details on the now familiar core techniques of PRA, and the principles behind them can be found in Chambers (1997) and various issue of *RRA/PLA Notes*.
3. Bina Desai (2004) notes how farmers in Rajasthan are less willing to give trust (*vishwas*, belief) to government extensionists imparting scientifically valid knowledge and receiving secure state salaries, than to private company salesmen whose sales and livelihood depends upon the practical outcome of a crop, and who would not risk selling low-quality products to valued customers.
4. The same can be said of national discourses of tribal underdevelopment (cf. Brow 1990, Gellner 1991), a point developed in Ankur Datta's MA dissertation, 'Constructing and reconstructing a nation: the cultural politics of identity in the movement for Jharkhand , India' (SOAS, 2002).
5. For example, Monthly Progress Report (MPR), March 1993: 17.
6. This is not to say that others did not also benefit from check dams, for example, as sources of domestic water, or even irrigation from pumping schemes; and they were popular for this reason.
7. See Mosse (1994) for fuller discussion of authority in PRA.
8. A point made in regard to social research more generally by Ardener (1975a, 1975b), who also provided the concepts of 'muting' and 'inarticulateness' used below; for details see Mosse (1994).
9. *Jankars*, rather than staff, were promoted to give public representation of the project in wider forums (e.g. the National Sharing Workshop on Women in Agriculture) and in 1998 *jankars* were included in the team to do an evaluation study of the government watershed programme in Jhabua whose findings were presented to *sarpanchs*, top district government, public representatives, MLAs (Members of the Legislative Assembly), and MPs.
10. These connections were important to compensate for the disadvantages of youth or being female (cf. Jackson 1997: 64).
11. As Christoplos notes of PRA analyses in the Mekong Delta in Vietnam, these 'did not reveal an alternative to the official view of poverty ... but served to further legitimise (the official discourse) with farmer testimonies' (1995: 17–18).
12. Accepting Weisgrau's point and indicating the first urgency of wages does not imply that farmers were unaware of, or uninterested in, the long-term fertility gains from SWC work.
13. The project did work on 'encroached' land where cultivation was not actually illegal but condoned through yearly 'fines' to the Forest Department, and in some cases even helped farmers regularise their land title.
14. Village PRA reports, 1992–2000: *passim*.
15. In one women's group 37 species were ranked in relation to eight different uses.

16. Of course the initial PRAs were not free of omission or selectivity. Fruit trees, for example emerged as an important priority but were not mentioned during the initial tree matrix exercises (Bezkorowajnyj et al. 1994).

17. As a cash crop eucalyptus has been shown to be a strong preference of men (see Baviskar 1995: 20, 22). Women's unarticulated experience of burdensome labour and time devoted to the collection of fuel and fodder (for which eucalyptus is not a first choice) or the economic and nutritional importance of forest species and the collection of non-timber forest produce (over which women had more control than cash tree crops) did not overly shape programme choices, even though they clearly featured in separate informal PRAs.

18. This relationship changed over time, and correspondingly the proportion of eucalyptus seedlings raised declined over the years of the project.

19. Quarterly Progress Report (QPR), Nov. 1992–March 1993: 14.

20. The PRA maps and transect diagrams removed to the project office assumed a physical world '"uncontaminated" by cultural and social meaning' (Pottier 1991: 9). Practical forms of knowledge could be overlooked entirely.

21. In another example of project-related 'short-termism' Starkloff (1996) shows how participatory mechanisms generate support for 'coping mechanisms' rather than addressing underlying environmental problems.

22. See Appadurai (1990) and Ludden (1992) for analysis of the historical construction of scientific agriculture in India in terms of a separation of the knower and knowledge. As Ludden argues, agriculture became:

    an object for development by being abstracted from society and culture, broken into input–output data, translated out of vernaculars in the English of scientific semantics, and projected back onto farmers by institutions that have imagined localities only as identically empirical units, passive under their gaze, objects of observation and responsibility. (1992: 271)

23. To project actors who perceive criticism and would try to defend themselves, I should emphasise that these are social effects that are below the level of awareness, and therefore not countered or managed by the application of 'best practice' (review PRAs, issue-focused PRAs and the like).

24. PRA information on the technical expertise possessed by Bhil women, and their part in agricultural decision making, for example, was used to make an argument for giving them a more prominent role in project activities such as credit, input supply or crop development.

25. The last included adjustable implements without the spanners to adjust them, and iron machinery too heavy for bullocks to pull.

26. Robert Chambers (1983, Chambers et al. 1989), however, popularised the idea of 'complex, diverse and risk-prone' to emphasise that poor people in marginal areas were sophisticated, dealt with complicated systems

and were therefore appropriate intellectual partners for development experts.

27. As Abdelrahman and Apthorpe (2002) note, 'aid remains supply driven even if it is also demand driven [since] demand ... is developed within a larger culture of supply ... [and] supply has a tendency to create and sustain demand for it'.

28. Tushaar Shah, fieldnotes for IBRFP Mid-Term Evaluation, August 1995.

5   IMPLEMENTATION: REGIME AND RELATIONSHIPS

1. On the mutual contribution of ethnography and organisational studies see Gellner and Hirsch (2001), Wright (1994), and Mosse (1998a) for discussion and further references.

2. Note on Planning, Annex C, 5 June 1993.

3. Chapter 6 looks at the fate of a selection of consultant ideas, debates and models.

4. Arce and Long (1992) examine in some detail the way in which a Mexican fieldworker (a *tecnico* or technical agronomist) devises his own strategies of intervention in both the village and official administrative arenas, which enable him to retain legitimacy in the eyes of both villagers and bureaucrats. See also Goetz 1996 and Lipsky 1980 on fieldworker discretion.

5. Evident in lively monthly meetings.

6. As the project aged, there were known solutions to many problems and senior experienced staff were able to offer guidance and instructions to juniors in review meetings.

7. By September 1996, even though the forms completed in the field had been reduced from six to one, 600–800 working groups in 50 villages undertaking SWC would still 'generate 1200–1600 pages of Measurement Book each week' (Consultant report, September 1996). In 2001 the project worked in five times that number of villages.

8. Internal memo, 5 March 1994.

9. Pressure of programme delivery led to some gravitation away from difficult or complex hamlets/villages and towards those able to present themselves as effective clients. In KBCL's Eastern India project I noticed sharp gradients of declining participation away from key accessible villages (Mid-Term Review Study, 1999).

10. Project monitoring data summarised in the Report of the Mid-Term Evaluation, January 1996 (Shah et al. 1996).

11. Compare the effects of incentives to maximise repayment rates on the practices of fieldworkers in women's credit programmes in Bangladesh (Goetz 1996).

12. As Baviskar (forthcoming) points out, private collaboration (between *jankars* and COs) is an easier way of getting things done than collective action.

13. Fieldworkers' assertions of status or demands for deference feature in recent descriptions of NGO and state programmes. This is not only a characteristic of men; women fieldworkers, especially those recruited

locally and close in socio-economic status to 'beneficiaries' also assert rank over beneficiaries (Goetz 1996, Heaton 2001).

14. Standing by a new brick-built compost pit, in my role as donor evaluator, I ask: 'Is it given free [by the project]?' 'No sir', comes the quick reply (via a CO), 'there is participation' – an answer that played on the ambiguity of *bhagidari*.

15. As COs involved pointed out. On average each household gained about 75 days employment on SWC work (including communal land): 48 in year one of the project, 15 in year two, and 11 in year three (Smith 1998).

16. Consultant Report, September 1996; Progress Report 4, Annex 6, 1994, p. 13.

17. In a sister KBCL project, women in a Bihar village had themselves requested that the project support an interlinked package of activities – ducks, goats, *rabi* seeds and a pump set (Social Development Consultant's report no. 5, 1996).

18. A project–client group administrative view also made inter-group or inter-village inequalities invisible. For similar reasons non-participants easily disappeared from view.

19. In fact the project had at least three distinctive modes of investment: (a) *giving to groups* (e.g. for flour mills, tree nurseries or other group income generation activities); (b) *giving to individuals by means of groups* (e.g. livestock, bio-gas, smokeless stoves, where the end beneficiaries are individuals); and (c) *giving to groups by means of individuals* (e.g. the digging/repair of private wells/ponds for collective use).

20. This proportion increased from 5 per cent in 1996 to 13–19 per cent in 1998.

21. This was necessary because farmer savings were always inadequate to meet the simultaneous demand from all members for cultivation loans. Initially the project advanced seed and fertiliser in kind on a pro-rata basis of Rs 500 per household.

22. According to studies in IBRFP's sister project in eastern India, by Thilo Glebe, group-based income-generation projects were over-financed with 60 per cent more working capital than was needed (1998: 74ff), finance having been used as an incentive to start activities. Income-generation projects in western India were similarly over-financed and under-appraised, a point repeatedly made in consultant and donor reports, most recently in DFID's Annual Review Mission of April 2002.

23. D'Arcy Mackenzie has helped me understand that all money is in reality obligation.

24. Recent (January 2001) records of 479 groups in Rajasthan show as little as 15 per cent of group funds in circulation. In a few cases the placement of money in high-interest deposit accounts and borrowing at a lower interest rate from banks is a deliberate strategy. But these are rare. The hot/cold distinction is one that some South Asian credit groups make to distinguish between, on the one hand, funds from their own savings, which imply a high degree of obligation, indicated by high interest rates and strong pressure to repay, and, on the other, externally granted capital, attaching weaker obligations.

25. While there were few available data on repayment rates, it was clear that, despite close supervision by project staff, the seasonal repayment rates for rotating crop loans (project capital) were very poor, although most were eventually repaid from migrant earnings. Based on data compiled for 22 villages, between *rabi* 1993 and *rabi* 1995 *seasonal* repayment rates were between 20 per cent and 100 per cent. Although the overall average was 74 per cent, only 36 per cent (8/22) of villages had consistently repaid 75 per cent or more of their loan amount by the end of the season. Only four villages had achieved this repayment rate for three or more cycles. The project's records of repayment of crop loans for the 1996 *kharif* showed a worsening of the situation over the 1993–5 period, with large outstanding loan amounts after a year or even 18 months. Project records do not easily allow more recent repayment rates on group loans to be calculated.

26. The limited use of SHG funds as a source of credit also had to do with the limited amount of credit they could offer. As Tushaar Shah put it, 'what could a loan of Rs 100 mean to Jaliben [a Dahod village woman and migrant construction worker] who proudly announced that she can climb eight floors with headloads of cement and concrete and therefore got paid Rs 70/day? What could [a group] loan of Rs 200 at 6 per cent/month mean to Gajubhai who offers a '*chandla*' of Rs 1,000 in a friend's wedding' (fieldnotes for IBRFP Mid-Term Evaluation, August 1995).

27. I should note that IBRFP project managers maintain that a relaxation in accounting procedures from 1996/7 allowed funds routinely to be channelled through SHGs without staff involvement. This view was not corroborated by my own work, or the views of field staff I interviewed. It is true that from 1997–9 *jankars* began to take a greater role in SWC payments, that a few groups were established as seed production centres, managing large-scale operations (with project assistance), and that some were recipients of funds from non-project state schemes. But anyway the issue is not whether funds are channelled through groups (or handled by *jankars*), but whether SHGs have authority to approve plans and expenditure, or to allocate a village development budget. KBCL procedures did not allow this. Even in April 2001, the only exception was a state watershed development scheme implemented by the project in which village committees were required to approve plans and expenditure and to manage funds. In the same year, IBRFP groups formed eight years earlier had only just begun to function independently of the project, but still looked to it for inputs. There is nothing exceptional here. The failure of bureaucratic participatory development (NGO or state) to trust people's organisations (or to promote those they can control) is almost universal. In India it has also exposed such programmes to criticism for by-passing local political institutions, the panchayats (Baviskar 2004, Manor 2002, see Chapter 8, note 38).

28. Consultant's report September 1996.

29. One former CO recalls defiance in face of 'terrible pressure': 'I said, "I am not going to discuss anything about mushrooms in my villages. If you terminate me, terminate right now." I think I am the only CO who did not discuss about mushrooms. And I challenged [them], it's not going to be a success, and you see now there is only archaeological evidence!'

30. Foot dragging can be a weapon of the strong as well as the weak (cf. Scott 1990a).
31. QPR July–September 1998. Quantification, as Appadurai (1997) notes, is important to 'the illusion of bureaucratic control'.
32. A metaphor like the 'tall poppy' used by a consultant colleague.
33. In IBRFP, the culture of fear of failure was perpetuated, for one, by insecure terms and conditions of employment of staff, expressed in contracts which were brief on entitlements and professional roles and expansive on the many and various forms of failure that would give the organisation occasion to terminate employment, and, for another, by the style of visiting senior managers who rarely missed an opportunity to underline threat and insecurity as a means of motivating performance. Senior KBCL managers would not hesitate to publicly reprimand junior staff. Some acquired reputations for the arbitrary exercise of power; those who argued or contradicted them, or who failed to meet their personal demands, could find their names withdrawn from the privilege of overseas training or promotion.
34. Scott uses the Greek word to refer to knowledge or practical skill embedded in local experience (1998: 311).
35. While practically critical, the economy of informal processes is not only ignored, but rigorously denied. Scapegoats are made of those (lacking adequate political protection) whose misjudgements or errors inadvertently reveal them. It is a sad irony that such a case lost the project manager his job after making an unmanageable project function for twelve years.
36. A point made by Bina Desai (2004).
37. A KBCL Director, recalling his advice to project staff. Interview, Delhi March 2001.
38. Meeting minute, 12 Dec. 2000.
39. A relational view pervades project practice. For instance on International Women's Day development oaths were made by women, symbolised by hand impressions on muslin cloth displayed on the project office wall.
40. At a corporate level, the project as a whole is a trophy, which the project manager has to deliver to KBCL's senior management. As a consultant colleague put it, the project was 'like a trinket on a shelf that they could bring down every so often and say to the government, "Oh hold this isn't it pretty," and then put it back on the shelf again. So long as nobody disturbed the shelf and so long as the trinket kept maybe growing a bit bigger, or getting a little bit more beautiful over time, that was all they were concerned about.'
41. As noted earlier, at the end of Phase I, 37 per cent of total project costs had gone on Technical Cooperation consultancy and overseas training (and the procurement of computers and evaluation services in India) (Phase II PEC Submission, p. 18).
42. As Baviskar concludes regarding a state participatory watershed programme in the same region, 'decentralisation is subverted by the administrative imperatives of demonstrating success and the related need to stay in control' (forthcoming: 13).

6 CONSULTANT KNOWLEDGE

1. Later, water resources and livestock specialisms were added.
2. Not all consultants working on the project were foreigners. Those specialising in gender and organisational issues were Indian nationals. One or two had longer stays with the project, but all were outsiders whose presence disrupted work routines.
3. Of course this assumes continuity of external support to a development programme over time, which is actually rather rare.
4. Comments like: 'the suggestions or ideas you made were never implemented ... [or] they launched into things that we actually said don't do ... [or] ideas and innovations never got off the ground [unless they] fitted into the general scheme of things ... it became development by rote in the end to an extent ... ' (interviews May–June 2001)
5. Between 1997 and 1999 the consultant team actually drafted and redrafted the *same* 'End of Project Report' giving cast-iron stability to the interpretation of strategies, activities, achievements and issues.
6. I realise that in arguing below that the effect of consultants was to shape representations rather than behaviour, I may be guilty of 'an insider's perspective that typically notes that power is always located somewhere else and not in one's own domain' (Eyben 2003). Certainly it should not be forgotten, in what follows, that consultants were instruments of the ODA/DFID contributing to a broader relationship of donor power and patronage (disguised as technical expertise); nor should it be assumed that consultants did not have other roles than model building. The consultant team leader, in particular, had a key political role in pushing donor interests vis-a-vis the project agency. Our actions did not cease to be political though their effects were constrained, often because of the relative weakness of our networks within the project system.
7. Mid-Term Report, April 1996, Annex 10: Irrigation Programme.
8. Mid-Term Report, Annex 11, added that 'it is worth noting that the introduction of simple recording on dairy farms in the U.K. in 1914 increased cow yields on those farms by 50 per cent in 5 years'.
9. Mid-Term Report, Annex 11.
10. 'Participatory Research on Fodder and Fuelwood Improvement and Management' (PROFFIM). This was a piece of 'centrally funded' DFID research linked to the project 'to identify appropriate management techniques for tree and fodder grass species'. It used sophisticated digital Global Positioning and Geographical Information Systems (GPS/GIS) to collect and analyse social and bio-physical information which 'provided insight into the perceived needs of the communities ... namely lack of fodder and fuelwood', and its results suggested which species could be grown and how, and recommended revival of the traditional practice of harvesting *lac*, among other NTFPs (non-timber forest produce) with commercial potential.
11. Mid-Term Report, April 1996, Annex 8, p. 10.
12. Mid-Term Report, April 1996, Annex 8, pp. 7–9.
13. The IBRFP Crops Specialist, Arun Joshi, was particularly crucial to this programme.

14. The identification of improved varieties first involved consultants searching nationwide among official national and state releases, within the private sector, among cultivars in the advanced stages of testing and plant breeders' advanced lines for varieties to match farmers' criteria.

15. Mid-Term Report, Annex 7, Crops Programme.

16. ' ... thin husks, grains that remained unbroken on dehulling, and grain that would fetch a higher market price than that of the local landraces' (Joshi and Witcombe 1996: 469).

17. PVS was extended to experiments with 'seed priming' – the practice of soaking seeds in water before sowing to increase successful germination – which was tested with farmers, who discovered higher yields and earlier ripening. Primed seeds grew faster, flowered earlier, avoided the effects of dry spells and formed grain earlier ('On farm seed priming: a key technology to improve the livelihoods of resource-poor farmers in India', Plant Sciences Research Programme and KRIBP, DFID, c. 1999).

18. The PVS model was premised on the idea that genetics alone, in the absence of additional inputs of fertiliser or changed agronomic practices, would significantly increase yields. In this, it consciously departed from prevailing input package (or 'mini-kit') approaches. Effectively, the design denied the politics of technology *application*, even as it emphasised the politics of technology *development* through agricultural research. The core problem was getting appropriate technology to farmers.

19. In the case of just one crop, the rice variety Kalinga III, the financial return on project investment was estimated as 47–70 per cent, taking into account the total IBRFP PVS *costs* including technical assistance (i.e. UK consultants) and overseas training, and the *benefits* from Kalinga III spreading to potentially suitable land in a 15-year period (i.e. before some equivalent or better variety would reach the area). Chapter 9 will indicate that the 'conservative assumptions' employed in this analysis proved not to be so. Pursuing the abstract economic speculation it was estimated that the 'loss' to farmers in six upland rice-growing Indian states who were currently denied access to Kalinga III was Rs 10,702 million (£198 million) at 1996 discounted prices (Balgoun 1996, cited in Witcombe et al. 1999).

20. The paradox of this success is that it comes from challenging the scientific status of Indian agricultural research by recognising its context in institutional politics, while giving scientific status to farmer knowledge by ignoring *its* context. PVS/PPB does not simply re-label the 'local' as 'scientific'; rather it involves 'disembedding' farmer knowledge/ judgement so that it can acquire a global (scientific) significance, and then 're-localising' it (cf. van der Ploeg 1992, cited in Desai 2004). Farmers' judgements about the performance of new varieties are 'scientific', not just because they are based on relevant experience and wider criteria (duration, disease resistance, price etc.) but because they are separate from the context of institutional politics that distort conventional agricultural research and regulatory frameworks (see note 24 Chapter 2). But at the same time, the PPB/PVS construction of the rational scientific farmer necessarily ignores the kind of ethnographic evidence that indicates the complex and *contextual* way in which South Asian farmers actually make

judgements about technology, which may be 'founded upon precepts (concepts and actions) that incorporate social and moral (as well as economic) concepts. The concept of abundance, for example, differs from the economic concept of productivity as yield or worked output in that it encompasses specific moral ideas of social obligation, share, and gift' (Mosse 2003: 237–8, citing Vasavi 1994). PVS/PPB could not allow that farmer technical knowledge was hybrid, imbued with 'relational properties', that crops may be judged in terms of 'appropriateness' between variety, soil *and* persons framed in terms of shared substance or humoral balance; or by taking simultaneous account of the politics of relations with kin, project, moneylender, state institutions and others (Daniel 1984, Gatter 1993, Gupta 1998) because this would make it 'unscientific'.

21. Yapa writes from a critical political ecology perspective, noting that 'seeds can become a means of dominating people and nature' (1996: 71). That is to say 'seeds of plenty' tie people in new ways to suppliers of seed, credit, fertiliser and other inputs; new relations of production that create new scarcity (of credit, inputs), new poverty, and serve the interests of agribusiness, and producers of fertiliser or irrigation pumps. Seeds also sustain professional identities and scientific careers, or enforce hierarchies between experts and farmers. In this sense the official 'regulatory frameworks', which institutionalise standards of technology evaluation (Witcombe et al. 1998), ensure that societal and professional relations (and biases) are built into seeds. New seeds are what Langdon Winner (1999) calls 'political technologies', that is forms of social ordering and political phenomena in their own right, embodiments of power and authority. But there is no reason to preconceive the effects of new technology. Precisely *because* technology is political, new 'smart seeds' can also emancipate (Paul Richards, pers. comm.), as indeed was the intention of PVS/PPB, by identifying crop improvements not dependent upon additional inputs of fertiliser, pesticide or water.

22. In fact, from 1997 there was a dramatic increase in seed supply for new maize and rice varieties by the project (given free or sold), as a result of many more introductory trials and in response to demand. But this supply depended upon project systems that were disrupted at the end of Phase I (see Chapter 8) and only put back on track with consultant support later in Phase II.

23. Consultant advice on SWC came both from a specialist soil scientist and from 'social development' consultants, including myself.

24. End of Project Report (Phase I), Soil and Water Conservation, April 1998.

25. While doing piece-rate work villagers could actually earn at twice the local daily wage-rate. But, by budgeting with the government's Schedule of Rates for earthworks (roughly double local wage rates), farmers could be represented as contributing 50 per cent of labour costs, amounting to substantial 'participation'. For example, in the August 1998 Monthly Progress Report, farmers were reported as contributing 11 million rupees, or 46 per cent of the total SWC costs.

26. IBRFP paid 10 per cent of costs into a maintenance fund and 5 per cent for *jankars*; 3 per cent of wages were deducted for personal savings accounts and 2 per cent for a group account. The project paid full wages for work on common lands, but deducted 25 per cent for group maintenance funds.

27. See Smith (1998) for a full discussion of the issue.

28. Aide Memoire of SWC consultant, May 1995. Later impact assessment studies involving crop-cutting measurements claimed that the cost of labour inputs into SWC could be paid back in increased yields in 2–3 years, especially in *nallah* (valley) areas (given a fair monsoon).

29. Notably Myrada in south India (Fernandez 1993).

30. With soil erosion rates of between 10 and 30 tonnes per hectare per year, 'if erosion remains unchecked, yields will diminish to minimal levels within 50 to 150 years' (Smith 1998).

31. Wide experience and a growing literature already dealt with local institutions as a *means* to an end (to form villager capital through savings, to manage assets, to supply inputs or to link to other agencies); or as an *end* in their own right, being the 'social capital' that enabled the poor to defend their interests, access political power, hold officials accountable or deal with injustice (e.g. Bhatt 1989, Ostrom 1990, Runge 1986, Unia 1991, Uphoff 1986, Wade 1987).

32. IBRFP's Village Development Societies were first created as an accounting mechanism to hold funds arising from the sale of nursery seedlings, the repayment of crop loans and the hiring of diesel pumps. They had only a paper or accounting reality (i.e. named bank accounts).

33. If the vain hope of the VDSs was to neutralise allegiance to clan, kin or faction, the aim of the *falia* groups was to fulfil 'natural' associations – both were strategies with colonial antecedents (Fiedrich 2002: 27). The replacement of imposed VDSs with 'natural affinity' *falia* groups did not, however, resolve the problem of women's exclusion. For example, kin-groups comprised of male 'in-laws' constrained younger women, who had to observe approved codes of conduct towards them.

34. This was considerably encouraged by the fact that NABARD (the National Bank for Agriculture and Rural Development) had just established a refinance facility to allow banks to lend to 'self-help groups' without collateral or the need to specify purpose.

35. Summarised from various local institutional development consultancy reports, 1994–6.

36. There is an analogy here with the relationship between Foucault's 'physics of power', its instrumentalities, technique and machineries; 'opaque power that has no possessor ... [and is] almost autonomously effective' – that is the power of institutional operations, and the ideology (our policy models) which 'all the while ... babbles on' (de Certeau 1984: 46).

37. Progress Report, June 1994.

38. A point made forcefully in the project's Mid-Term Evaluation (Shah et al. 1996); see Chapter 7.

39. It was conceded that women did offer on-the-spot influence through labouring, some worked as trained *jankars* setting out contours,

and that there was significant strategic value in the project norm of equal wages.

40. Gendered hierarchies of productive/domestic, technology/tradition pervade development agencies. The technical and the social, is the 'hard' against the 'soft', professional/secretarial or male against female. These are social/institutional hierarchies that have only recently been questioned or, more rarely, even reversed.

41. Mona Mehta's work was particularly important in this, and in analysing gender-based exclusions from project activities.

42. I should note that current project management insists that much has changed in recent years, in targeting benefits to women (through women's groups, appropriate technologies and work with women *jankars*), in the institutionalising of gender specialists and training (internally and through local NGOs), and in addressing the problems of women staff (e.g. posting women with women, sexual harassment policy).

43. Even when the project did recruit livestock specialists, these tended to be professional vets unable to address the professional border-zones of fodder–livestock management.

44. In ways that resemble Mitchell's analysis of the 'rule of experts' our work helped bring about or enforce a distinction between practices and policy by securing a sphere of rational intention or abstract design which appeared external to (and generative of) events. Our writing, models and maps erased the personal, contingent, hybrid agencies, struggles, connections and interactions of actual practice by portraying events as the outcome of rational intention guided by our expertise (or deviation from it) (cf. Mitchell 2002: 77). Perhaps our status as development experts depended upon the abstraction of principles, models, design and science from messy practice securing the status of ex ante plans (2002: passim).

45. Rossi makes a similar point in a recent conference paper (2003).

46. In April 2001, Supriya Akerkar and I obtained written responses (in Hindi and English) from 68 project staff to questions seeking views on the problems people face in the region, the changes desired as a result of the project and their own working roles.

47. Or '[keeping] village soil in the village; village's water in the village; village's money in the village' (*gaon ki mitti gaon me; gaon ka pani gaon me, gaon ka paisa gaon me*). Current DFID policy trends were evident in a number of responses that emphasised 'linkage with government schemes and line departments' and non-land-based income generation (see Chapter 8).

48. In our rough survey, only 29 per cent of staff identified gender relations as an aspect of the project context and objectives, whereas nearly 60 per cent gave a clear natural resources-based 'self-reliance' view of project goals. A small section of staff (12–15 per cent) expressed a narrow 'activity perspective' in which the project is viewed as delivering specific inputs and assets. A significant minority (a third) had a more complex view of livelihood problems and changes.

49. The notion of the 'project idea', a forceful representation distinct from the exigencies of practice, finds a parallel in the 'state idea' in the work on the anthropology of the state (see note 8 in Chapter 1, Abrams 1988).

7 THE SOCIAL PRODUCTION OF DEVELOPMENT SUCCESS

1. It is the blurring of meaning and ontology characteristic of the world of development projects that makes it possible to talk of 'reality' in this way. Of course, projects that have lost their reality (as projects) do not cease to have material effects.
2. The new National Watershed Development Programme among them.
3. As the project and its approach became a marketing success in its own right, KBCL managers showed less and less interest in the sorts of agricultural marketing opportunities that they had originally hoped for. Technical consultants repeatedly failed to get the organisation interested in the processing and marketing of new crops such as niger or sunhemp.
4. By 1995, earlier problems such as low tree survival rates and SWC works washed away by monsoon rains because of misaligned contours, inadequate compaction or surplusing arrangements had been overcome.
5. And the growth of farmer organisations was too important to rely on uncertain member savings.
6. Reviewing community-driven development, Mansuri and Rao (2004) also identify the specific difficulty of establishing causal relations in participatory development, that is between participation or group activity on the one hand and project effectiveness and sustainability on the other.
7. This is not to say that reporting was not inventive. On the contrary it had to be in order to track changing outside expectations. So, when *participation* is emphasised, SWC work is reported in terms of farmers' contributions to physical structures, when the concern shifts to *drought relief*, it is the number of wage-labour days generated that is recorded (Monthly Progress Report, February 2001).
8. Report on the Annual Monitoring of the Western India (KBCL) Rainfed Farming Project, 23–28 January 1995.
9. One expert, quite misunderstanding the principle of PVS, commented that 'the standard of agronomy practices in the participatory field experiments ... was not sufficiently rigorous'; another commented that 'a greater emphasis on the collection and use of meteorological data at all locations ... would strengthen the scientific approach'; and a third senior visitor concluded that 'there is no concept of disease among farmers'(!) Others, with their own social development concerns could deride such comments. Visitors were clearly of different kinds having different levels of experience and able to contribute more or less useful ideas.
10. MPR, August 1998, p. 2.
11. MPR, Gujarat, January 2001.
12. Public spectacles of this sort are a feature of development in many places, often serving to legitimise state power. Amita Baviskar (forthcoming) notes a strange inversion of rituals of state when, to advertise its

watershed development programme, the district administration in Jhabua
(an IBRFP district) adopts practices more commonly associated with social
movements. It launches its mission in new villages with rallies 'where
officials exhort people to shout slogans and sing songs composed by
the administration, and arm them with placards and banners painted
by hired artists'. Officers eschew official vehicles to walk in the rallies
(*padyatras*).

13. MPR, July–August 1995. Republic Day 1997 was celebrated as 'Women
Jankars' Day'.

14. MPR, May 1995.

15. Initially in the state's Integrated Watershed Development Programme,
but later for state programmes at district level, for example, through
the UNICEF-funded Community Based Convergence Services (CBCS) in
Banswara district (Rajasthan), the DWCRA, World Food Programme and
others.

16. From the start it was accepted that 'the economic viability of the project
depends on the approach being replicable elsewhere in India'. Annual
Report, 1992, p. 26.

17. MPR, Oct.–Dec. 1996. This is not to deny that individual IGFRI
scientists learned from visits to the project and especially from informal
conversations with *jankars*.

18. 'Utmost care needs to be taken during the writing of progress reports',
insisted the project manager in one staff meeting, 'the style of reporting
should be such that it does not give a different meaning to the readers.
One should be careful to include all the names of government officials
and other personalities who have actively supported the project' (Meeting
minutes, 6 Sept. 1993).

19. As an NGO director working in the same region pointed out to me:

> when we work with the government we work under such stress ...
> Whenever the Assembly session is on in Bhopal, every other day
> we receive a letter, an urgent fax from the District Administration
> [saying] send this information, or send that information because some
> MLAs have asked ... like, how many boulder check[dam]s you have
> made in your watersheds, each village-wise, and that too financial
> year-wise ...

Latour captures the same general process when he writes that 'the more
a technological project progresses, the more the role of technology
decreases in relative terms: such is the paradox of development'
(1996: 126).

20. MPR, May 1995. Note that the same report also noted that 'SWC work was
at its peak during the month with the construction of 649 cubic metres
of earth field bunds and 751 earth *nallah* (valley-bottom) bunds.'

21. Regarding improved varieties the question is whether, to take Kalinga
III, the 46 per cent yield advantage demonstrated in paired comparisons
and controlled crop-cutting experiments could be reproduced across a
village in the normal cultivation of upland rice. Yield differences with
local varieties on equivalent land would depend upon the rainfall, sowing

time, inputs, labour and credit availability. Certainly there was a gap between the consistently high yield advantage demonstrated in farmer trials, and the more mixed perception in village-level studies (Chapter 9). There were (and are) solid grounds for rejecting the conclusions that the yield advantage of Kalinga III over local varieties was only 6 per cent; but the point here is that the very *existence* of this study destabilised 'success'.

22. India Country Strategy Paper, 1995, Overseas Development Administration.

23. ODA Assistance to Renewable Natural Resources in India, Sept. 1994.

24. ODA Assistance to Renewable Natural Resources in India, Sept. 1994.

25. The studies of Bhil livelihoods were organised around a 'model of change' linking project inputs (e.g. physical works), outputs (e.g. SWC bunds), outcomes (e.g. yield increases) and impacts (e.g. food security).

26. By 1998 a new livelihoods model presented ODA (now DFID)'s rural development goals in terms of enhancing and maintaining a balance between five 'livelihood capital assets': a 'pentagon' of natural capital, social capital, human capital (health, education etc.), financial capital and physical capital (basic infrastructure). DFID's 1998 Natural Resources Advisers Conference endorsed this model of 'SRL' (sustainable rural livelihoods). For sources on the considerable recent UK literature on 'sustainable livelihoods' see the Overseas Development Institute website at www.odi.org.uk; for a critique of the model's capacity to grasp the value contestations that underpin people's livelihood interests and experiences see Arce (2003).

27. 'Draft Rural Development Strategy – India', internal memo, Delhi, 14 Oct. 1998.

28. Perhaps most importantly, the livelihood framework was in keeping with new poverty-reduction policy goals. To expand the chief adviser's comment:

> OK, we've got many objectives and many ideas, but there is one overall theme for agriculture and rural space, and that's what do we do about poor people. And then you start realising that the really poor people, the ones we said in India we couldn't help because they didn't have a cow, actually have multiple livelihood options and indeed most people in rural space did many different things. The forests weren't really separate from the rice paddies, and they weren't separate from carrying bricks in urban areas, which is why we found the idea of a livelihood attractive.

29. The Rural Development Group, note, August 2000.

30. Successful development projects are to policy models, what exemplars are to scientific paradigms in Kuhn's usage (see Fine 2002: 2061). The importance of an exemplar, a worldview and a body of supporting professionals (capable of switching allegiance) gives policy models a superficial resemblance to paradigms, and policy change to 'paradigm shift' (2002: 2061).

31. Western India Rainfed Farming Project (WIRFP) Phase II. PEC Submission, June 1998, DFID.
32. WIRFP Phase II. PEC Submission, June 1998.
33. Persisting concern about KBCL's accounting and personnel procedures and their incompatibility with project goals did eventually (in 1997) result in an independent consultancy study commissioned to look into alternative institutional arrangements for the project, although this partial examination of operational systems was really intended as a contribution to planning the next phase.
34. Staff shared this perception. As one commented:

> ... the project management agency thought that ODA is measuring success, which was not true. ODA was not measuring success ... [they, ODA] should have said [that] what we are measuring is entirely different, for our own internal consumption, to satisfy our government, to satisfy our tax payers, to satisfy the whole range of people who are not involved in what you are doing. It is not your success assessment.

35. Report of the final Annual Review of Phase 1, DFID, New Delhi, December 1998.

8   AID POLICY AND PROJECT FAILURE

1. For an account of rapid policy change and continuity of institutionally grounded practice in the health sector in India following the Cairo Summit see Cleves (2000).
2. These demands became built into the design of the second phase (WIRFP Phase II, PEC Submission, June 1998).
3. Annex 1 – Project Approach, WIRFP Phase II Project Document, June 1998.
4. Institutional appraisal, WIRFP Phase II Project Document, June 1998.
5. Both 'rituals of unity' and 'carnivals of division' are from Spencer's (1990) analysis of modes of public life in rural Sri Lanka.
6. An alternative might have been to support the general state-relief measures.
7. W.S. Atkins Consultants' Report no. 34 (August 2001).
8. An outbreak of malpractice and embezzlement by *jankars* when COs were absent in the period between Phase I and Phase II showed just how vulnerable some of these groups were.
9. This was clearly the case in 'India: Rural Livelihoods Programme: Concept Note', circulated to programme managers and chief advisers outlining new rural livelihood programmes at the time.
10. ODA India: Country Review Paper, 1993, cf. Shepherd et al. (2000).
11. This was one among other strands of the new aid policy including a new role for the private sector, policy consistency – which meant 'joining up' development aid, human rights, ethical trade and foreign policy – and

the replacement of an earlier 'value for money' rubric with the language of moral duty.

12. Dahl asks the question of Swedish aid, can 'partnership' provide the mobilising metaphor for aid in contrast to charity that 'solidarity' earlier did (2001: 15–17)? She points out that the 'partnership' is a complex and clever signifier that conveys the radical idea of solidarity or equality while also meeting a neo-liberal demand for contract, responsibility and self-interest that fits with a new business environment without losing old supporters (2001: 13). The appeal to 'New Labour' in Britain is self-evident.

13. In fact already, in the 1995 India Country Strategy Paper, 'the overall objective of the aid programme [was] to help GoI reduce poverty and address environmental issues on a sustainable basis'. Indeed the post-White Paper country strategy simply formalised existing trends towards policy coherence, strategic influence, focus states, decentralised aid management and a poverty focus, monitored by increasing numbers of 'institutional' as well as social development advisers (cf. Shepherd et al. 2000: 23).

14. My interviews suggest, however, that quite a few people disagreed with the idea that the best way to exert influence over state systems was to work *within* them. Research scientists interviewed pointed to the importance of international research independent of state bureaucracy, and NGOs to the success of innovations such as joint forest management, which began beyond the state.

15. If the IBRFP was born in a 1990s policy climate favouring the market and private sector against the state (the 'Washington Consensus'), it now faced a post-Washington Consensus which reaffirmed the importance of the regulatory structures of the state and governance to the elimination of poverty. This was the latest in a series of worldwide policy changes succinctly summarised by Barry Ireton (I paraphrase a quote in Foster 2000): in the 1960s newly independent governments in a hurry displaced the private sector; in the 1970s donors in a hurry displaced government systems; in the 1980s governments returned ownership to the private sector; in the 1990s donors began to return ownership to governments.

16. An extension of the same argument says that too much aid is *bilateral*, and that more aid should be pooled internationally with greater power-sharing in the governance of multilateral organisations that handle it through integrated budget frameworks (Maxwell 2002).

17. These had grown out of a decade of experimental collaboration between government and NGOs. The watershed programmes fitted DFID's history of natural resources-based approaches to rural development (see Farrington et al. 1999). Other donors, building on other traditions, worked with credit and financial institutions (e.g. the Swiss with NABARD).

18. The Western Orissa Rural Livelihoods Project (£32 million) and the Andhra Pradesh Rural Livelihoods Project (£50 million). See Turton (2000b) for a critical review of India's watersheds programmes from a rural livelihoods perspective, examining the gains and losses of poor men and women dependent upon common property or seasonal migration.

19. State partnerships also required reform of the system of aid flows to make it possible to finance regional state governments directly. Earlier, when all aid finance went to the centre and was turned into *loans* to state governments paid as part of their devolved budgets, there were few incentives at the state level to attract foreign donor assistance. Indeed, the quantum of committed but unutilised foreign aid funds reached 10 billion rupees at one point (INTRAC 1998: 53). Reforms bringing new fiscal pressures gave state governments a new incentive to compete for inward investment and to enter into policy dialogue with donors.

20. The emphasis here on the selection of aid partners is a departure from the earlier ineffective and politically unacceptable forms of aid 'conditionality' (Boyce 2002: 241; Slater and Bell 2002: 345). The downside of the 'selectivity' approach (or aid as reward) is that policy dialogue is effective where it is not necessary and aid flows gravitate away from weak states with political instability or violence, factors which are themselves major contributors to poverty (cf. Pronk 2001).

21. 'Upstream' implied a shift from judging achievements in terms of logframe outputs and purposes towards giving attention to *programme goals* ('more effective policies and programmes to reduce poverty...' in the case of IBRFP; cf. Shepherd et al. 2000: 34).

22. Interview in London, June 2001. Some reactions to new policy directions among DFID-India staff implied concern that experiences and models from African countries were being misapplied to Indian states. Others in the aid policy world worried about the marginalisation of area development projects as 'throwing the baby out with the bathwater' (Farrington et al. 2002).

23. The project manager of a DFID urban development programme in Hyderabad spoke of vulnerability in the absence of DFID staff as 'an external cushion'.

24. When AP's 'Vision 2020' received condemnation by representatives of poor farmers in a 'citizen's jury' (*prajateerpu*) (Pimbert and Wakefield 2002), criticism was made in the British national press and questions were raised in the UK parliament. DFID objected to the representation of its India programme and demanded removal of the Prajateerpu document from the research websites (IIED/IDS) on which it was posted. There is an interesting dilemma here. As donor agencies like DFID develop state-level partnerships their agendas inevitably have to converge, to some degree, with those of their partner states (otherwise there's no partnership). And, to the extent that these partnerships are successful, it becomes difficult clearly to identify separate bits with donor country flags on them (which is as it should be). But the consequence, as the Prajateerpu controversy shows, is that such donors cannot easily avoid exposure to criticism levelled at the broader development policies and strategies of their state partners. It is still unclear how DFID will balance the conflicting demands of partnership and policy coherence, or how it will deal with domestic (i.e. UK) political responses to the state policies (e.g. in AP) with which they are associated, however tenuously. The dilemma here is being caught between accusations of undemocratic suppression of debate, and neo-colonial interference in domestic (i.e. Indian state) policy discussion.

25. This is a view I have from interviews with senior government officials in Hyderabad and Bhopal, in September 2001.
26. Financial services for women's groups is one such fashion, often promoted with inadequate attention to the reality of limited opportunities for enterprise. 'Any donor would like to be associated with a programme that is empowering five million women', commented a senior bureaucrat in Hyderabad.
27. Gould (2003) discusses the importance of 'scale making' (scale is always socially constructed), and shifts in resolution in development.
28. Internal DFID memo on 'The Future of the Rainfed Farming Project', 2 Feb. 2000.
29. India: Rural Livelihoods Programme: Concept Note, June 1998.
30. Some of my DFID interlocutors maintain this is an unjustified interpretation of a DFID-sponsored event. I wonder, the marginalisation of IBRFP, and projects in general, in DFID policy circles at the time was unmistakable.
31. Email from head of DFID-India to the DFID director general (in response to a paper of mine).
32. In September 2001 I engaged in work concerned with setting up a Challenge Fund (CF) through which various agencies – NGOs, researchers, community-based organisations, panchayats – would help the state administration address critical constraints to implementing its new (large-scale) decentralised panchayat- and community-led development initiatives. Linking this initiative to IBRFP (as manager of the CF) provided the means (i) to reconnect the project to DFID's legitimising policy framework; and (ii) to increase the project's symbolic capital by conveying an image of the project as a source of experience and innovation for government. Typically, the effect of the consultancy was more to improve the project as a system of representations than to modify its operations or practice.
33. Watershed development, drought relief, joint forest management among others, usually designed around community-based approaches and requiring NGO implementing agencies. IBRFP (and its *jankars*) also provided government with consultancy services, for example, for programme monitoring, PRA training and research.
34. Shepherd et al. are correct when they note that 'efforts of the flagship IBRFP were appreciated by government officers because it was seen as an honest organisation, not because it had a distinctive development strategy' (2000: 86).
35. Still, as development contractors project staff might be able to challenge corrupt practices; and they did help extend and converge government resources in remote areas. Moreover, the project learned things from implementing government programmes.
36. While the project promoted client user-groups and SHGs, DFID's institutional advisers in Delhi had an a priori commitment to work within the framework of state policy on political decentralisation, that is through panchayati raj institutions (PRIs). The tension (or contradiction) between donor-promoted associations and institutions shaped by electoral politics is the focus of an important contemporary debate on democracy and

development in rural India (see Manor 2002, Saxena 2001). On the one hand, there is the fear that well-resourced SHGs/federations undermine poorly resourced PRIs; on the other, there is the suspicion that linking federations to panchayats will result in their 'politicisation'. In its second phase, the IBRFP project policy tries to resolve the tension in two ways: (1) by enabling SHGs to act as pressure groups representing the interests of marginal groups or influencing the use of tied funds in panchayats; and (2) offering support and training on local democracy to PRI leaders.

37.   It is perhaps not surprising that the DFID advisers responsible for the project contest my analysis of both the crisis facing the project in 1999–2000 and the ruptures of policy change. Regarding the first, they emphasise 'internal project reasons' (delays in establishing the Trust, slow recruitment, lack of strategic direction) and the contingent factors of leadership, personality and an eruption of casteism in KBCL rather than the effects of DFID's shifting policy agenda and its failure to deal with institutional complexity. On the second, their analysis of policy change overlooks rupture in favour of a view of the long-term integration and compatibility of the components of an ongoing aid portfolio (letter, 23 January 2004, and pers. comm.). The disjunctures of development are easily lost in renewed policy optimism.

38.   Craig and Porter argue that the ranked goals of global economic integration, good governance, poverty reduction and safety nets amount to a convergence 'optimising economic, juridical and social governance in order to create ideal conditions for international finance and investment … with a *disciplined* inclusion of the poor', which 'represents an attempt to generate a level of global to local integration, discipline and technical management of marginal economies, governance and populations unprecedented since colonial times' (2003: 54–5, emphasis in original).

39.   There are also risks and naiveties in promoting a policy package in which 'all good things go together' – popular participation, democracy, poverty reduction, economic growth, good governance.

40.   As de Certeau points out: 'The ministers of knowledge have always assumed that the whole universe was threatened by the very changes that affected their ideologies and their positions. They transmute the misfortune of their theories into theories of misfortune. When they transform their bewilderment into "catastrophies", when they seek to enclose the people in the "panic" of their discourse, are they once more necessarily right?' (1984: 95–6).

9   ASPIRATIONS FOR DEVELOPMENT

1.   There were eight carefully selected village case-studies, each an intensive participatory piece of research undertaken over 6 to 9 months by a team of researchers facilitated by experienced COs familiar with the village concerned. The research drew on extensive project documentation and available baseline data and involved updated household surveys (of all households), farming system and livelihood modelling, a range of

PRA exercises differentiated according to topic, and the gender, age and socio-economic status of the participants, and household-level interviews (of participants and non-participants). The research was structured to allow attention to inter- and intra-household differences, and each study ended with the presentation to villagers of a book of sketches, photos and findings, whose accuracy was discussed at a series of feedback meetings. The studies were coordinated by our consultancy team, but in large measure undertaken and written by ODA 'Associate Professional Officers', Julia Rees, Jessica Dart and R. Petre along with the IBRFP project team. Special acknowledgement should go to Meera Shahi and Kalpesh Soni for this work. (Department for International Development 'IBRFP' Phase I, Impact Assessment Reports, vols 1 and 2, Village Studies, KBCL, Centre for Development Studies, University of Wales. New Delhi, December 1999.)

2. Chatra Khuta village study.
3. In fact the PVS approach halved the time normally taken to make improved varieties available to farmers.
4. The spread of Kalinga III was carefully tracked by the project (Witcombe et al. 1999). From three villages in 1994 seed had spread to 41 villages by 1996 and to over 100 project and non-project villages by 1997. Spread *within* villages meant that the area under Kalinga III nearly doubled reaching between 20 and 65 per cent of all rice grown in selected villages. Spreading seed is also an insurance for future supply in the event of crop failure, especially in villages without a project supplier.
5. Chatra Khuta village study.
6. Mahunala village study.
7. I will comment on the *distribution* of this gain below. The survey relied on farmer memory and a purposefully selected sample of 48 households across 'wealth rank' categories in the project area. ('Project Impact on Farming Systems Livelihoods: Changes in Net Income' [draft], IBRFP, December 1998.)
8. Mahunala village study.
9. For this farmer manure was also short because cow dung was burned owing to a shortage of fuel wood. Chatra Khuta village study.
10. One farmer interviewed gave up urea altogether in the belief that yields were declining, and that the soil was losing its capacity to retain moisture, and began using more compost (Ratanmal village study). These are perspectives which elsewhere have led farmers to disparage new seed technology, using 'hybrid' ('hybrid times', 'hybrid people') as a metaphor for weakness, vulnerability, high cost and in need of constant attention (Vasavi 1994, writing on dryland Karnataka).
11. Bijori village study.
12. Consultants hoped that this variation would decline as farmers became more careful about where they planted varieties like Kalinga III (Joshi and Witcombe 1996: 470).
13. Jharola village study.
14. One farmer in Mahunala village concluded that 'given the choice of local seed or project seed from [the] group [on] credit, I would have taken project seed in *rabi* and local seed in *kharif*' (Mahunala village study).

15. This was the crux of the disagreement in 1995 between consultants and mid-term evaluators who judged the yield advantage of Kalinga III respectively as 46 and 6 per cent (see Chapter 7). Project consultants complained that by comparing Kalinga III grown on poor land with local varieties grown on more favourable sites, the evaluators had failed to discover the advantages revealed in their own paired comparisons (Joshi and Witcombe 1995, 1996).

16. Some new varieties, such as the black gram (*arad*), were generally unpopular.

17. Mahunala village study.

18. Kalinga III accounted for only 13 per cent of rice grown in 1996. When, by 2001, the variety was still far from dominant, the consultant suggested that the intervening drought years had knocked back its uptake so that the impact was far less than the figures that were projected in Witcombe et al. (1999). Witcombe informs me that in 2003, post-drought, Kalinga III adoption rates were up to or exceeded the predicted rate of 25–45 per cent of upland rice in Madhya Pradesh and Gujarat, although it is now replaced by new rice varieties developed in the Phase II project (pers. comm.).

19. The point is not that the yield advantage of new varieties over local ones is in doubt (or under-perceived by farmers, although it may be), but that yield advantage does not translate into income gains for Bhil households in an unmediated way, but depends upon landholding, moisture conditions, crop management and fertiliser use, sowing times, access to inputs, debt and credit relations, among other things. Second, the fact that new crop technology is 'recontextualised' in this way challenges attempts such as Vasavi's (1994) to distinguish between context-sensitive traditional cultivation and context-free modern agriculture, and populist models such as Vandana Shiva's in which the latter displaces the former (see Akhil Gupta [1998] for further comments on the hybrid nature of agricultural knowledge and practice in India).

20. To date, one adoption study shows over half of farmers given seed in 1998 still growing the variety on nearly 40 per cent of their maize land in 2000 (Witcombe et al. 2003).

21. It has to be noted that this man was disgruntled at having been evicted from his encroached Forest Department land. 'Baripada' village study.

22. Bijori and Ratanmal village studies.

23. Mahunala village study. And also, as some women pointed out, because men would not permit them to spend money on fuel.

24. Palasiapada village study.

25. Naganwat Choti village study.

26. Mahunala village study.

27. Some, though, felt that threshers wasted straw by chopping it too fine.

28. Bijori village study. Significantly, virtually every claim here is open to a counter-claim. Some, for instance, insisted that SWC work reduces weeding because water stands for longer in the fields and eliminates the task of clearing the field of stones.

29. In practice it is very difficult to determine who the poor or better off are. The project's 'wealth rank' socio-economic classification into 'better off',

'medium', 'poor' and 'very poor' was a crude and unreliable classification; it was inadequately differentiated – unable for example to distinguish the poor but socially mobile, or life-cycle related poverty, and also incapable of capturing enormous mobility between the categories. A family could slip downwards as result of a single episode – a bad harvest, a heavy loan, ill-health, the partition of the household and division of land, or divorce – or its position could improve simply as a result of domestic cycle shifts which improved dependency ratios. Such categorisations – common in participatory projects – do little to capture the dynamics of poverty (related to domestic cycles, debt cycles, etc.). Based on established perceptions of well-being and peasant identities (shared by villagers and staff), they often over-emphasise agricultural production-subsistence criteria of 'wealth', and take less account of market-based exchanges, and 'common property' or forest collection, or of social exclusion or health and physical weakness (cf. Social Development Consultant's reports for IBRFP's sister East India project, *passim*).

30. In its sample of villages/households, the survey found that agricultural incomes of the top three of four wealth rank categories had increased by 30–40 per cent, while those of the poorest by only 17 per cent (in some sample villages the agricultural incomes of the poorest had actually *declined*). In absolute terms the increase in agricultural incomes of the poorest was only a quarter as much as that of 'better-off' families. By its own admission, this survey bristled with difficult assumptions, including those associated with wealth-ranking mentioned earlier ('Project Impact on Farming Systems Livelihoods: Changes in Net Income' [draft], IBRFP, December 1998).
31. Mahunala village study.
32. Ratanmal village study.
33. Interviews from various village studies.
34. Mahunala village study.
35. Jharola village study. This was a major factor in almost all village studies such that one researcher concluded that 'the amount of seed purchased is not a good indicator of farmer preferences, showing as it does farmer preference for low interest seeds' (Mahunala study, p. 49). The high proportion of new varieties sown from home-saved seed (between 25 and 98 per cent) would be a better indicator, although the higher figure here comes from a village in which seed provided through a project-established seed bank in the village was also classified as 'home-saved' in the survey (Chatra Khuta study, pp. 47–48).
36. Jharola and Naganwat Choti village studies.
37. Naganwat Choti village study.
38. In one group, farmers spoke of yield increases of 25 to 50 per cent simply from planting maize 3–7 days earlier and applying small amounts of urea.
39. Jharola village study.
40. Time as a resource is emphasised locally, but largely excluded from universal technical agricultural knowledge. The time–labour implications of new technology are typically under-emphasised, especially when it is women's time that is concerned. While official variety release systems

emphasise yield, *duration* is often of more importance to marginal farmers. In a broader frame, Appadurai illustrates an historical shift from a situation in which time and calendrical-ritual cycles set the periodicity of agriculture to one in which time is subject to the labour cash and climatic needs of commercial crops (1990: 210, see also Lansing 1991).

41. Ratanmal village study.

42. Naganwat Choti village study.

43. Women's acquisition of new independent sources of income (e.g. through vegetable cultivation or income-generation activities) was also sometimes viewed as reducing conflict over household resources.

44. Project interventions also had the effect of reducing *inter*-village obligations. During the resurgence of the goddess cult in 1992–3 (Chapter 4) Mataji (the goddess) travelled from village to village, manifesting herself in each village through the possession of female devotees. A *puja* (worship) was given and coconuts offered to the goddess. The coconuts were carried to the next village where twice the number of coconuts were to be offered and so on. Under the influence of the project, some village leaders began to break the chain, refusing the obligation and expense of supplying coconuts and completing the ritual in their villages, bringing 'enthusiasm to the project team' and 'intensifying and strengthening relations with the project' (Project note: 'Case Studies: Successes and Failures', Dahod, October 1993).

45. However, such change also needs to be placed in a broader context. As historical transitions, the erosion of forms of reciprocal labour exchange, the emergence of a more open labour market, and agrarian differentiation, as well as a shift to more exploitative relationships between adivasis and *sahukars*, are analysed in Jan Breman's work over three decades (1974, 1985, 1996).

46. While SHGs are an aspect of modernity or urbanity for villagers, for those outsiders who promote them, they are often the reverse – signs of tradition. These are often metropolitan professionals (such as myself) whose romantic/nostalgic attachment to the collective perhaps has something to do with the fact that their own lives have never been less communal or more individual: living in nuclear families, dependent upon contractual services (etc.) – a point made by Fiedrich (2002).

47. Comments from interviews in Bijori and Jharola village studies.

48. The idea of cultural difference understood in terms of being of another time derives from Fabian (1983). See commentaries by Skaria (2003) and Moore (2003: 174). Placed in a wider political economy of development, these developments resonate with colonial history and imperial discourses of improvement (Moore 2003: 175).

49. Jharola village study.

50. I am suggesting a shift in analysis here away from the dominant focus on the condition of poverty and livelihoods, towards the aspirations, mobilising passions and dreams of 'the poor', and their expression through *consumption and lifestyles*. The question is, how are valued lifestyles produced? Consumption is then a matter of reproducing lifestyles; and lifestyles are for creating social networks. Goods (as Mary Douglas argued) are for mobilising people, connecting through things

to other people. One of the advantages of focusing on consumption and lifestyles rather than the 'othering' discourses of poverty and livelihoods in the analysis of development is that it enables the driving forces of *high* levels of consumption in 'the West' to be considered in the same frame as poverty in the South.

51. Jharola village study.
52. Mahunala and Palasiapara village studies.
53. Mahunala village study.
54. Jharola village study.
55. Commenting on her efforts to speak to women of such empowerment, one fieldworker admitted that 'Women were listening to us because they respected us; but they were not adopting ... [or] practising what we were saying. They were laughing at us ... you know saying "This is not what happens in our culture, what you are talking about."' Still this fieldworker believed that the project had a gradual, unnoticed impact on women.
56. Mahunala case study.
57. Palasiapara village study.
58. Bijori, Jharola and Palasiapara village studies.
59. See Chapter 4 and Mosse (1994), on dominant views in participatory research methods.
60. That is households with at least one member migrating (Sarjumi village study).
61. The programme aims to provide welfare support to migrants (shelter, water, education and childcare), to enhance their ability to get work (e.g. through labour exchanges) and in the longer-term work with government, labour unions and industry to enable a highly exploited section of the labour force to realise basic rights – to minimum wages, freedom from bondage, sexual exploitation, compensation for injury or death, to associate and seek protection and redress. As noted in Chapter 8, this work, requiring a 'rights-based' approach and alliances with NGOs and unions, would prove hard to negotiate within KBCL higher management.
62. Mahunala village study.
63. I should note that, without the constraints of drought or heavy monsoons, with additional new varieties, and improved capacity in seed supply, the project's technical consultants are today still optimistic about their earlier economic projections for upland rice. They are also convinced that investing in improved genetics for higher-yielding, risk-reducing, input-responsive varieties – which, they argue, make changes in agronomy more attractive – is the best and most cost-effective approach to long-term agricultural development (pers. comm.). My point is not to dismiss this green revolution view (and certainly not the importance of PVS/PPB), but to emphasise, as indeed Bhil farmers did in our impact studies, the prior importance of changes in the networks of social relations and patronage to the adoption and impact of any technology.
64. For this reason, effort went into getting PVS or PPB varieties certified as state releases. The important outcome of the project from this point of view was the proven superiority of PVS over conventional replicated trials – given that data from participatory trials still 'do not command

the scientific respectability of data from replicated yield trials' – and its spread to other areas (Joshi and Witcombe 1995: 11, 1996: 476). In this respect, the project was more successful in influencing crop research systems outside India (in Nepal and West Africa) than within it. Even though PVS methodologies were validated and taken up under a major World Bank-funded participatory extension programme, the approach was significantly weakened, becoming in practice relabelled front-line trials and mini-kits (interview).

65. Some project observers felt that the low-input, low-return activities (pump operations, grain banks, shops, etc.) would never increase the income of the poorest. An anti-poverty strategy, they argued, required instead more capital-intensive, high-return activities involving wider linkages beyond the project for finance (from banks), technology, materials and marketing.

10 CONCLUSIONS AND IMPLICATIONS

1. The expression borrowed from Raymond Apthorpe (pers. comm.) is perhaps also inaccurate in that, following Ricoeur (1978), metaphors are vehicles for both understanding and managing reality, even if they do not shape events in the way that is claimed. I am grateful to Ingie Hovland for this point.

2. Mitchell's work extends the point by showing how, through the fabrication of ideas of 'national economy', 'free market', 'neoliberal reform', the 'self-regulating market', 'privatisation' or 'globalisation' (i.e. processes that follow a global logic) policy discourse abstracts from and misrepresents the actual 'multilayered political re-adjustment of rents, subsidies, and the control of resources' in particular places, concealing (in his case of Egypt) the hand of US or government interventions, protection, force and political repression, informal and clandestine economic activity (2002: 277).

3. We have seen, for example, how professional identities, alliances, divisions within the project, consultant and donor agencies were structured around the making and interpretation of policy which provided the idioms of speech, reporting and villager claims on the project.

4. See Ellerman (2002) for further discussion of the contradiction between the promotion of official views ('branded knowledge', 'best practices', 'funded assumptions', 'science') and the capacity to promote learning in development organisations.

5. Drawing on Rose (1993), Dahl refers to the neo-liberal 'therapeutic model of self improvement' employed in empowerment rhetoric which diverts attention from the structural issues or the need for changes in the allocation of resources (2001: 24).

6. De Certeau draws a distinction between the *tactics* of consumption and *strategies*, which have some connection with power. As consultants what we developed were participation strategies; they were changed by the *tactics* of practice.

7. Rather, as Foucault says of the idea of justice, development is 'an idea which has been invented and put to work in different types of societies as an instrument of a certain political and economic power *or as a weapon against that power ...* ' (cited in Rabinow 1984: 6, emphasis added).

8. Cox (1987) makes a similar kind of distinction between the normative, the pragmatic and the reflexive (cited in Eyben 2003: 28). Eyben comments on the way in which individually held moral and value-laden ideas take technical form in the transition to administration. Values remain, but submerged.

9. For reviews of this debate in anthropology see Agrawal (1996), Apthorpe (1996a), Autumn (1996), Bennett (1996), Escobar (1991), Gardener and Lewis (1996), Grillo (1997), Little and Painter (1995), Mosse (1998a).

Bibliography

Abdelrahman, Maha and Raymond Apthorpe. 2002. *Contract-financed technical co-operation and local ownership: Egypt country study report.* Stockholm: Swedish International Development Cooperation Agency.

Abraham, Anita and Jean-Philippe Platteau. 2004. Participatory development: where culture creeps in. In Vijayendra Rao and Michael Walton (eds) *Culture and public action.* Stanford, CA: Stanford University Press.

Abrams, Philip. 1988. Notes on the difficulty of studying the state. *Journal of Historical Sociology* 1(1): 58–89.

Abramson, David. 1999. A critical look at NGOs and civil society as means to an end in Uzbekistan. *Human Organisation* 58(3): 240–50.

Agarwal, Bina. 1994. *A field of one's own.* Cambridge: Cambridge University Press.

Agarwal, Bina. 1997. Environmental action, gender equity and women's perspectives. *Development and Change* 28: 1–43.

Agrawal, Arun. 1995. Dismantling the divide between indigenous and scientific knowledge. *Development and Change* 26: 413–39.

Agrawal, Arun. 1996. Poststructuralist approaches to development: some critical reflections. *Peace and Change* 21(4): 464–77.

Ahmad, Mokbul Morshed. 2002. Who cares? The personal and professional problems of NGO fieldworkers in Bangladesh. *Development in Practice* 12(2): 177–91.

Alexander, Catherine. 2001. Legal and binding: time, change and long-term transactions. *Journal of the Royal Anthropological Institute* (NS) 7(3): 467–85.

Alvesson, Mats. 1993. *Cultural perspectives on organisations.* Cambridge: Cambridge University Press.

Amanullah, Md. and S.C. Sharma. 1987. *Indebtedness among tribals of Jhabua District: a case study.* Bhopal: Tribal Research Institute.

Appadurai, Arjun. 1990. Technology and the reproduction of values in rural western India. In F.A. Marglin and S.A. Marglin (eds) *Dominating knowledge: development, culture and resistance.* Delhi: Oxford University Press.

Appadurai, Arjun. 1997. *Modernity at large: cultural dimensions of globalization.* Delhi: Oxford University Press.

Appadurai, Arjun. 2004. The capacity to aspire: culture and the terms of recognition. In Vijayendra Rao and Michael Walton (eds) *Culture and public action.* Stanford, CA: Stanford University Press.

Apthorpe, Raymond. 1996a. Reading development policy and policy analysis: on framing, naming, numbering and coding. In R. Apthorpe and Des Gasper (eds) *Arguing development policy: frames and discourses.* London and Portland, OR: Frank Cass.

Apthorpe, Raymond. 1996b. Policy anthropology as expert witness. *Social Anthropology* 4(2): 163–79.

Apthorpe, Raymond. 1997. Writing development policy and policy analysis plain or clear: on language, genre and power. In S. Shore and S. Wright (eds)

Anthropology of policy: critical perspectives on governance and power. London and New York: Routledge.

Arce, Alberto. 2003. Value contestations in development interventions: community development and sustainable livelihoods approaches. *Community Development Journal* 38(3): 199–212.

Arce, Alberto and Norman Long. 1992. The dynamics of knowledge: interfaces between bureaucrats and peasants. In N. Long and A. Long (eds) *Battlefields of knowledge: the interlocking of theory and practice in social research and development.* London: Routledge.

Arce, Alberto and Norman Long. 2000. Consuming modernity: mutational processes of change. In Alberto Arce and Norman Long (eds) *Anthropology, development and modernities: exploring discourses, counter-tendencies and violence.* London and New York: Routledge.

Ardener, E. 1975a. Belief and the problem of women. In S. Ardener (ed.) *Perceiving women.* London: Dent; New York: John Wiley.

Ardener, E. 1975b. The 'problem' revisited. In S. Ardener (ed.) *Perceiving women.* London: Dent; New York: John Wiley.

Ardener, S. 1978. Introduction: the nature of women in society. In *Defining females.* London: Croom Helm.

Asad, Talal. 1986. The concept of cultural translation in British social anthropology. In James Clifford and George E. Marcus (eds) *Writing culture: the poetics and politics of ethnography.* Berkeley: University of California Press.

Astha. 1987. A review of the training programmes and an identification of the training needs in the DWCRA programme in Rajasthan. Unpublished report. Astha: Udaipur.

Aurora, G.S. 1972. *Tribe, caste, class encounters.* Hyderabad: Administrative Staff College of India.

Autumn, S. 1996. Anthropologists, development and situated truth. *Human Organisation* 55(4): 480–84.

Balaguru, T., K. Venkateswarlu and M. Rajagopalan. 1988. Implementation of World Bank-aided National Agricultural Research Project in India: a case study. *Agricultural Administration and Extension* 29: 135–47.

Baviskar, Amita. 1995. *In the belly of the river: tribal conflicts over development in the Narmada valley.* Delhi: Oxford University Press.

Baviskar, Amita. 1997. Tribal politics and discourses of environmentalism. *Contributions to Indian Sociology* 31(2): 195–223.

Baviskar, Amita. 2003. Politics of development. *Biblio* 8(1–2): 31–33.

Baviskar, Amita. 2004. Between micro-politics and administrative imperatives: decentralization and the Watershed Mission in Madhya Pradesh, India. *European Journal of Development Research* 16(1): 26–40.

Baviskar, Amita. forthcoming. The dream machine: the model development project and the remaking of the state. In Amita Baviskar (ed.) *Waterscapes: the cultural politics of a natural resource.* Delhi: Permanent Black.

Bebbington, Anthony, Scott Guggenheim, Elizabeth Olson and Michael Woolcock. 2004. Exploring social capital debates at the World Bank. *Journal of Development Studies* 40(5): 33–42.

Bennett, J.W. 1996. Applied and action anthropology: ideological and conceptual aspects. *Current Anthropology* 36: S23–S53.

Bezkorowajnyj, P.G., S. Jones, J.N. Khare and P.S. Sodhi. 1994. A participatory approach to developing village tree programmes: the KRIBP experience. Paper presented at the Agroforestry into the Twenty-First Century Conference, New Delhi, November.

Bhabha, Homi. 1994. *The location of culture*. London: Routledge.

Bhatt, Anil. 1989. *Development and social justice: micro action by weaker sections*. Delhi: Sage Publications.

Biggs, Stephen. 1995. Participatory technology development: reflections on current advocacy and past technology development. Paper prepared for the workshop on Participatory Technology Development (PTD). 'The limits of participation', Intermediate Technology, Institute of Education, London, March.

Biggs, Stephen, and Sally Smith. 2003. A paradox of learning in project cycle management and the role of organisational culture. *World Development* 31(10): 1743–57.

Bloch, M. 1991. Language, anthropology and cognitive science. *Man* 26(2): 183–98.

Booth, David (ed.) 1994. *Rethinking social development: theory, research and practice*. Harlow: Longman Scientific and Technical.

Bourdieu, P. 1977. *Outline of a theory of practice*, trans. R. Nice. Cambridge: Cambridge University Press.

Bourdieu, P. 1984. *Distinction: a social critique of the judgement of taste*. Cambridge: Cambridge University Press.

Boyce, James L. 2002. Unpacking aid. *Development and Change* 33(2): 239–46.

Brass, Paul. 1997. *Theft of an idol: text and context in the representation of collective violence*. Princeton, NJ: Princeton University Press.

Breman, J. 1974. *Patronage and exploitation*. Berkeley: University of California Press.

Breman, J. 1978. Seasonal migration and co-operative capitalism: the crushing of cane and of labour by the sugar factories of Bardoli, South Gujarat. *Economic and Political Weekly* 13: 1317–60.

Breman, J. 1985. *Of peasants, migrants and paupers: rural labour circulation and capitalist production in West India*. Delhi: Oxford University Press.

Breman, J. 1996. *Footloose labour*. Cambridge: Cambridge University Press.

Brinkerhoff, D.W. 1996. Process perspectives on policy change: highlighting implementation. *World Development* 24(9): 1395–401.

Brow, James. 1990. The incorporation of a marginal community within the Sinhalese nation. *Anthropological Quarterly* 63(1): 7–17.

Brundtland, H. 1987. *Our common future*. Oxford: Oxford University Press, for the World Commission on Environment and Development.

Burawoy, Michael. 2001. Manufacturing the global. *Ethnography* 2(2): 147–59.

Burghart, Richard. 1993. His lordship at the cobblers' well. In Mark Hobart (ed.) *An anthropological critique of development: The growth of ignorance*. London: Routledge.

Carney, Diane (ed.). 1998. Sustainable rural livelihoods: what contribution can we make? (Papers presented at the DFID Natural Resources Advisers

Conference, London, July) London: Department for International Development.

Chambers, Robert. 1983. *Rural development: putting the last first*. Harlow: Longman.

Chambers, Robert. 1997. *Whose reality counts? Putting the first last*. London: Intermediate Technology.

Chambers, R., A. Pacey and L.-A. Thrupp. 1989. *Farmer first: farmer innovation and agricultural research*. London: Intermediate Technology Publications.

Chauhan, B.R. 1978. Tribalisation. In N.N. Vyas, R.S. Mann and N.D. Chaudhary (eds) *Rajasthan Bhils*. Udaipur: M.L.V. Tribal Research and Training Institute.

Chhotray, Vasudha. 2004. The negation of politics in participatory development projects, Kurnool, Andhra Pradesh. *Development and Change* 35(2): 327–52.

Christoplos, I. 1995. *Representation, poverty and PRA in the Mekong Delta*, Research Report No. 6. Environment Policy and Society (EPOS), Linköping University.

Clay, E.J. and B.B. Schaffer (eds). 1984. *Room for manoeuvre: an exploration of public policy in agriculture and rural development*. London: Heinemann Educational.

Cleves, Julia. 2000. Making and implementing reproductive health policy: delivering the Cairo programme of action in India 1994–99. PhD Thesis, University of Wales, Swansea.

Cohn, Bernard S. 1996. *Colonialism and its forms of knowledge: the British in India*. New Delhi: Oxford University Press.

Cook, Bill and Uma Kothari. 2001. *Participation, the new tyranny?* London: Zed Books.

Cooper, F. and R. Packard. 1997. *International development and the social sciences: essays in the history and politics of knowledge*. Berkeley: University of California Press.

Corbridge, Stuart and John Harriss. 2001. *Reinventing India: liberalization, Hindu nationalism and popular democracy*. New Delhi: Oxford University Press.

Cowen, Michael and Robert Shenton. 1995. The invention of development. In Jonathan Crush (ed.) *Power of development*. London and New York: Routledge.

Cox, R.W. 1987. *Production, power and world order: social forces in the making of history*. New York: Columbia University Press.

Craig, David and Doug Porter. 1997. Framing participation: development projects, professionals, and organisations. In D. Eade (ed.) *Development and patronage: a development in practice reader*. Oxford: Oxfam, pp. 50–57.

Craig, David and Doug Porter. 2003. Poverty reduction strategy papers: a new convergence. *World Development* 31(1): 53–69.

Crewe, Emma and Elizabeth Harrison. 1998. *Whose development? An ethnography of aid*. London: Zed Books.

Dahl, Gudrun. 2001. *Responsibility and partnership in Swedish aid discourse*. Uppsala: The Nordic Africa Institute.

Daniel, E.V. 1984. *Fluid signs: being a person the Tamil way*. Berkeley: University of California Press.

Das, Veena. 1995. *Critical events: anthropological perspectives on contemporary India*. Delhi: Oxford University Press.

Davis-Case, D'Arcy. 1989. *Community forestry: participatory assessment, monitoring and evaluation*. Rome: Food and Agriculture Organisation of the United Nations.

de Certeau, Michel. 1984. *The practice of everyday life*. Berkeley: University of California Press.

Deliège, Robert. 1985. *The Bhils of western India: some empirical and theoretical issues in anthropology in India*. New Delhi: National Publishing House.

Desai, Bina. 2004. Local brokers: knowledge, trust and organisation in the practice of agricultural extension for small and marginal farmers in Rajasthan, India. PhD thesis, University of London.

DFID. 1997. *Eliminating world poverty: a challenge for the 21st century*. Government White Paper on International Development, Cm 3789. London: Department for International Development.

DFID. 1999. India country strategy. New Delhi: Department for International Development.

DFID. 2000. *Eliminating world poverty: making globalisation work for the poor: Government White Paper on International Development*. London: Department for International Development.

Dirks, N. 2001. *Castes of mind: colonialism and the making of modern India*. Princeton, NJ: Princeton University Press.

Doshi, J.K. 1978. *Processes of tribal unification and integration: a case study of the Bhils*. Delhi: Concept Publishers.

Doshi, S.L. 1971. *Bhils: between societal self-awareness and cultural synthesis*. Delhi: Sterling.

Doshi, S.L. 1990. *Tribal ethnicity, class and integration*. Jaipur: Rawat.

Doshi, S.L. 1997. *More on feudalism and subaltern tribals*. New Delhi: Himanshu Publications.

Douglas, Mary. 1980. *Evans-Pritchard*. Glasgow: Fontana Modern Masters.

Douglas, Mary and B. Isherwood. 1978. *The world of goods: towards an anthropology of consumption*. London: Routledge.

Dube, S.C. 1958. *India's changing villages: human factors in community development*. London: Routledge and Kegan Paul.

Duffield, Mark. 2001. *Global governance and the new wars: the merging of development and security*. London: Zed Books.

Edwards, Michael. 1989. The irrelevance of development studies. *Third World Quarterly* 11(1): 116–35.

Edwards, Michael. 1999. *Future positive: international co-operation in the 21st century*. London: Earthscan Publications.

Edwards, Michael. 1994. NGOs in the age of information. *IDS Bulletin* 25(2): 117–24.

Eldridge, P. nd. The political role of voluntary organisations and action groups in Gujarat. Unpublished paper, University of Tasmania (c. 1989).

Ellerman, David. 2002. Should development agencies have official views? *Development in Practice* 12(3–4): 285–97.

Erskine, K.D. 1908. *Rajput Gazetteers*, Volume II-A *The Mewar Residency*. Ajmer: Scottish Mission Industries Co. Inc.

Escobar, Arturo. 1991. Anthropology and the development encounter: the making and marketing of development anthropology. *American Ethnologist* 18(4): 16–40.

Escobar, Arturo. 1992. Planning. In Wofgang Sachs (ed.) *The development dictionary: a guide to knowledge as power.* Johannesburg: Witwatersrand University Press; London and New Jersey: Zed Books.

Escobar, Arturo. 1995. *Encountering development: the making and unmaking of the Third World.* Princeton, NJ: Princeton University Press.

Eyben, Rosalind. 2003. Donors as political actors: fighting the Thirty Years War in Bolivia. *IDS Working Paper no. 183,* April. Brighton: Institute of Development Studies.

Fabian, Johannes. 1983. *Time and the other: how anthropology makes its object.* New York: Columbia University Press.

Fairhead, James. 1991. Methodological notes on exploring indigenous knowledge and management of crop health. *RRA Notes* 14: 39–42.

Fairhead, James. 2000. Development discourse and its subversion: decivilisation, depoliticisation and dispossession in West Africa. In Alberto Arce and Norman Long (eds) *Anthropology, development and modernities: exploring discourses, counter-tendencies and violence.* London and New York: Routledge.

Fairhead, James and Melissa Leach. 1996. *Misreading the African landscape: society and ecology in a forest–savannah mosaic.* Cambridge: Cambridge University Press.

Fairhead, James and Melissa Leach. 1997. Webs of power and the construction of environmental policy problems: forest loss in Guinea. In R.L. Stirrat and R. Grillo (eds) *Discourses of development: anthropological perspectives.* Oxford/New York: Berg Publishers.

Fairhead, James and Melissa Leach. 2002. Introduction: changing perspectives on forests: science/policy processes in wider society. *IDS Bulletin* 33(1): 1–12.

Fardon, Richard. 1999. *Mary Douglas: an intellectual biography.* London and New York: Routledge.

Farrington, John, Roger Blench, Ian Christoplos, Karin Ragsgard and Anders Rudqvist. 2002. Do area development projects have a future? *ODI Natural Resources Perspectives paper* No. 82. London: Overseas Development Institute.

Farrington, John, Catheryn Turton and A.J. James. 1999. *Participatory watershed development: challenges for the twenty-first century.* New Delhi: Oxford University Press.

Feldman, J. and J. March. 1981. Information in organisations as signal and symbol. *Administrative Science Quarterly* 26: 171–86.

Ferguson, J. 1994. *The anti-politics machine: development, de-politicisation and bureaucratic power in Lesotho.* Minneapolis: University of Minnesota Press.

Ferguson, J. 1997. Anthropology and its evil twin: development in the constitution of a discipline. In F. Cooper and R. Packard (eds) *International development and the social sciences: essays in the history and politics of knowledge.* Berkeley: University of California Press.

Fernandez, A.P. 1993. *The Myrada experience: the interventions of a voluntary agency in the emergence and growth of people's institutions for sustained and equitable management or micro-watersheds*. Bangalore: Myrada.

Fernandez, A.P. 1995. Self-help groups: the concept. *Myrada Rural Management Systems Paper* No. 22. Bangalore: Myrada.

Fiedrich, Marc. 2002. Domesticating modernity: understanding women's aspirations in participatory literacy programmes in Uganda. DPhil thesis, University of Sussex, UK.

Fine, Ben. 2002. Economics imperialism and the new development economics as Kuhnian paradigm shift? *World Development* 30(12): 2057–70.

Fletcher, Robert. 2001. What are we fighting for? Rethinking resistance in a Pewenche community in Chile. *Journal of Peasant Studies* 28(3): 37–66.

Foster, Mick. 2000. New approaches to development co-operation: what can we learn from experience with implementing sector-wider approaches? *ODI Working Paper no. 140*. London: Overseas Development Institute.

Foucault, M. 1979a. *Discipline and punish: the birth of the prison*. New York: Vintage.

Foucault, M. 1979b. *Power/knowledge: selected interviews and other writings 1972–77*, ed. Colin Gordon. New York and London: Prentice Hall.

Foucault, M. 1986. Of other spaces. *Diacritics – a review of contemporary criticism* 16(1): 22–27.

Francis, Paul. 2001. Participatory development at the World Bank: the primacy of process. In Bill Cook and Uma Kothari (eds) *Participation: the new tyranny?* London: Zed Books.

Friedman, Jonathan. 1992. The past and the future: history and the politics of identity. *American Anthropologist* 94(4): 837–59.

Friedman, Jonathan. 1993. The simplicity of the global and the complexity of the local. ASA IV Decennial Conference, Oxford, 26–31 July.

Fuller, C.J. and John Harriss. 2000. For an anthropology of the modern Indian state. In C.J. Fuller and Veronique Bénéï (eds) *The everyday state in modern India*. New Delhi: Social Science Press.

Gadgil, Madhav and Ramachandra Guha. 1992. *This fissured land: an ecological history of India*. Delhi: Oxford University Press.

Gadgil, Madhav and Ramachandra Guha. 1995. *Ecology and equity: the use and abuse of nature in contemporary India*. London and New York: Routledge.

Gaikwad, V.R. 1981. Community development in India. In R. Dore and Z. Mars (eds) *Community development: comparative case studies in India, the Republic of Korea, Mexico and Tanzania*. London: Croom Helm.

Gardner, K. and D. Lewis. 1996. *Anthropology, development and the post-modern challenge*. London: Pluto.

Gardner, Katy and David Lewis. 2000. Dominant paradigms overturned or 'business as usual'? Development discourse and the White Paper on International Development. *Critique of Anthropology* 20(1): 15–29.

Gasper, Des. 1996. Analysing policy arguments. In R. Apthorpe and Des Gasper (eds) *Arguing development policy: frames and discourses*. London: Frank Cass.

Gasper, Des and Raymond Apthorpe. 1996. Introduction: discourse analysis and policy discourse. In R. Apthorpe and Des Gasper (eds) *Arguing development policy: frames and discourses*. London: Frank Cass.

Gatter, Philip. 1993. Anthropology in farming systems research: a participant observer in Zambia. In J. Pottier (ed.) *Practising development: social science perspectives*. London: Routledge.

Gellner, David N. 1991. Hinduism, tribalism and the position of women: the problem of Newar identity. *Man* 26(1): 105–25.

Gellner, David and Eric Hirsch (eds) 2001. *Inside organisations: anthropologists at work*. Oxford and New York: Berg.

Gibson, James W. 1986. *The perfect war: technowar in Vietnam*. Boston, MA: Atlantic Monthly Press.

Gidwani, V.K. and K. Sivaramakrishnan. nd. Body politics: circular migration and subaltern identities in India. Manuscript.

Glebe, Thilo. 1998. Economic impact assessment. KBCL Indo-British Rainfed Farming Project (East), Ranchi, India. Unpublished consultant report.

Goetz, A.-M. 1996. Local heroes: patterns of fieldworker discretion in implementing GAD policy in Bangladesh. *IDS Discussion Paper* 358. Brighton: Institute of Development Studies.

Goldman, Michael. 2001. The birth of a discipline: producing authoritative green knowledge, World Bank style. *Ethnography* 2(2): 191–217.

Gould, Jeremy. 2003. Timing, scale and style: capacity as governmentality in Tanzania. Paper presented at the EIDOS Workshop on 'Order and disjuncture: the organisation of aid and development', SOAS, London 26–28 Sept.

Grammig, Thomas. 2002. *Technical knowledge and development: observing aid projects and processes*. London: Routledge.

Green, Maia. 2000. Participatory development and the appropriation of agency in southern Tanzania. *Critique of Anthropology* 20(1): 67–89.

Green, Maia. 2002. Social development: issues and approaches. In Uma Kothari and Martin Monogue (eds) *Development theory and practice: critical perspectives*. Basingstoke: Palgrave.

Grillo, R.D. 1997. Discourses of development: the view from anthropology. In R.L. Stirrat and R.D. Grillo (eds) *Discourses of development: anthropological perspectives*. Oxford and New York: Berg Publishers.

Guha, Ramachandra. 1999. *Savaging the civilized: Verrier Elwin, his tribals, and India*. New Delhi: Oxford University Press.

Gupta, Akhil. 1997. Agrarian populism in the development of a modern nation (India). In F. Cooper and R. Packard (eds) *International development and the social sciences: essays in the history and politics of knowledge*. Berkeley: University of California Press.

Gupta, Akhil. 1998. *Postcolonial developments: agriculture in the making of modern India*. Durham, NC and London: Duke University Press.

Gupta, Akhil and James Ferguson. 1997. Culture, power, place: ethnography at the end of an era. In A. Gupta and J. Ferguson (eds) *Culture, power, place: explorations in critical anthropology*. Durham, NC and London: Duke University Press.

Gupta, Anil and M. Schroff. 1990. *Rural banking – learning to unlearn: an action research enquiry*. New Delhi: Oxford and IBH Publishing.

Haas, P. 1990. *Saving the Mediterranean*. New York: Columbia University Press.

Hall, Stuart. 1996. On postmodernism and articulation: an interview with Stuart Hall, edited by Lawrence Grossberg. In David Morley and Kuan-Hsing Chen (eds) *Stuart Hall: critical dialogues in cultural studies.* London: Routlege.

Hardiman, D. 1987a. *The coming of Devi.* New Delhi: Oxford University Press.

Hardiman, D. 1987b. The Bhils and sahukars of Eastern Gujarat. In Ranajit Guha (ed.) *Subaltern studies V: writings on South Asian history and society.* New Delhi: Oxford University Press.

Hardiman, D. 1996. *Feeding the Baniya: peasants and usurers in western India.* Delhi: Oxford University Press.

Harper, Ian. 2003. Mission, magic and medicalisation: an anthropological study into public health in contemporary Nepal. PhD thesis, University of London.

Heaton, Celayne. 2001. Our differences don't make a difference: practising 'civil society' in Nepal's non-governmental sector. Unpublished PhD thesis, University of London.

Heller, P. 2001. Moving the state: the politics of democratic decentralisation in Kerala and South Africa, and Porto Alegre. *Politics and Society* 29(1): 131–63.

Herzfeld, Michael. 1992. *The social production of indifference.* New York and Oxford: Berg

Heyman, Josiah McC. 1995. Putting power in the anthropology of bureaucracy. *Current Anthropology* 36(2): 261–87.

Hobart, M. (ed.). 1993. *An anthropological critique of development: The growth of ignorance.* London: Routledge.

Hobart, M. 1995. Black umbrellas: the implication of mass media in development. Unpublished paper presented at EIDOS Workshop on Globalisation and Decivilisation, Agricultural University of Wageningen.

INTRAC. 1998. Participatory approaches learning study (PALS) – India study: a report for the Department of International Development (DFID). Oxford: The International NGO Training and Research Centre (INTRAC).

Jackson, Cecile. 1997. Sustainable development at the sharp end: field-worker agency in a participatory project. In D. Eade (ed.) *Development and patronage: a Development in Practice reader.* Oxford: Oxfam, pp. 58–67.

Jain, L.C. 1985. *Grass without roots: rural development under government auspices.* Delhi, London: Sage Publications.

Jain, P.C. 1991. *Social movements among tribals: a sociological analysis of Bhils of Rajasthan.* Jaipur: Rawat Publications.

James, Wendy. 1999. Empowering ambiguities. In Angela Cheater (ed.) *The anthropology of power: empowerment and disempowerment in changing structures.* London: Routledge.

Jeffrey, Roger and Nandini Sundar (eds). 1999. *A new moral economy for India's forests: discourses of community and participation.* New Delhi: Sage Publications.

Johnston, James. 2002. Qualities of development: discourse, governmentality and translation of education policy in the People's Republic of China. MA dissertation, SOAS, University of London.

Jones, Emma. 2000. Constructing transformative spaces, transforming gendered lives. MPhil dissertation, Institute of Development Studies, MP22, University of Sussex.

Jones, Steve. 1978. Tribal underdevelopment in India. *Development and Change* 9: 41–70.

Jones, S., J.N. Khare, D. Mosse, P. Smith, P.S. Sodhi and J. Witcombe. 1994. The Indo-British Rainfed Farming Project: issues in the planning and implementation of participatory natural resources development. *KRIBP Working Paper no. 1*. Centre for Development Studies, University of Wales, Swansea.

Joshi, Arun and J.R. Witcombe. 1995. Farmer participatory research for the selection of rainfed rice cultivars. *KRIBP Working Paper No. 4*, Research Issues in Natural Resource Management, Swansea: Centre for Development Studies, University of Wales Swansea.

Joshi, Arun and J.R. Witcombe. 1996. Farmer participatory crop improvement II: participatory varietal selection, a case study in India. *Experimental Agriculture* 32: 461–77.

Kamat, Sangeeta. 2002. *Development hegemony: NGOs and the state in India.* New Delhi: Oxford University Press.

Karlsson, B.G. 1999. Entering into the Christian dharma: contemporary 'tribal' conversions in India. Paper presented at the Conference on 'Cultural Interactions', Oxford, September.

Karlsson, B.G. 2000. *Contested belonging: an indigenous people's struggle for forest and identity in sub-Himalayan Bengal.* London: Curzon Press.

Karlsson, B.G. 2002. Anthropology and the 'indigenous slot': claims to and debates about indigenous people's status in India. Paper presented at the EASA conference 'Engaging the World', Copenhagen, August.

Kaufmann, Georgia. 1997. Watching the developers: a partial ethnography. In R.G Grillo and R.L. Stirrat (eds) *Discourses of development: anthropological perspectives.* Oxford and New York: Berg.

Klenk, Rebecca. 2003. 'Difficult work': becoming developed. In K. Sivaramakrishnan and Arun Agrawal (eds) *Regional modernities: the cultural politics of development in India.* New Delhi: Oxford University Press.

Kothari, Rajni. 1986. NGOs, the state and world capitalism. *Economic and Political Weekly* 21(50):

Kuhn, Thomas S. 1962. *The structure of scientific revolutions.* Chicago: University of Chicago Press.

Kumar, Sanjay and Stuart Corbridge. 2002. Programmed to fail? Development projects and the politics of participation. *Journal of Development Studies* 29(2): 73–103.

Lal, R.B. nd. *Role of minor forest produce in tribal life and culture.* Ahmedabad: Tribal Research and Training Institute.

Lambert, Helen. 1996. Caste, gender and locality in rural Rajasthan. In C.J. Fuller (ed.) *Caste today.* New Delhi: Oxford University Press.

Lansing, S. 1991. *Priests and programmers: technologies of power in the engineered landscape of Bali.* Princeton, NJ: Princeton University Press.

Latour, Bruno. 1996. *Aramis, or the love of technology*, trans. Catherine Porter. Cambridge, MA and London: Harvard University Press.

Latour, Bruno. 2000. When things strike back: a possible contribution of science studies. *British Journal of Sociology* 5(1): 105–23.

Law, J. 1994. *Organising modernity.* Oxford: Blackwell Publishers.

Leach, Melissa and James Fairhead. 2000. Fashioned forest pasts, occluded histories? International environmental analysis in West African locales. *Development and Change* 31(1): 35–59.

Lewis, David. 1998. Partnership as process: building an institutional ethnography of an inter-agency aquaculture project in Bangladesh. In D. Mosse, J. Farrington and A. Rew (eds) *Development as process: concepts and methods for working with complexity.* London and New York: Routledge.

Li, Tania Murray. 1996. Images of community: discourse and strategy in property relations. *Development and Change* 27(3): 501–27.

Li, Tania Murray. 1997. Boundary work: a response to 'Community in conservation: beyond enchantment and disenchantment' by Arun Agrawal. In Arun Agrawal (ed.) *Community in conservation: beyond enchantment and disenchantment.* CDF Discussion paper. Gainesville, FL: Conservation and Development Forum, pp. 69–82.

Li, Tania Murray. 1999. Compromising power: development, culture and rule in Indonesia. *Cultural Anthropology* 14(3): 295–322.

Li, Tania Murray. 2000. Articulating indigenous identity in Indonesia: resource politics and the tribal slot. *Comparative Studies in Society and History* 42(1): 149–79.

Li Tania Murray. 2002. Government through community and the practice of politics. Paper presented at Agrarian Studies, University of Yale, October.

Lipsky, M. 1980. *Street-level bureaucracy: dilemmas of the individual in public service.* New York: Russell Sage.

Lipton, M. 1996. Growing mountain, shrinking mouse? Indian poverty and British bilateral aid. *Modern Asian Studies* 30(3): 481–522.

Little, Peter and Michael Painter. 1995. Discourse, politics, and the development process: reflections on Escobar's 'Anthropology and the development encounter'. *American Ethnologist* 22(3): 602–16.

Lobo, Lancy. 2002. Adivasis, Hindutva and post-Godhra riots in Gujarat. *Economic and Political Weekly* 30 November.

Long, Norman. 1977. *An introduction to the sociology of rural development.* London: Tavistock Publications.

Long, Norman. 1992. From paradigm lost to paradigm regained? The case for an actor-oriented sociology of development. In N. Long and A. Long (eds) *Battlefields of knowledge: the interlocking of theory and practice in social research and development.* London: Routledge.

Long, Norman. 2001. *Sociology of development: actor perspectives.* London and New York: Routledge.

Long, N. and A. Long (eds). 1992. *Battlefields of knowledge: the interlocking of theory and practice in social research and development.* London: Routledge.

Ludden, David. 1992. India's development regime. In N.B. Dirks (ed.) *Colonialism and culture.* Ann Arbor: University of Michigan Press.

Ludden, David (ed.). 1994. *Agricultural production and Indian history.* Delhi: Oxford University Press.

Luthra, Sangeetha. 2003. Educating entrepreneurs, organizing for social justice: NGO development strategies in New Delhi *bastis.* In K. Sivaramakrishnan and Arun Agrawal (eds) *Regional modernities: the cultural politics of development in India*. New Delhi: Oxford University Press.

McCurdy, David W. 1964. A Bhil village of Rajasthan. PhD dissertation. Department of Anthropology, Cornell University.

Manor, James. 2002. User committees: a potentially damaging second wave of decentralisation. Draft paper, accessed via www.panchayats.org, December 2002.

Mansuri, Ghazala and Vijayendra Rao. 2004. Community-based (and driven) development: a critical review. *World Bank Research Observer* 19(1): 1–39.

Marcus, G. 1995. Ethnography in/of the world system: the emergence of multi-sited ethnography. *Annual Review of Anthropology* 24: 95–117.

Marcus, G. 1998. *Ethnography through thick and thin*. Princeton, NJ: Princeton University Press.

Masavi, M. nd. Problem of land alienation among tribals in Gujarat. Vidyapith, Ahmedabad: Tribal Research Institute.

Massey, Doreen. 1993. Power, geometry and a progressive sense of place. In Jon Bird et al. (eds) *Mapping the futures: local cultures, global change*. London: Routledge, pp. 59–69.

Mathur, L.P. 1988. *Resistance movement among the tribals in India: a case of the Bhils of Rajasthan in the 19th century*. Udaipur: Himanshu Publications.

Maxwell, Simon. 2002. More aid? Yes – and use it to reshape aid architecture. *Overseas Development Institute – Opinions Series* no. 3, February.

Mehta, Mona. 1999. Suppressed subjects? Gender dynamics in the context of agrarian change and seasonal labour migration in Dahanu Taluka, Maharashtra. PhD thesis, Institute of Social Studies, The Hague. Maastricht: Shaker Publications BV.

Mikkelsen, B. 1995. *Methods for development work and research*. London: Sage.

Mines, Mattison and Vijayalakshmi Gourishankar. 1990. Leadership and individuality in South Asia: the case of the south Indian big-man. *Journal of Asian Studies* 49(4): 761–86.

Mintzberg, Henry. 1979. *The structuring of organisations*. Englewood Cliffs, NJ: Prentice-Hall.

Mitchell, Timothy. 2002. *Rule of experts: Egypt, techno-politics, modernity*. Berkeley: University of California Press.

Moore, Donald S. 2000. The crucible of cultural politics: reworking 'development' in Zimbabwe's eastern highlands. *American Ethnologist* 26(3): 654–89.

Moore, Donald S. 2003. Beyond blackmail: multivalent modernities and the cultural politics of development in India. In K. Sivaramakrishnan and Arun Agrawal (eds) *Regional modernities: the cultural politics of development in India*. New Delhi: Oxford University Press.

Moore, Henrietta L. 1988. *Anthropology and feminism*. Cambridge: Polity Press.

Moore, Henrietta L. 1999. *Anthropological theory today*. Cambridge: Polity Press.

Moore, Sally Falk. 2001. The international production of authoritative knowledge: the case of drought-stricken West Africa. *Ethnography* 2(2): 161–90.

Moser, C.O.N. and C. Levy. 1986. A theory and methodology of gender planning: meeting women's practical and strategic needs, Gender and Planning Working Paper. London: Development Planning Unit, UCL, London.

Mosse, David. 1994. Authority, gender and knowledge: theoretical reflections on the practice of Participatory Rural Appraisal. *Development and Change* 25(3): 497–525.

Mosse, David (with the IBRFP Project team). 1995. Social analysis in participatory rural development. *PLA Notes* 24: 27–33.

Mosse, David. 1996a. The social construction of 'people's knowledge' in participatory rural development. In S. Bastian and N. Bastian (eds) *Assessing participation: a debate from South Asia*. New Delhi: Konark Publishers.

Mosse, David (with the IBRFP project team). 1996b. Local institutions and farming systems development: thoughts from a project in tribal western India. *ODI Agren Network Paper* No. 64. London: ODI.

Mosse, David. 1997. The ideology and politics of community participation. In R.L. Stirrat and R. Grillo (eds) *Discourses of development: anthropological perspectives*. Oxford and New York: Berg Publishers.

Mosse, David. 1998a. Process-oriented approaches to development practice and social research: an introduction. In D. Mosse, J. Farrington and A. Rew (eds) *Development as process: concepts and methods for working with complexity*. London: Routledge.

Mosse, David. 1998b. Process documentation and process monitoring: cases and issues. In D. Mosse, J. Farrington and A. Rew (eds) *Development as process: concepts and methods for working with complexity*. London: Routledge.

Mosse, David. 1999. Colonial and contemporary ideologies of community management: the case of tank irrigation development in south India. *Modern Asian Studies* 33(2): 303–38.

Mosse, David. 2001. 'People's knowledge', participation and patronage: operations and representations in rural development. In Bill Cook and Uma Kothari (eds) *Participation – the new tyranny?* London: Zed Press.

Mosse, David. 2002. Adivasi migrant labour support: a collaborative programme. Consultant's report, Western India Rainfed Farming Project, DFID, India, May.

Mosse, David. 2003a. The making and marketing of participatory development. In Philip Quarles van Ufford and Ananta K. Giri (eds) *A moral critique of development: in search of global responsibilities*. London and New York: Routledge.

Mosse, David. 2003b. *The rule of water: statecraft, ecology and collective action in south India*. New Delhi: Oxford University Press.

Mosse, David. 2003c. Supporting rural communities in the city: Adivasi migrant labour support programme. Consultant's report, Western India Rainfed Farming Project, DFID, India, May.

Mosse, David and Mona Mehta. 1993. Genealogies as a method of social mapping in participatory rural appraisal. *RRA Notes* No. 18: 5–11.

Mosse, David and Mona Mehta. 1996. More questions than answers: gender in farming systems development. Draft paper presented at workshop on Gender in Agricultural Research, ICRSAT, Hyderabad.

Mosse, D., T. Ekande, P. Sodhi, S. Jones, M. Mehta and U. Moitra. 1994. Approaches to participatory planning: a review of the KRIBP experience. *KRIBP Working Paper No. 5*, Centre for Development Studies, University of Wales, Swansea.

Mosse, David, J. Farrington and A. Rew (eds). 1998. *Development as process: concepts and methods for working with complexity.* London and New York: Routledge.

Mosse, David, Sanjeev Gupta, Mona Mehta, Vidya Shah, Julia Rees and the KRIBP Project Team. 2002. Brokered livelihoods: debt, labour migration and development in tribal western India, *Journal of Development Studies* 38(5): 59–88.

Naik, T.B. 1956. *The Bhils: a study.* Delhi: Bharatiya Adimjati Seva Sang.

Nelson, N. and S. Wright. 1995. *Power and participatory development: theory and practice.* London: Intermediate Technology Publications.

Novellino, Dario. 2003. From seduction to miscommunication: the confession and presentation of local knowledge in 'participatory development'. In Johan Pottier, Alan Bicker and Paul Sillitoe (eds) *Negotiating local knowledge: power and identity in development.* London: Pluto Press.

Nuijten, Monique and Jilles van Gastel. 2003. The reinvention of ownership at the Dutch Ministry of Development Cooperation. Paper given at conference on 'Order and Disjuncture: The Organisation of Aid and Development'. London, SOAS, September.

ODI. 1998. The UK White Paper on international development – and beyond. *ODI Briefing Paper* (2) May (ISSN 0140–8682).

OECD. 1996. *Shaping the 21st century: the contribution of development co-operation.* Development Assistance Committee. Paris: OECD.

Olivier de Sardan, Jean-Pierre. forthcoming. Introduction: the three approaches in the anthropology of development. In *Anthropology and development.* London: Zed Press. (First published in French: *Anthropologie et développement: essai en socio-anthropologie du changement.* Paris: Karthala, 1995.)

Osella, F. and C. Osella. 1996. Articulation of physical and social bodies in Kerala. *Contributions to Indian Sociology* (ns) 30(1): 37–68.

Ostrom, E. 1990. *Governing the commons: the evolution of institutions for collective action.* Cambridge: Cambridge University Press.

Ouroussoff, Alexandra. 2001. What is an ethnographic study? In David Gellner and Eric Hirsch (eds) *Inside organisations: anthropologists at work.* Oxford and New York: Berg.

Padel, Felix. 2000. *The sacrifice of human being: British rule and the Konds of Orissa.* Delhi: Oxford University Press.

Panayiotopoulis, Prodomos. 2002. Anthropology consultancy in the UK and community development in the Third World: a difficult dialogue. *Development in Practice* 12(1): 45–58.

Parkin, David. 1995. Latticed knowledge: eradication and dispersal of the unpalatable in Islam, medicine and anthropological theory. In Richard Fardon (ed.) *Counterworks: managing the diversity of knowledge.* London and New York: Routledge.

Peet, R. and M. Watts (ed.) 1996. *Liberation ecologies: environment, development and social movements.* London and New York: Routledge.

Pels, D. 2000. On reflexivity. *Theory, Culture & Society* 17(3): 1–25.

Pels, P. and L. Nencel. 1991. Introduction: critique and the deconstruction of anthropological authority. In P. Pels and L. Nencel (eds) *Constructing knowledge: authority and critique in social science.* London: Sage.

Perrow, Charles. 1986. *Complex organisations: a critical essay*, 3rd edn. New York: McGraw-Hill.

Phillips, Sue and Richard Edwards. 2000. Development, impact assessment and the praise culture. *Critique of Anthropology* 20(1): 47–66.

Pickering, Andrew. 2002. Cybernetics and the mangle: Ashby, Beer and Pask. Available online at www.soc.uiuc.deu/faculty/pickerin/cybernetics.pdf. (To be published in French in A. Dahan and D. Pestre (eds). forthcoming. *La Reconfiguration des sciences pour l'action dans les années*, Paris: Presses de l'EHESS.)

Pigg, Stacy Leigh. 1992. Inventing social categories through place: social representations and development in Nepal. *Comparative Studies in Society and History* 34: 491–513.

Pigg, Stacy Leigh. 1996. The credible and the credulous: the question of 'villagers' beliefs' in Nepal, *Cultural Anthropology* 99(2): 160–201.

Pigg, Stacy Leigh. 1997. Found in most traditional societies – traditional medical practitioners between culture and development. In F. Cooper and R. Packard (eds) *International development and the social sciences: essays in the history and politics of knowledge.* Berkeley: University of California Press.

Pimbert, Michel P. and Tom Wakefield. 2002. Prajateerpu: a citizen's jury/ scenario workshops on food and farming futures for Andhra Pradesh, India. London: International Institute of Environment and Development and Brighton: Institute of Development Studies.

Pinch, T. and Bijker, W. 1984. The social construction of facts and artefacts: or how the sociology of science and the sociology of technology might benefit each other. *Social Studies of Science* 14(3): 399–441.

Porter, Doug J. 1995. Scenes from childhood: the homesickness of development discourse. In Jonathan Crush (ed.) *Power of development.* London and New York: Routledge.

Porter, Doug, B. Allen and G. Thompson. 1991. *Development as practice: paved with good intentions.* London: Routledge.

Pottier, Johan. 1991. Representation and accountability: understanding social change through rapid appraisal, unpubl. ms. School of Oriental and African Studies, London.

Pottier, Johan (ed.). 1993. *Practicing development: social science perspectives.* London: Routledge.

Pottier, Johan. 2003. Negotiating local knowledge: an introduction. In Johan Pottier, Alan Bicker and Paul Sillitoe (eds) *Negotiating local knowledge: power and identity in development.* London: Pluto Press.

Power, M. 1997. *The audit society: rituals of verification.* Oxford: Oxford University Press.

Pronk, Jan P. 2001. Aid as catalyst. *Development and Change* 32(4): 611–29.

Quarles van Ufford, Philip. 1988a. The hidden crisis in development: development bureaucracies in between intentions and outcomes. In P. Quarles van Ufford, D. Kruijt and T. Downing (eds) *The hidden crisis in development: development bureaucracies.* Tokyo and Amsterdam: United Nations and Free University Press.

Quarles van Ufford, Philip. 1988b. The myth of rational development policy: evaluation versus policy making in Dutch Protestant donor agencies. In P. Quarles van Ufford, D. Kruijt and T. Downing (eds) *The hidden crisis in development: development bureaucracies*. Tokyo and Amsterdam: United Nations and Free University Press.

Quarles van Ufford, Philip. 1993. Knowledge and ignorance in the practices of development policy. In M. Hobart (ed.) *An anthropological critique of development: the growth of ignorance*. London and New York: Routledge.

Quarles van Ufford, Philip and Dik Roth. 2003. The Icarus effect: the rise and fall of development optimisms in a regional development project in Luwu District, South Sulawesi, Indonesia. In Philip Quarles van Ufford and Ananta K. Giri (eds) *A moral critique of development: in search of global responsibilities*. London and New York: Routledge.

Quarles van Ufford, Philip, Ananta Kumar and David Mosse. 2003. Interventions in development: towards a new moral understanding of our experiences and an agenda for the future. In Philip Quarles van Ufford and Ananta Giri (eds) *A moral critique of development: in search of global responsibilities*. London and New York: Routledge.

Rabinow, Paul. 1984. *The Foucault reader: an introduction to Foucault's thought*. London: Penguin Books.

Raheja, Gloria Goodwin and Ann Grodzins Gold. 1994. *Listen to the heron: re-imagining gender and kinship in N. India*. Berkeley: University of California Press.

Rajora, S.C. 1987. *Social structure and tribal elite*. Udaipur. Himanshu Publications.

Raman, K.V. and T. Balaguru. 1988. NARP – an innovative approach towards FSR in India. *Agricultural Administration and Extension* 30: 203–13.

Rao, A. 1988. *Tribal social stratification*. Udaipur: Himanshu Publications.

Rao, Vijayendra and Michael Walton. 2004. Culture and public action: an introduction. In V. Rao and M. Walton (eds) *Culture and public action*. Stanford, CA: Stanford University Press.

Rew, A.W. 1997. The donors' discourse: official social development knowledge in the 1980s. In R.L. Stirrat and R. Grillo (eds) *Discourses of development: anthropological perspectives*. Oxford/New York: Berg Publishers.

Rew, Alan and Martin Rew. 2003. Development models 'out-of-place': social research on methods to improve livelihoods in eastern India. *Community Development Journal* 38(3): 213–24.

Richards, Paul. 1985. *Indigenous agricultural revolution*. London: Allen and Unwin.

Ricoeur, Paul. 1978. *The rule of metaphor: multi-disciplinary studies of the creation of meaning in language*, trans. Robert Czerny with Kathleen McLaughlin and John Costello. London: Routledge and Kegan Paul.

Robertson, A.F. 1984. *People and the state: an anthropology of planned development*. Cambridge: Cambridge University Press.

Roe, Emery M. 1991. Development narratives, or making the best of blueprint development. *World Development* 19(4): 287–300.

Roe, Emery. 1994. *Narrative policy analysis: theory and practice*. Durham, NC and London: Duke University Press.

Rondinelli, Dennis A. 1983. *Development projects as policy experiments*. London: Methuen.

Rose, Nicholas. 1993. Government, authority and expertise in advanced liberalism. *Economy and Society* 22 (3): 283–99.

Rossi, Benedetta. 2003. Global governance and hidden transcripts: unveiling development rhetorics in Keita (Niger). Paper presented at the EIDOS Workshop on 'Order and Disjuncture: The Organisation of Aid and Development', SOAS, London 26–28 Sept.

Runge, C.F. 1986. Common property and collective action in economic development. *World Development* 16(5): 623–35.

Rutherford, Stuart. 2000. *The poor and their money*. Delhi: Oxford University Press.

Sachs, Wolfgang (ed.). 1992. *The development dictionary: a guide to knowledge as power*. London: Zed Books.

Sahlins, Marshall. 1999. Two or three things that I know about culture. *Journal of the Royal Anthropological Institute* 5(3): 399–421.

Said, E. 1978. *Orientalism*. New York: Pantheon Books.

Samantaray, Ranjan K. 1994. Evaluation of social forestry programmes in Panchmahals for KBCL Project. Centre for Arid Zones Studies, University of Wales, Bangor.

Saxena, N.C. 2001. Issues in panchayats. Draft paper accessed via www.panchayats.org. 13 Sept.

Sayer, Derek. 1994. Everyday forms of state formation: some dissident remarks on 'hegemony'. In Gilbert M. Joseph and Daniel Nugent (eds) *Everyday forms of state formation: revolution and the negotiation of rule in modern Mexico*. Durham, NC: Duke University Press.

Scheper-Hughes, Nancy. 1992. *Death without weeping: the violence of everyday life in Brazil*. Berkeley and Los Angeles: University of California Press.

Scoones, I. 1998. Sustainable rural livelihoods: a framework for analysis. *IDS Working Paper* no. 72.

Scott, D. 1992. Criticism and culture: theory and post-colonial claims on anthropological disciplinarity. *Critique of Anthropology* 12(4): 371–94.

Scott J.C. 1990a. *Weapons of the weak: everyday forms of peasant resistance*. Delhi: Oxford University Press.

Scott J.C. 1990b. *Domination and the arts of resistance: hidden transcripts*. New Haven, CT: Yale University Press.

Scott J.C. 1998. *Seeing like a state: how certain schemes to improve the human condition have failed*. New Haven, CT and London: Yale University Press.

Shah, A. 1995. 'Impact of IBRFP's Soil and Water Conservation Programme: Some Policy Implications', Centre for Development Studies, University of Wales, UK.

Shah, T., S. Chandra, S. Ladbury, S. Parthasarthy and A. Shah. 1996. *Indo-British Rainfed Farming Project (IBRFP): Report of the Mid-Term Evaluation, January 1996*. London: Overseas Development Administration.

Sharma, B.K. 1990. *Peasant movements in Rajasthan (1920–1949)*. Jaipur: Pointer Publishers.

Sharrock, G., Charles Clift and George Dwyer. 1985. Fertiliser extension in eastern India: the Indo-British Fertiliser Education Project. *Agricultural Administration* 20: 73–84.

Shepherd, Andrew, with Richard Slater, Aasha Kapur Mehta, Alicia Herbert, Amita Shah, Manju Senapaty. 2000. *Evaluation of DFID's Support to Poverty Reduction: India Country Study*. London: DFID.

Sherring, Revd M.A. 1872. *Hindu tribes and castes, together with an account of the Mohammadan tribes of the North West Frontier and of the aboriginal tribes of the Central Provinces*. Reprinted Delhi: Cosmo Publications, 1974.

Shiva, Vandana. 1989. *Staying alive: women, ecology and development*. London: Zed Books.

Shore, C. and S. Wright (eds). 1997. *Anthropology of policy: critical perspectives on governance and power*. London and New York: Routledge.

Shrikant, L.M. 1967. *Cooperative movement among the tribals*. New Delhi.

Singh, Vikas (with ASA team). 1998. *Joint Forest Management in Jhabua District (M.P.): a process study of two Village Protection Committees*. Dahod: Action for Social Advancement.

Sivaramakrishnan, K. 1999. *Modern forests: statemaking and environmental change in colonial eastern India*. Delhi: Oxford University Press.

Sivaramakrishnan, K. 2000. Crafting the public sphere in the forests of West Bengal: democracy, development and political action. *American Ethnologist* 27(2): 431–61.

Sivaramakrishnan, K. and Arun Agrawal (eds). 2003. *Regional modernities: the cultural politics of development in India*. New Delhi: Oxford University Press (forthcoming with Stanford University Press).

Sjöblom, D.K. 1999. Land matters: social relations and livelihoods in a Bhil community in Rajasthan, India. PhD thesis, School of Development Studies, University of East Anglia.

Skaria, Ajay. 1999. *Hybrid histories: forests, frontiers and wildness in Western India*. Delhi: Oxford University Press.

Skaria, Ajay. 2003. Development, nationalism and the time of the primitive: the Dangs darbar. In K. Sivaramakrishnan and Arun Agrawal (eds) *Regional modernities: the cultural politics of development in India*. New Delhi: Oxford University Press.

Slater, David and Morag Bell. 2002. Aid and the geopolitics of the post-colonial: critical reflections on New Labour's overseas development strategy. *Development and Change* 33(2): 335–60.

Smith, P.D. 1998. The use of subsidies for soil and water conservation: a case study from western India. *Agricultural Research and Extension Network Paper 87*. London: Overseas Development Institute, July.

Smith P.D., D.S. Virk, J.R. Witcombe, A.J. Packwood and T. Looms. 1998. The Indian cultivar database. Paper prepared for GBDL/IAALD/CTA/ NITRANET'98 'The Role of Agriculture Information in Decision Making in Research and Practice'. Kardinal-Döpfner-Haus, Fresing, Germany, 2–5 June.

Sodhi, P.S., T. Ekande, S. Jones, A. Joshi, U. Moitra and D. Mosse. 1993. Manual on participatory planning, *KRIBP Working Paper No. 3*, Centre for Development Studies, University of Wales, Swansea.

Spencer, Jonathan. 1990. *A Sinhala village in a time of trouble: politics and change in rural Sri Lanka*. Delhi: Oxford University Press.

SPS. 1988. *Whither common lands? Rural poor or industry? Who should benefit from common lands forestry? A case study of people's resistance to the take-over of their common lands and forestry by the government and industry.* Dharwad: Samaj Parivartana Samudaya et al.

Starkloff, Ralf. 1996. Participatory discourse and practice in a water resources crisis in Sri Lanka. In S. Bastian and N. Bastian (eds) *Assessing participation: a debate from South Asia.* New Delhi: Konark Publishers.

Steins, Natalie. 2001. New directions in natural resources management: the offer of actor-network theory. *IDS Bulletin* 32(4): 18–25.

Stirrat, R.L. 2000. Cultures of consultancy. *Critique of Anthropology* 20(1): 31–46.

Stoller, Paul. 1994. Ethnographies as texts/ethnographies as griots. *American Ethnologist* 21(2): 353–66.

Strum, Shirley and Bruno Latour. 1999. Redefining the social link: from baboons to humans. In Donald MacKenzie and Judy Wajcman (eds) *The social shaping of technology,* 2nd edn. Buckingham: Open University Press.

Sundar, Nandini. 2000. Unpacking the 'joint' in Joint Forest Management. *Development and Change* 31: 255–79.

Sutton, Rebecca. 1999. The policy process: an overview. *ODI Discussion Paper* no. 118.

Tiffin, M. and M. Mortimore. 1994. *More people less erosion.* New York: Praeger.

Tod, James. 1839. *Travels in western India.* London: WH Allen.

Tsing, Anna. 1993. *In the realm of the diamond queen.* Princeton, NJ: Princeton University Press.

Turton, Cathryn. 2000a. Sustainable livelihoods and project design in India. *ODI Working Paper 127.* London: Overseas Development Institute.

Turton, Cathryn. 2000b. Enhancing livelihoods through participatory watershed development in India. *ODI Working Paper 131.* London: Overseas Development Institute.

Unia, P. 1991. Social action group strategies in the Indian sub-continent. *Development in Practice* 1(2): 84–96.

Uphoff, N.T. 1986. *Local institutional development.* West Hartford, CT: Kumarian Press.

Van der Ploeg, J.D. 1992. The reconstitution of locality: technology and labour in modern agriculture. In T.K. Marsden et al. (eds) *Labour and locality: critical perspectives on rural change,* vol. 4. London: Fulton.

Van Maanen, John. 2001. Natives 'r' us: some notes on the ethnography of organisations. In David Gellner and Eric Hirsch (eds) *Inside organisations: anthropologists at work.* Oxford and New York: Berg.

Varma, S.C. 1978. *The Bhil kills.* Delhi: Kunj Publishing House.

Vasavi, A.R. 1994. Hybrid times, hybrid people: culture and agriculture in south India. *Man* 29(2): 283–332.

Vyas, N.N. 1980. *Bondage and exploitation in tribal India.* Jaipur: Rawat Publications

Vyas N.N. and N.D. Chaudhary. 1968. Sagri – an economic institution among the Bhils of Rajasthan. *Tribe* 5(3): 14–36.

Wade, Robert. 1987. *Village republics: economic conditions for collective action in South India.* Cambridge: Cambridge University Press.

Watts, Michael. 1992. Space for everything (a commentary). *Cultural Anthropology* 7(1): 115–29.

Watts, Michael. 1995. A new deal in emotions: theory and practice and the crisis of development. In Jonathan Crush (ed.) *Power of development*. London and New York: Routledge.

Watts, Michael. 2001. Development ethnographies. *Etnography* 2(2): 283–300.

Weisgrau, Maxine K. 1997. *Interpreting development: local histories, local strategies.* Lanham, MD, New York and Oxford: University Press of America.

White, Sarah. 1996. Depoliticising development: the uses and abuses of participation. *Development in Practice* 6(1): 6–15.

White, Shirley A. and K. Sadanandan Nair. 1999. The catalyst communicator: facilitation without fear. In S.A. White (ed.) *The art of facilitating participation: releasing the power of grassroots communication.* New Delhi, Thousand Oaks, London: Sage Publications.

Winner, Langdon. 1999. Do artefacts have politics? In D. MacKenzie and J. Wajcman (eds) *The social shaping of technology*, 2nd edn. Buckingham: Open University Press.

Witcombe, J.R. 1999. Do farmer-participatory methods apply more to high-potential areas than to marginal ones? *Outlook on Agriculture* 28(1): 43–9.

Witcombe, John R., Daljit S.Virk and John Farrington (eds). 1998. *Seeds of choice: making the most of new varieties for small farmers.* London: Intermediate Technology Publications.

Witcombe, J.R., R. Petre, S. Jones and A. Joshi. 1999. Farmer participatory crop improvement, IV: the spread and impact of a rice variety identified by participatory varietal selection. *Experimental Agriculture* 35: 471–87.

Witcombe, J.R., A. Joshi and S.N. Goyal. 2003. Participatory plant breeding in maize: a case study from Gujarat, India. *Euphytica* 130: 413–22.

Wood, G.D. (ed). 1985. *Labelling in development policy: essays in honour of Bernard Schaffer.* London: Sage Publications.

Wood, G.D. 1998. Consultant behaviour: projects as communities: consultants, knowledge and power. *Project Appraisal* 16(1): 54–64.

Wood, G.D. 2003. Staying secure, staying poor: 'the Faustian bargain'. *World Development* 31(3): 455–71.

World Bank. 1990. India: agricultural research: prologue, performance and prospects. Report No. 8383-IN.

Wright, S. (ed.). 1994. *Anthropology of organizations.* London and New York: Routledge.

Yapa, Lakshman. 1996. Improved seeds and constructed scarcity. In R. Peet and M. Watts (ed.) *Liberation ecologies: environment, development and social movements.* London and New York: Routledge.

Index